GOSPEL OVER GODS

JESUS CHRIST, THE FALLEN ANGELS, & THE SUPERNATURAL WAR OF THE BIBLE

by

TYLER GILREATH

For my loving wife (Nikki)
& precious children.

CONTENTS

INTRODUCTION

FAMILIAR BIBLE STORIES HAVE CAPTIVATED COUNTLESS generations. Stories of a talking serpent and ancient gardens. Whispers of a watery flood and tales of a tower built to the heavens. Rumors of giants in the Promised Land and Israelites in the Red Sea. You've wondered, and been in wonder, of angels from heaven and demons from the deep. The Bible is fascinating… and it is in no way fiction. Although we didn't walk the holy mountains with Elijah or watch Jesus bleed, we believe (John 20:29). But let me ask you a question—have you ever felt like something in the Bible was missing? Primarily, a common thread that ties the entire narrative together from Genesis to Revelation? I certainly did.

That missing link was the war of the unseen realm.

The supernatural struggle between God and His fallen angels had always seemed obscure in the biblical narrative, if not completely absent altogether. Admittedly, reading the Bible felt a bit like watching a failed blockbuster movie where the hero and villain rarely cross paths, let alone interact or confront one another in battle. Instead, the entire "film" was seemingly nothing but random scenes of a supporting cast merely filling space and time. This often left me asking, "Wait, that's it? There has to be more to the story, right? Is the Bible really just a collection of unrelated accounts that seem to have little to no bearing on one another? Is there no metanarrative in the Bible, no detailed storyline that captures the big picture?" I'm embarrassed to say Bible study soon became a "required" burden instead of a real blessing. As a Christian minister, this was a "Houston, we have a problem" moment!

My theological world was rocked when a dear friend challenged my grasp of Jesus' good news and its supernatural implications by asking me several pointed questions. I began to dig deeper, much deeper than I ever had before, to find answers to those questions. In Jesus' Sermon on the Mount, He told His disciples, "You have heard that it was said, but I say unto you…" For many months, I felt like I lived on that mountain, listening to Jesus' words on repeat. Like the disciples, I too was in the classroom of the master Teacher, experiencing the hardest part of learning: unlearning. What I discovered on my journey truly changed me. The Bible wasn't missing anything—I was. I was missing the "eyes to see" (Matt 13:16). I was missing my first-century glasses.

The reality is "your gospel" (Gal 1:8) is too modern; it's filtered through hundreds of years of opinions and traditions, just like mine was. Unknowingly and unintentionally, Jesus' sheep have been led to brown pastures by many well-intentioned preachers and teachers. The epidemic of the modern gospel has invaded all of Christendom, including your church. I wrote this book to lead a new generation back to the beginning, back to the green pastures, and back to the original good news.

Our journey back in time will lead us to the ancient world, a world very different than the one we call home. I must warn you, however—this journey will demand everything of you. Like Abraham, you will be faced with the decision to raise your knife and sacrifice something you hold most dear at the turn of every page—your beliefs, your convictions, and your context. I assure you, when you finish this literary journey, your faith will soar to the heavens, and so will your love for reading the Bible.

Together, we will retrace the biblical narrative and point out important (and often overlooked) markers along the way—clues the inspired biblical writers, ancient Israelites, first-century Christians, the church fathers, and even historians left for seeking souls to find

(Matt 7:7). As you'll soon discover, the connectivity of all Scripture is shocking, and so is the forgotten story of the ancient gospel.

But what is the ancient gospel? Well, I'm so glad you asked. It's breathtaking and life-giving. It's supernatural and saving. It's gospel over gods.

CHAPTER 1

THE GUARDIAN CHERUB, THE TREE OF LIFE, AND THE REIGN OF DEATH

For God doth know that in the day ye eat thereof, then your eyes shall be opened, and ye shall be as gods, knowing good and evil. (Gen 3:5, KJV)

READING THE STORY

IN THE BEGINNING, THE ETERNAL WORD of God (John 1:1–3, 14) set our world into motion by releasing His thunderous voice into a new dimension (Ps 33:9). As heaven peered into the dark, dysfunctional void (Gen 1:2), the sons of God, His heavenly angels, looked on with amazement as they lifted up their voices in song (Job 38:7) as the Creator spoke.

> "Then God said, "Let there be light," and there was light. God saw that the light was good, and God separated the light from the darkness. God called the light "day," and the darkness he called "night." There was an evening, and there was a morning: one day. Then God said, "Let there be an expanse between the waters, separating water from water." So God made the expanse and separated the water under the expanse from the water above the expanse. And it was so. God called the expanse "sky." Evening came and then morning: the second day. Then God said, "Let the water under the sky be gathered into one place, and let the dry land appear." And it was so. God called the dry land "earth," and the gathering of the water he called "seas." And God saw that it was good. Then God said, "Let the earth produce vegetation: seed-bearing plants and fruit trees on the earth bearing fruit with seed in it according to their kinds." And it was so. The earth produced vegetation: seed-bearing plants according to their kinds and trees bearing fruit with seed in it according to their kinds. And God saw that it was good. Evening came and then morning: the third day. Then God said, "Let there be lights in the expanse of the sky to separate the day from the night. They will serve as signs for seasons and for days and years. They will be lights in the expanse of the sky to provide light on the earth." And it was so. God made the two great lights—the greater light to rule over the day and the lesser light to rule over the night—as well as the stars. God placed them in the expanse of the sky

to provide light on the earth, to rule the day and the night, and to separate light from darkness. And God saw that it was good. Evening came and then morning: the fourth day. Then God said, "Let the water swarm with living creatures, and let birds fly above the earth across the expanse of the sky." So God created the large sea-creatures and every living creature that moves and swarms in the water, according to their kinds. He also created every winged creature according to its kind. And God saw that it was good. God blessed them: "Be fruitful, multiply, and fill the waters of the seas, and let the birds multiply on the earth." Evening came and then morning: the fifth day. Then God said, "Let the earth produce living creatures according to their kinds: livestock, creatures that crawl, and the wildlife of the earth according to their kinds." And it was so. So God made the wildlife of the earth according to their kinds, the livestock according to their kinds, and all the creatures that crawl on the ground according to their kinds. And God saw that it was good. Then God said, "Let us make man in our image, according to our likeness. They will rule the fish of the sea, the birds of the sky, the livestock, the whole earth, and the creatures that crawl on the earth." So God created man in his own image; he created him in the image of God; he created them male and female. God blessed them, and God said to them, "Be fruitful, multiply, fill the earth, and subdue it. Rule the fish of the sea, the birds of the sky, and every creature that crawls on the earth." God also said, "Look, I have given you every seed-bearing plant on the surface of the entire earth and every tree whose fruit contains seed. This will be food for you, for all the wildlife of the earth, for every bird of the sky, and for every creature that crawls on the earth—everything having the breath of life in it—I have given every green plant for food." And it was so. God saw all that he had made, and it was very good indeed. Evening came and then morning: the sixth day." (Gen 1:3–31, CSB)

Oh, to be a heavenly fly on the wall, right?! For the heavenly hosts to witness the inception of this new realm, the innumerable galaxies in it, and the many creatures that were given the breath of life was quite the gift (Gen 1:20, 30; 2:7). To stand in God's presence and take it in must have been truly remarkable. But to at least one of God's supernatural sons—His anointed, winged guardian cherub (Ezek 28:14)—it was the start of a multidimensional war that directly affects you. I'm speaking of "the serpent," of course.

> *The adversary in the garden is the nachash, which is the word translated into English as "serpent." It's based on an adjective that means "bright or brazen, like shiny brass."*[1]

In the mind of the "shining serpent," he had outgrown his position among God's heavenly host. As the "fairest of them all," his inflated ego demanded he become something else—someone else. In Israel's taunt toward Babylon, the garden's infamous serpent is in view. Notice what Isaiah revealed about the devil's pompous heart.

> [13] You said to yourself, "I will ascend to the heavens; **I will set up my throne above the stars of God. I will sit on the mount of the gods' assembly**, in the remotest parts of the North. [14] I will ascend above the highest clouds; **I will make myself like the Most High**." (Isa 14:13–14, CSB)

Talk about high aspirations! They were out of this world, literally. He wanted to be equal to the Creator Himself and above "the stars of God," also known as "the angels of God" (Job 38:7). Satan wanted to rule heaven and earth, both the seen and unseen realms. To pull it off, he would soon recruit some supernatural help along the way. For now, however, he slithered alone.

---

1 Derek P. Gilbert, *The Great Inception: Satan's Psyops from Eden to Armageddon* (Crane, MO: Defender, 2017), Kindle edition.

Back to the story.

> The two were naked, both Adam and his wife, and they did not feel shame. Now the serpent was wiser than all the wild animals that were upon the land that the Lord God made. And the serpent said to the woman, "Why is it that God said, 'You may never eat from every tree of the garden?' " The woman said to the serpent, "From every tree of the garden we may eat, but from the fruit of the tree that is in the middle of the paradise God said, 'You will not eat from it, nor may you ever touch it, in order that you might not die.' " The serpent said to the woman, "You certainly will not die; for God knows that in the day you eat from it, your eyes will be opened, and you will be as gods who know good and evil." The woman saw that the tree was good for food and that it was pleasing to the eyes to look at and it was seasonable to look at, and after taking some of its fruit, she ate. She also gave to her husband with her, and they ate. Then the eyes of the two were opened, and they realized that they were naked, and they sewed together fig-tree leaves and made for themselves loincloths. They heard the sound of the Lord God walking about in the paradise in the evening, and both Adam and his wife hid from the face of the Lord God in the middle of the tree of the paradise. And Lord God summoned Adam and said to him, "Adam, where are you?" He said to him, "I heard the sound of you walking about in the paradise, and I was afraid because I am naked, and I hid." He said to him, "Who announced to you that you are naked? Unless you have eaten from the tree of which I commanded you 'From this one alone, do not eat.' " Adam said, "The woman whom you gave with me, she gave to me from the tree, and I ate." The Lord God said to the woman, "What is this you have done?" The woman said, "The serpent deceived me, and I ate." (Gen 3:1–13, LES)

Eating from the forbidden tree may seem like a small infraction, but it's quite the contrary. Eve's sin opened the floodgates for unrighteousness to rule in the hearts of men. For the first time in human history, mankind had sinned against their Creator.

As the Bible then reveals, the Lord curses the reptilic deceiver to a low status of existence.

> "So the LORD God said to the serpent: Because you have done this, **you are cursed** more than any livestock and more than any wild animal. You will move on your belly and **eat dust** all the days of your life. (Gen 3:14, CSB)

God's judgment of the serpent addressed his pride head-on.

> *The point being made by the curse is that the nachash, who wanted to be "most high," will be "most low" instead—cast away from God and the council to earth, and even under the earth. In the underworld, the nachash is even lower than the beasts of the field. He is hidden from view and from life in God's world. His domain is death.*[2]

Because of this judgment, the serpent would crawl on his belly and be forced to lick the dust all the days of his life (Mic 7:17). The prophet Ezekiel catalogued God's chiding of his anointed guardian cherub in Ezekiel 28:13–16.

> "You were in Eden, the garden of God. Every kind of precious stone covered you: carnelian, topaz, and diamond, beryl, onyx, and jasper, lapis lazuli, turquoise and emerald. Your mountings and settings were crafted in gold;

---

2 M. S. Heiser, *The Unseen Realm: Recovering the Supernatural Worldview of the Bible*, 1st ed. (Bellingham, WA: Lexham Press, 2015), 91.

> they were prepared on the day you were created. **You were an anointed guardian cherub**, for I had appointed you. You were on the holy mountain of God; you walked among the fiery stones. From the day you were created you were blameless in your ways until wickedness was found in you. Through the abundance of your trade, you were filled with violence, and you sinned. **So I expelled you in disgrace from the mountain of God**… (Ezek 28:13–16, CSB)

God continued,

> "I will put hostility between you and the woman, and **between your offspring and her offspring**. He will strike your head, and you will strike his heel. (Gen 3:15, CSB)

God's angelic sons undoubtedly looked on as Satan was then slung from the holy mountain of Eden. The cat was out of the bag. All of creation had just witnessed the first supernatural battle between good and evil. Satan's façade of loyalty to God was now evident to all beings of heaven and earth. As you'll soon see, his diabolical plan to steal, kill, and destroy (John 10:10) would pick up speed as he recruited his initial angelic allies, who would also rebel against their Creator and pledge their loyalty to the Satanic cause of human corruption.

ANSWERING YOUR QUESTIONS

WHAT DOES GENESIS 3:15 MEAN?

God told Satan,

> 15 I will put hostility between you and the woman, and **between your offspring and her offspring**. He will strike your head, and you will strike his heel. (Gen 3:15, CSB)

This prophecy packs a powerful punch. God knew there would be a continued struggle between the offspring of women and the offspring of Satan.

> *The rest of the biblical story doesn't consist of humans battling snake people. That's no surprise, since the enemy of humanity wasn't a mere snake. The Bible does, however, describe an ongoing conflict between followers of Yahweh and human and divine beings who follow the spiritual path of the nachash.*[3]

More will be revealed about this topic in the next chapter. As God revealed in Genesis 3:15,

> *A descendant of Eve would come forth who would someday undo the damage caused by the divine rebel, the nachash. That this descendant is linked to Eve implies that the score will be settled through her bloodline.*[4]

We now know the aim of this prophecy was centered around an intimate conflict between Satan and Jesus, the son of Mary. The pinnacle of their struggle would end with both parties being fatally "wounded." Jesus would be "bruised" by Satan in His death, and the serpent would be cosmically "crushed" by the resurrected Son of Man. While this prophecy is easy to unravel after the fact, it was very mysterious throughout the Old Testament, undoubtedly by strategic design.

WHY THE TWO TREES?

In God's infinite wisdom, He gave His human imagers free choice. The tree of life and the tree of the knowledge of good and evil were

---

3 Heiser, *The Unseen Realm*, 90.

4 Heiser, *The Unseen Realm*, 89.

visually and functionally a representation of that choice. Eat from the tree of life, and you will perpetuate immortality. Eat from the tree of the knowledge of good and evil, and you'll experience death. It was really that simple. Severian of Gabala (fifth century), a historically highly-esteemed preacher in Constantinople, stated,

> *The Tree of Life stood in the middle of paradise like a trophy. The Tree of Knowledge stood as a contest. If you keep the commandment of this tree, you will receive a prize. So consider this marvelous thought: Every tree in paradise was in bloom, and fruit was in abundance everywhere. Only in the center are the duo of competition and struggle.*[5]

Even now, the contest is still ongoing for your heart. God wants to win your heart willingly, not by force. However, the Lord does put abundance in our lives so that, hopefully, we will come to know and accept His love. St. Ephrem the Syrian (fourth century A.D.) wrote of the abundance our Creator had given Adam and Eve so that they, too, would always choose to live life with God in His beautiful paradise garden.

> *Even though God had given them everything else out of Grace, He wished to confer on them, out of Justice, the immortal life which is granted through eating of the Tree of Life. He therefore laid down this commandment. Not that it was a large commandment, commensurate with the superlative reward that was in preparation for them; no,* ***He only withheld from them a single tree, just so that they might be subject to a commandment****. But He gave them the whole of*

5 Andrew Louth and Marco Conti, eds., *Genesis 1–11* (Downers Grove, IL: InterVarsity Press, 2001), 61.

> *Paradise, so that they would not feel any compulsion to transgress the law.*[6]

Many have asked, "Whatever happened to the garden of Eden and the tree of life?" While God doesn't exactly give us its longitude and latitude, we know it still exists, tucked away for the saints who die in the Lord. Fittingly, the Bible both begins and ends with God's human imagers eating from the tree of life and living in the garden of paradise. Note the following passages in the book of Revelation:

Revelation 2:7 (CSB)	Revelation 22:2 (CSB)	Revelation 22:14 (CSB)	Revelation 22:19 (CSB)
7 "Let anyone who has ears to hear listen to what the Spirit says to the churches. To the one who conquers, I will give the right to eat from the **tree of life**, which is in the paradise of God.	2 down the middle of the city's main street. The **tree of life** was on each side of the river, bearing twelve kinds of fruit, producing its fruit every month. The leaves of the tree are for healing the nations,	14 "Blessed are those who wash their robes, so that they may have the right to the **tree of life** and may enter the city by the gates.	19 And if anyone takes away from the words of the book of this prophecy, God will take away his share of the **tree of life** and the holy city, which are written about in this book.

As the *Baker Encyclopedia of the Bible* so beautifully points out,

---

6 Ephrem, *Hymns on Paradise*, 209 (Brock).

> *The way to the tree of life which was closed in Genesis 3 is open again for God's believing people in Revelation. This has been made possible by the second Adam, Jesus Christ. Those who have washed their robes in the blood of Christ (cf. Rv 7:14), and have sought forgiveness of their sin through the redemptive work of Christ receive the right to the tree of life (22:14), but the disobedient will have no access to it.*[7]

Indeed, Christ has removed all roadblocks to the tree of life for believers who seek its fruit, including its mysterious protector, the "flaming sword" that God commissioned to "stand guard" after the fall. Origen of Alexandria (185–254 A.D.) wrote,

> *For who else could remove "the flaming turning sword which was placed to guard the tree of life" and the gates of paradise? What other sentinel was able to turn the "cherubim" from their incessant vigil, except only he to whom "was given all power in heaven and in earth." As, I say, no one else could do these things besides him [Christ]...*[8]

CONNECTING THE GOSPEL

SEPARATION & THE SECOND DEATH

Since God cannot lie (Heb 6:18), man surely died as a result of their sin. You may be asking, "Well, then why didn't they?"

Some have falsely assumed God got cold feet and "presidentially" pardoned them from execution. However, that line of thinking is completely off-base. It's important to understand that God never

---

7 W. A. Elwell and B. J. Beitzel, "Tree of Life," *Baker Encyclopedia of the Bible* 2:2105.

8 Origen, *Homilies on Leviticus 1–16*, 185 (Barkley).

specified when or how they would "surely die." Just that they *would* die. Their punishment is best summed up in one word—separation.

How does separation from God lead to death? Getting to the bottom of this question is crucial as we're introduced to the ancient gospel. Due to the fall of man, two connected yet distinct deaths plague us all. The first and most obvious is physical death.

> [27] And just as it is appointed for people to die once—and after this, judgment—[28] so also Christ, having been offered once to bear the sins of many, will appear a second time, not to bear sin, but to bring salvation to those who are waiting for him. (Heb 9:27–28, CSB)

Eventually, everyone is forced to walk in the valley of the shadow of death (Ps 23:4). Like the sage Solomon said, there's "a time to be born, and a time to die" (Eccl 3:2, ESV).

For Adam and Eve, things just got real. All they've ever known is Eden's paradise and God's holy presence filling it. As God addressed His divine council of holy angels (Ps 89:6–7), He made the executive decision. Mankind would have to be moved out of the garden and severed from the tree of life. We left Him no choice.

> [22] The Lord God said, "Since the man has become like one of us, knowing good and evil, he must not reach out, take from the tree of life, eat, and live forever." [23] So **the Lord God sent him away from the garden of Eden** to work the ground from which he was taken. [24] He drove the man out and stationed the cherubim and the flaming, whirling sword east of the garden of Eden to guard the way to the tree of life. (Gen 3:22–24, CSB)

Their immortal status had been revoked. No tree of life meant no immortality. Eventually, they would die. Every time someone grasps death's chilling hand, they have the lord of the dead to thank for it. Every spouse, every child, and every parent who stands over a grave and grieves is reminded of this indescribable pain that was born out of Satan's deception.

As painful as dying is for all parties involved, it's what comes after death, however, that will haunt the souls of those who reject the gospel: the second death.

> 8 But the cowards, faithless, detestable, murderers, sexually immoral, sorcerers, idolaters, and all liars—their share will be in **the lake that burns with fire and sulfur, which is the second death**." (Rev 21:8, CSB)

The biggest downside to being kicked out of God's garden wasn't losing their lunch card to the tree of life, though; it was the newfound realization that, for the first time, they would be separated from God's holy presence. They would no longer hear the rustling grass as their Creator walked with them (Gen 3:8) in the beautiful paradise garden. It was all due to their "partaking" in sin. Sin separates—it always has. Paul taught that those who experience the second death will be cast away from the presence of the Lord.

> 8 with burning flame giving punishment to those who do not know God and who do not obey the gospel of our Lord Jesus,
> 9 who will pay the penalty of eternal destruction, **away from the presence of the LORD** and from the glory of his strength, (2 Thess 1:8–9, LEB)

The resemblance between the debacle in Eden and eternal punishment is undeniable. Adam and Eve's punishment created a template with everlasting effects. This template of separation, as a means of punishment for the ungodly, is littered throughout both the Old and New Testaments. Here's what Jesus said about it in Matthew 7.

> [21] Not every one that saith unto me, Lord, Lord, shall enter into
> the kingdom of heaven; but he that doeth the will of my Father
> which is in heaven. [22] Many will say to me in that day, Lord,
> Lord, have we not prophesied in thy name? and in thy name have
> cast out devils? and in thy name done many wonderful works?
> [23] And then will I profess unto them, I never knew you: **depart
> from me**, ye that work iniquity. (Matt 7:21–23, KJV 1900)

Hell is real and was originally built for the devil and his angels. However, it will also be, by default, the eternal home of everyone who isn't liberated from the serpent (Matt 23:33), as Justin Martyr (100–165 A.D.) wrote in the First Apology 28:

> *For with us the prince of the evil spirits is called a serpent, and Satan, and the devil, as you may learn even from an examination of our writings; who, Christ has foretold, will be sent into fire with his host, and the men who are his followers, there to be tormented to an endless eternity.*[9]

As Leo the Great (400–461 A.D.) pointed out,

> *...unless the Almighty God did deign to do this, no kind of righteousness, no form of wisdom could rescue any one from the devil's bondage and from the depths of eternal death. For the condemnation that passes with sin from one upon all would remain, and our nature, corroded by its deadly wound, would discover no remedy, because it could not alter its state in its own strength.*[10]

---

9 G. A. Jackson, *The Apostolic Fathers and the Apologists of the Second Century*, ed. G. P. Fisher (New York: D. Appleton and Company, 1879), 156.

10 Leo the Great, *Sermons*, 135 (Feltoe).

Our journey into the past is about giving you a future hope, one that's far away from Satan, his angels, and the lake of fire. God has made that possible through the Savior, Jesus Christ.

> [1] For we know that if our earthly tent we live in is destroyed, we have a building from God, an eternal dwelling in the heavens, not made with hands. (2 Cor 5:1, CSB)

> [3] Blessed be the God and Father of our Lord Jesus Christ, who according to his great mercy has caused us to be born again to a living hope through the resurrection of Jesus Christ from the dead, [4] into an inheritance imperishable and undefiled and unfading, reserved in heaven for you (1 Pet 1:3–4, LEB)

I assure you, you can escape eternal death and its dark lord! It all starts with realizing and acknowledging what the fruit of your sin has borne—separation.

> [2] But your sins make a separation between you and God, and because of your sins he has turned his face away from you, to show no mercy. [3] For your hands have become defiled with blood, and your fingers with sins, and your lips have uttered lawlessness, and your tongue gives heed to injustice… [12] For our lawlessness is great before you, and our sins are set against us, for our lawless acts are with us, and we know our unjust acts. (Isa 59:2–3, 12, LES)

Isaiah's words hit like a ton of bricks. Like Adam and Eve, we are dead men and women who long for life, yet we innately lack the ability to create it. But, by God's grace, there is good news! Paul sees "the man Jesus" as the means of overthrowing death's reign, which gained its foothold through "the man Adam."

> 12 Therefore, just as sin entered the world through one
> man, and death through sin, in this way death spread to all
> people, because all sinned. 13 In fact, sin was in the world
> before the law, but sin is not charged to a person's account
> when there is no law. 14 Nevertheless, death reigned from
> Adam to Moses, even over those who did not sin in the
> likeness of Adam's transgression. He is a type of the Coming
> One. 15 But the gift is not like the trespass. For if by the
> one man's trespass the many died, how much more have the
> grace of God and the gift which comes through the grace
> of the one man Jesus Christ overflowed to the many. 16 And
> the gift is not like the one man's sin, because from one sin
> came the judgment, resulting in condemnation, but from
> many trespasses came the gift, resulting in justification.
> 17 If by the one man's trespass, death reigned through
> that one man, how much more will those who receive the
> overflow of grace and the gift of righteousness reign in life
> through the one man, Jesus Christ. 18 So then, as through
> one trespass there is condemnation for everyone, so also
> through one righteous act there is justification leading to
> life for everyone. 19 For just as through one man's disobe-
> dience the many were made sinners, so also through the
> one man's obedience the many will be made righteous.
> 20 The law came along to multiply the trespass. But where
> sin multiplied, grace multiplied even more 21 so that, just
> as sin reigned in death, so also grace will reign through
> righteousness, resulting in eternal life through Jesus Christ
> our Lord. (Rom 5:12–21, CSB)

We'll pick up additional layers to the gospel along our journey. For now, know that Jesus can save us from all sin and from the white knuckles of Satan's death grip.

LOOKING AHEAD

After the fall of man, there was a new sheriff in town: the devious devil. His reign over humanity was certain. He was inaugurated as the god of this world after just one bite (2 Cor 4:4).

As Adam and Eve descended down the precipitous side of Eden and off God's holy mountain, they were no longer exclusively the Creator's. Satan had laid claim to their souls and was looking to collect in the event of their "unfortunate" deaths. As the first family set out into the unknown, one thing was certain—there was blood in the water. The war for heaven and earth had begun.

CHAPTER 2

THE SONS OF GOD, THE DAUGHTERS OF MEN, AND A GIANT PROBLEM

The angels of God, having seen the daughters of humans, that they were beautiful, took for themselves women from all whom they picked out. (Genesis 6:2, LES)

READING THE STORY

MAN WAS RESILIENT. THE CHANGE IN ZIP code didn't annul their allegiance to their Maker. They understood their role in the circle of life. Adam and Eve had children, a quiver full of them (Ps 127:5). This is precisely what God asked them to do back in the garden—be fruitful and multiply (Gen 1:28). Their procreation was essential for populating the earth.

Do you recall the Lord's scathing rebuke to the serpent in our previous chapter?

> 15 I will put hostility between you and the woman, and between **your offspring** and **her offspring**. He will strike your head, and you will strike his heel. (Gen 3:15, CSB)

Though vague, God was firm; one of their descendants would defeat the lord of the dead. This brought hope into the world and helped them navigate the dangerous highways of family tragedy and dark days (Gen 4). They spent much of their time running on the fumes of love and hope. Unknown to them, thousands of years would pass before Jesus, the silent assassin (Isa 53:7), would slay the dragon (Isa 27:1).

The question that needs to be answered is, "Who are the serpent's seed, what was their origin, and why would they fight with men?" Most Bible teachers make the messianic connection and move on. "Nothing to see here, move along, Bible student." In the rare event that it is discussed, a metaphorical application is often made, saying this represents anyone who aligns themselves with Satan. This isn't an unfair analysis. Passages in the Bible paint the picture of people making the devil their spiritual father quite frequently (John 8:44; 1 John 3:12). However, this isn't the whole story.

What happens next may come as a shock to your modern ears, but it will provide tremendous clarity to the "serpent's seed" issue. More importantly, it will enlighten you about the ancient context of Genesis 6.

> When man began to multiply on the face of the land and daughters were born to them, the **sons of God** saw that the daughters of man were attractive. And **they took as their wives** any they chose. (Gen 6:1–2, ESV)

As the sons of God—His holy angels (Job 1:6–8; 2:1–4; 38:4–7)—fixated on beautiful human women, they were drawn away by lust and enticed. These angelic rebels abandoned their proper dwelling (Jude 1:6) and pledged their loyalty to the Satanic cause. The sexual mingling of the celestial angels and human women produced monstrous giants called the Nephilim, the mighty warriors of old.

> The Nephilim were on the earth in those days, and also afterward, when the sons of God came in to the daughters of man and **they bore children to them**. These were the mighty men who were of old, the men of renown. (Gen 6:4, ESV)

Heaven was heartbroken over the angels' pursuit of unnatural desire (Jude 1:7) and many women's apparently willing participation in it (Dan 11:37). The Lord was cut to the heart and was sorrowful that He had made man (Gen 6:6). The addition of human "imagers" (Gen 1:27) proved to be too much for many of God's heavenly host.

With a broken heart, God said to the angelic faithful who fled fornication (1 Cor 6:18),

> … "I will blot out man whom I have created from the face of the land, man and animals and creeping things and birds of the heavens, for I am sorry that I have made them." (Gen 6:7, ESV)

Tough decisions were becoming the status quo as of late; the devil was forcing God's hand.

> "The LORD saw that the wickedness of man was great in the earth, and that every intention of the thoughts of his heart was only evil continually. (Gen 6:5, ESV)

The earth had become a breeding ground for sexual sin and false teaching. Satan's newest angelic recruits were at the helm of the sinking ship of morality (Job 4:18). Unfortunately, humanity had become their loyal deckhands. It was official—the heavens couldn't be trusted (Job 15:15). Sin was rampant in all realms.

ANSWERING YOUR QUESTIONS

HOW DO WE KNOW "THE SONS OF GOD" ARE "THE ANGELS OF GOD?"

A good rule of thumb for parsing interpretations of any given text is to let the Bible dictate its own terms and definitions. It's sinful and irresponsible to do otherwise (2 Tim 2:15). One should always ask, "Are there other passages in Scripture that speak directly to this issue?" Do they contain the exact words or similar phrases to the controversial passage under consideration? In other words, serious Bible students yield to inspiration (2 Tim 3:16), not their preferences or pet views; those they're willing to sacrifice. Truth-seekers speak where the Word speaks and are silent where it is silent.

Using these guidelines with Genesis 6:1–8, it becomes apparent that the "sons of God" **(benê [ha]ʾelōhîm)** of the Old Testament are always divine members of God's heavenly host. The "sons of God" language of Genesis 6 appears four other times in the Hebrew Bible. Three of the occurrences are in the book of Job.

In Job 38, God asked Job,

> 4 Where were you when I established the earth? Tell me, if you have understanding. 5 Who fixed its dimensions? Certainly

> you know! Who stretched a measuring line across it? [6] What
> supports its foundations? Or who laid its cornerstone [7] **while
> the morning stars sang together and all the sons of God
> shouted for joy**? (Job 38:4–7, CSB)

Clearly, in this text, angelic beings are "the sons of God." Mankind wasn't even in existence when God laid the foundation of the earth, only the angels. The phrase, "the sons of God," is also used twice in the early chapters of Job.

> [6] One day **the sons of God came to present themselves before
> the Lord, and Satan also came with them.** [7] The Lord asked
> Satan, "Where have you come from?" "From roaming through
> the earth," Satan answered him, "and walking around on it."
> (Job 1:6–7, CSB)

> [1] One day **the sons of God came again to present themselves
> before the Lord, and Satan also came with them to present
> himself before the Lord**. [2] The Lord asked Satan, "Where
> have you come from?" "From roaming through the earth," Satan
> answered him, "and walking around on it." (Job 2:1–2, CSB)

The "sons of God" who presented themselves before the Lord of heaven are, unambiguously, angelic beings.

The last occurrence where the sons of God are unquestionably the angels of God is found in Deuteronomy 32:8–9. However, we'll have more to say about that in a future chapter.

There's not a single passage in all of the Old Testament where the "sons of God" (**benê [ha]ʾelōhîm**) are mere humans, including Genesis 6:1-4. The early church understood who the sons of God were in Genesis 6. Their use of the Septuagint, the Greek translation of the Hebrew Scriptures, preserves the original context of the passage—the sons of God = the angels of God. The Lexham English Septuagint reads,

> [1] And Noah lived five hundred years, and Noah fathered three sons: Shem, Ham, and Japheth. And it happened, when humans began to become numerous upon the land, and they had daughters, [2] **the angels of God**, having seen the daughters of humans, that they were beautiful, **took for themselves women** from all whom they picked out. (Genesis 6:1–2, LES)

WHAT DID ANCIENT JEWS AND EARLY CHRISTIANS BELIEVE?

On our journey to discover the ancient gospel, you will be tempted to reach for the shelf and grab a "trusty" twentieth-century commentary. You may even get squirmy enough to call your minister to set things straight. You should resist this urge. Blindly listening to modern teachers and preachers is what got us all into this mess to begin with. It's not our job to "decide" the meaning of a passage, but to "discover" how the original readers understood it.

I'm not suggesting that you burn your library and shun your preacher. I simply want you to come to grips with the fact that the Bible wasn't written to you—it was written for you (Rom 15:4). It wasn't written to your parents, grandparents, or great-grandparents. It wasn't even written to the PhD scholar down the street; it was written to ancient Jews and early Christians. Their context matters more than yours, mine, or anyone else you've ever known. As we seek to restore the old paths, I humbly ask that you acknowledge this and give a listening ear to a cloud of ancient witnesses who, though dead, still speak (Heb 11:4).

Flavius Josephus was a well-informed and respected Jewish historian who was born in Jerusalem in 37 A.D. The writings he left behind are invaluable to our understanding of ancient history and have been cited for centuries by countless theologians, scholars, and ministers alike. In his book Antiquities of the Jews, Josephus commented on Genesis 6 by saying,

> *(73)* ***for many angels of God accompanied with women****, and* ***begat sons*** *that proved unjust, and despisers of all that was good, on account of the confidence they had in their own strength; for the tradition is, That these men did what resembled the acts of those whom the Grecians call* ***giants****. (74) But Noah was very uneasy at what they did; and, being displeased at their conduct, persuaded them to change their dispositions and their acts for the better;—but, seeing that they did not yield to him, but were slaves to their wicked pleasures, he was afraid they would kill him, together with his wife and children, and those they had married; so he departed out of that land.*[1]

Irenaeus (130–203 A.D.) of Gaul was a disciple of Polycarp, who was a disciple of the apostle John. He expounded on Genesis 6 by saying,

> *And for a very long while wickedness extended and spread, and reached and laid hold upon the whole race of mankind, until a very small seed of righteousness remained among them: and* ***illicit unions*** *took place upon the earth, since* ***angels were united with the daughters of the race of mankind; and they bore to them sons who for their exceeding greatness were called giants.***[2]

Athenagoras (c. 133–190 A.D.) was known as "the Christian philosopher of Athens." He's famous for his Apology in 177 A.D., which was

---

1 Flavius Josephus, *The Works of Josephus: Complete and Unabridged*, 32 (Whiston).

2 Irenæus, *The Demonstration of the Apostolic Preaching*, 85 (Robinson).

written to Emperor Marcus Aurelius and defended the Christian faith. He commented on Genesis 6 by writing,

> *And just as with men who have power to choose good or evil—for you would not honour the virtuous and punish evildoers if vice and virtue were not within their free choice—some are found zealous for what they are entrusted with by you, and others remiss,* ***so it is with these angels too****: some remained at the task for which they were created and to which they were appointed by God (for they had received free will from God), while others acted wantonly towards their own nature and their charge, that is, the ruler of this realm of matter and of the forms that are in it, and others that were in charge of the first firmament. Pray, realize that we tell of nothing without evidence, but expound what the prophets have declared. Well then,* ***these angels fell a-lusting after maidens and yielded to fleshly desires****, and he, the chief of them, became heedless and wicked in the administration of his charge.* ***Thus by those that went after maidens were the so-called giants begotten***[3]

Justin Martyr (100–165 A.D.) was a prominent Christian defender of the second century. He started two Christian schools in Ephesus and Rome. Eventually, he was "martyred" for his beliefs. He wrote,

> *God, when He had made the whole world, and subjected things earthly to man, and arranged the heavenly elements for the increase of fruits and rotation of the seasons, and appointed this divine law—for these things also He evidently made for man—committed the care of men and of all things under heaven to*

3 Athenagoras, *Athenagoras: Embassy for the Christians, The Resurrection of the Dead*, 62–63 (Crehan).

> *angels whom He appointed over them. But* ***the angels transgressed this appointment, and were captivated by love of women...***[4]

Commodian was a Latin Christian poet of the third century. He commented on the angelic fall of Genesis 6 by stating,

> ***Such was the beauty of women, that it turned them [the angels] aside****; so that, being contaminated, they could not return to heaven. Rebels from God, they uttered words against Him. Then the Highest uttered His judgment against them; and* ***from their seed giants are said to have been born.***[5]

Clement of Rome (c. 35–99 A.D.), the believed associate of Peter, Paul, and John, is sometimes linked with a series of sermons called The Clementine Homilies. It expounds on the angelic sin of Genesis 6:

> *yet having become in all respects men,* ***they [the angels] also partook of human lust****, and being brought under its subjection they fell into cohabitation with women; and being involved with them, and sunk in defilement and altogether emptied of their first power, were unable to turn back to the first purity of their proper nature... "But* ***from their unhallowed intercourse spurious men sprang, ranch greater in stature than ordinary men, whom they afterwards called giants.***[6]

Quintus Septimius Florens Tertullian (160–220 A.D.) was "the father of Latin theology."

---

4 Justin Martyr, *The Second Apology of Justin*, 190 (Roberts and Donaldson).

5 Commodian, *The Instructions of Commodianus*, 203 (Wallis).

6 PSEUDO-Clement of Rome, *The Clementine Homilies*, 273 (Smith).

> *Trained as a lawyer, Tertullian converted to the Christian faith shortly before 197. He became a leading *apologist for the church and argued eloquently for imperial toleration of Christians, who, he urged, were not enemies of the state. He also made the case that Christianity was vastly superior to other religions.*[7]

Tertullian discussed the angelic sin of Genesis 6 on multiple occasions. In On Idolatry 9, he said "those angels, the deserters from God, the lovers of women…" Furthermore, in his writing On the Veiling of Virgins, he argued that Paul's reference to women wearing a head covering (a symbol of authority), "because of the angels" (1 Cor 11:10) refers to the sexual enticement of angels. He wrote at length,

> *If "the woman ought to have power upon the head," all the more justly ought the virgin, to whom pertains the essence of the cause (assigned for this assertion). For if (it is) on account of* ***the angels****—those, to wit,* ***whom we read of as having fallen from God and heaven on account of concupiscence after females****—who can presume that it was bodies already defiled, and relics of human* **lust***, which such angels yearned after, so as not rather to have been inflamed for virgins, whose bloom pleads an excuse for human lust likewise? For thus does Scripture withal suggest: "And it came to pass," it says, "when men had begun to grow more numerous upon the earth, there were withal daughters born them; but* ***the sons of God, having descried the daughters of men, that they were fair, took to themselves wives of all whom they elected****." For here the Greek name of women does seem to have the sense "wives," inasmuch as mention is made of marriage. When, then, it says "the daughters of men," it manifestly purports virgins,*

---

7 N. P. Feldmeth, *Pocket Dictionary of Church History: Over 300 Terms Clearly and Concisely Defined* (Downers Grove, IL: IVP Academic, 2008), 131.

> *who would be still reckoned as belonging to their parents—for wedded women are called their husbands'—whereas it could have said "the wives of men:" in like manner not naming the angels adulterers, but husbands, while they take unwedded "daughters of men," who it has above said were "born," thus also signifying their virginity: first, "born;" but here,* ***wedded to angels****. Anything else I know not that they were except "born" and subsequently wedded. So perilous a face, then, ought to be shaded, which has* ***cast stumbling-stones even so far as heaven****: that, when standing in the presence of God, at whose bar it stands accused of the* ***driving of the angels from their (native) confines****, it may blush before the other angels as well; and may repress that former evil liberty of its head,—(a liberty) now to be exhibited not even before human eyes. But even if they were females already contaminated whom those angels had desired, so much the more "****on account of the angels****" would it have been the duty of virgins to be veiled,* ***as it would have been the more possible for virgins to have been the cause of the angels' sinning****. If, moreover, the apostle further adds the prejudgment of "nature," that redundancy of locks is an honour to a woman, because hair serves for a covering, of course it is most of all to a virgin that this is a distinction; for their very adornment properly consists in this, that, by being massed together upon the crown, it wholly covers the very citadel of the head with an encirclement of hair.*[8]

The "CD," also known as the "Cairo Document" or the "Damascus Document," discusses the sin of the Heavenly Watchers of Genesis 6. Copies of the CD were found at Qumran among the Dead Sea Scrolls. In a stern warning to Qumran's community members about sexual purity, CD-A Col. ii:14–21 states,

---

8 Tertullian, *On the Veiling of Virgins*, 31–32 (Thelwall).

14 And now, hear me, O children, that I may open your eyes to see and to understand the acts of 15 God, to choose what He desires, and to despise what He hates, [to observe the statutes of God with the loving covenant], to walk perfectly 16 in all His ways and not to wander into thoughts inclining toward transgression with eyes of whoredom, since many 17 have gone astray in these matters. Mighty armies have stumbled into them from the time of old until now. ***While walking in the stubbornness of 18 their heart the Watchers of Heaven fell. In it (whoredom) were seized those who have not obeyed the commandments of God 19 along with their children, whose height was like that of the cedars.*** *And their bodies were piled up like mountains, because 20 all flesh which was on the dry land fell, for they died and were as if they had never been, because they were following 21 their passions.*[9]

Clement of Alexandria (150–215 A.D.) was an author, teacher, and true defender of the Christian faith in the second to third century. He referenced Genesis 6 in his Miscellanies.

To which also we shall add, that ***the angels*** *who had obtained the superior rank,* ***having sunk into pleasures, told to the women*** *the secrets which had come to their knowledge;*[10]

Lactantius (240–320 A.D.), the Christian rhetorician of North Africa, wrote in his literary work, The Divine Institutes,

Therefore, while they ***[the angels]*** *abode among men, that most deceitful ruler of the earth, by his very association, gradually*

9 B. Embry, R. Herms, and A. T. Wright, eds., vol. 2 of *Early Jewish Literature: An Anthology* (Grand Rapids, MI: William B. Eerdmans Publishing Company, 2018), 137.

10 Clement of Alexandria, *The Stromata, or Miscellanies*, 446 (Roberts).

> *enticed them to vices, and polluted them by* ***intercourse with women****. Then, not being admitted into heaven on account of the sins into which they had plunged themselves, they fell to the earth.* ***Thus from angels the devil makes them to become his satellites and attendants.***[11]

If we truly want to read the Bible through first-century glasses, then we must be prepared to accept what we find in antiquity. In the case of Genesis 6:1–4, we consistently find a supernatural interpretation in both ancient Judaism and throughout the first several centuries of the early church.

HOW CAN SPIRITUAL BEINGS REPRODUCE WITH HUMAN WOMEN?

Many have asked the question, "How can spiritual heavenly beings procreate with female human beings?" This is a valid question. To answer it, we need to unlearn common misguided understandings about angels.

By nature, angels are ministering spirits (pneumata). They are described as "winds" and flames of fire (Ps 104:4; Heb 1:7) who are greater in might and power (2 Pet 2:11). However, they can also take on physical embodiment and perform physical tasks.

Here's a small sampling of God's "holy ones" (qedôšîm) doing physical things.

1. An angel struck Peter to wake him up during his prison break experience.

> 6 And when Herod was about to bring him out, that night Peter was sleeping, bound with two chains between two soldiers; and the guards before the door were keeping the prison. 7 Now behold, **an angel of the Lord stood by him**, and a light shone

11 Lactantius, *The Divine Institutes*, 64 (Fletcher).

in the prison; and **he struck Peter on the side and raised him up**, saying, "Arise quickly!" And his chains fell off his hands. (Acts 12:6–7, NKJV)

2. Angels ate food, washed their feet, and stayed in Lot's house.

[1] Now the **two angels** came to Sodom in the evening, and Lot was sitting in the gate of Sodom. When Lot saw them, he rose to meet them, and he bowed himself with his face toward the ground. [2] And he said, "Here now, my lords, please turn in to your servant's house and **spend the night, and wash your feet**; then you may rise early and go on your way." And they said, "No, but we will spend the night in the open square." [3] But he insisted strongly; so they turned in to him and entered his house. Then he made them a feast, and baked unleavened bread, and **they ate**. (Gen 19:1–3, NKJV)

3. Angels sat at the tomb of Jesus as they talked with Mary concerning the whereabouts of Jesus' body.

[1] Now after the Sabbath, at the dawning on the first day of the week, Mary Magdalene and the other Mary came to view the tomb. [2] And behold, there was a great earthquake, for **an angel of the Lord descended from heaven and came up and rolled away the stone and sat down on it**. (Matt 28:1–2, LEB)

[11] But Mary stood outside at the tomb, weeping. Then, while she was weeping, she bent over to look into the tomb, [12] and she saw **two angels** in white, **seated one at the head and one at the feet** where the body of Jesus had been lying. [13] And they said to her, "Woman, why are you weeping?" **She said to them**, "They have

> taken away my Lord, and I do not know where they have put him!" (John 20:11–13, LEB)

While angels are spiritual beings, their ability to take on physical form cannot be denied. Our lack of understanding about how the supernatural works is not a valid reason to deny its existence or interaction with our world. Somehow, the supernatural world can link to the natural. Nothing about the supernatural world can be explained by modern science or by any laws of nature because it's not natural—it's supernatural. The reality is angels can walk, talk, eat, sit, sleep, and yes, even reproduce if they so choose.

According to the Testaments of Reuben and Naphtali, two of twelve volumes in a second-century B.C. Jewish set titled The Testaments of the Twelve Patriarchs, the angelic Watchers of Genesis 6 chose flesh over spirit, changed their nature, and fulfilled their sinful lust.

> *Testament of Reuben 5:6 – For it was thus that they charmed the Watchers, who were before the Flood. As they continued looking at the women, **they were filled with desire for them** and perpetrated the act in their minds. Then **they were transformed** into human males, and while the women were cohabiting with their husbands they appeared to them. Since **the women's minds were filled with lust for these apparitions, they gave birth to giants**. For the Watchers were disclosed to them as being as high as the heavens.*[12]

> *Testament of Naphtali 3:5 – Likewise **the Watchers departed from nature's order**; the Lord pronounced a curse on them at*

12 J. H. Charlesworth, vol. 1 of *The Old Testament Pseudepigrapha* (New York; London: Yale University Press, 1983), 784.

> *the Flood. On their account he ordered that the earth be without dweller or produce.*[13]

WHAT ABOUT THE SETHITE VIEW?

The Sethite view is a non-supernaturalist interpretation of Genesis 6:1–4. This belief teaches that the godly sons of Seth (the sons of God) married the rebellious daughters of Cain (the daughters of man). Most modern Christians hold this view. To say this "interpretation" has a bevy of issues is an understatement.

1. To say the sons of God are the sons of Seth and to say the daughters of man are the daughters of Cain is to totally ignore what the text actually says. The Hebrew words are especially important here. Moses uses the word ʿādām (translated "man/mankind") several times in the text. This Hebrew word describes "all humanity."

> 1 When man (**ʿādām** – all mankind) began to multiply on the face of the land and daughters were born to them, 2 the sons of God saw that the daughters of man (**ʿādām** – all mankind) were attractive. And they took as their wives any they chose. (Gen 6:1–2, ESV)

If Moses wanted us to know the sons of God were the sons of Seth, he used the wrong Hebrew word. He should have used the Hebrew word for Seth (***sheth***). Did he make a mistake? Likewise, if Moses wanted his readers to know the daughters of men were the daughters of Cain, he should have used the Hebrew word for Cain (***qayin***). Is the inspired Word wrong? No.

2. Second, "Seth" is not "God," and "Men" are not "Cain." What if your minister or pastor shuffled names in and out of the biblical text by saying Adam was married to Evelyn, not Eve?

---

13 Charlesworth, *The Old Testament Pseudepigrapha*, 812.

While this may generate some laughs among part of the congregation, many would question if the speaker was feeling okay. If this continued week after week, it would lead to a disgruntled body who grew impatient with him changing the Word of God. He would soon be forced to resign, or he would be fired.

Do you think the Lord would be pleased if everywhere else in the Bible where Jesus' name is found, we swapped it out with the name "Seth?" Should we teach that Seth created the heavens and the earth or that Seth died for our sins? I think you get the point; every jot and tittle, every letter and word, is important (Matt 5:18).

3. Third, are we supposed to believe that Cainite men never married Sethite women? If so, why wasn't that an issue?
4. Fourth, how does the Sethite interpretation contribute to the mass corruption upon all flesh? In other words, how did marital unions between the sons of Seth and the daughters of Cain (which weren't forbidden by God) lead to worldwide corruption and the decay of morality?
5. Fifth, how did marriages between these two human families suddenly start producing giants/Nephilim on the earth?

For centuries, readers have been misled by the Sethite interpretation. The biblical writers and people of antiquity knew nothing of the Sethite view. Like most false teaching, it slithered into the church and reared its ugly head hundreds of years after the church was established. While Julius Africanus was the first to mention the Sethite view (third century), Augustine of Hippo (354–430 A.D.) was the first to popularize it. As the Lexham Bible Dictionary points out concerning Augustine,

> *His work is also seen as a transition point between the ancient view of the world and the medieval one.*[14]

---

14 M. Wierenga, "Church Fathers," *Lexham Bible Dictionary*.

Teaching any view of Genesis 6:1–4 that originated centuries years after the church was established cannot honestly be considered as teaching about these verses in context.

WHAT ABOUT MATTHEW 22:30?

Defenders of the "Sethite" view use Matthew 22:30 in an attempt to "prove" that it is impossible for angels to marry or procreate. This Scripture states,

> 23 The same day came to him the Sadducees, which say that there
> is no resurrection, and asked him, 24 Saying, Master, Moses said,
> If a man die, having no children, his brother shall marry his
> wife, and raise up seed unto his brother. 25 Now there were with
> us seven brethren: and the first, when he had married a wife,
> deceased, and, having no issue, left his wife unto his brother:
> 26 Likewise the second also, and the third, unto the seventh.
> 27 And last of all the woman died also. 28 Therefore in the resur-
> rection whose wife shall she be of the seven? for they all had her.
> 29 Jesus answered and said unto them, Ye do err, not knowing
> the scriptures, nor the power of God. 30 For in the resurrection
> they neither marry, nor are given in marriage, **but are as the
> angels of God in heaven**. (Matt 22:23–30, KJV 1900)

Note: Jesus made sure to clarify to which set of angels He referred—the angels of God in heaven. The fallen angels of Genesis 6 are not among the faithful in heaven. Since they were "wandering stars" (Matt 24:29; Mark 13:25; Jude 1:13) who left "their proper dwelling," they were locked under gloomy chains of darkness. Peter and Jude taught this when they referred back to the Genesis 6 episode.

> 4 For if God did not spare angels **when they sinned**, but cast them into hell and **committed them to chains of gloomy**

> **darkness** to be kept until the judgment; [5] if he did not spare **the ancient world**, but preserved Noah, a herald of righteousness, with seven others, **when he brought a flood upon the world of the ungodly**; (2 Pet 2:4–5, ESV)

> [6] And the angels who did not stay within their own position of authority, but **left their proper dwelling, he has kept in eternal chains under gloomy darkness until the judgment of the great day—** [7] **just as** Sodom and Gomorrah and the surrounding cities, **which likewise indulged in sexual immorality and pursued unnatural desire**, serve as an example by undergoing a punishment of eternal fire. (Jude 6–7, ESV)

Sulpicius Severus (363–425 A.D.) was born of nobility in Aquitaine and became a writer and hagiographer of the early church. He identified the "certain angels" who left their "proper dwelling,"

> *When by this time the human race had increased to a great multitude,* ***certain angels, whose habitation was in heaven, were captivated by the appearance of some beautiful virgins,*** *and cherished illicit desires after them, so much so, that filling beneath their own proper nature and origin,* ***they left the higher regions*** *of which they were inhabitants, and* ***allied themselves in earthly marriages.*** *These angels gradually spreading wicked habits, corrupted the human family, and from their alliance giants are said to have sprung, for* ***the mixture with them of beings of a different nature,*** *as a matter of course,* ***gave birth to monsters.***[15]

Peter and Jude have no hesitation accusing certain angels of committing "sexual immorality" and indulging in "unnatural desire" in the days

15 Sulpicius Severus, *The Sacred History of Sulpitius Severus*, 71–72 (Roberts).

of Noah. Like the sexually sick cities of Sodom and Gomorrah, the sons of God of Genesis 6 will spend eternity in the lake of fire (Matt 25:41).

WHAT DOES "NEPHILIM" MEAN?

The word "Nephilim" in Genesis 6:4 is often translated "giants" in many versions of the Bible, such as the KJV and the LES (Lexham English Septuagint). However, some versions, such as the ESV, don't translate the word—they leave "Nephilim" in the text.

Genesis 6:4 (KJV 1900)	Genesis 6:4 (LES)	Genesis 6:4 (ESV)
4 There were **giants** in the earth in those days; and also after that, when the sons of God came in unto the daughters of men, and they bare children to them, the same became mighty men which were of old, men of renown.	4 Now **giants** were upon the land in those days, and after that, whenever the sons of God visited the daughters of humans, they fathered children for themselves; those were the **giants** who were from long ago, the people of renown.	4 The **Nephilim** were on the earth in those days, and also afterward, when the sons of God came in to the daughters of man and they bore children to them. These were the mighty men who were of old, the men of renown.

No one really debates the fact that there were giants before the flood. The interest usually centers around the meaning of the word "Nephilim." For many years, scholars said it meant "fallen ones" because of the belief that "Nephilim" comes from the Hebrew root naphal, which means to "cast down" or "to fall." This understanding has come under fire in recent years, largely due to Dr. Michael S. Heiser, a leading scholar in ancient languages, and his attention to Hebrew morphology. Heiser explains,

In the form we find it in the Hebrew Bible, if the word nephilim came from Hebrew naphal, it would not be spelled as we find it. The form nephilim cannot mean "fallen ones" (the spelling would then be nephulim). Likewise nephilim does not mean "those who fall" or "those who fall away" (that would be nophelim). The only way in Hebrew to get nephilim from naphal by the rules of Hebrew morphology (word formation) would be to presume a noun spelled naphil and then pluralize it. I say "presume" since this noun does not exist in biblical Hebrew—unless one counts Genesis 6:4 and Numbers 13:33, the two occurrences of nephilim—but that would then be assuming what one is trying to prove! However, in Aramaic the noun naphil(a) does exist. It means "giant," making it easy to see why the Septuagint (the ancient Greek translation of the Hebrew Bible) translated nephilim as gigantes ("giant").[16]

CONNECTING THE GOSPEL

BECOMING SONS OF GOD

Understanding who the "sons of God" *(benê [ha]'elōhîm)* are in the Old Testament is crucial in restoring the ancient context of Genesis 6. As we've established, the *(benê [ha]'elōhîm)* in the Hebrew Scriptures are angelic beings, members of God's heavenly hosts. When we turn our attention to the Greek New Testament, the "sons of God" terminology expands to include people, and there is a fundamental reason why.

Before we discuss the tie-in between the sons of God of both testaments, let's first acknowledge *the* Son of God, Jesus Christ, our Lord. In the New Testament, Jesus is called the Son of God. Jesus' sonship was

---

16 Michael S. Heiser, "The Nephilim," SITCHIN IS WRONG.COM, n.d., http://www.sitchiniswrong.com/nephilim/nephilim.htm.

unique and one-of-a-kind. He was the "only begotten" (Gk: *monogenḗs*) Son of God (John 3:16).

> *"The term monogenes is related to Greek monos, "only," and genes, "offspring, race, kind," suggesting the meaning "only one of its kind, unique" for monogenes."*[17]

Jesus as the only begotten doesn't negate the fact that there are other children of God. This terminology merely sets him far above everything and everyone, even the angels in Heaven. None of the angels are described as "begotten" or fathered by the Creator (Hebrews 1:5). This is why the Hebrews writer elevates Jesus over the angels (Hebrews 1:5-8).

While Christ came as the begotten Son of God, His coming in the likeness of men made it possible for humans to experience a heavenly sonship. It's only because of Christ that men can now be called "the sons of God" (Gk: τεκνα Θεου), as John reveals in the New Testament.

> 12 But as many as **received him, to them gave he power to**
> **become the sons of God** (*τεκνα Θεου*), even to them that believe
> on his name: 13 Which were born, not of blood, nor of the will
> of the flesh, nor of the will of man, but of God. (John 1:12–13,
> KJV 1900)

Our heavenly sonship is highlighted throughout the New Testament. Note the following passages.

> 5 having predestined us to **adoption as sons by Jesus Christ**
> to Himself, according to the good pleasure of His will, 6 to the

---

17 E. R. Clendenen and Church Chris, "Only Begotten," *Holman Illustrated Bible Dictionary* 1223.

> praise of the glory of His grace, by which He made us accepted in the Beloved. [7] In Him we have redemption through His blood, the forgiveness of sins, according to the riches of His grace (Eph 1:5–7, NKJV)

> [15] For you did not receive the spirit of slavery to fall back into fear, **but you have received the Spirit of adoption as sons**, by whom we cry, "Abba! Father!" [16] The Spirit himself bears witness with our spirit that we are children of God, [17] and if children, then heirs—heirs of God and fellow heirs with Christ, provided we suffer with him in order that we may also be glorified with him. (Rom 8:15–17, ESV)

> [4] But when the fullness of the time had come, God sent forth His Son, born of a woman, born under the law, [5] to redeem those who were under the law, **that we might receive the adoption as sons.** [6] And **because you are sons, God has sent forth the Spirit of His Son into your hearts**, crying out, "Abba, Father!" [7] Therefore you are no longer a slave but a son, and if a son, then an heir of God through Christ. (Gal 4:4–7, NKJV)

The "sons of God" terminology in both testaments carries the idea of being *divinely created.* Being divinely created is the common denominator between angels, Christians, even Jesus Christ. For example, all the heavenly sons of God*(benê [ha]ʾelōhîm)*, both loyal and rebellious, were once *created* by our Lord. No. They are not the byproduct of marriage or procreation. This much is seen in Colossians 1:16-17.

> [16] For by him were **all things created**, that are in heaven, and that are in earth, visible and **invisible, whether they be thrones, or dominions, or principalities, or powers: all things were**

> **created by him**, and for him: [17] And he is before all things, and **by him all things consist**. (Colossians 1:16–17, KJV 1900)

The same was true of Jesus Christ. While Christ was the eternal Word of God who always existed (John 1), His being born of a virgin was also a powerful demonstration of *divine creation*. But, where does that leave us? We weren't born of a virgin or spoken into existence. We have earthly parents who brought us into the world by natural means. The Bible has the answer.

The thread that ties the sons of God, both human and angelic, together is the idea of being directly and divinely *created*. Through Christ Jesus, humans are divinely *recreated* into a new creation. God affords man the opportunity to "trade-in" our fallen status and earthly origin for something much better. We're allowed to become the sons and daughters of God. Let's unpack how this crucial transition takes place.

Before we can grasp the *new creation* concept, we must first be introduced to what Christ called the *new birth*. Notice what Jesus said to Nicodemus in John 3.

> [1] There was a man from the Pharisees named Nicodemus, a ruler of the Jews. [2] This man came to him at night and said, "Rabbi, we know that you are a teacher who has come from God, for no one could perform these signs you do unless God were with him." [3] Jesus replied, "Truly I tell you, **unless someone is born again, he cannot see the kingdom of God**." [4] "How can anyone be born when he is old?" Nicodemus asked him. "Can he enter his mother's womb a second time and be born?" [5] Jesus answered, "Truly I tell you, **unless someone is born of water and the Spirit, he cannot enter the kingdom of God**. [6] Whatever is born of the flesh is flesh, and whatever is born of the Spirit is spirit. [7] Do not be amazed that I told you that you must be born again. (John 3:1–7, CSB)

This new birth is a spiritual one. Jesus said there are two components of the new birth—one must be born of water and the Spirit. A Syrian theologian named John of Damascus (675–749 A.D.) explained the two components in the following way:

> *For since man's nature is twofold, consisting of soul and body, He [Jesus] bestowed on us a twofold purification, of water and of the Spirit: the Spirit renewing that part in us which is after His image and likeness, and the water by the grace of the Spirit cleansing the body from sin and delivering it from corruption, the water indeed expressing the image of death, but the Spirit affording the earnest of life.*[18]

Chromatius, a bishop of Aquileia in 388 A.D., also wrote of the new birth and described baptism as a "spiritual womb":

> *Fleshly then is the birth from a human being; spiritual is the birth from God.... That one gives birth [procreat] to a person in the world; this one generates [generat] for God.... This spiritual birth is accomplished altogether invisibly, even as that birth is visible. Now it is certainly seen that one who is baptized is dipped and is seen to come up from the water. But what is done in that bath is not seen. The church of the faithful alone understand spiritually that a sinner goes down into the font but comes up clean from all sin.... Those who are regenerated [regenerantur] by baptism are reborn [renascuntur] in innocence, having put away the old error and malice of sin. For* ***it is the spiritual womb*** *of the church* ***that conceives and bears sons for God****. (Sermon 18.2–3)*[19]

18 John Damascene, *An Exact Exposition of the Orthodox Faith*, 78 (Salmond).

19 E. Ferguson, *Baptism in the Early Church: History, Theology, and Liturgy in the First Five Centuries* (Grand Rapids, MI; Cambridge, U.K.: William B. Eerdmans Publishing Company, 2009), 658–659.

Ancient Syrian hymn-writer Ephraem of Nisibis (306–373 A.D.) wrote hymns to combat his theological opposers and their diatribe. In *Hymns on Virginity*, he also calls baptism a "womb" and does so by personifying baptism as a mother who births her children in the "threefold pangs" of the Father, the Son, and the Holy Spirit.

> *With visible colors*
> *is the royal portrait formed,*
> *and formed with visible oil*
> *the invisible picture of our invisible King.*
> *In those marked,* ***baptism,***
> ***who bears them in her womb,***
> *will replace the picture of the first Adam,*
> *corrupted, transformed into the new picture*
> *and birth them in the threefold pangs*
> *of the three precious names*
> *of the Father, the Son, and the Holy Spirit.20*

While we are all products of natural, human procreation, we are the sons of God (*τεκνα Θεου*) because we have been *born again*, not of corruptible seed, but of *incorruptible*. This new birth occurs when we are born again in the spiritual womb of baptism. In the words of Fourth-century preacher Theodore of Mopsuestia,

> *In [the one Godhead]* ***we believe and are baptized*** *and through it we become one body, according to the working on us of the Holy Spirit,* ***in baptism****, which makes us children of God and one body of Christ our Lord, whom we consider our head. (14, p. 64).*[21]

---

20 A. B. McGowan, *Ancient Christian Worship: Early Church Practices in Social, Historical, and Theological Perspective* (Grand Rapids, MI: Baker Academic, 2014), 172.

21 Ferguson, *Baptism in the Early Church*, 531.

Our being "sons" of God is also well demonstrated in Luke 20:30-36, the parallel account to Matthew 22:30. In this passage, Jesus reveals that resurrected saints will be counted *equal* to the angels, being called sons of God.

> 30 And the second took her as wife, and he died childless. 31 Then the third took her, and in like manner the seven also; and they left no children, and died. 32 Last of all the woman died also.
> 33 Therefore, in the resurrection, whose wife does she become? For all seven had her as wife." 34 Jesus answered and said to them, "The sons of this age marry and are given in marriage.
> 35 But those who are counted worthy to attain that age, and the resurrection from the dead, **neither marry** nor are given in marriage; 36 **nor can they die** anymore, **for they are equal to the angels and are sons of God, being sons of the resurrection**. (Luke 20:30–36, NKJV)

Clearly, Jesus considered angels to be sons of God. If he didn't believe that, then his comments are senseless. The Lord used holy angels as an Old Testament touchpoint to teach us that sons of the resurrection are indeed also "sons of God." As Jesus articulated, we will be like our angelic counterparts in form (no death), status (sons of God), and function (not given in marriage). The Jews at Qumran envisioned a united destiny with *the spirits*, full of worship alongside the angels (i.e., the holy ones, the sons of heaven).

> *22 You created from the dust for the eternal council. The perverse spirit You have cleansed from great transgression, that he might take his stand with 23* ***the host of the holy ones****, and enter together (or in the Yahad) with the congregation of the* ***sons of heaven. And for man, You have allotted an eternal destiny with the spirits*** *24 of knowledge, to praise Your name*

> *together with shouts of joy, and to recount Your wonders before all Your creatures.*[22]

As Jesus taught, this will be our reality. As we look forward to a blissful eternity with the hosts of heaven, praising our God together, we do so because we share a similar divine origin with the angels. Just as our Lord *created* the Old Testament's angelic sons of God, the New Testament similarly describes Christians as a *new creation* in Christ Jesus. Paul wrote,

> [10] For we are His workmanship, **created in Christ Jesus** for good works, which God prepared beforehand that we should walk in them. (Eph 2:10, NKJV)

> [17] Therefore **if anyone is in Christ, he is a new creation**; the old things have passed away; behold, new things have come. (2 Cor 5:17, LEB)

God loves us and proudly considers us to be among His children. Though we are distinct from angels, we are given an exalted status *equal* to angels. We are sons of God because we've been divinely *recreated* into something new. As His sons, we should count our blessings and thank God that he didn't limit his amazing love to only spiritual beings, but that he extended His devotion to the entire race of fallen humanity as well. John writes,

> [1] See what sort of love the Father has given to us: that **we should be called children of God** *(τεκνα Θεου)*, and we are! Because of this the world does not know us: because it did not know

---

22 M. O. Wise, M. G. Abegg, Jr., and E. M. Cook, eds., *The Dead Sea Scrolls: A New Translation* (New York: HarperOne, 2005), 182.

> him. [2] Dear friends, **now we are children of Go***d (τεκνα Θεου)*, and what we will be has not yet been revealed. We know that whenever he is revealed we **will be like him**, because we will see him just as he is. (1 John 3:1–2, LEB)

LOOKING AHEAD

With God's creation corrupted by the angels, any hope for redeeming fragile man was slipping away. The rising wrath of God was about to be released on all the ungodly of heaven and earth. Everyone aboard the ship of immorality wouldn't survive the deluge of punishment that was about to be rained down by Almighty God. Would this be the end of all mankind and God's promised seed? Unless someone found grace in God's eyes soon, tragically, it would be.

CHAPTER 3

ENOCH, THE FLOOD, & THE ANGELIC PRISON

For if God did not spare the angels who sinned, but held them captive in Tartarus with chains of darkness and handed them over to be kept for judgment, and did not spare the ancient world, but preserved Noah, a proclaimer of righteousness, and seven others when he brought a flood on the world of the ungodly, (2 Peter 2:4–5, LEB)

READING THE STORY

MAN COULDN'T SERVE TWO MASTERS (MATT 6:24), and eventually, everyone simply quit trying. They walked to the drum of satisfaction—the lust of the eyes, the lust of the flesh, and the pride of life—as they marched in the infantry of the slithering serpent. His pursuit of worldwide corruption and the nullification of God's "crushed head" prophecy was nearly complete. There was only one small problem—Noah found grace in the eyes of God (Gen 6:8).

Noah had the faith of his great-grandfather, Enoch. When Moses recorded the generations of Adam in Genesis 5, he listed **Enoch as being the seventh** from Adam.

> "Jared was 162 years old when he fathered Enoch. Jared lived 800 years after he fathered Enoch, and he fathered other sons and daughters. So Jared's life lasted 962 years; then he died. Enoch was 65 years old when he fathered Methuselah. And after he fathered Methuselah, Enoch walked with God 300 years and fathered other sons and daughters. So Enoch's life lasted 365 years. Enoch walked with God; then he was not there because God took him. (Gen 5:18–24, CSB)

Enoch was a special servant. He and Elijah were the only two in all of the Bible to be translated to heaven prior to death (2 Kgs 2:10–12). What an honor! His uniqueness cannot be overstated. According to the apostle Jude, Enoch was a prophet of God. Jude cites one of Enoch's prophecies in Jude 14-15. Notice what he says:

Jude 14–15 (ESV)	Enoch 1:9 (LES)
[14] It was also about these that Enoch, the seventh from Adam, prophesied, saying, "Behold, the Lord comes with ten thousands of his holy ones, [15] to execute judgment on all and to convict all the ungodly of all their deeds of ungodliness that they have committed in such an ungodly way, and of all the harsh things that ungodly sinners have spoken against him."	[9] For he comes with his ten thousands and his holy ones to enact judgment against all. He will destroy everyone who is ungodly and reproach all flesh concerning all works of the ungodly: the things they did impiously, the harsh words that they spoke and all that ungodly sinners spoke against him."

The same book from which the apostle Jude quoted provides incredible insight regarding the decline of morality before the flood. While the book of Enoch is not in the Bible, the story you are about to hear was in the minds of ancient Jews and early Christians. The book of Enoch was widely circulated in antiquity and became synonymous with Genesis 6:1-4. Indeed, the Enochic tradition of "the Watchers" who descended on Mount Hermon was believed to be factual and true in both ancient Judaism and the early church. More will be said about this later in the chapter. 1 Enoch 6-9 states,

> "And it came to pass when the children of men had multiplied that in those days were born unto them beautiful and comely daughters. [2.] And **the angels** [*the Watchers*]**, the children of the heaven,** saw and lusted after them, and said to one another: 'Come, let us choose us wives from among the children of men and beget us children.' [3.] And Semjâzâ, who was their leader, said unto them: 'I fear ye will not indeed agree to do this deed, and I alone shall have to pay the penalty of a great sin.' [4.] And they all answered him and said: 'Let us all swear an oath, and all bind

ourselves by mutual imprecations not to abandon this plan but to do this thing.' 5. Then sware they all together and bound themselves by mutual imprecations upon it. 6. **And they were in all two hundred; who descended in the days of Jared on the summit of Mount Hermon**, and they called it Mount Hermon, because **they had sworn and bound themselves by mutual imprecations** upon it. 7. And these are the names of their leaders: Sêmîazâz, their leader, Arâkîba, Râmêêl, Kôkabîêl, Tâmîêl, Râmîêl, Dânêl, Êzêqêêl, Barâqîjâl, Asâêl, Armârôs, Batârêl, Anânêl, Zaqîêl, Samsâpêêl, Satarêl, Tûrêl, Jômjâêl, Sariêl. 8. These are their chiefs of tens.

VII. 1. And all the others together with them **took unto themselves wives, and each chose for himself one, and they began to go in unto them and to defile themselves with them**, and they taught them charms and enchantments, and the cutting of roots, and made them acquainted with plants. 2. And **they became pregnant, and they bare great giants**, whose height was three thousand ells: 3. Who consumed all the acquisitions of men. And when men could no longer sustain them, 4. **The giants turned against them and devoured mankind.** 5. And they began to sin against birds, and beasts, and reptiles, and fish, **and to devour one another's flesh, and drink the blood.** 6. Then the earth laid accusation against the lawless ones.

VIII. 1. And **Azâzêl taught men to make swords, and knives, and shields**, and breastplates, and made known to them the metals ‹of the earth› and the art of working them, and bracelets, and ornaments, and the use of antimony, and the beautifying of the eyelids, and all kinds of costly stones, and all colouring tinctures. 2. And there arose **much godlessness**, and they **committed fornication**, and they were led astray, and became **corrupt in all their ways**. 3. Semjâzâ **taught enchantments**, and root-cuttings, 'Armârôs the **resolving of enchantments**, Barâqîjâl (taught) **astrology**, Kôkabêl **the constellations**, Ezêqêêl **the knowledge**

> **of the clouds**, ‹Araqiêl **the signs of the earth**, Shamsiêl **the signs of the sun**›, and Sariêl **the course of the moon**. 4. And as men perished, they cried, and their cry went up to heaven…
>
> IX. 1. And then Michael, Uriel, Raphael, and Gabriel looked down from heaven and saw much blood being shed upon the earth, and all lawlessness being wrought upon the earth. 2. And they said one to another: 'The earth made without inhabitant cries the voice of their crying up to the gates of heaven. 3. And now to you, the holy ones of heaven, the souls of men make their suit, saying, "Bring our cause before the Most High".' 4. And they said to **the Lord of the ages: 'Lord of lords, God of gods, King of kings ‹and God of the ages›**, the throne of Thy glory (standeth) unto all the generations of the ages, and Thy name holy and glorious and blessed unto all the ages! 5. Thou hast made all things, and power over all things hast Thou: and all things are naked and open in Thy sight, and all things Thou seest, and nothing can hide itself from Thee. 6. Thou seest what **Azâzêl** hath done, who hath **taught all unrighteousness on earth and revealed the eternal secrets** which were (preserved) in heaven, which men were striving to learn: 7. And Semjâzâ, to whom Thou hast given authority to bear rule over his associates. 8. And **they have gone to the daughters of men upon the earth, and have slept with the women**, and have defiled themselves, and revealed to them all kinds of sins. 9. **And the women have borne giants, and the whole earth has thereby been filled with blood and unrighteousness**. (1 Enoch 6:1–9:9)[1]

The violence and sinful passion the Watchers incited among men was a pandemic. Even the "righteous lines of Seth" were corrupted, as Jewish Historian Josephus pointed out.

---

1 R. H. Charles, ed., *The Book of Enoch or 1 Enoch: Translation*, trans. R. H. Charles (Oxford: The Clarendon Press, 1912), 13–21.

> *(72) Now this posterity of Seth continued to esteem God as the Lord of the universe, and to have an entire regard to virtue, for seven generations; but in process of time they were perverted, and forsook the practices of their forefathers, and did neither pay those honors to God which were appointed them, nor had they any concern to do justice towards men. But for what degree of zeal they had formerly shown for virtue, they now showed by their actions a double degree of wickedness; whereby they made God to be their enemy,*[2]

To Satan's surprise and disappointment, he couldn't corrupt the last man standing—Enoch's great-grandson, Noah.

It was time for the world, the Watchers, and their bastard children (the mighty Nephilim/giants) to experience justice.

> Then God said to Noah, "I have decided to put an end to every creature, for the earth is filled with wickedness because of them; therefore I am going to destroy them along with the earth. "Make yourself an ark of gopher wood. Make rooms in the ark, and cover it with pitch inside and outside. This is how you are to make it: The ark will be 450 feet long, 75 feet wide, and 45 feet high. You are to make a roof, finishing the sides of the ark to within eighteen inches of the roof. You are to put a door in the side of the ark. Make it with lower, middle, and upper decks. "Understand that I am bringing a flood—floodwaters on the earth to destroy every creature under heaven with the breath of life in it. Everything on earth will perish. But I will establish my covenant with you, and you will enter the ark with your sons, your wife, and your sons' wives. You are also to bring into the ark two of all the living creatures, male and female, to keep them alive with you. Two

---

2 Josephus, *The Works of Josephus*, 32.

> of everything—from the birds according to their kinds, from the livestock according to their kinds, and from the animals that crawl on the ground according to their kinds—will come to you so that you can keep them alive. Take with you every kind of food that is eaten; gather it as food for you and for them." And Noah did this. He did everything that God had commanded him. (Gen 6:13–22, CSB)

As Noah built the ark, he preached to the perishing (2 Pet 2:5), but no one listened. Time was up, and so was the opportunity for repentance. With the animals in place (Gen 7:2–5), 600-year-old Noah (Gen 7:11), his wife, his sons (Shem, Ham, and Japheth), and their wives entered the ark. The Lord shut them in, supernaturally sealing the entrance (Gen 7:16). No amount of rain, no strong giants, not even an innumerable number of angels could unseal the ark of deliverance. They were totally secure in God's saving hands.

Seven days later (Gen 7:10), the foundations of the great deep suddenly burst forth, and the windows of the heavens were opened; it rained for forty days and forty nights (Gen 7:12). As each drop of rain tumbled from the heavens, and as the waters emerged from the deep, Noah's ark climbed and conquered the high crests of the raging waters (Gen 7:18–20). Everything wicked drowned, every defiant village was washed away, and "the mighty men of old" (Gen 6:4), the giant Nephilim, trembled under the flood as they gasped for air. The rebel sons of God helplessly looked on as their mutant children perished in the flood (1 Enoch 12:6).

Job 26:5–6 (Brenton LXX En)	Job 26:5 (NKJV)
5 Shall **giants** be born from **under the water** and the inhabitants thereof? 6 Hell is naked before him, and destruction has no covering.	5 "The dead ***rěpāʾîm***) tremble, Those under the waters and those inhabiting them.

Ezekiel 32:27 (Brenton LXX En)	Ezekiel 32:27 (ESV)
[27] And they are laid with **the giants that fell of old**, who went down to Hades **with their weapons of war**: and they laid their swords under their heads, but their iniquities were upon their bones, because they terrified all men during their life.	[27] And they do not lie with **the mighty**, the fallen from among the uncircumcised, who went down to Sheol **with their weapons of war**, whose swords were laid under their heads, and whose iniquities are upon their bones; for the terror of **the mighty men** was in the land of the living.

Notice how these events are described by King David, the Psalmist, generations later.

Psalm 29:1–3, 10–11 (Brenton LXX En)	Psalm 29:1–3, 10–11 (CSB)
[1] Bring to the Lord, **ye sons of God**, bring to the Lord young rams; bring to the Lord glory and honour. [2] Bring to the Lord glory, due to his name; worship the Lord **in his holy court**. [3] The voice of the Lord is **upon the waters**: the God of glory has thundered: the Lord is upon **many waters.** [10] **The LORD will dwell on the waterflood: and the LORD will sit a king for ever.** [11] The Lord will give strength to his people; the Lord will bless his people with peace.	[1] Ascribe to the LORD, you **heavenly beings**, ascribe to the LORD glory and strength. [2] Ascribe to the LORD the glory due his name; worship the LORD in the splendor of his holiness. [3] The voice of the LORD is **above the waters**. The God of glory thunders— the LORD, **above the vast water**, [10] **The LORD sits enthroned over the flood; the LORD sits enthroned, King forever**. [11] The LORD gives his people strength; the LORD blesses his people with peace.

The sons of God (heavenly beings) were called to recognize and worship God, the wielder of the mighty flood. Like the psalmist depicted, the

King of the heavenly court sat enthroned over the flood and its many corpses for 150 days (Gen 7:24). God had spoken. The runaway train of immorality and corruption came to a screeching halt. With all the tyrannical giants gone and wicked humanity deceased, Noah and his family could now live in peace. But what happened to "the angels who sinned," the celestial fathers of the mighty giants? Peter and Jude both reveal that they were locked away under gloomy chains of darkness.

> 4 For if God did not spare the angels who sinned, but held them captive in Tartarus with chains of darkness and handed them over to be kept for judgment, 5 and did not spare the ancient world, but preserved Noah, a proclaimer of righteousness, and seven others when he brought a flood on the world of the ungodly, (2 Pet 2:4–5, LEB)

> 6 And the angels who did not stay within their own position of authority, but left their proper dwelling, he has kept in eternal chains under gloomy darkness until the judgment of the great day— 7 just as Sodom and Gomorrah and the surrounding cities, which likewise indulged in sexual immorality and pursued unnatural desire, serve as an example by undergoing a punishment of eternal fire. (Jude 6–7, ESV)

Furthermore, according to Enoch, Azâzêl was bound in the desert, and Semjâzâ and the other angels who made the vitriolic vow on Mount Hermon were cast into the deepest abyss of "Tartarus."

> "And again the Lord said to Raphael: 'Bind Azâzêl hand and foot, and cast him into the darkness: and make an opening in the desert, which is in Dûdâêl, and cast him therein. 5. And place upon him rough and jagged rocks, and cover him with darkness, and let him abide there for ever, and cover his

> face that he may not see light. 6. And on the day of the great judgement he shall be cast into the fire.
>
> 11. And the Lord said unto Michael: 'Go, bind Semjâzâ and his associates who have united themselves with women so as to have defiled themselves with them in all their uncleanness. 12. And, when their sons have slain one another, and they have seen the destruction of their beloved ones, **bind them** fast for seventy generations in the valleys of the earth, till the day of their judgement and of their consummation, till the judgement that is for ever and ever is consummated. 13. **In those days they shall be led off to the abyss of fire**: ‹and› to the torment and **the prison in which they shall be confined for ever**. 14. And whosoever shall be condemned and destroyed will from thenceforth be bound together with them to the end of all generations. (1 Enoch 10:4–6, 11–14)[3]

Sorrowful over their punishment, they called for undying Enoch and asked that he appeal to God on their behalf to free them from their gloomy prison.

> Then I went and spoke to them all together, and **they were all afraid, and fear and trembling** seized them. 4. And they besought me to draw up a petition for them **that they might find forgiveness, and to read their petition in the presence of the Lord of heaven.** 5. For from thenceforward they could not speak (with Him) nor lift up their eyes to heaven for shame of their sins for which they had been condemned. 6. Then I wrote out their petition, and the prayer in regard to their spirits and their deeds individually and in regard to their requests that they should have forgiveness and length. (1 Enoch 13:3–6)[4]

---

3 Charles, *The Book of Enoch or 1 Enoch: Translation*, 22–25.

4 Charles, *The Book of Enoch or 1 Enoch: Translation*, 29–31.

After bringing their petition before God and His heavenly court, Enoch descended back to the spirits in prison with a single message. He preached a sermon of finality to them. To their dismay, it was one of condemnation, not salvation; they wouldn't be getting out.

> And **your petition** on their behalf **shall not be granted**, nor yet on your own: even though you weep and pray and speak all the words contained in the writing which I have written. (1 Enoch 14:7)

ANSWERING YOUR QUESTIONS

DID ENOCH WRITE THE BOOK OF ENOCH?

While there are many noncanonical and secular sources the biblical writers quote and reference (Ps 24; Acts 17:27–28; etc.), these sources are never referred to as "prophecies"—the exception is a citation from the the book of Enoch. Jesus' brother Jude does in fact call Enoch's words "prophecy," the same words found in 1 Enoch 1:9.

Jude 14–15 (ESV)	1 Enoch 1:9
14 It was also about these that **Enoch**, the seventh from Adam, **prophesied**, saying, "**Behold, the Lord comes with ten thousands of his holy ones,** 15 **to execute judgment on all and to convict all the ungodly of all their deeds of ungodliness...**	9 **And behold! He cometh with ten thousands of His holy ones To execute judgement upon all, And to destroy all the ungodly.**[5]

5 Charles, *The Book of Enoch or 1 Enoch: Translation*, 7–8.

One would think the book of Enoch is definitely the source of Jude's reference when comparing the two passages. However, some argue Jude isn't using the book of Enoch as his source. Their argument is that Jude never said Enoch "wrote" the words found in Jude 1:9—only that he "prophesied" them. The suggestion is that, by inspiration, Jude was given divine insight into prophetic words uttered by Enoch before the flood. Could this happen? Certainly. This explanation is not without its own set of problems, however. If Jude only knew Enoch's prophecy by divine revelation, then how did the uninspired writer of the book of Enoch *also* know what Enoch uttered before the flood? Lucky guess? Not a chance. He certainly couldn't have copied off Jude's homework since the book of Enoch is much older than Jude's letter.

This argument is problematic. No. There is nothing unusual about the way Jude introduces Enoch's prophecy. Jesus introduces the prophet Isaiah's writing in the same way that Jude does Enoch's.

Matthew 15:7–8 (KJV)	Jude 14–15 (KJV)
Ye hypocrites, well did **Esaias prophesy of you, saying**, This people draweth nigh unto me with their mouth, and honoureth me with their lips; but their heart is far from me.	And **Enoch** also, the seventh from Adam, **prophesied of these, saying**, Behold, the Lord cometh with ten thousands of his saints, to execute judgment upon all, and to convince all that are ungodly among them of all their ungodly deeds which they have ungodly committed, and of all their hard speeches which ungodly sinners have spoken against him.

Should we conclude that Jesus' source was something else besides the book of Isaiah since He didn't specify He was quoting from Isaiah's *book*? No. The way Jude introduces Enoch's prophecy doesn't rule out the book of Enoch as his being his source.

Others have suggested Jude did quote Enoch's prophecy from a written source, but his source was not the book we know as the book of Enoch; it was something else entirely. This would certainly solve the problem surrounding the origin of Jude's citation and point to the fact that the book of Enoch is an imposter whose author merely parroted a divine writing. However, the notion that there was some other mysterious book or source from which Jude quoted is not evidential. No smoking gun has ever been found. This stance is based entirely on supposition, not proof. Most scholars don't even entertain this idea. In fact, scholars have pointed out there are many Enochic echoes throughout the entire New Testament, not only in Jude, as we will soon explore.

Perhaps most damning of all to the authenticity of the book of Enoch is the notion that there are several acclaimed theological issues with the book. These "issues" have been well-documented by scholars for decades and should be taken very seriously. Truth does not contradict itself; it is unified in the ideas it sets forth. Of course, perceived contradictions don't mean *real* inconsistencies are present. Many atheists point to many *supposed* contradictions in the Bible, particularly in the synoptic gospels; that doesn't make these critics right. There are many factors that must be considered before ideas can be proven contradictory. The same holds true for the book of Enoch.

A final argument against the authenticity of the book of Enoch is that it's not part of the Jewish canon. This is true, so case closed, right? Not quite. The oldest known copies of 1 Enoch were found in the Qumran Caves near the Dead Sea, hidden alongside other ancient biblical scrolls. In 1947, a young Bedouin shepherd boy stumbled across the sacred scrolls while tending to his sheep. It's believed that a Jewish sect, the Essenes, were the preservers of the ancient texts. In fragment *4Q559* found at Qumran, notice what was believed about the preservation of Enoch's book:

*Col. 2 3[... Abraham was] nin[ety-nine ye]ars old 4[when he fathered Isaac. Is]aac was [sixty years o]ld [when he fathered] 5[Jacob. Jacob was] sixty-five y[ears old when he fathered Levi.] 6[**He gave to Levi the Book of the Words of] Enoch [to preserve and pass on**] 7[to his own descendants. Levi was thirty-f]ive when he fa[thered Kohath.] 8[Kohath was twenty-ni]ne when he fathered Am[r]am. Amr[am was] 9[one hundred and twenty-three when he fathered] Aaron. Aaro[n] left Egy[pt] 10[with the priests,] who [totaled] eleven thousand five hundred and thirty-six.*[6]

Nickelsburg, a scholar who devoted his life to studying the book of Enoch and Enochic texts, discussed how the Jews at Qumran perceived and preserved the controversial book.

Qumran provides an identifiable location in ancient Judaism for the substantial use and influence of the Enochic traditions. The evidence is diverse. Cave 4 yielded eleven manuscripts of various parts of 1 Enoch, dating from the early second century B.C.E. to the early first century C.E. (see §2.1.2.1–2). Also preserved are fragments of nine manuscripts of the Enochic Book of Giants, dating from the first half of the first century B.C.E. to the early first century C.E. (see §2.1.2.3). Thus the Enochic tradition was alive and well at Qumran...

The proliferation of Enochic and quasi-Enochic material in the Qumran library suggests two scenarios. (1) The Qumran community attracted people who prized the Enochic texts and others closely related to them, and who brought their copies of these texts with them. (2) The community provided an ambience

6 Wise, Abegg, Jr., and Cook, *The Dead Sea Scrolls*, 565.

> *that fostered the copying and use of these texts and the incorporation of their traditions into new texts.*[7]

Indisputably, the Jews at Qumran believed in the content of the book of Enoch and worked diligently to preserve it as they did the Old Testament Scriptures. Additionally, up until the first or second century, there was no closed Jewish canon or finalized list that well-defined what was inspired and what was apocryphal. Canonization was an evolving process that likely wrapped up after the establishment of the church. When a new generation of Jews drew the final canonical line in the sand, the book of Enoch didn't make the cut. The question is, did it ever make the cut to the Jews in any time period? What about the Jews at Qumran?

The story rarely told is that, diametric to the Jewish canon, many Christians in the first and second centuries *embraced* the book of Enoch as inspired of God and fought for its canonicity, largely due to Jude's use of it. They primarily attributed the Jews' rejection of the book of Enoch to its many Christological connections and the practical difficulty of the book surviving the flood. Tertullian (160–220 A.D.), a second-century Christian, wrote,

> ***I am aware that the Scripture of Enoch [1 Enoch], which has assigned this order (of action) to angels, is not received by some, because it is not admitted into the Jewish canon either.*** *I suppose they did not think that, having been published before the deluge, it could have safely survived that world-wide calamity, the abolisher of all things. If that is the reason (for rejecting it), let them recall to their memory that Noah, the survivor of the deluge,*

7 George W. E. Nickelsburg, "1 Enoch: A Commentary on the Book of 1 Enoch," in *Hermeneia Commentary Series—A Critical and Historical Commentary on the Bible*, ed. Klaus Baltzer (Minneapolis, MN: Fortress, 2001), 76–77.

> *was the great-grandson of Enoch himself; and he, of course, had heard and remembered, from domestic renown and hereditary tradition, concerning his own great-grandfather's "grace in the sight of God," and concerning all his preachings; since Enoch had given no other charge to Methuselah than that he should hand on the knowledge of them to his posterity. Noah therefore, no doubt, might have succeeded in the trusteeship of (his) preaching; or, had the case been otherwise, he would not have been silent alike concerning the disposition (of things) made by God, his Preserver, and concerning the particular glory of his own house.*
>
> ***But since Enoch in the same Scripture has preached likewise concerning the Lord, nothing at all must be rejected by us which pertains to us; and we read that "every Scripture suitable for edification is divinely inspired." By the Jews it may now seem to have been rejected for that (very) reason, just like all the other (portions) nearly which tell of Christ.*** *Nor, of course, is this fact wonderful, that they did not receive some Scriptures which spake of Him whom even in person, speaking in their presence, they were not to receive. To these considerations is added the fact that* ***Enoch possesses a testimony in the Apostle Jude.***[8]

Is Tertullian's argument a valid one? How much credence should we give a generation of Jews who rejected Christ and the gospel itself? How much stock should Christians put in the Jewish canon versus a possible testimony of an apostle and the brother of Jesus? This was the predicament of the early church.

Later Christians such as Augustine of Hippo (354–430 A.D.), a champion of the Sethite View, distanced themselves from the writings

---

8 M. S. Heiser, Reversing Hermon: *Enoch, The Watchers & The Forgotten Mission of Jesus Christ* (Bellingham, WA: Lexham Press, 2017), 188–189.

of Enoch due to its "unverified origin" and teachings on the identity of the sons of God (benê [ha]ʾelōhîm) of Genesis 6, considering the book of Enoch (Henoch) an apocryphal work. Augustine wrote,

> *Thus, although it is undeniable that some writings left by Henoch in the seventh generation after Adam were divinely inspired, since Jude the Apostle, in a canonical Epistle says so,* ***nevertheless the writings of Henoch were omitted****, and not without good reason, from the canon of Scripture which was carefully preserved by the priestly line in the Temple of the Hebrew people.* ***Their very antiquity made them suspect, for no one could tell whether the writings were those of Henoch, since they were not claimed as such by those who could be shown to have been so careful in preserving, generation after generation, the canonical tradition. That is why the writings which ran under the name of Henoch, and contain the fables about giants not having men for their fathers, are not believed to be his by those who are capable of judging.***[9]

By and large, around the third to fourth century, the overwhelming majority of Christendom came to agree with their Jewish counterparts—Enoch did not write the book of Enoch. Outside of the Ethiopic canon of Scripture, the book of Enoch is not a part of the canon.

Indeed, the origin of the book of Enoch was, and still is, a source of great controversy. However, as Augustine admitted,

> *"There is, of course, some truth to be found in these apocryphal writings..."*[10]

9 Augustine of Hippo, *The City of God, Books VIII–XVI*, 474 (Walsh and Monahan).

10 Augustine of Hippo, *The City of God, Books VIII–XVI*, 474.

While most scholars today don't consider the book of Enoch a product of inspiration, they do agree the book's wide, sweeping influence is felt across much of the New Testament landscape, as it was in Jude 14–15. That much is certain! One cannot simply ignore the direct quotes, content patterns, and many echoes of the book of Enoch in the New Testament because of the controversy surrounding this book. Inspired or not, Jesus Christ and the New Testament writers presupposed their audience and readers to be familiar with the ubiquitous book of Enoch (which they were) and recycled many of its *truths*—keyword: *TRUTHS*—in their teachings and inspired writings. Yes, books can contain truths, even if they aren't products of inspiration. Here is a brief list of some of the written echoes that scholars believe tie the book of Enoch and the New Testament together.

THE NEW TESTAMENT	THE BOOK OF ENOCH
It was also about these that Enoch, the seventh from Adam, prophesied, saying, **"Behold, the Lord comes with ten thousands of his holy ones, to execute judgment on all and to convict all the ungodly..."** (Jude 14–15, ESV)	9. **And behold! He cometh with ten thousands of His holy ones To execute judgement upon all, And to destroy all the ungodly:**[11]
And **the angels** which kept not their first estate, but **left their own habitation...** (Jude 6, KJV 1900)	And go, say to **the Watchers [the angels]** of heaven... Wherefore have ye **left the high, holy, and eternal heaven...** (Enoch 15:2–3)[12]

11 Charles, *The Book of Enoch or 1 Enoch: Translation*, 7–8.

12 Charles, *The Book of Enoch or 1 Enoch: Translation*, 35.

THE NEW TESTAMENT	THE BOOK OF ENOCH
And **the angels**… he hath **reserved in everlasting chains under darkness** unto **the judgment of the great day.**" (Jude 6, KJV 1900)	… **bind them [the angels]** fast for seventy generations in the valleys of the earth, **till the day of their judgement.** (Enoch 10:12)[13] …And **darkness** shall be their dwelling, (Enoch 46:6)[14]
When **the Son of man shall come** in his glory, and all the holy angels with him, then shall he **sit upon the throne of his glory:** (Matthew 25:31, KJV 1900)	For **that Son of Man has appeared**, And **has seated himself on the throne of his glory…** (Enoch 69:29)[15]
For we wrestle not against flesh and blood, but **against principalities, against powers**, against the rulers of the darkness of this world, **against spiritual wickedness in high places.** (Ephesians 6:12, KJV 1900)	And He will summon all the host of the heavens… and all **the angels of power**, and **all the angels of principalities**, and the Elect One, and **the other powers on the earth (and) over the water.** (Enoch 61:10)[16]
For the Father judgeth no man, but hath **committed all judgment unto the Son:** (John 5:22, KJV 1900)	And he sat on the throne of his glory, And the **sum of judgement was given unto the Son** of Man,[17]

13 Charles, *The Book of Enoch or 1 Enoch: Translation*, 24–25.

14 Charles, *The Book of Enoch or 1 Enoch: Translation*, 89.

15 Charles, *The Book of Enoch or 1 Enoch: Translation*, 141.

16 Charles, *The Book of Enoch or 1 Enoch: Translation*, 121.

17 Charles, *The Book of Enoch or 1 Enoch: Translation*, 140.

THE NEW TESTAMENT	THE BOOK OF ENOCH
The Son of man goeth as it is written of him: but woe unto that man **by whom the Son of man is betrayed! it had been good for that man if he had not been born**. (Matthew 26:24, KJV 1900)	... And where the resting-place of those who have **denied the Lord** of Spirits? **It had been good for them if they had not been born**. (Enoch 38:2)[18]
and then the lawless one will be revealed. **The Lord Jesus will destroy him with the breath of his mouth** and will **bring him to nothing** at the appearance of his coming. (2 Thessalonians 2:8, CSB)	And the **Lord of Spirits** seated him on the throne of His glory, And the spirit of righteousness was poured out upon him, And **the word of his mouth slays all the sinners**, And **all the unrighteous are destroyed** from before his face. (Enoch 62:2)[19]
And he carried me away in the spirit to a great and high mountain, and shewed me that great city, the holy Jerusalem, descending out of heaven from God, Having the glory of God: and her light was like unto a stone most precious, even like a jasper stone, **clear as crystal**; (Revelation 21:10–11, KJV 1900)	**And he translated my spirit into the heaven of heavens**, And I saw there as it were a structure **built of crystals**, And between those **crystals** tongues of living fire.[20]

18 Charles, *The Book of Enoch or 1 Enoch: Translation*, 71.

19 Charles, *The Book of Enoch or 1 Enoch: Translation*, 123.

20 Charles, *The Book of Enoch or 1 Enoch: Translation*, 143.

THE NEW TESTAMENT	THE BOOK OF ENOCH
In my Father's house are many **mansions**: if it were not so, I would have told you. I go to prepare a place for you. (John 14:2, KJV 1900)	And there I saw the **mansions** of the elect and the **mansions** of the holy… (Enoch 41:2)[21]
And **I saw the dead, small and great, stand before God;** and **the books were opened:** and **another book was opened, which is the book of life:** and the dead were judged out of those things which were written in the books, according to their works. (Revelation 20:12, KJV 1900)	In those days **I saw the Head of Days** when He seated himself upon the throne of His glory, **And the books of the living were opened before Him:** And **all His host which is in heaven above and His counsellors stood before Him,** (Enoch 47:3)[22]
Then they also which are **fallen asleep in Christ** are perished. (1 Corinthians 15:18, KJV 1900)	… And the spirit of those who have **fallen asleep in righteousness.** (Enoch 49:3)[23]
And **his raiment became shining, exceeding white as snow;** so as no fuller on earth can white them. (Mark 9:3, KJV 1900)	And the Great Glory sat thereon, and **His raiment shone more brightly** than the sun and **was whiter than any snow.**[24]
And the fifth angel sounded, and **I saw a star fall from heaven** unto the earth: and to him was given the key of the bottomless pit. (Revelation 9:1, KJV 1900)	And again **I saw** with mine eyes as I slept, and I saw the heaven above, and behold **a star fell from heaven,** (Enoch 86:1)[25]

21 Charles, *The Book of Enoch or 1 Enoch: Translation*, 79.

22 Charles, *The Book of Enoch or 1 Enoch: Translation*, 91–92.

23 Charles, *The Book of Enoch or 1 Enoch: Translation*, 96.

24 Charles, *The Book of Enoch or 1 Enoch: Translation*, 34.

25 Charles, *The Book of Enoch or 1 Enoch: Translation*, 187.

THE NEW TESTAMENT	THE BOOK OF ENOCH
Likewise, I say unto you, **there is joy** in the presence of **the angels of God** over one sinner that repenteth. (Luke 15:10, KJV 1900)	… And the faces of [all] **the angels in heaven** shall be lighted **up with joy.**[26]
And I saw a **new heaven** and a new earth: for **the first heaven** and the first earth **were passed away;** and there was no more sea. (Revelation 21:1, KJV 1900)	And **the first heaven shall depart and pass away,** And a **new heaven** shall appear, (Enoch 91:16)[27]
Ye **have lived** in pleasure on the earth, and been wanton; ye have nourished your hearts, as in a **day of slaughter.** (James 5:5, KJV 1900)	And **have become ready** for the **day of slaughter,** And the day of darkness and the day of the great judgement. (Enoch 94:9)[28]
And the sea gave up the dead which were in it; and **death and hell delivered up the dead which were in them:** and they were judged every man according to their works. And death **and hell** were cast into the lake of fire. This is the second death. And whosoever was not found written in the book of life was cast into the lake of fire. (Revelation 20:13–15, KJV 1900)	**And in those days shall the earth also give back that which has been entrusted to it,** And **Sheol also shall give back that which it has received, And hell** shall give back that which it owes. For in those days the Elect One shall arise, And he shall choose the righteous and holy from among them: For the day has drawn nigh that they should be saved.[29]

26 Charles, *The Book of Enoch or 1 Enoch: Translation*, 100.

27 Charles, *The Book of Enoch or 1 Enoch: Translation*, 233.

28 Charles, *The Book of Enoch or 1 Enoch: Translation*, 235.

29 Charles, *The Book of Enoch or 1 Enoch: Translation*, 98–100.

THE NEW TESTAMENT	THE BOOK OF ENOCH
And beside all this, between us and you there is a **great gulf fixed:** so that **they which would pass from hence to you cannot;** neither can they pass to us, that would come from thence. (Luke 16:26, KJV 1900)	And he answered me and said unto me: And such **a division has been made** for the spirits of the righteous... And such has been made for sinners when they die and are buried in the earth and judgement has not been executed on them in their lifetime... **Here their spirits shall be set apart** (Enoch 22:9–13)[30]
Then said the king to the servants, **Bind him hand and foot, and take him away, and cast him into outer darkness;** there shall be weeping and gnashing of teeth. (Matthew 22:13, KJV 1900)	And again the Lord said to Raphael: **'Bind Azâzêl hand and foot, and cast him into the darkness**: (Enoch 10:4)[31]

As we will discover throughout the course of our literary journey, additional *truths* from the book of Enoch have *significant* ties to what is written in your Bible. We will note them along the way.

WHAT DID THE ANCIENTS SAY ABOUT GIANTS?

The following quotes will give you a sampling of the consensus view of Genesis 6:1–4 among the ancient Jews hundreds of years before and during the time of Christ and among Christians for centuries after Christ. Let's start with Jubilees. The Book of Jubilees (second century B.C.) comments on Genesis 6. It essentially serves as a Jewish commentary book that retells and summarizes the history found in the

30 Charles, *The Book of Enoch or 1 Enoch: Translation*, 49–50.

31 Charles, *The Book of Enoch or 1 Enoch: Translation*, 22–23.

books of Genesis and Exodus. It's often referred to by scholars as "The Little Genesis."

> *And it came to pass when the children of men began to multiply on the face of the earth and daughters were born unto them,* ***that the angels of God*** *saw them on a certain year of this jubilee, that they were beautiful to look upon; and* ***they took themselves wives of all whom they chose, and they bare unto them sons and they were giants****. 2. And lawlessness increased on the earth and all flesh corrupted its way, alike men and cattle and beasts and birds and everything that walks on the earth—all of them corrupted their ways and their orders, and they began to devour each other, and lawlessness increased on the earth and every imagination of the thoughts of all men (was) thus evil continually. 3. And God looked upon the earth, and behold it was corrupt, and all flesh had corrupted its orders, and all that were upon the earth had wrought all manner of evil before His eyes. 4. And He said: "I shall destroy man and all flesh upon the face of the earth which I have created." 5. But Noah found grace before the eyes of the Lord. 6. And against the angels whom He had sent upon the earth, He was exceedingly wroth, and He gave commandment to root them out of all their dominion, and He bade us to bind them in the depths of the earth, and behold they are bound in the midst of them, and are (kept) separate. (Jubilees 5:1-6)* [32]

Third Maccabees also mentions the giants before the flood. It's one of four Jewish writings (The Books of Maccabees) that catalog Jewish

---

32 R. H. Charles, ed., *The Book of Jubilees*, trans. R. H. Charles (London: Adam and Charles Black, 1902), 43–44.

life and history prior to the rise of rabbinic Judaism and Christianity. It notes,

> [4] *Those who previously did wrong—among whom were giants, who trusted in Rome and arrogance—you destroyed, bringing on them immeasurable water. (3 Maccabees 2:4, LES)*

Another Jewish text that briefly brushes on the subject of the giants of Genesis 6 is 1 Baruch. The book of Baruch is an apocryphal book that was written to Jewish exiles in Babylon. It was included in the Septuagint, the ancient Greek Old Testament, but has been dropped in most modern Bibles. It claims to have been written by Baruch, a secretary to the prophet Jeremiah. It states,

> *24 O Israel, how great is the house of God! and how large is the place of his possession! 25 Great, and hath none end; high, and unmeasurable. 26* ***There were the giants famous from the beginning, that were of so great stature, and so expert in war****.*
> *27 Those did not the Lord choose, neither gave he the way of knowledge unto them: 28 but they were destroyed, because they had no wisdom, and perished through their own foolishness. (Baruch 3:24–28, Brenton LXX En)*

Eusebius (260–339 A.D.) also commented on Genesis 6:1–4 in his commentary on Isaiah. He's known for producing the first comprehensive written history of the church as well as the *Onomasticon*, the geographical catalog that matched biblical cites to biblical stories. He wrote,

> *...the "angels" who came down from heaven, from whom "the giants were born." The Scripture of Moses mentions them when it says: "the sons of God saw that the daughters of men were fair; and they took to wife such of them as they chose."21 Then*

> *it says that "those born" from them were "those who were named giants forever."*[33]

WAS NOAH'S BLOODLINE (DNA) CORRUPTED BY THE FALLEN ANGELS?

No. The Bible makes this abundantly clear.

> 6 These are the generations of Noah. Noah was a righteous man, **blameless** in his generation. Noah walked with God. (Gen 6:9, ESV)

Moses wrote that Noah was "blameless" (**tâmîym**) in "his generations." "Blameless" carries a dual meaning. Sometimes, "blameless" denotes righteousness.

> *The Hebrew term* תָּמִים *(tamim, "blameless") is used of men in Gen 17:1 (associated with the idiom "walk before," which means "maintain a proper relationship with," see 24:40); Deut 18:13 (where it means "blameless" in the sense of not guilty of the idolatrous practices listed before this; see Josh 24:14); Pss 18:23, 26 ("blameless" in the sense of not having violated God's commands); 37:18 (in contrast to the wicked); 101:2, 6 (in contrast to proud, deceitful slanderers; see 15:2); Prov 2:21; 11:5 (in contrast to the wicked); 28:10; Job 12:4.*[34]

Noah was certainly a righteous man; however, his generation being "blameless" carries a deeper meaning. The Faithlife Study Bible comments on Genesis 6,

---

33 Eusebius of Caesarea, *Commentary on Isaiah*, 72 (Armstrong).

34 The NET Bible First Edition Notes (Richardson, TX: Biblical Studies Press, 2006), Gen 6:9.

> *The Hebrew word used here, tamim, refers to being free from defect; it is often used in sacrificial contexts to describe an unblemished animal presented to God (Exod 12:5; Lev 1:3, 10; 3:1, 6).*[35]

Biblical scholar Dr. E. W. Bullinger drives this point home in Appendix 26 of his timeless literary work, the Companion Bible. He argued that "blameless" spoke of Noah's physical pedigree being intact.

> *The Heb. word tāmīm means without blemish, and is the technical word for bodily and physical perfection, and not moral. Hence it is used of animals of sacrificial purity. It is rendered without blemish in Ex. 12:5; 29:1; Lev. 1:3, 10; 3:1, 6; 4:3, 23, 28, 32; 5:15, 18; 6:6; 9:2, 3; 14:10; 22:19; 23:12, 18; Num. 6:14; 28:19, 31; 29:2, 8, 13, 20, 23, 29, 32, 36; Ezek. 43:22, 23, 25; 45:18, 23; 46:4, 6, 13.*
>
> *Without spot. Num. 19:2; 28:3, 9, 11; 29:17, 26.*
>
> *Undefiled. Ps. 119:1.*
>
> *This shows that Gen. 6:9 does not speak of Noah's moral perfection, but tells us that he and his family alone had preserved their pedigree and kept it pure, in spite of the prevailing corruption brought about by the fallen angels. See Ap. 23 and 25.*[36]

This would be crucial since Noah and his family would be the progenitors of all mankind after the flood. Noah was a righteous man whose human "pedigree" wasn't tainted by the mingling of angels and women. He was one hundred percent human and loved God with one hundred percent of his heart.

---

35 Faithlife Study Bible (Bellingham, WA: Lexham Press, 2012, 2016), Gen 6:9.

36 E. W. Bullinger, vol. 2 of *The Companion Bible: Being the Authorized Version of 1611 with the Structures and Notes, Critical, Explanatory and Suggestive and with 198 Appendixes* (Bellingham, WA: Faithlife, 2018), 28.

CONNECTING THE GOSPEL

"SAVED BY WATER"

What do water baptism, Noah, Jesus, and Enoch have in common? More than you might think. Understanding how it's all interconnected is paramount in comprehending the ancient gospel. Notice what Peter wrote.

> 18 For **Christ** also suffered once for sins, the righteous for
> the unrighteous, that he might bring us to God, being put to
> death in the flesh but made alive in the spirit, 19 in which **he**
> **went and proclaimed to the spirits in prison**, 20 because they
> formerly did not obey, when God's patience waited **in the days**
> **of Noah**, while the ark was being prepared, in which a few,
> that is, **eight persons, were brought safely through water**.
> 21 **Baptism, which corresponds to this, now saves you**, not as
> a removal of dirt from the body but as an appeal to God for
> a good conscience, through the resurrection of Jesus Christ,
> 22 who has gone into heaven and is at the right hand of God,
> **with angels, authorities, and powers having been subjected to**
> **him**. (1 Pet 3:18–22, ESV)

Dr. Michael S. Heiser has done extensive research into ancient Near Eastern texts, Semitic languages, and the context of the ancient world. Notice his comments on Peter's passage:

> *Just as Jesus was the second Adam for Paul, Jesus is the second Enoch for Peter. Enoch descended to the imprisoned fallen angels to announce their doom. First Peter 3:14–22 has Jesus descending to these same "spirits in prison" to tell them they were still defeated, despite his crucifixion. God's plan of salvation and kingdom rule had not been derailed—in fact, it was right on schedule. The*

> *crucifixion actually meant victory over every demonic force opposed to God. This victory declaration is why 1 Peter 3:14–22 ends with Jesus risen from the dead and set at the right hand of God—above all angels, authorities and powers. The messaging is very deliberate, and has a supernatural view of Genesis 6:1–4 at its core.*[37]

Peter wants his readers to realize that baptism corresponds to the eight souls saved by water and to the defeat of the sinister forces of evil. We will dive deeper into baptism's reiteration of doom for the fallen angels in the next section. The very element (water) that destroyed every living thing was the same element that saved the world.

Peter's not denying faith, God's grace, or the ark's role in their deliverance from the prediluvian world; he's simply highlighting the role water played in their deliverance. In *Against Heresies 4.36.4*, Irenaeus (130–203 A.D.) discussed the dualistic role water played in both "destroying" the giants and "saving" mankind. He wrote,

> *in the days of Noah* ***He justly brought on the deluge for the purpose of extinguishing*** *that most infamous race of men then existent, who could not bring forth fruit to God, since the angels that sinned had commingled with them, and [acted as He did] in order* ***that He might put a check upon the sins of these men, but [that at the same time] He might preserve the archetype, the formation of Adam.***[38]

The watery flood sent by the Lord was Noah's saving grace, saving all eight souls aboard the ark while washing away corruption. Peter wanted

---

37 Heiser, *The Unseen Realm*, 338.

38 Irenaeus of Lyons, *The Writings of Irenæus*, 30 (Roberts and Rambaut).

his readers to know that water baptism did the same for them. This is well-demonstrated through the idea of "washing."

Ancient Christian writer Justin Martyr (c. 100–c. 165 A.D.) wrote extensively about the "washing" one receives in the waters of baptism.

> *(61.3) Then they are led by us to where there is water, and in the manner of the regeneration [ἀναγεννήσεως] by which we ourselves were regenerated [ἀνεγεννήθημεν] they are regenerated [ἀναγεννῶνται]. For at that* ***time they are washed [λουτρὸν ποιοῦνται] in the water*** *in the name of God the Master and Father of all, and of our Savior Jesus Christ, and of the Holy Spirit. (4) For Christ also said, "Unless you are regenerated [ἀναγεννηθῆτε] you cannot enter into the kingdom of heaven." ...*
>
> *(9) And we have learned from the apostles the reason for this practice. (10) Since at our first birth we have been born without our knowledge or choice from the moist seed at the union of our parents with each other and have existed in bad habits and evil conduct, in order that we might not remain children of ignorance and necessity but become children of choice and knowledge and might obtain the forgiveness of sins committed in the past, there is called in the water upon the one who chooses to be regenerated [ἀναγεννηθῆναι] and who repents of sins the name of God the Master and Father of all. The one leading the* ***person being washed [λουσόμενον] to the bath [λουτρόν]*** *speaks only this name ...*
>
> *(12) This bath [λουρὸν] is called illumination [φωτισμός], since those who learn these things are illuminated in their understanding. (13) And the person who is illuminated [φωτιζόμενος]* ***is washed [λούεται] in the name of Jesus Christ,*** *who was crucified under Pontius Pilate, and in the name of the Holy Spirit, who through the prophets foretold all the things about Jesus....*

> *(65.1)* ***After we thus wash [λοῦσαι] the person*** *who has been persuaded and who has given consent, we lead this one to where those called brothers and sisters have gathered together to make fervent prayers in common on behalf of themselves and of the one who has been illuminated [φωτισθέντος] and of all others everywhere. We pray that having learned the truth we may be accounted worthy and through our deeds be found good citizens and guardians of what is commanded in order that we may be saved with eternal salvation.*
>
> *(66.1) This food is called by us eucharist, of which no one is allowed to partake except the one who believes the things taught by us to be true,* ***was washed [λουσαμένῳ] in the bath [λουτρόν] for forgiveness of sins and regeneration*** *[ἀναγέννησιν], and who lives in the manner Christ taught. (1 Apology 61.3–13; 65.1; 66.1))*[39]

Justin understood baptism is a washing away of sins. He didn't invent this aspect of salvation—he read it in the Bible.

> 12 Someone named Ananias, a devout man according to the law, who had a good reputation with all the Jews living there,
> 13 came and stood by me and said, 'Brother Saul, regain your sight.' And in that very hour I looked up and saw him. 14 And
> he said, 'The God of our ancestors has appointed you to know his will, to see the Righteous One, and to hear the words from
> his mouth, 15 since you will be a witness for him to all people of what you have seen and heard. 16 And now, why are you delaying? **Get up and be baptized, and wash away your sins, calling on his name.**' (Acts 22:12–16, CSB)

---

39 Ferguson, *Baptism in the Early Church*, 237–238.

As students of the modern gospel, this can be really confusing. If you've been taught baptism was something you do after you are saved, then I'm sorry—you've been misled. An early defender of the faith was Tertullian (160–220 A.D.), properly called Quintus Septimius Florens Tertullian. Tertullian was aware of a wicked woman who argued that baptism was unnecessary to gain spiritual life. He wrote,

> *And in fact a certain viper from the Cainite group, who recently spent some time here, carried off a good number with her exceptionally poisonous doctrine, above all destroying baptism. Obviously this is according to her nature: for vipers and asps as a rule, and even serpents, seek out arid and waterless places. But we little fishes, following Jesus Christ our ichthus, begin our life in the water, and can only be safe remaining in water. (1.2–3)*[40]

Many moderns mock the idea that spiritual life begins in the water and argue it implies we are saved by works, and not by grace through faith (Eph 2:8–9). The original Christians didn't see it that way and parsed Peter's words exactly as he articulated them. They knew "baptism now saves us" not because of "what" one does or earns in the water, per se (i.e., merit), but because of "who" one puts on in the water—Jesus Christ and the Holy Spirit (i.e., grace through faith).

> 26 For ye are all **sons of God**, through faith, in Christ Jesus.
> 27 **For as many of you as were baptized into Christ did put on Christ**. (Gal 3:26–27, ASV 1901)

> 4 But when the kindness of God our Savior and his love for mankind appeared, 5 **he saved us**—not by works of righteousness that we had done, but according to his mercy—**through the**

40 McGowan, *Ancient Christian Worship*, 164.

> **washing of regeneration and renewal by the Holy Spirit.** [6] He poured out his Spirit on us abundantly through Jesus Christ our Savior [7] so that, having been justified by his grace, we may become heirs with the hope of eternal life. (Titus 3:4–7, CSB)

"BAPTISM AS A PLEDGE OF ALLEGIANCE"

Peter wrote in 1 Peter 3:21 that baptism was an "appeal" or "pledge" (Gk: ἐπερώτημα, ĕpĕrōtēma) of good conscience made to God. The Theological Lexicon of the New Testament notes,

> *"This oath of allegiance [baptism] is antithetical to the disobedience of Noah's contemporaries; it is the pledge of a person regenerated by the power of Christ's resurrection, in which the believer shares through the baptismal rite (1 Pet 1:3; Rom 6:4; Col 2:12).*[41]

In baptism, one is pledging their allegiance to the God of heaven while casting off the powers of darkness from Hell. Peter's audience would have understood that water baptism not only "corresponded" to the saving of Noah's family, but that it also "corresponded" to the chained "spirits in prison" (2 Peter 2:4-5; Jude 6-7) of Genesis 6, to whom Jesus preached (1 Peter 3:18-22). Switching sides and allegiance through water baptism adds insult to the imprisoned angel's past defeat and reiterates their eternal doom. Dr. Michael S. Heiser writes,

> *But in addition to that, it [baptism] is also a visceral reminder to the defeated fallen angels. Every baptism is a reiteration of their doom in the wake of the gospel and the kingdom of God. Early*

---

41 Ceslas Spicq and James D. Ernest, *Theological Lexicon of the New Testament* (Peabody, MA: Hendrickson Publishers, 1994), 33.

> *Christians understood the typology of this passage and its link back to the fallen angels of Genesis 6.*[42]

Again, when one is baptized, they are, in essence, switching sides and renouncing their loyalty to the devil and his condemned angels. This public proclamation is against all the members of Satan's demonic regime, chained and unchained. This was the understanding in the ancient world, but it has, unfortunately, been forgotten in the modern age. In an ancient third century text titled On the *On the Holy Theophany*, water baptism is understood as a renunciation of Satan:

> *The one who with faith goes down to the bath [λουτρόν] of regeneration [ἀναγεννήσεως], separates from the Evil One and associates himself with Christ, renounces the Enemy and confesses that Christ is God, puts off the bondage and puts on the adoption, comes up from baptism bright as the sun ..., a son of God and joint-heir with Christ.*[43]

In 392 A.D., Theodore of Mopsuestia wrote,

> *"Through the gift of the holy baptism you are separating yourselves from the servitude of the Tyrant, which all our fathers from the time of Adam downwards received, and in which they lived"*[44]

Origen of Alexandria (185–254, A.D.), a prolific Christian influencer in the early church, also spoke of baptism being connected to a turning from "the Tyrant," or the devil.

---

42 Heiser, *The Unseen Realm*, 338–339.

43 Ferguson, *Baptism in the Early Church*, 335.

44 Ferguson, *Baptism in the Early Church*, 527.

> *We come to that moment we made these promises, this declaration to the devil. Each of the faithful recalls when he came to the waters of baptism, when he received the first seal of the faith and approached the fount of salvation, the words that he pronounced then; he recalls his renunciation of the devil. He promised to resort to none of his pomps and his works and not to submit to any of his servitudes and his pleasures. (Homilies on Numbers 12.4)*[45]

Fourth-century preacher Chromatius of Aquileia preached that confession and baptism was a renunciation of the world in the presence of the Lord's holy angels.

> *Before you came to baptism, one asked you if you renounced the world, its pomps, and its works. And you responded that you renounced them. And so you came to the grace of eternal baptism. Your words are preserved before God. Your response is written in heaven. (Sermon 14.4)*
>
> *You made a sworn promise of your faith to God. You swore your promise in the presence of angels, because angels are present when you are asked about your faith. See what you did. If something promised to a human being is binding, what about that which is solemnly pledged to God? (Sermon 14.4)*[46]

LOOKING AHEAD

"In the six hundred first year, in the first month, on the first day of the month, the water that had covered the earth was dried up. Then Noah removed the ark's cover and saw that

---

45 Ferguson, *Baptism in the Early Church*, 423.

46 Ferguson, *Baptism in the Early Church*, 423.

> the surface of the ground was drying. By the twenty-seventh day of the second month, the earth was dry. Then God spoke to Noah, "Come out of the ark, you, your wife, your sons, and your sons' wives with you. Bring out all the living creatures that are with you—birds, livestock, those that crawl on the earth—and they will spread over the earth and be fruitful and multiply on the earth." So Noah, along with his sons, his wife, and his sons' wives, came out. All the animals, all the creatures that crawl, and all the flying creatures—everything that moves on the earth—came out of the ark by their families. (Gen 8:13–19, CSB)

It was a turning page for Noah and his family. For the first time in many generations, the earth and the heavens were largely pure in God's sight. With Satan's angelic recruits locked away under gloomy chains of darkness and his monstrous Nephilim annihilated, the serpent of Eden was, once again, forced to continue his sinful quest alone.

> "God blessed Noah and his sons and said to them, "Be fruitful and multiply and fill the earth. The fear and terror of you will be in every living creature on the earth, every bird of the sky, every creature that crawls on the ground, and all the fish of the sea. They are placed under your authority. (Gen 9:1–2, CSB)

After reiterating the Edenic order to be fruitful and multiply, God quickly established some new ground rules for mankind.

> "Every moving thing that lives shall be for you as food. As I gave the green plants to you, I now give you everything. Only you shall not eat raw flesh with blood in it. And your lifeblood I will require; from every animal I will require

> it. And from the hand of humankind, from the hand of each man to his brother I will require the life of humankind. "As for the one shedding the blood of humankind, by humankind his blood shall be shed, for God made humankind in his own image. (Gen 9:3–6, LEB)

As man once again set out into the unknown, God made a binding promise—He would never send a global flood to destroy all flesh ever again.

> "But you, be fruitful and multiply; spread out over the earth and multiply on it." Then God said to Noah and his sons with him, "Understand that I am establishing my covenant with you and your descendants after you, and with every living creature that is with you—birds, livestock, and all wildlife of the earth that are with you—all the animals of the earth that came out of the ark. I establish my covenant with you that never again will every creature be wiped out by floodwaters; there will never again be a flood to destroy the earth." And God said, "This is the sign of the covenant I am making between me and you and every living creature with you, a covenant for all future generations: I have placed my bow in the clouds, and it will be a sign of the covenant between me and the earth. Whenever I form clouds over the earth and the bow appears in the clouds, I will remember my covenant between me and you and all the living creatures: water will never again become a flood to destroy every creature. The bow will be in the clouds, and I will look at it and remember the permanent covenant between God and all the living creatures on earth." God said to Noah, "This is the sign of the covenant that I have established between me and every creature on earth." (Gen 9:7–17, CSB)

A vibrant rainbow hung in the misty sky. It was a beautiful promise, a constant reminder that God would never destroy the earth with a cataclysmic flood again. As the rainbow faded, so did a future generation's trust in God and His eternal promise. Something big was coming, and it all started in a high tower far away.

CHAPTER 4

THE HIGH TOWER, THE RULE OF THE GODS, AND THE DIVORCEMENT OF SEVENTY NATIONS

When the Most High divided
the nations, when he separated
the sons of Adam, he set the
bounds of the nations according to
the number of the angels of God.
(Deuteronomy 32:8, Brenton LXX En)

READING THE STORY

THE EARTH WAS BEAUTIFUL, AND SO was man's relationship with God. The flood had cleansed the earth of Nephilim giants and wicked people, just as God intended. As the waters receded, Noah's ark rested in the mountains of Ararat (Gen 8:4). Noah and his family had to press on and say goodbye to the boat that had become their salvation. Now, it was just an empty ark that could tell the tale of a lost world, but would not.

Undoubtedly, Noah, Shem, Ham, Japheth, and their respective families were all truly thankful the Lord had saved them from an array of evil angels, towering giants, corrupt humans, and the cataclysmic flood. As they settled into their new normal, Noah's youngest son, Ham (Gen 9:22–24), soon had four children of his own.

> 6 Ham's sons: Cush, Mizraim, Put, and Canaan. (Gen 10:6, CSB)

Ham's oldest son, Cush, also eventually married and was blessed with a baby boy named Nimrod.

> “Cush's sons: Seba, Havilah, Sabtah, Raamah, and Sabteca. And Raamah's sons: Sheba and Dedan. Cush fathered **Nimrod**, who began to be powerful in the land. **He was a powerful hunter in the sight of the** LORD. That is why it is said, “Like Nimrod, a powerful hunter in the sight of the LORD.” (Gen 10:7–9, CSB)

Nimrod's love for hunting soon transformed into a passion for building. He was the chief architect for many of the civilizations in the ancient world, including the city of Erech (modern-day Iraq).

> “Now, **the beginning of his kingdom was Babel**, Erech, Akkad, and Calneh, in the land of Shinar. From that land he went out to Assyria, and he built Nineveh, Rehoboth-Ir,

> Calah, Resen between Nineveh and Calah; that is the great city. (Gen 10:10–12, LEB)

Shamefully, he used his talent of masonry for a terrible evil. Nimrod and his proud heart built, from the ground up, the ancient cities of Shinar (Sumer). What happened next changed the landscape of our world forever. In fact, it would drive the narrative of the rest of the Bible.

As Nimrod's obsession with "kingdom building" grew, so did his following. He had a vision for greatness, no doubt. Disastrously, his greatness wouldn't be of God, but of the devil. Interestingly enough, the name "Nimrod" means, "We shall rebel." Nimrod announced a new building project to his legion of rebellious masons: the Tower of Babel. Notice what Josephus, the Jewish Historian, said about Nimrod.

> *Now it was **Nimrod** who excited them to such an affront and contempt of God. He was the grandson of Ham, the son of Noah,—a bold man, and of great strength of hand. He persuaded them not to ascribe it to God as if it was through his means they were happy, but to believe that it was their own courage which procured that happiness. He also gradually changed the government into tyranny,—seeing no other way of turning men from the fear of God, but to bring them into a constant dependence upon his power. He also said he would be revenged on God, if he should have a mind to drown the world again; for that he would build a tower too high for the waters to be able to reach! and that he would avenge himself on God for destroying their forefathers!*[1]

---

1 Josephus, *The Works of Josephus*, 35.

Up to this moment, everyone communicated in a common language and, for the most part, served God with a singleness of heart. But that was all about to change, along with God's relationship status with all the nations of the earth.

> **Now the whole world had one language and a common speech**. As people moved eastward, they found a plain in Shinar and settled there. They said to each other, "Come, let's make bricks and bake them thoroughly." They used brick instead of stone, and tar for mortar. Then they said, "**Come, let us build ourselves a city, with a tower that reaches to the heavens**, so that we may make a name for ourselves; otherwise we will be scattered over the face of the whole earth." But the Lord came down to see the city and the tower the people were building. (Gen 11:1–5, NIV)

Before leaving the royal court of heaven, the Lord met with His holy angels, the sons of God.

> The Lord said, "If as one people speaking the same language they have begun to do this, then nothing they plan to do will be impossible for them. **Come, let us go down and confuse their language so they will not understand each other**." So the Lord scattered them from there over all the earth, and they stopped building the city. That is why it was called Babel—because **there the** Lord **confused the language of the whole world**. From there the Lord scattered them over the face of the whole earth. (Gen 11:6–9, NIV)

There's one important detail left out by Moses in the Genesis chronology of the Tower of Babel. He includes it, however, in his fifth and final book of the Pentateuch—the book of Deuteronomy.

Deuteronomy 32:8 (ESV)	Deuteronomy 32:8 (Brenton LXX En)
8 When the Most High gave to the nations their inheritance, when he divided mankind, he fixed the borders of the peoples **according to the number of the sons of God.**	8 When the Most High divided the nations, when he separated the sons of Adam, he set the bounds of the nations **according to the number of the angels of God.**

As God visited the tower of man, He was more than disappointed; He was put out with his human imagers. Their arrogance and faithlessness were as horrific as Nimrod's twisted tower. Shockingly, God did something no one saw coming—He divorced the nations and allotted them "according to the number of the sons of God (benê [ha]ʾelōhîm)," thus lining up with the Septuagint's rendering, "according to the number of the angels of God (angelōn theou)." These were not rebellious angels; they were "holy angels" (malākîm qôdeš), loyal sons of God. We know the number was at least seventy because that's how many nations were "spread abroad on the earth" in the table of nations listed in Genesis 10. Philo of Alexandria (20 B.C.–50 A.D.), a contemporary of Jesus Christ Himself, attested to this in *On the Posterity of Cain and His Exile 91*:

> *When God was dividing and drawing a wall between the nations of the soul, separating those who spoke different languages; and when establishing the sons of the earth in their abodes, he dispersed them and removed to a distance from himself those whom he called the sons of Adam; then he fixed the boundaries of the offspring of virtue,* ***making them equal in number to the angels; for as many angels of God as there are****, so many nations and species of virtue are there.*[2]

---

2 Philo of Alexandria, *The Works of Philo: Complete and Unabridged*, 140 (Yonge).

Yahweh would no longer be their God, and they would no longer be His people. From now on, each of the seventy nations would be governed by a divinely appointed angelic viceroy. These tutelary spirits were to act as shepherds and guides for all the nations of the ancient world until the "fullness of time had come" (Gal 4:4–7). Tragically, the angels over the nations (Dan 10:13–21) would betray their heavenly Father and fall in league with the serpentine dark lord (Matt 25:41), becoming the evil small-G gods of the Old Testament.

ANSWERING YOUR QUESTIONS

WHAT DID THE ANCIENTS SAY?

In the early third century, Origen of Alexandria (185–254 A.D.) wrote quite extensively on the angelic allotment at Babel:

> *Whence* ***also those angels have been roused to wrath who held each individual nation under their authority****. "For when the Most High divided the nations* ***according to the number of the angels of God****, then Jacob became his portion and Israel the lot of his inheritance." For Christ, to whom the Father had said: "Ask of me and I will give you the nations for your inheritance and the utmost parts of the earth for your possession,"* ***expelling those very angels from the authority and domination which they had among the nations****, provoked them to wrath. And for this reason Scripture says: "The kings of the earth stood up, and the princes met together, against the Lord and against his Christ." Therefore they resist us also and stir up struggles and strife against us. Hence also the Apostle of Christ: "* ***Our struggle is not against flesh and blood, but against principalities and powers and rulers of this world****." For this reason, therefore, we must be watchful and act carefully, because "our adversary, as a roaring lion, goes about*

> *seeking whom he may devour." Unless we shall resist him "strong in faith," he shall again recall us into captivity. If this should happen to us, we will make thankless the work of him who "fastened to his cross principalities and powers, confidently triumphing over them in himself" and who came "to set at liberty the captives."*[3]

Additionally, Origen highlighted the angels' "reign" in *Homilies on Genesis and Exodus.*

> *I say even something more. You will discover also in the divine dispensations something like this to have taken place in that which Moses says: "When the Most High divided the nations and distinguished the boundaries of the nations, he established them* ***according to the number of the angels of God****, and Jacob became the Lord's portion, and Israel the lot of his inheritance." You see, therefore, that* ***the reign of angels was established deservedly for each nation****, but the people of Israel became "the Lord's portion."*[4]

He notes in his Commentary on the Epistle to the Romans,

> ***These angels, to whom a portion of the nations had been distributed in some manner, seduced each individual nation away from being the Lord's portion. And by corrupting them they made them stumble*** *so that the Lord said through the prophet, "My desired portion has become a curse to me."*[5]

In *Philocalia 22.9*, Origen referenced Nimrod and his builders of the wicked tower, saying,

---

3 Origen, *Homilies on Genesis and Exodus*, 153–154 (Heine).

4 Origen, *Homilies on Genesis and Exodus*, 216–217.

5 Origen, *Commentary on the Epistle to the Romans, Books 6–10*, 169 (Scheck).

> *let them severally...be delivered to angels of more or less severity, and of such and such dispositions, until they have paid the penalty for their audacity; and we will further suppose them to be severally* ***led by the angels****, who give them their own language, to various parts of the earth according as they deserve; some, let us say, to a scorching hot country, others to one so bitterly cold that it punishes its inhabitants, some to a land hard to cultivate, others to one not so hard, some to a land full of wild beasts, and others to one with not so many.*[6]

Finally, he wrote in De Principiis 1.5.2,

> *"The portion of the Lord is His people Jacob; Israel is the cord of His inheritance."* ***Other nations, moreover, are called a part of the angels****; since "when the Most High divided the nations, and dispersed the sons of Adam, He fixed the boundaries of the nations according to the number of the angels of God."*[7]

The Book of Jubilees (second century B.C.) also alludes to the divine allotment of Deuteronomy 32:8–9.

> *31. And He sanctified it, and gathered it from amongst all the children of men; for there are many nations and many peoples, and all are His, and over all hath* ***He placed spirits in authority****...*
> *32. But over Israel He did not appoint any angel or spirit, for He alone is their ruler, and He will preserve them and require them at the hand of His angels and His spirits, and at the hand of all His powers in order that He may preserve them and bless them, and*

6 Origen, *The Philocalia of Origen*, 170–171 (Lewis).

7 Origen, *De Principiis*, 257 (Crombie).

> *that they may be His and He may be theirs from henceforth for ever. (Jubilees 15:31–32)*[8]

Clement of Alexandria (150–215 A.D.) commented on Deuteronomy 32:8–9 in *Miscellanies*:

> *For by an ancient and divine order* ***the angels are distributed among the nations****. But the glory of those who believe is "the Lord's portion."*[9]

Eusebius (260–339 A.D.) also referenced the "guardians of the nations" in his work, The Proof of the Gospel 4.7:

> *In these words surely he names first the Most High God, the Supreme God of the Universe, and then as Lord His Word, Whom we call Lord in the second degree after the God of the Universe. [d] And their import is that all the nations and the sons of men, here called sons of Adam, were distributed among the* ***invisible guardians of the nations, that is the angels****, by the decision of the Most High God, and His secret counsel unknown to us.*[10]

Basil of Caesarea (330–379 A.D.) wrote of the angelic allotment and connected it to Daniel 10:

> *In addition, Moses taught us in the song that certain angels preside over entire nations: When the Most High divided the nations, when he scattered the sons of Adam, he fixed the limits of the*

---

8 Charles, *The Book of Jubilees or The Little Genesis*, 111–112.

9 Clement of Alexandria, *The Stromata, or Miscellanies*, 524.

10 Eusebius of Cæsarea, *The Proof of the Gospel: Being the Demonstratio Evangelica of Eusebius of Cæsarea*, 176 (Ferrar).

> *nations according to the number of his angels [Dt 32:8]. In his vision of the angel, the wise Daniel heard him saying: The prince of the kingdom of the Persians has made a stand before me, and behold! Michael, one of the chief princes, came to help me, and I left him there with the prince of the kingdom of the Persians [Dn 10:13]. A little further on, the same one says: And the prince of the Greeks was coming [Dn 10:20].*[11]

As the centuries passed, scholars such as Rabanus Maurus (c. 780–856 A.D.), a Frankish monk, continued to highlight the angelic allotment that took place at Babel ages ago. Maurus wrote,

> *We may interpret that the rulers placed by God over every people are the angels to whom he entrusted the care of each people, according to that word of Deuteronomy, "He set the boundaries of the peoples according to the number of the angels of God." And one reads in the book of Daniel that there is a head of the Greeks and a head of the Persians*[12]

What's powerfully telling is the allotment at Babel was not forgotten by the Gentile nations of the world. They were telling the same story as the Hebrews and shared the same cosmology: an "allotment of gods" worldview. Athenian philosopher Plato (428–348 B.C.) wrote in *Critias 109*,

> *In the days of old,* ***the gods had the whole earth distributed among them by allotment****. There was no quarrelling; for you cannot rightly suppose that the gods did not know what was proper for each of them to have, or, knowing this, that they would seek to procure*

---

11 Basil of Caesarea, *Against Eunomius*, 187 (Radde-Gallwitz).

12 S. J. Voicu, ed., *Apocrypha* (Downers Grove, IL: InterVarsity Press, 2010), 259.

> *for themselves by contention that which more properly belonged to others. They all of them by just apportionment obtained what they wanted, and* ***peopled their own districts****; and when they had peopled them they tended us, their nurselings and possessions, as shepherds tend their flocks, excepting only that they did not use blows or bodily force, as shepherds do, but governed us like pilots from the stern of the vessel, which is an easy way of guiding animals, holding our souls by the rudder of persuasion according to their own pleasure;—thus did they guide all mortal creatures.* ***Now different gods had their allotments in different places which they set in order.***[13]

Believers such as Eusebius, having read Plato's words, recognized Plato alluded to Deuteronomy 32:8–9. Eusebius wrote in *The Preparation of the Gospel 11.26*,

> *[c] Also the oracle of Moses which said, *'When the Most High was dividing the nations, when He was separating the children of Adam, He set the bounds of the nations according to the number of the angels of God,' seems to be directly paraphrased by Plato in the words whereby he defined* ***the whole human race to be 'the possessions of gods and daemons.'***[14]

ARE THE GODS REAL?

Our modern minds have been conditioned to reject the idea of divine plurality at all costs. We've been taught there is only one God and that "God" is His name. G-O-D is not His name; it's what He is—a spiritual being (ʾelōhîm). His name is Yahweh. He is one of many spirit beings in the unseen realm (John 4:24). While Yahweh is an

13 Plato, vol. 3 of *The Dialogues of Plato*, 530 (Jowett).

14 Eusebius of Caesarea, *Evangelicae Praeparationis Libri XV*, 595 (Gifford).

ʾelōhîm, no other ʾelōhîm is Yahweh. He is "species" unique and incomparable to all others.

> 6 "**You alone are Yahweh**. You alone have made the heavens, the heavens of the heavens, and all of their army, the earth and all that is in it, the waters and all that is in them. You give life to all of them, and **the army of the heavens worship you**. (Neh 9:6, LEB)

> 8 **There is none like you among the gods**, O Lord, and there are no works like yours. (Ps 86:8, LEB)

The exceptionality of our God cannot be overstated. The Father, the Son, and the Spirit are from everlasting to everlasting (1 Chr 16:36); yet, while separate, they are one (Deut 6:4). These truths serve as the foundation of Christianity.

However, it's incorrect to say there is only one "god." The apostle Paul said there are many gods (***theoi***) and lords (***kurioi***).

> 5 For though **there be** that are called **gods**, whether in heaven or in earth, (**as there be gods many, and lords many**,) (1 Cor 8:5, KJV 1900)

Paul follows that statement with an important clarifier—we serve the one God who created all things and all beings, both supernatural and human.

> 6 But to us there is but **one God**, the Father, **of whom** are **all things**, and we in him; and one Lord Jesus Christ, **by whom** are **all things**, and we by him. (1 Cor 8:6, KJV 1900)

Origen, in his *Homilies on Genesis and Exodus*, wrote,

> *Scripture itself will be able to teach us the reason for "many gods" or "many lords" if you listen attentively and patiently. For the same Moses says in the song of Deuteronomy, "When the Most High divided the nations and scattered the sons of Adam, he set the boundaries of the nations in accordance with the number of the angels of God. And his people Jacob became the portion of the Lord, the lot of his inheritance Israel." It is evident, therefore, that the angels to whom the Most High entrusted the nations to be ruled are called either gods or lords; gods as if given by God and lords as those who have been alloted power from the Lord.*[15]

Furthermore, Moses points out that demonic spirits are also "gods" (*ʾ**elōhîm***).

> 17 They sacrificed to devils, and not to God; to gods (ʾ**elōhîm**) whom they knew not: new and fresh gods came in, whom their fathers knew not. (Deut 32:17, Brenton LXX En)

To be clear, there is only one omnipresent, omniscient, and omnipotent God who created all things, including all the "gods" (*ʾ**elōhîm***) and "spirits" (***rûaḥôṯ***) of the unseen realm (Jas 1:17; Ps 148:1–5). Yahweh, the God of the Bible, is the God (*ʾ**elōhîm***) of gods (*ʾ**elōhîm***) and serves as King over them.

Psalm 95:3 (LEB)	Psalm 94:3 (Brenton LXX En)
3 For **Yahweh** is the great God, and **the great king over all gods,**	3 For **the Lord** is a great God, and a great **king over all gods:** for the Lord will not cast off his people.

15 Origen, *Homilies on Genesis and Exodus*, 319.

Deuteronomy 10:17 (LEB)	Deuteronomy 10:17 (Brenton LXX En)
17 For Yahweh your God, he is **God of the gods** and **Lord of the lords**, the great and mighty God, the awesome one who is not partial, and he does not take bribes.	17 For the Lord your God, **he is God of gods**, and **Lord of lords**, the great, and strong, and terrible God who does not accept persons, nor will he by any means accept a bribe:

The language chosen by the biblical writers is illuminating. They believed the small-G gods (*ʾelōhîm*) were real spiritual beings. Strangely, while we moderns have embraced angels and demons, we've rejected the realness of "the gods." The biblical writers didn't; they embraced their existence. Tellingly, the translators of the Septuagint (LXX), the Greek translation of the Hebrew Scriptures, often translated "gods" as "angels." They understood who the gods were in these contexts and didn't think it to be an egregious substitution. As you read the following passages, ask yourself, "How can these verses be true if the gods don't exist?" The answer is simple; they can't. No. The Bible is not lying. It means what it says. There are good ʾelōhîm (gods/angels) and bad ʾelōhîm (gods/angels). Obviously, the rebellious ones are evil, and the righteous ones are good. Yahweh, the God (ʾelōhîm) of gods (ʾelōhîm) is Lord overall.

Deuteronomy 32:43 (ESV)	Deuteronomy 32:43 (Brenton LXX En)
43 "Rejoice with him, **O heavens**; **bow down to him, all gods...**"	43 Rejoice, **ye heavens, with him**, and **let all the angels of God worship him**...
Psalm 138:1 (ESV)	**Psalm 137:1 (Brenton LXX En)**
1 I give you thanks, O LORD, with my whole heart; **before the gods** I sing your praise;	1 I will give thee thanks, O Lord, with my whole heart; and I will sing psalms to thee **before the angels**; for thou hast heard all the words of my mouth.

Psalm 97:7, 9 (ESV)	Psalm 96:7, 9 (Brenton LXX En)
7 All worshipers of images are put to shame, who make their boast in **worthless idols**; **worship him, all you gods**! 9 For you, O LORD, are most high over all the earth; you are exalted **far above all gods**.	7 Let all that worship graven images be ashamed, who boast of their **idols**; **worship him, all ye his angels**. 9 For thou art Lord most high over all the earth; thou art greatly exalted **above all gods**.
Psalm 96:4–5 (ESV)	**Psalm 95:4–5 (Brenton LXX En)**
4 For great is the LORD, and greatly to be praised; **he is to be feared above all gods**. 5 For all the **gods of the peoples are worthless idols**, but the LORD made the heavens.	4 For the Lord is great, and greatly to be praised: **he is terrible above all gods**. 5 **For all the gods of the heathen are devils**: but the Lord made the heavens.
Psalm 86:8 (ESV)	**Psalm 85:8 (Brenton LXX En)**
8 There is none like you **among the gods**, O Lord, nor are there any works like yours.	8 There is none like to thee, O Lord, **among the gods**; and there are no works like to thy works.
2 Chronicles 2:5 (LEB)	**2 Chronicles 2:5 (Brenton LXX En)**
5 And the house that I am building will be great, for **our God is greater than all gods**.	5 And the house which I am building is to be great: for the Lord **our God is great beyond all gods**.
Psalm 136:2 (LEB)	**Psalm 135:2 (Brenton LXX En)**
2 Give thanks to the **God of gods**, for his loyal love endures forever.	2 Give thanks to the **God of gods**: for his mercy endures for ever.
Micah 4:5 (LEB)	**Micah 4:5 (Brenton LXX En)**
5 For **all the nations** walk, each in the name of **its god**, but we **will walk** in the name of **Yahweh our God**, forever and ever.	5 For **all other nations** shall walk every one in **his own way**, but **we will walk** in the name of **the Lord our God** for ever and ever.

Deuteronomy 4:19–20 (ESV)	Deuteronomy 4:19–20 (Brenton LXX En)
[19] And beware lest you raise your eyes to heaven, and when you see the sun and the moon and the stars, **all the host of heaven**, you be drawn away and **bow down to them and serve them**, things that the LORD your God has **allotted to all the peoples** under the whole heaven. [20] But the LORD has taken you and brought you out of the iron furnace, out of Egypt, **to be a people of his own inheritance**, as you are this day.	[19] and lest having looked up to the sky, and having seen the sun and the moon and the stars, and **all the heavenly bodies**, thou shouldest go astray and **worship them**, and **serve them**, which the Lord thy God has **distributed to all the nations** under heaven. [20] But God took you, and led you forth out of the land of Egypt, out of the iron furnace, out of Egypt, **to be to him a people of inheritance**, as at this day.
Exodus 15:11 (LEB)	**Exodus 15:11 (Brenton LXX En)**
[11] **Who is like you among the gods, Yahweh**? Who is like you—glorious in holiness, awesome in praiseworthy actions, doing wonders?	[11] **Who is like to thee among the gods, O Lord**? who is like to thee? glorified in holiness, marvellous in glories, doing wonders.
Deuteronomy 3:24 (ESV)	**Deuteronomy 3:24 (Brenton LXX En)**
[24] 'O Lord GOD, you have only begun to show your servant your greatness and your mighty hand. For **what god** is there in heaven or on earth who **can do such works and mighty acts as yours**?	[24] Lord God, thou hast begun to shew to thy servant thy strength, and thy power, and thy mighty hand, and thy high arm: for **what God** is there in heaven or on the earth, **who will do as thou hast done**, and according to thy might?

1 Kings 8:23 (LEB)	3 Kingdoms 8:23 (Brenton LXX En)
[23] and he said, "**O Yahweh, God of Israel, there is no god like you** in the heavens above or on the earth beneath, keeping the covenant and the loyal love for your servants who are walking before you with all their heart.	[23] and he said, **Lord God of Israel, there is no God like thee** in heaven above on the earth beneath, keeping covenant and mercy with thy servant who walks before thee with all his heart;

"NO GOD BESIDES ME?"

What about the verses that say, "There are no gods besides Me?"

> [39] See, now, that I, even I am he, and **there is not a god besides me**; I put to death and I give life; I wound and I heal; there is not one who delivers from my hand! (Deut 32:39, LEB)

> [6] Thus says Yahweh, the king of Israel, and its redeemer, Yahweh of hosts: "I am the first, and I am the last, and **there is no god besides me.** [7] And who is like me? Let him proclaim it! And let him declare it and set it in order for me since I established an eternal people and things that are to come, and let them tell them the things that are coming. (Isa 44:6–7, LEB)

Do these verses contradict what we've learned elsewhere? No. When the Bible says, "There is no god besides Me," it's not a statement of deniability, but of incomparability. There are similar phrases claimed by the nations of Babylon and Nineveh.

> [8] Now therefore hear this, you lover of pleasures, who sit securely, who say in your heart, "**I am, and there is no one besides me**; I shall not sit as a widow or know the loss of children": (Isa 47:8, ESV)

> [15] This is the jubilant city that lives in security, that says to herself: **I exist, and there is no one else**. What a desolation she has become, a place for wild animals to lie down! Everyone who passes by her scoffs and shakes his fist. (Zeph 2:15, CSB)

Biblical scholar Dr. Michael S. Heiser wrote about this phrase:

> *Isaiah 47:8 and Zephaniah 2:15 have, respectively, Babylon and Nineveh saying "there is none besides me." Are we to believe that the point of the phrase is to declare that no other cities exist except Babylon or Nineveh? That would be absurd. The point of the statement is that Babylon and Nineveh considered themselves incomparable, as though no other city could measure up to them. This is precisely the point when these same phrases are used of other gods—they cannot measure up to Yahweh. The Bible does not contradict itself on this point. Those who want to argue that the other elohim do not exist are at odds with the supernatural worldview of the biblical writers.*[16]

WHAT ABOUT IDOLS?

There are some verses that depict the nations' gods as simply lifeless idols—nothing more, nothing less. For example, listen to the language of Psalm 135:15–18.

> [15] The idols of the heathen are silver and gold, The work of men's hands. [16] They have mouths, but they speak not; Eyes have they, but they see not; [17] They have ears, but they hear not; Neither is there any breath in their mouths. [18] They that make them are like unto them: So is every one that trusteth in them. (Ps 135:15–18, KJV 1900)

---

16 Heiser, *The Unseen Realm*, 35.

However, we must take into account the sum of Scripture. Earlier in the book of Psalms, Psalm 106:36–39 reveals the idol worshipers were sacrificing to demonic entities.

> 36 and **served their idols**, which became a snare to them. 37 **They even sacrificed their sons and daughters to the demons**, 38 and they poured out innocent blood, the blood of their sons and daughters, whom they sacrificed to the idols of Canaan, and so the land was defiled with the blood. 39 And they became unclean by their works, and were unfaithful in their deeds. (Ps 106:36–39, LEB)

Their idolatry was merely symbolic for who they really worshiped—angels and demons, the panoply of the powers of darkness. Note the following verses:

1 Corinthians 10:18–21 (LEB)	Revelation 9:20 (ESV)
18 Consider Israel according to the flesh: are not the ones who eat the sacrifices sharers in the altar? 19 Therefore, what am I saying? That food sacrificed to idols is anything, or that an idol is anything? 20 No, but that **the things which they sacrifice, they sacrifice to demons** and not to God, and **I do not want you to become sharers with demons.** 21 You are not able to drink the cup of the Lord and the cup of demons. **You are not able to share the table of the Lord and the table of demons.**	20 The rest of mankind, who were not killed by these plagues, did not repent of the works of their hands nor **give up worshiping demons and idols** of gold and silver and bronze and stone and wood, which cannot see or hear or walk,

Isaiah 65:11 (LES)	Colossians 2:18 (KJV 1900)
[11] But you who have forsaken me and who forget my holy mountain and who **prepare a table for a demon** and fill up a mixture to Fortune,	[18] Let no man beguile you of your reward in a voluntary humility and **worshipping of angels,** intruding into those things which he hath not seen, vainly puffed up by his fleshly mind,

Early Christians, even after the first century, understood these truths. Tertullian (155–220 A.D.) linked idolatry with the supernatural in his literary work titled *On Idolatry.*

> *"You who serve stones, and ye who make images of gold, and silver, and wood, and stones and clay, and serve phantoms, and demons, and spirits" Tertullian Idolatry 1.4*[17]

At times, even God's allotted portion, Israel, venerated these same spirit gods. Uncoincidentally, this is revealed in—drum roll, please—Deuteronomy 32.

> [17] **They sacrificed to demons**, which were not God, to gods they did not know, **to new gods that had come in recently**, which your ancestors had not feared. [18] Of the Rock that bore you, you were unmindful, and you forgot the God who gave you birth. [19] And the Lord saw it, and rejected them, because of the provocation of his sons and his daughters. [20] And he said, "I will hide my face from them, I will see what their end shall be; for they are a very perverse generation, children in whom there is no faithfulness [21] They have moved me to jealousy with what is no God; they have

17 Ken Johnson, *Ancient Paganism*, Biblefacts.org, Kindle edition, 39–40.

> provoked me to anger with their idols; and I will move them to jealousy with those that are not a people; I will provoke them to anger with a foolish nation. (Deut 32:16–21, The Dead Sea Scrolls Bible)[18]

The Gentile nations knew, without a shadow of a doubt, that they were worshiping real, supernatural, higher entities. They payed homage to their gods through their idols. These graven images, or statues, were often sculpted to mirror their god's likeness or perceived attributes (Dan 3:25). Idols functioned as divine abodes for spiritual beings. Consequently, idol worshipers thought of graven images as access points to their gods, as Hundley describes:

> *Within the divine abode, the divine presence often was concretized in a cult image, which served loosely as a divine body to which the divine essence was symbiotically joined…*
>
> *It is thus a misconception to assume that by making a statue, people believed they were making a god. Instead, the statue provided an access point to the god who already existed, yet was out of the suppliant's reach and control.*[19]

Hundley further explains,

> *Although the deity theoretically could be distinguished from its statue, there was generally little impetus to do so (see briefly Hundley 2013a: 367–371). As their primary access point to the divine, people tended to identify the statue-deity symbiosis as their god and treat it accordingly with care and petitions even if*

---

18 Wise, Abegg, Jr., and Cook, *The Dead Sea Scrolls*, Deut 32:16–21.

19 Michael B. Hundley, "Divine Presence in Ancient Near Eastern Temples," *Religion Compass* 9.7 (2015): 205–206, doi: 10.1111/rec3.12154.

> *they theoretically envisioned the god as far more than its image. To treat it as any less would be to minimize their access point and thus their access.*[20]

Lactantius (240–320 A.D.) alluded to the presence of the gods in their temples during sacrificial offerings to their images in *Divine Institutes 2.17.*

> *And that they [the gods] may easily entice them,* ***they conceal themselves in the temples, and are close at hand at all sacrifices****; and they often give prodigies, that men, astonished by them,* ***may attach to images a belief in their divine power and influence.***[21]

Minucius Felix (second century), a converted Roman lawyer and apologist for Christ, wrote in his book *Octavius* that impure spirits,

> *"...lurk in hiding beneath consecrated statues and images... Sometimes, as they haunt their shrines, they suggest prophecies to soothsayers; at other times they animate the fibres of entrails, direct the flight of birds, manage the drawing of lots, and produce oracles enveloped in a multitude of lies.*[22]

The following cuneiform text was found in Nineveh and dates back to 680 B.C.E. It's quite eye-opening. It distinguishes a clear difference between the people's actual gods and their idols. Both are given reverence.

---

20 Hundley, "Divine Presence in Ancient Near Eastern Temples," 207.

21 Lactantius, *The Divine Institutes*, 66.

22 Minucius Felix, *The Octavius of Marcus Minucius Felix*, 101 (Clarke).

I:1–18 Esarhaddon, king of the world, king of Assyria, governor of Babylon, king of Sumer and Akkad, the pious prince, worshiper of ***Nabu and Marduk****: Before my time, in the reign of an earlier king, there were evil forces in Sumer and Akkad. The people who dwelt in Babylon answered each other yes (when they meant) no, speaking lies all the time. They stretched out their hands for the property of Esagila,* ***the temple of the gods****, and gave away (its) gold, silver, and gems to Elam as payment.*

I:19–II:11 ***Marduk, lord of the gods, was enraged. He set his mind to leveling the land and destroying its people.*** *The Arachtu Canal, [Col. II] a river of abundance, of waters mighty like the Flood, was brought up and it poured into the city where he dwelled, and into his sanctuary, and turned it into a ruin.* ***The gods (and) goddesses who dwelled there went up to heaven****. The people who lived there, having been dealt captivity and degradation, went into slavery.*

II:12–18 He had recorded seventy years as the period of its desolation. ***But the merciful Marduk—after his heart was calmed—transposed (the number) and ordered its repopulation in the eleventh year.***

II:19–III:8 You truly called me, Esarhaddon, from among my older brothers in order that these things might be restored, [Col. III] and you set your good, protecting shadow over me. All who hate me, you have flattened like the Flood; all of my enemies, you have defeated. You have caused me to reach my goal. In order to give rest to the heart of your great divinity, to put your mind at ease, you entrusted the shepherding of Assyria to my hands.

III:9–13 At the beginning of my reign, in my first regnal year, when I took my seat upon the royal throne in majesty, favorable signs appeared in the heavens (and) on earth. Concerning the resettlement of the city and the renovation of his sanctuary, he sent his sign.

III:14–IV:2a I was fearful (and) anxious about undertaking that task. **I knelt down before Shamash, Adad, and Marduk, the chief justices of the gods, my lords.** *By the sacrificial food bowls of the diviners, positive omens were revealed—he caused liver-omens to be written concerning the rebuilding of Babylon (and) the restoration of Esagila. [Col. IV] I trusted that these were reliable.*

IV:2b–15 I summoned all of my experts and the whole population of Babylonia. I made them wield the hoe and imposed forced labor upon them. I sprinkled its retaining walls with good oil, honey, butter, beer, choice wine, (and) pure mountain beer. I took the construction-basket upon my head and I carried it myself. In a brick mold of ivory, ebony, boxwood and sissoo (?), I had (them) make bricks all year.

IV:16–27 I had Esagila, **the temple of the gods**, *rebuilt from its foundations to its peak—together with its shrines, Babylon the special city, Imgur-Enlil, its wall, Nimitti-Enlil, its outer wall—I made them bigger, higher, and more majestic. I restored* **the statues of the great gods**, *and had them* **reinstalled in their sanctuaries, their eternal dwellings**. *I reestablished their interrupted offerings.*

IV:28–34 I gathered together the sons of Babylon who had been enslaved, who were in captivity and degradation, and I counted them as Babylonians; I reestablished their special status.[23]

---

23 C. B. Hays, *Hidden Riches: A Sourcebook for the Comparative Study of the Hebrew Bible and Ancient Near East*, 1st ed. (Louisville, KY: Westminster John Knox Press, 2014), 280–281.

WHAT WAS THE TOWER OF BABEL?

Scholars have suggested the Tower of Babel was a ziggurat temple structure common in Mesopotamia.

> *Archaeological excavations have provided information about the building of towers for temples called ziggurats. The excavation of a number of such towers has made it clear they were structures consisting of several platforms, each of lesser dimensions than the one immediately below it. The top platform served as the location for a small temple dedicated to the particular deity of the builder or of the city in which it was built.*[24]

As we've learned, the Hebrews called the city, "Babel" (***bābel***), which is similar to the Hebrew word that means, "confuse" (***bālal***). "Babel" derives from the Akkadian word, "***Bāb-ilu***," which means "gate of the gods," as Derek Gilbert points out in his insightful book, *The Great Inception.*[25]

Hundley also described these temple structures as "bridging the gap" between the seen and unseen realms. He wrote,

> *The temple was constructed to provide a more direct, regular, and regulated access point. It served as a cosmic axis that united heaven and earth and, in Mesopotamia, was literally the navel of the world both vertically and horizontally (see Maul 1997). While the gods continued to dwell in their natural habitats, they also came to dwell in temples, thereby bridging the gap between human and divine worlds.*[26]

---

24 W. A. Elwell and B. J. Beitzel, "Babel," *Baker Encyclopedia of the Bible* 1:243.

25 Gilbert, *The Great Inception.*

26 Hundley, "Divine Presence in Ancient Near Eastern Temples," 204.

This is precisely what Nimrod and his mob of masons were trying to build: a bridge to the heavenly dimension. To their credit, it worked—God and his angels "came down."

WHY DOES MY BIBLE SAY, "ACCORDING TO THE NUMBER OF THE SONS OF ISRAEL?"

Many English Bibles, such as the NIV, have mankind being divided according to the number of the "sons of Israel" in Deuteronomy 32:8–9.

Deuteronomy 32:8 (NIV)	Deuteronomy 32:8 (ESV)	Deuteronomy 32:8 (Brenton LXX En)
8 When the Most High gave the nations their inheritance, when he divided all mankind, he set up boundaries for the peoples **according to the number of the sons of Israel.**	8 When the Most High gave to the nations their inheritance, when he divided mankind, he fixed the borders of the peoples **according to the number of the sons of God.**	8 When the Most High divided the nations, when he separated the sons of Adam, he set the bounds of the nations **according to the number of the angels of God.**

However, Israel wasn't even a nation at the time, nor was it listed in the table of nations in Genesis 10. God didn't call Abraham until after the fact, in Genesis 12. How can you divide the nations according to something that doesn't exist? The discovery of the Dead Sea Scrolls exposed the corrupted "sons of Israel" rendering and provided some much-needed clarity to puzzled Bible students. The DSS has man being divided "according to the number of the **sons of God** *(benê [ha]'elōhîm)*," thus lining up with the Septuagint's rendering, "according to the number of the **angels of God** *(angelōn theou)*." Both are divine beings.

CONNECTING THE GOSPEL

BABEL & PENTECOST

There are major gospel connections between Babel and Pentecost. Acts 2 is the lynchpin of the Bible; it's where everything comes together. It's the first time Peter used his kingdom keys (Matt 16:19) to preach the gospel to a lost audience who asked the question, "Men and brothers, what shall we do?" (Acts 2:37).

> 38 And Peter said to them, "**Repent and be baptized** every one of you in the name of Jesus Christ **for the forgiveness of your sins**, and you will **receive the gift of the Holy Spirit**. (Acts 2:38, ESV)

This was the first time thousands of people believed the gospel (Rom 10:10–11), obeyed it (Rom 10:16; 2 Thess 1:8), and were added to Jesus' church (Acts 2:41).

In Acts 2, God is signaling a complete abrogation and nullification of His divorce of the nations back at Babel. Luke, the beloved physician (Col 4:14) and penman of the book of Acts, wants his readers to pick up on the significance of the Spirit lifting the language barrier that God formerly instituted at Babel. The Holy Spirit's action telegraphed the end of Babel and the commencement of the kingdom of God (Col 1:13). John MacArthur wrote in his book, *Strange Fire*,

> *In Genesis 11, at the Tower of Babel, the Lord had confused the languages of the world as a judgment on humanity. In contrast, on the day of Pentecost, the curse of Babel was miraculously undone, demonstrating that the wonderful words of God, including the gospel of Jesus Christ, were to be taken throughout the whole world to those in every nation. This is precisely how*

early Christians, in the centuries after the apostles, understood the miracle of languages.[27]

MacArthur goes on to cite an early and eloquent preacher of Christianity, John Chrysostom (349–407 A.D.), also known as "golden mouth," to prove his point.

And as in the time of building the tower [of Babel] the one tongue was divided into many; so then [at Pentecost] the many tongues frequently met in one man, and the same person used to discourse both in the Persian, and the Roman, and the Indian, and many other tongues, the Spirit sounding within him: and the gift was called the gift of tongues because he could all at once speak divers languages.[28]

Luke is deliberate and surgical in his selection of specific words. He uses the Greek LXX (En. Septuagint) translation of the Hebrew Scriptures as a literary blueprint to tear down the Tower of Babel and its far-reaching consequences. This is intertextuality at its finest.

First, notice how he uses the same Greek word when he relays the idea of "confusion" (**sugchĕō, *συγχέω***) in Acts 2.

Genesis 11:7 (Brenton LXX En)	Acts 2:6 (ASV 1901)
7 Come, and having gone down let us there confound (**sugchĕō, *συγχέω***) their tongue, that they may **not understand each the voice of his neighbour**.	6 And when this sound was heard, the multitude came together, and were confounded (**sugchĕō, *συγχέω***), because that **every man heard them speaking in his own language**.

---

27 J. F. MacArthur, Jr., *Strange Fire: The Danger of Offending the Holy Spirit with Counterfeit Worship* (Nashville: Thomas Nelson, 2013).

28 MacArthur, Jr., *Strange Fire: The Danger of Offending the Holy Spirit with Counterfeit Worship.*

The crowd was confused in Acts 2 because they heard the apostles speak in their native tongues.

> [7] They were astounded and amazed, saying, "Look, aren't all these who are speaking Galileans? [8] How is it that each of us can hear them **in our own native language**? [9] Parthians, Medes, Elamites; those who live in Mesopotamia, in Judea and Cappadocia, Pontus and Asia, [10] Phrygia and Pamphylia, Egypt and the parts of Libya near Cyrene; visitors from Rome (both Jews and converts), [11] Cretans and Arabs—we hear them declaring the magnificent acts of God in our own tongues." [12] They were all astounded and perplexed, saying to one another, "**What does this mean**?" (Acts 2:7–12, CSB)

It meant God was finally taking back "all flesh" (Acts 2:17, 21). This was prophesied in Isaiah 2:2. Luke wants his readers to realize that Pentecost functioned as the launchpad to prophetic fulfillment.

Isaiah 2:2 (KJV 1900)	Acts 2:5 (KJV 1900)
[2] And it shall come to pass in the last days, That the mountain of the Lord's house shall be established in the top of the mountains, And shall be exalted above the hills; And all nations shall flow unto it.	[5] And there were dwelling at Jerusalem Jews, devout men, out of every nation under heaven.

Some six hundred years before Pentecost, the Jews were exiled and scattered among all the nations due to their idolatry and veneration of other gods, as Jerome (347–419 A.D.), the translator of the Latin Vulgate, recorded in *Commentary on Isaiah 16.5*.

> *Sacred history narrates that Israel offered victims to* ***the gods of the nations*** *upon high mountains and hills, and like the*

> *most brazen prostitute* ***she spread her legs to all the demons*** *[cf. Ezek 16:25].*[29]

Origen noted that this harlotry on Israel's part gave rise to the Gentiles' ability to enter into a covenant relationship with Yahweh. He wrote,

> *So long as that portion of the Lord [Israel] was abiding in its status it was not possible for us who were Gentiles to enter into the inheritance of God and to succeed to the rights of his scepter. On account of this, therefore, God allows blindness to occur to a part, i.e., not to all, but to some from Israel, a blindness, doubtless, inflicted under the pretext of* ***envious jealousy by those angels who had been allotted the ruling sovereignty over the other nations****. God allowed this then and, though he was able to hinder it, he was unwilling, in order that in place of those who had slipped, having been deceived by blindness, i.e., by the hardness of heart,* ***God would make his own portion from those [angels] who had deceived these portions****; so that, in a certain way, in that by which they had set a trap they were trapped. For, by turning away the people of God unto themselves through the allurements of sin,* ***they made room for the Gentiles to enter into the inheritance of God****, with God holding judgment with them by a sort of common and most equitable right so that, as long as they were oppressing the people of God, in captivity to blindness, the number of the Gentiles was being added in place of those whom the angels, from the beginning, had stolen from the portion of God and from his segregated inheritance."*[30]

---

29 Jerome, *St. Jerome: Commentary on Isaiah: Including St. Jerome's Translation of Origen's Homilies 1–9 on Isaiah*, 724 (Scheck).

30 Origen, *Commentary on the Epistle to the Romans*, 182–183.

The Jews' exile actually helped accelerate Yahweh's plan to rescue the Gentiles. That plays out here, in Acts 2.

> *In other words, the tribes of Israel had become so intermingled with the Gentile nations that for Diaspora Jews to return to Jerusalem and follow Messiah constituted the nations being drawn into the new covenant kingdom of God. According to the apostle Luke, Pentecost of AD 30 was not only the ingathering of the tribes of Israel, it was the beginning of the inheritance of the Gentile nations. Pentecost, AD 30, was the beginning of regathering the scattered Jews AND the reclamation of the divided nations. Pentecost was the undoing of both Exile and Babel.*[31]

While the Pentecost list of nations in Acts 2:7–12 isn't comprehensive of all seventy disinherited nations listed in Genesis 10, it does, however, represent them from east to west. Dr. Michael S. Heiser wrote,

> *the Pentecost list confirms God's evangelism strategy articulated by Paul, who said that the gospel was for the Jew first, and then the Gentile (Rom 1:16). Three thousand Jews came to believe in Jesus as a result of the events at Pentecost (Acts 2:41), and those three thousand Jewish converts went back to their homelands after the Pentecost pilgrimage. These new disciples were the seeds of the gospel, Yahweh's plan to reclaim the nations.*[32]

The second clue in the Babel/Pentecost connection is Luke's inclusion of the word "divided" (διαμερίζω, diamĕrizō).

---

31 Brian Godawa, *When Watchers Ruled the Nations: Pagan Gods at War with Israel's God and the Spiritual World of the Bible* (Los Angeles, CA: Embedded Pictures Publishing, 2020), Kindle edition, 75.

32 Heiser, *The Unseen Realm*, 302.

Deuteronomy 32:8 (Brenton LXX En)	**Acts 2:1, 3–4 (ESV)**
8 When the Most High divided (**διαμερίζω, diamĕrizō**) the nations, when he separated the sons of Adam, he set the bounds of the nations according to the number of the angels of God.	1 When the day of Pentecost arrived, they were all together in one place. 3 And divided (**διαμερίζω, diamĕrizō**) tongues as of fire appeared to them and rested on each one of them. 4 And they were all filled with the Holy Spirit and began to speak in other tongues as the Spirit gave them utterance.

At Babel, "the nations" were divided according to the number of the angelic sons of God. At Pentecost, "the tongues" were divided according to the number of human sons of God. Babel's punishment of division and rejection was swallowed up by Pentecost's message of unification and acceptance. For the first time in 3,000 years, all nations were, once again, being called to unite under their Creator, through Jesus Christ, our Lord (Heb 4:14–16).

LOOKING AHEAD

As the nations marched off to their appointed boundaries, they no longer belonged to Yahweh. He had given them up (Rom 1:27–29). From now on, they looked to their allotted angels for guidance. Seemingly, God had no one to call His own; that is, until He would call a particular man to be "His portion" and "His allotted heritage." As you'll learn in the next chapter, the promises God made this man were extravagant and actually involve you receiving a mysterious and divine inheritance (2 Pet 1:4).

CHAPTER 5

GOD'S PORTION & ABRAHAM'S PROMISE

For Yahweh's portion was his people,
Jacob the share of his inheritance…
Yahweh alone guided him, and there
was no foreign god accompanying
him. (Deuteronomy 32:9, 12, LEB)

READING THE STORY

MANKIND WAS LEFT WHOLLY IN THE hands of other gods; Yahweh had no one to call His own. It appeared God's promise to crush Satan was all but lost, especially now that the gods over the nations had gone rogue and poisoned men's hearts (Ps 58). However, a glimmer of hope was on the horizon. Exactly ten generations from Noah, God found a man who would soon teem with faith—Abram (Gen 12). The Lord appeared to Abram in ancient Mesopotamia (Acts 7:2) in a Sumerian city called Ur (Gen 15:7).

> "The LORD said to Abram: Go from your land, your relatives, and your father's house to the land that I will show you. I will make you into a great nation, I will bless you, I will make your name great, and you will be a blessing. I will bless those who bless you, I will curse anyone who treats you with contempt, and all the peoples on earth will be blessed through you. So Abram went, as the LORD had told him, and Lot went with him. Abram was seventy-five years old when he left Haran. (Gen 12:1–4, CSB)

Without any real introduction, the Lord called Abram for a very important purpose. Surprisingly, Abram wasn't full of questions such as, "Who are you and where are we going?" Abram knew there was something unique about Yahweh—He was different from the Mesopotamian gods he and his family worshiped (Josh 24:2). Full of faith, he moved seven hundred miles northwest to Haran with his wife Sarai, his father Terah, and his nephew Lot. They lived in Haran until Abram's father, Terah, died at the ripe old age of 205 years old (Gen 11:32). Without the guidance of his father, Abram was at a major crossroads in life. He had several options.

Option 1: Stay put in Haran.

Option 2: Get sentimental and return to his roots in Ur.

There was a third option, however, albeit very uncertain. He could finish what he started and complete his heavenly Father's call to the land of Canaan. At age seventy-five, Abram did the hardest thing he could have done—by faith, he moved his family 450 miles southwest into the unknown.

> And Abram took Sarai his wife, and Lot his nephew, and all their possessions that they had gathered, and all the persons that they had acquired in Haran, and they went out to go to the land of Canaan. And they went to the land of Canaan. (Gen 12:5, LEB)
>
> Yet he gave him no inheritance in it, not even a foot's length, but promised to give it to him as a possession and to his offspring after him, though he had no child. (Acts 7:5, ESV)

While God was insistent that Abram and Sarai would have this "promised child," they knew their biological clocks were ticking. Their lack of patience soon led to a disastrous relationship.

> Abram's wife, Sarai, had not borne any children for him, but she owned an Egyptian slave named Hagar. Sarai said to Abram, "Since the LORD has prevented me from bearing children, go to my slave; perhaps through her I can build a family." And Abram agreed to what Sarai said. So Abram's wife, Sarai, took Hagar, her Egyptian slave, and gave her to her husband, Abram, as a wife for him. This happened after Abram had lived in the land of Canaan ten years. He slept with Hagar, and she became pregnant. When she saw that she was pregnant, her mistress became contemptible to her. (Gen 16:1–4, CSB)

> So Hagar gave birth to Abram's son, and Abram named his son (whom Hagar bore) Ishmael. Abram was eighty-six years old when Hagar bore Ishmael to him. (Gen 16:15–16, CSB)

God didn't throw away Abram or rescind His promises; He extended him forgiveness and grace. Thirteen long years later, the Lord came down from heaven and appeared to Abram, who was now ninety-nine years old, and said,

> "I am God Almighty; walk before me faithfully and be blameless. Then I will make my covenant between me and you and will greatly increase your numbers." Abram fell facedown, and God said to him, "As for me, this is my covenant with you: **You will be the father of many nations**. No longer will you be called Abram; **your name will be Abraham**, for I have made you a father of many nations. I will make you very fruitful; I will make nations of you, and kings will come from you. I will establish my covenant as an **everlasting covenant between me and you and your descendants after you for the generations to come**, to be your God and the God of your descendants after you. The whole land of Canaan, where you now reside as a foreigner, I will give as an everlasting possession to you and your descendants after you; and **I will be their God**." Then God said to Abraham, "As for you, you must keep my covenant, you and your descendants after you for the generations to come. This is my covenant with you and your descendants after you, the covenant you are to keep: Every male among you shall be circumcised. You are to undergo circumcision, and it will be the sign of the covenant between me and you. (Gen 17:1–11, NIV)

> And God said to Abraham, "as for Sarai your wife, you shall not call her name Sarai, for Sarah shall be her name. And I will bless

> her; moreover, I give to you from her a son. And I will bless her, and she shall give rise to nations. Kings of peoples shall come from her." And Abraham fell upon his face and laughed. And he said in his heart, "Can a child be born to a man a hundred years old, or can Sarah bear a child at ninety?" And Abraham said to God, "Oh that Ishmael might live before you!" And God said, "No, but **Sarah your wife shall bear a son for you, and you shall call his name Isaac**. And I will establish my covenant with him as an everlasting covenant to his offspring after him. And as for Ishmael, I have heard you. Behold, I will bless him and I will make him fruitful, and I will multiply him exceedingly. He shall father twelve princes, and I will make him a great nation. But my covenant I will establish with Isaac, whom Sarah shall bear to you at this appointed time next year." When he finished speaking with him, God went up from Abraham. (Gen 17:15–22, LEB)

As God promised, Sarah became pregnant.

> "And she conceived, and Sarah bore to Abraham a son in his old age at the appointed time that God had told him. And Abraham called the name of his son who was born to him, whom Sarah bore to him, Isaac. And Abraham circumcised Isaac his son when he was eight days old, as God had commanded him. And Abraham was one hundred years old when Isaac his son was born to him. (Gen 21:2–5, LEB)

The birth of Isaac was the spark that ignited the growth of the twelve patriarchs.

> "...And so Abraham became the father of Isaac, and circumcised him on the eighth day, and Isaac became the father of **Jacob**, and Jacob of the **twelve patriarchs**. (Acts 7:8, ESV)

Yahweh was no longer "peopleless." Jacob and his descendants were known as "Israel" (Gen 32:28) and were the Lord's portion and His allotted heritage, antithetical to the gods' "allotted" portions (i.e., the nations of the world). As Moses wrote, "no foreign god" was with Israel.

Deuteronomy 32:9–14 (ESV)	Deuteronomy 32:9–14 (LEB)
9 But **the Lord's portion is his people, Jacob his allotted heritage.** 10 "He found him in a desert land, and in the howling waste of the wilderness; he encircled him, he cared for him, he kept him as the apple of his eye. 11 Like an eagle that stirs up its nest, that flutters over its young, spreading out its wings, catching them, bearing them on its pinions, 12 **the Lord alone guided him, no foreign god was with him.** 13 He made him ride on the high places of the land, and he ate the produce of the field, and he suckled him with honey out of the rock, and oil out of the flinty rock. 14 Curds from the herd, and milk from the flock, with fat of lambs, rams of Bashan and goats, with the very finest of the wheat— and you drank foaming wine made from the blood of the grape.	9 **For Yahweh's portion was his people, Jacob the share of his inheritance.** 10 He found him in a desert land, and in a howling, desert wasteland; he encircled him, he cared for him, he protected him like the apple of his eye. 11 As an eagle stirs up its nest, hovers over its young, spreads out its wings, takes them, carries them on its pinions, 12 **so Yahweh alone guided him, and there was no foreign god accompanying him.** 13 And he set him on the high places of the land, and he fed him the crops of the field, and he nursed him with honey from crags, and with oil from flinty rock, 14 With curds from the herd, and with milk from the flock, with the fat of young rams, and rams, the offspring of Bashan, and with goats along with the finest kernels of wheat, and from the blood of grapes you drank fermented wine.

The psalmist understood the nation of Israel stood humbly on the blessing ground of Yahweh, King of the gods, while the rest of the world's nations didn't. Their god was not the Lord; they served lesser gods (*ʾelōhîm*) allotted to them at Babel. As the Psalmist put it,

> [12] Blessed is the nation whose God is Yahweh, the people he has chosen for his inheritance. (Ps 33:12, LEB)

ANSWERING YOUR QUESTIONS

WHAT DID THE ANCIENTS SAY?

In Philippians 4, Paul mentions a man by the name of Clement and calls him his fellow laborer whose name is written in the book of life.

> [1] So then, my dearly loved and longed for brothers and sisters, my joy and crown, in this manner stand firm in the Lord, dear friends. [2] I urge Euodia and I urge Syntyche to agree in the Lord. [3] Yes, I also ask you, true partner, to help these women who have contended for the gospel at my side, **along with Clement and the rest of my coworkers whose names are in the book of life**. (Phil 4:1–3, CSB)

According to the early church fathers, this Clement is the author of a lengthy letter written in 96 A.D. to the church at Corinth. First Clement 29:1–3 references the angelic allotment that's written about in Deuteronomy 32:8–9. It also emphasizes that God kept an allotted portion for Himself, as we've learned in this chapter.

> *1 LET us then approach him in holiness of soul, raising pure and undefiled hands to him, loving our gracious and merciful Father, who has made us the portion of his choice for himself. 2 For thus*

> *it is written: "When the most high divided the nations, when he scattered the sons of Adam, he established the bounds of the nations according to the number of the angels of God. His people Jacob became the portion of the Lord, Israel was the lot of his inheritance." 3 And in another place he says "Behold the Lord taketh to himself a nation from the midst of nations, as a man taketh the first-fruit of his threshing-floor, and the Holy of Holies shall come forth from that nation."*[1]

Cyril of Alexandria (378–444 A.D.) also discussed this in *Festal Letters 22.4:*

> *For the law given through Moses was imposed, not on everyone on earth, but only on those from Israel, and the family from Abraham was called God's chosen portion. For it is written: "When the Most High divided the nations, when he separated the sons of Adam, he set the boundaries of the nations according to the number of God's angels, and the Lord's people became his portion, Israel the allotment of his inheritance."*[2]

Cyril commented in another place,

> *God reminds Israel of the honor and glory bestowed on them, as well as the mercy and love shown them. They were worthy of the highest privileges, for they alone had been called from among all the nations to have intimate fellowship with God and become God's portion and lot. Therefore inspired Moses cried out: The heaven of heavens belongs to the* Lord *your God. The* Lord *has chosen you*

---

1 I. P. Clement, S. Ignatius, Bishop of Antioch, S. Polycarp, and Bishop of Smyrna, vol. 1 of *The Apostolic Fathers*, 57–59 (Lake).

2 Cyril of Alexandria, *Festal Letters, 13–30*, 123 (Amidon).

> *from all the nations to be his people (Deut 10:14; 7:6). And again: When the Most High divided the nations, when he separated the sons of Adam, he fixed the bounds of the people according to the number of the sons of God, and his people Jacob became the portion of the LORD, Israel his allotted heritage (Deut 32:8–9).*
>
> *It was necessary then that those who were honored, elected, and selected to be God's chosen lot should not turn away from God's law nor disappoint the God who loved them and bestowed on them the best and most desirable things.*[3]

Yahweh's decision to portion out a people for Himself not only blessed Abraham and his immediate descendants, but it also foreshadowed the body of believers Jesus eventually named "the church," or "the called out." Clement wrote in 1 Clement 30:1,

> *1 SEEING then that we are the portion of one who is holy, let us do all the deeds of sanctification, fleeing from evil speaking, and abominable and impure embraces, drunkenness and youthful lusts, and abominable passion, detestable adultery, and abominable pride.*[4]

CONNECTING THE GOSPEL

THE GOSPEL & ABRAHAM

The good news about the gospel is it's for all. It's colorblind and multilingual, showing no partiality (Rom 2:11). While it was first preached

---

3 Cyril of Alexandria, *Isaiah: Interpreted by Early Christian and Medieval Commentators*, 358 (Wilken, Christman, and Hollerich).

4 Clement et al., *The Apostolic Fathers*, 59.

to the masses at Pentecost, it was technically preached ages before to Abraham.

> [8] And the Scripture, foreseeing that God would justify the Gentiles by faith, **preached the gospel beforehand to Abraham**, saying, "In you shall all the nations be blessed." (Gal 3:8, ESV)

The bad news was the nations were following the small-G gods and were without hope in the world (Eph 2:12). By God preaching the gospel to Abraham, it brought humanity a much-needed hope. Abraham would be the conduit through which all the disinherited nations would, once again, be blessed.

The perpetuation of Abraham's seed would eventually bring about the Christ child. In modern terms, Jesus would be a part of Abraham's family tree. This was the essence of the seed promise God made Abraham and Sarah; through "their seed," all families of the earth would be "blessed" (Gen 12:3). The blessings God referred to were, primarily, spiritual blessings. As Paul pointed out, all spiritual "blessings" are found in Christ (Eph 1:3). Notice what Paul writes later on in Galatians 3.

> [29] And if you belong to Christ, then you are Abraham's seed, heirs according to the promise. (Gal 3:29, CSB)

If we are Christ's, we are grafted into Abraham's family tree. As a result, we are spiritually related to Abraham, the father of faith (Rom 4:16), having mimicked the essence of his faith. This brings us to the heart of the gospel—being justified "by faith." Justification by faith is something the Israelites struggled to understand. They sought justification by merit, not by faith. In their minds, if they kept the Law of Moses faithfully, they "deserved" justification. The issue was the sacrifices God commanded in Moses's Law couldn't take away their sins (Heb 10:4). The Law was only designed to cast a shadow of things to come (Heb 10:1). Animal sacrifices in the Mosaic Law merely telegraphed the coming Lamb of God who would take away the sins of the world (John 1:29); they themselves weren't the answer to sin. Elsewhere in Galatians 3, Paul exposes the "justification by merit" mentality and praises Abraham's "justification by faith" approach.

> 10 For all who rely on the works of the law are under a curse, because it is written, Everyone who does not do everything written in the book of the law is cursed. 11 Now it is clear that **no one is justified before God by the law**, because the righteous will live by faith. 12 But **the law is not based on faith; instead, the one who does these things will live by them**. 13 Christ redeemed us from the curse of the law by becoming a curse for us, because it is written, Cursed is everyone who is hung on a tree. 14 **The purpose was that the blessing of Abraham would come to the Gentiles by Christ Jesus, so that we could receive the promised Spirit through faith**. 15 Brothers and sisters, I'm using a human illustration. No one sets aside or makes additions to a validated human will. 16 Now the promises were spoken to Abraham and to his seed. He does not say "and to seeds," as though referring to many, but referring to one, and to your seed, who is Christ. 17 My point is this: The law, which came 430 years later, does not invalidate a covenant previously established by God and thus cancel the promise. 18 For if the inheritance is based on the law, it is no longer based on the promise; but **God has graciously given it to Abraham through the promise**. (Gal 3:10–18, CSB)

All would agree we are saved in the likeness of Abraham—"by faith." But what exactly does "by faith" mean? Biblical faith necessitates trusting obedience. Notice what James wrote about Abraham's faith.

> 21 Wasn't Abraham our father justified by works in offering Isaac
> his son on the altar? 22 You see that **faith was active together**
> **with his works, and by works, faith was made complete,** 23 and
> the Scripture was fulfilled that says, Abraham believed God, and
> it was credited to him as righteousness, and he was called God's
> friend. (Jas 2:21–23, CSB)

Abraham wouldn't be a friend of God had he not trusted and obeyed God's call for his life.

> 8 **By faith Abraham**, when he was called, **obeyed and set out**
> **for a place that he was going to receive as an inheritance.**
> He went out, even though he did not know where he was going.
> 9 **By faith he stayed as a foreigner in the land of promise**, living
> in tents as did Isaac and Jacob, coheirs of the same promise.
> (Heb 11:8–9, CSB)

Abraham also demonstrated this same "trusting obedience" when God called him to sacrifice his son Isaac on Mount Moriah (Gen 22).

> 17 **By faith Abraham**, when he was tested, **offered up Isaac**. He
> received the promises and yet he was offering his one and only
> son, 18 the one to whom it had been said, Your offspring will be
> traced through Isaac. 19 He considered God to be able even to
> raise someone from the dead; therefore, he received him back,
> figuratively speaking. (Heb 11:17–19, CSB)

Prolific writer and theologian Dr. John Piper points to the necessity of Abraham's trusting obedience in his becoming the father of faith.

> *Obedience is the necessary outcome of truly trusting in God's promises, and so obedience is made a condition of inheriting God's*

> *promises which are granted by grace and through faith. This means that the covenant of Abraham is just like the new covenant under which we live. For it too is conditional—not on works, but on the obedience of faith. John 3:36 says: "He who does not obey the Son shall not see life, but the wrath of God rests upon him"; and Hebrews 5:9, "Christ became the source of eternal salvation to all who obey him." The Covenant of Abraham and the New Covenant under which we live today are one covenant of grace, because in both gracious promises are made to sinners who receive them through faith—a faith which banks so completely on the wisdom and power and love of God that it inevitably obeys his commands.*[5]

So, what about passages such as Ephesians 2:8–9, which teach we are saved by grace through faith and not by works?

> [8] For you are saved by grace through faith, and this is not from yourselves; it is God's gift—[9] not from works, so that no one can boast. (Eph 2:8–9, CSB)

Is this a contradiction of Scripture? Absolutely not. The wider context of Ephesians 2:8–9 is important. Paul is writing to Gentile converts who formerly served under the gods over the nations. Paul emphasizes to these brethren that they were predestined to receive the adoption as sons through Jesus Christ (Eph 1:5). This "predestination" terminology echoes back to the time when "the gospel was preached to Abraham," meaning there would be an eventual joining of the disinherited Gentiles and God's allotted portion, Israel. For generations, this remained hidden. The "mystery" of the gospel was solved for these Ephesian brethren when they witnessed two things: the dethroning of

---

5 John Piper, "The Covenant of Abraham," *Desiring God* (website), 18 October 1981, https://www.desiringgod.org/messages/the-covenant-of-abraham.

the small-G gods at Christ's resurrection and the elevation of Christ far above their former spiritual rulers.

> [18] (the eyes of your hearts having been enlightened), so that you may know what is the hope of his calling, what are the riches of the glory of his inheritance among the saints, [19] and what is the surpassing greatness of his power toward us who believe, according to the working of his mighty strength [20] which he has worked in Christ, **raising him** from the dead and seating him at his right hand in the heavenly places, [21] **above all rule and authority and power and lordship and every name named**, not only in this age but also in the coming one, [22] and **he subjected all things under his feet** and gave him as head over all things to the church, [23] which is his body, the fullness of the one who fills all things in every way. [1] And you, although you were dead in your trespasses and sins, [2] in which **you formerly walked according to the course of this world, according to the ruler of the authority of the air, the spirit now working in the sons of disobedience**, [3] among whom also we all formerly lived in the desires of our flesh, doing the will of the flesh and of the mind, and we were children of wrath by nature, as also the rest of them were. (Eph 1:18–2:3, LEB)

The way Abraham was saved became a template for the way the Gentiles would be saved. Abraham was "called out" of the world (i.e., Mesopotamia) and into God's marvelous light. This was exactly what God had called these Ephesian brethren to do (Eph 5:8). Peter alludes back to the matrix of ideas in Deuteronomy 32:8–9, 9–14, where Jacob (Israel) was Yahweh's allotted portion. Peter understands that God's allotted portion isn't national Israel anymore, but spiritual Israel, the "called out" (i.e., the church). Today, we are "His portion" and "His possession."

> 9 But you are a **chosen** race, a royal priesthood, a holy nation,
> **a people for his possession**, so that you may proclaim the
> praises of the one who **called you out of darkness into his**
> **marvelous light**. 10 Once **you were not a people, but now you**
> **are God's people**; you had not received mercy, but now you
> have received mercy. (1 Pet 2:9–10, CSB)

With a trusting and obedient faith like that of Abraham, the Ephesian brethren abandoned the gods that had enslaved them and were liberated, being united with Christ. Their salvation was not of merit, but of grace. While meritorious works don't save, an obedient faith which trusts completely in God's grace does. This kind of faith was the faith of Abraham, and we are all immeasurably blessed because of it.

> 18 and in your offspring shall all the nations of the earth be blessed, because you have obeyed my voice." (Gen 22:18, ESV)

The question is, will we squander this blessing? Or will we walk in Abraham's "by faith" footsteps? Didymus the Blind (313–398 A.D.), the head of the catechetical school of Alexandria eons ago, became blind when he was five years old. If anyone understood what it meant to walk by faith and not by sight, it was him. He once wrote of the opportunity Christ has afforded everyone who walks by faith—to be freed from fallen angels and forgiven in Christ. He wrote,

> *When the Most High apportioned the nations, when he dispersed the sons of Adam, he fixed the boundaries of the nations according to the number of God's angels." When this covenant was canceled by Christ, and the angels of the nations were no longer in command, all the nations became the heritage and portion of the*

one who cast aside the beautiful staff to dissolve the covenant with all the peoples [Christ].

This excellent achievement was effected on the day arranged by the sun of justice, which the ***father of all the believing nations, Abraham****, was most glad to see. That is to say,* ***everyone who composed the nations was blessed in his offspring, provided they had his faith****, which was reckoned as righteousness.*[6]

Have you been saved by faith?

LOOKING AHEAD

It was certain: The way of faith would lead to the path of promise. But Israel's journey to promise would be plagued with problems. As we'll discover in the next chapter, Abraham's descendants were about to be locked in the nefarious nation of Egypt, a garrison for the gods, for the next four hundred years.

> As the sun was setting, a deep sleep came over Abram, and suddenly great terror and darkness descended on him. Then the LORD said to Abram, "Know this for certain: Your offspring will be resident aliens for four hundred years in a land that does not belong to them and will be enslaved and oppressed. However, I will judge the nation they serve, and afterward they will go out with many possessions. But you will go to your ancestors in peace and be buried at a good old age. (Gen 15:12–15, CSB)

---

6 Didymus the Blind, *Commentary on Zechariah*, 272 (Hill).

CHAPTER 6

MOSES, A BURNING BUSH, AND HOLY GROUND

And Yahweh saw that he turned aside to see, and God called to him from the midst of the bush, and he said, "Moses, Moses." And he said, "Here I am." And he said, "You must not come near to here. Take off your sandals from on your feet, because the place on which you are standing, it is holy ground." (Exodus 3:4–5, LEB)

READING THE STORY

GOD HAD CHOSEN ABRAHAM TO REIGNITE His earthly family. As God's beloved elect, Abraham's family began to flourish just as God promised they would. Our story now picks up when Abraham's grandson, Jacob (i.e., Israel), journeyed to Beersheba and offered sacrifices to the God of heaven. As the sun slipped under the horizon and the moon began its nightly reign, God had a message for Jacob, His allotted portion.

> "And God spoke to Israel in a vision at night and said, "Jacob! Jacob!" "Here I am," he replied. "I am God, the God of your father," he said. "Do not be afraid to go down to Egypt, for I will make you into a great nation there. I will go down to Egypt with you, and I will surely bring you back again. And Joseph's own hand will close your eyes." (Gen 46:2–4, NIV)

To Jacob, this must have been shocking news. What did traveling to Egypt have to do with the Abrahamic promise? How would being the minority in a foreign land play a major role in making Israel a great nation? With little explanation from God, Jacob packed his bags for Egypt, the gift of the Nile.

> "So Jacob arose from Beersheba. And the sons of Israel carried their father Jacob, and their little ones and their wives in the wagons Pharaoh had sent to transport him. And they took their livestock and their possessions that they had acquired in the land of Canaan. And they came to Egypt, Jacob and all his offspring with him: his sons and his sons' sons with him, his daughters and his sons' daughters, and all his offspring he brought with him into Egypt. (Gen 46:5–7, LEB)

Upon their arrival in Egypt, Jacob was reunited with his favorite son, Joseph. Despite Joseph being sold into slavery by his jealous brothers, it was a sweet, forgiving, and graceful reunion. Joseph said to them,

> As for you, you planned evil against me, but God planned it for good, in order to do this—to keep many people alive—as it is today. So then, do not be afraid. I myself will provide for you and your little ones. And he consoled them and spoke kindly to them. (Gen 50:20–21, LEB)

Joseph reassured them that all would be well. He may have also explained to them his rise to power in Egypt and how the pharaoh had once said to him,

> ... "Since God has made all of this known to you there is no one as discerning and wise as you. You shall be over my house, and to your word all my people shall submit. Only with respect to the throne will I be greater than you." Then Pharaoh said to Joseph, "See, I have set you over all the land of Egypt." Then Pharaoh removed his signet ring from his finger and put it on the finger of Joseph. And he clothed him with garments of fine linen, and he put a chain of gold around his neck. And he had him ride in his second chariot. And they cried out before him, "Kneel!" And Pharaoh set him over all the land of Egypt. (Gen 41:39–43, LEB)

As time passed, so did Jacob, Joseph, and the rest of his sons (Exod 1:6). Even though this golden generation was claimed by death, all was not lost; God's portion had budded into a plentiful nation, just as was promised.

> But the Israelites were fruitful, increased rapidly, multiplied, and became extremely numerous so that the land was filled with them. (Exod 1:7, CSB)

This new generation of Israelites was met with stark opposition by the new generation of Egyptians. For the next three hundred years, God's chosen portion would take the brunt of a sudden changing of the wind, a turning of the tide. They were forced into slavery.

> "A new king, who did not know about Joseph, came to power in Egypt. He said to his people, "Look, the Israelite people are more numerous and powerful than we are. Come, let's deal shrewdly with them; otherwise they will multiply further, and when war breaks out, they will join our enemies, fight against us, and leave the country." So the Egyptians assigned taskmasters over the Israelites to oppress them with forced labor. They built Pithom and Rameses as supply cities for Pharaoh. But the more they oppressed them, the more they multiplied and spread so that the Egyptians came to dread the Israelites. They worked the Israelites ruthlessly and made their lives bitter with difficult labor in brick and mortar and in all kinds of fieldwork. They ruthlessly imposed all this work on them. (Exod 1:8–14, CSB)

This new pharaoh even made a decree for the Egyptian midwives to slaughter all the male children born to Hebrew women (Exod 1:15–17). Despite Pharaoh's royal decree, the midwives refused because they feared the Lord. Enraged, Pharaoh demanded that all male Hebrew babies were to be thrown into the Nile River (Exod 1:22). However, one mother was determined to save her baby boy. Little did she know, her desperate act of faith would one day be Israel's saving grace.

> "Now a man from the family of Levi married a Levite woman. The woman became pregnant and gave birth to a son; when she saw that he was beautiful, she hid him for three months. But when she could no longer hide him, she got a papyrus basket for him and coated it with asphalt and pitch. She

> placed the child in it and set it among the reeds by the bank of the Nile. Then his sister stood at a distance in order to see what would happen to him. Pharaoh's daughter went down to bathe at the Nile while her servant girls walked along the riverbank. She saw the basket among the reeds, sent her slave girl, took it, opened it, and saw him, the child—and there he was, a little boy, crying. She felt sorry for him and said, "This is one of the Hebrew boys." Then his sister said to Pharaoh's daughter, "Should I go and call a Hebrew woman who is nursing to nurse the boy for you?" "Go," Pharaoh's daughter told her. So the girl went and called the boy's mother. Then Pharaoh's daughter said to her, "Take this child and nurse him for me, and I will pay your wages." So the woman took the boy and nursed him. When the child grew older, she brought him to Pharaoh's daughter, and he became her son. She named him Moses, "Because," she said, "I drew him out of the water." (Exod 2:1–10, CSB)

Eighty long years later, God's chosen people were gasping for freedom. Their Egyptian taskmasters had nearly broken their spirits for good. Their aspirations of being blessed in some distant promised land were quickly fading. In desperation, they cried out to the God of their forefathers—Abraham, Isaac, and Jacob—one last time.

> "And then during those many days, the king of Egypt died, and the Israelites groaned because of the work, and they cried out, and their cry for help because of the work went up to God. And God heard their groaning, and God remembered his covenant with Abraham, with Isaac, and with Jacob, and God saw the Israelites, and God took notice. (Exod 2:23–25, LEB)

God knew it was time. The mighty nation of Israel was complete and so was their stay in Egypt—it was time to lead them home. An exodus out of Egypt would not be easy, though. As far as the pharaoh was concerned, they were his slaves and wouldn't be going anywhere without his permission. Meanwhile, in Midian, Moses was tending Jethro's sheep.

> Now Moses was tending the flock of Jethro his father-in-law, the priest of Midian, and he led the flock to the far side of the wilderness and came to Horeb, the mountain of God. (Exod 3:1, NIV)

If you're wondering why Moses was in Midian, let me explain. Despite growing up as an adopted Egyptian in Pharaoh's house, he never stopped identifying with his own people. The mistreatment of the Hebrews infuriated him.

> And then in those days when Moses had grown up, he went out to his brothers, and he saw their forced labor, and he saw an Egyptian man striking a Hebrew man, one of his brothers. And he turned here and there, and he saw no one, and he struck the Egyptian, and he hid him in the sand. And he went out on the second day, and there were two Hebrew men fighting, and he said to the guilty one, "Why do you strike your neighbor?" And he said, "Who appointed you as a commander and a judge over us? Are you intending to kill me like you killed the Egyptian?" And Moses was afraid, and he said, "Surely the matter has become known." And Pharaoh heard this matter, and he sought to kill Moses, and Moses fled from Pharaoh, and he lived in the land of Midian… (Exod 2:11–15, LEB)

Moses's pursuit to get out of dodge played out rather nicely for him. He started a new life in Midian, where he quickly settled down and married one of Jethro's seven daughters, Zipporah (Exod 2:21). After enjoying forty years of simply being a husband, father, and shepherd, Moses got the most unusual call by a very significant angel. This celestial angel taught Moses an invaluable lesson about sacred space in the unlikeliest of places—a burning bush.

> "Meanwhile, Moses was shepherding the flock of his father-in-law Jethro, the priest of Midian. He led the flock to the far side of the wilderness and came to Horeb, the mountain of God. Then **the angel of the** LORD appeared to him in a flame of fire within a bush. As Moses looked, he saw that the bush was on fire but was not consumed. So Moses thought, "I must go over and look at this remarkable sight. Why isn't the bush burning up?" When the LORD saw that he had gone over to look, God called out to him from the bush, "Moses, Moses!" "Here I am," he answered. "Do not come closer," he said. "Remove the sandals from your feet, for the place where you are standing is holy ground." Then he continued, "**I am the God of your father, the God of Abraham, the God of Isaac, and the God of Jacob**." Moses hid his face because he was afraid to look at God. (Exod 3:1–6, CSB)

ANSWERING YOUR QUESTIONS

WHO IS THE ANGEL OF THE LORD?

Exodus 3:1–6 is clear—the angel of the Lord was God incarnate. This isn't the only time God appeared to men as the angel of the Lord. In fact, Jacob, Joseph's father, had several encounters with this same angel. Jacob's first encounter with him was in a dream that's normally referred to as Jacob's ladder (Gen 28:10–22). This dream is revisited in Genesis 31.

> [11] Then **the angel of God said** to me in the dream, 'Jacob,' and I said, 'Here I am.' [12] And he said, 'Lift up your eyes and see—all the rams mounting the flock are streaked, speckled, and dappled, for I have seen all that Laban is doing to you. [13] **I am the God of Bethel** where you anointed a stone pillar, where you made a vow to me. Now get up, go out from this land and return to the land of your birth.'" (Gen 31:11–13, LEB)

Stunningly, the angel of the Lord says he is God. The plot thickens. In the very next chapter, Jacob wrestles with an unidentified, yet very important, "man."

> [22] That night he arose and took his two wives, his two female slaves, and his eleven children and crossed the ford of the Jabbok. [23] And he took them and sent them across the stream. Then he sent across all his possessions. [24] And Jacob remained alone, and **a man wrestled with him** until the breaking of the dawn. [25] And when he saw that he could not prevail against him, he struck his hip socket, so that Jacob's hip socket was sprained as he wrestled with him. [26] Then he said, "Let me go, for dawn is breaking." But he answered, "I will not let you go unless you bless me." [27] Then he said to him, "What is your name?" And he said, "Jacob." [28] And he said, "Your name shall no longer be called Jacob, but Israel, for **you have struggled with God** and with men and have prevailed." [29] Then Jacob asked and said, "Please tell me your name." And he said, "Why do you ask this—for my name?" And he blessed him there. [30] Then Jacob called the name of the place Peniel which means "**I have seen God face to face** and my life was spared." (Gen 32:22–30, LEB)

Jacob knew whom he wrestled—he wrestled God. Back in chapter 2 of our book, we learned angels can take on a physical body, like that of men. Could this be the same angel of the Lord he dreamt of? The prophet Hosea substantiates Jacob's claim that he wrestled with God Himself. However, he adds one significant detail.

> [3] In the womb he took his brother by the heel, and in his manhood **he strove with God [ʾelōhîm].** [4] **He strove with the angel [*malʾāk*] and prevailed**; he wept and sought his favor. **He met God at Bethel**, and there God spoke with us— (Hos 12:3–4, ESV)

Hosea lays any doubts to rest. Jacob wrestled with the angel of the Lord, who is none other than God Himself. This same angel is the one who appeared to Moses in the burning bush. Understanding it was God's literal presence in the bush helps us parse the "holy ground" piece in the passage.

WHAT IS HOLY GROUND?

From the midst of the bush, the angel of the Lord told Moses in Exodus 3:5 (ESV), "…Do not come near; take your sandals off your feet, for the place on which you are standing is **holy ground**." This is the same thing the angel of God, the commander of the Lord's army, told Joshua before taking the city of Jericho.

> [13] When Joshua was near Jericho, **he looked up and saw a man** standing in front of him with a drawn sword in his hand. Joshua approached him and asked, "Are you for us or for our enemies?" [14] "Neither," he replied. "**I have now come as commander of the LORD's army**." Then Joshua bowed with his face to the ground in homage and asked him, "What does my lord want to say to his servant?" [15] The commander of the LORD's army said to Joshua, "**Remove the sandals from your feet, for the place where you are standing is holy**." And Joshua did that. (Josh 5:13–15, CSB)

Holy ground was an important theological tenant in Israelite cosmology. Holy ground is simply the space where God is. That "space" is holy because God's presence deems it so (Rev 4:8).

The idea of holy ground was not unique, however, to just the Israelites. All the nations in the ancient Near East considered their gods and their lands holy. This is due to the cosmic geography established at Babel. There, God divided languages and "allotted" land and lesser gods to all the nations of the world (Deut 4:19–20; 32:8–9).

Cosmic geography is obvious in several Old Testament passages. First, consider the healing of Naaman, the commander of the Syrian army. Naaman had contracted leprosy and sought out the prophet Elisha to heal him. Elisha told him, nonchalantly, to go dip in the murky Jordan River seven times. To Naaman's surprise, it actually worked; he was fully healed. When he returned to Elisha, the man of God, things got interesting.

> 15 When he returned to the man of God, he and all of his
> army, he came and stood before him and said, "Please
> now, I know that there is no God in all of the world except
> in Israel. So then, please take a gift from your servant."
> 16 And he said, "As Yahweh lives, before whom I stand, I
> surely will not take it." Still he urged him to take it, but
> he refused. 17 Then Naaman said, "If not, then **please let a
> load of soil** on a pair of mules be given to your servants,
> for **your servant will never again bring a burnt offering
> and sacrifice to other gods, but only to Yahweh**. 18 As far
> as this matter, may Yahweh pardon your servant when my
> master goes into the house of Rimmon to worship there,
> and he is leaning himself on my arm, that I also bow down
> in the house of Rimmon: when I bow down in the house of
> Rimmon, may Yahweh please pardon your servant in this

> matter." [19] He said to him, "Go in peace," so he went from him a short distance. (2 Kgs 5:15–19, LEB)

As a newly-converted worshiper and loyalist to Yahweh, Naaman believed he needed to take back "holy ground" to his homeland. His understanding was that this "holy dirt" would provide blessings back in Syria and forgiveness from his pagan duties in the house of the god Rimmon. Elisha didn't laugh him out of his presence for an absurd parting request; happily, he granted Naaman's two mule-load request of dirt and sent him on his way.

Another instance where cosmic geography is in view is when the Philistines captured the ark of the covenant and displayed it in the house of their small-G god, Dagon.

> [1] Now the Philistines had captured the ark of God and brought it from Ebenezer to Ashdod. [2] Then the Philistines took the ark of God and brought it to the temple of Dagon and placed it beside Dagon. [3] When the Ashdodites got up early the next morning, **there was Dagon fallen** with his face to the ground **before the ark of Yahweh**! So they took Dagon and returned him to his place. [4] When they got up early in the morning the next day, **there was Dagon fallen again** with his face to the ground before the ark of Yahweh! The head of Dagon and the palms of his two hands were cut off, lying at the threshold; only the body of Dagon was left. [5] (**Therefore the priests of Dagon and all who come into the house of Dagon do not tread on the threshold of Dagon in Ashdod until this very day**.) (1 Sam 5:1–5, LEB)

The statue of Dagon falling on its face telegraphed to the pagan priests that this space was no longer held by the power of Dagon; it had been claimed by Yahweh, the God of Israel. As Scripture points out, they wouldn't dare walk on God's newly-claimed holy ground ever again. They avoided it.

Lastly, we learn a good deal about cosmic geography from an interaction that took place between David and King Saul. David was hurt and confused about why Saul wanted to kill him.

> [18] And he said, "Why does my lord pursue after his servant? For what have I done? What evil is on my hands? [19] Now therefore let my lord the king hear the words of his servant. If it is the LORD who has stirred you up against me, may he accept an offering, but if it is men, may they be cursed before the LORD, **for they have driven me out this day that I should have no share in the heritage of the** LORD**, saying, 'Go, serve other gods.'** [20] **Now therefore, let not my blood fall to the earth away from the presence of the** LORD, for the king of Israel has come out to seek a single flea like one who hunts a partridge in the mountains." (1 Sam 26:18–20, ESV)

David recognized that foreign lands were controlled by the small-G gods over the nations. And since he was driven away from Gibeah, Israel's headquarters during Saul's reign, he was outside of the circumference of God and Israel's heritage and inside the domain of the gods.

CONNECTING THE GOSPEL

THE SPIRIT & THE TEMPLE

The Spirit of God played a prominent role throughout the biblical narrative. His Spirit is equative with His divine presence. While God is omnipresent, His Spirit is often described as dwelling in specific locations throughout time. During the Mosaic dispensation, God dwelt with his portion, Israel, first in the tabernacle.

> 8 And let them make me a sanctuary, **that I may dwell in their midst**. (Exod 25:8, ESV)

Eventually, this tent of meeting (Exod 35:21) was replaced by a more permanent structure, the temple (1 Chr 28:11–12). King David passed on the plans to build the temple to his royal son—Solomon. As Solomon put the final touches on God's holy temple, he prayed to God. Notice what happened next.

> 1 And when Solomon finished praying, then fire came down from heaven and consumed the burnt offering and the sacrifices, and the glory of Yahweh filled the house.
> 2 And the priests were not able to go into the house of Yahweh, for the glory of Yahweh had filled the house. (2 Chr 7:1–2, LEB)

This was the arrangement of how men dwelt with God throughout the remainder of the Old Testament. But God's vision for communing with man was much larger and intimate. He wanted to reside in a temple that wasn't made with human hands. He wanted to live in each of His believers. As members of Christ's Body, we, the people, are living stones in the new spiritual temple of God.

> 5 you yourselves like **living stones** are being **built up as a spiritual house**, to be a holy priesthood, to offer spiritual sacrifices acceptable to God through Jesus Christ. (1 Pet 2:5, ESV)

Paul discusses this with Christ's believers in both of his letters to the church at Corinth in eye-opening detail.

> 16 Do you not know that you are God's temple and that God's Spirit dwells in you? (1 Cor 3:16, ESV)

> 19 Or do you not know that your body is a temple of the Holy Spirit within you, whom you have from God? You are not your own, (1 Cor 6:19, ESV)

> 16 What agreement has the temple of God with idols? For we are the temple of the living God; as God said, "I will make my dwelling among them and walk among them, and I will be their God, and they shall be my people. (2 Cor 6:16, ESV)

It's imperative that you understand the Spirit of God is our unique identifying mark. Without it, we can't belong to Christ.

> 9 You, however, are not in the flesh but in the Spirit, if in fact **the Spirit of God dwells in you. Anyone who does not have the Spirit of Christ does not belong to him.** 10 But if Christ is in you, although the body is dead because of sin, the Spirit is life because of righteousness. (Rom 8:9–10, ESV)

These verses are lifechanging. Spirit-filled believers are God's new sacred space. What an honor! We must guard this precious gift (2 Tim 1:14) and remember, as God's chosen portion, we renounced all ungodliness at our baptism. Every single day, we are called to live soberly, righteously, and godly in the present world (2 Tim 2:12). This is our vocation. We must try to walk worthy of it (Eph 4:1).

LOOKING AHEAD

As God called Moses from the burning bush, Moses was terribly afraid.

> "Then the Lord said, "I have observed the misery of my people in Egypt, and have heard them crying out because of their oppressors. I know about their sufferings, and I have come down to rescue them from the power of the Egyptians and

> to bring them from that land to a good and spacious land, a land flowing with milk and honey—the territory of the Canaanites, Hethites, Amorites, Perizzites, Hivites, and Jebusites. So because the Israelites' cry for help has come to me, and I have also seen the way the Egyptians are oppressing them, therefore, go. I am sending you to Pharaoh so that you may lead my people, the Israelites, out of Egypt." (Exod 3:7–10, CSB)

Would God's plan backfire? How would Pharaoh respond to hardline demands from an outlaw of Egypt? How would these demands sit with the gods of Egypt? With so much at stake, a supernatural smackdown was brewing by the Nile, and it would be a bloodbath for the ages.

CHAPTER 7

SHOOTOUT IN EGYPT: 10 PLAGUES AND 11 VICTORIES

while the Egyptians were burying all the firstborn among them whom Yahweh struck. Yahweh also executed punishments among their gods. (Numbers 33:4, LEB)

READING THE STORY

STARTLED AND A BIT DUMBFOUNDED BY his supernatural encounter with the Lord, Moses knew his simple life in Midian was over.

> And Moses went, and he returned to Jethro his father-in-law, and he said to him, "Please let me go, and let me return to my brothers who are in Egypt, and let me see whether they are yet alive. And Jethro said to Moses, "Go in peace." And Yahweh said to Moses in Midian, "Go, return to Egypt because all the men have died who were seeking your life." And Moses took his wife and his sons and had them ride on the donkey, and he returned to the land of Egypt, and Moses took the staff of God in his hand. And Yahweh said to Moses, "When you go to return to Egypt, see all of the wonders that I have put in your hand, and do them before Pharaoh, and I myself will harden his heart, and he will not release the people. (Exod 4:18–21, LEB)

As Moses began his northward journey, he was to meet up with his brother Aaron at the mountain of God, Sinai. Meanwhile, the Lord appeared to Aaron, Moses's older brother, and pointed him in the direction of the holy mountain.

> And Yahweh said to Aaron, "Go to the desert to meet Moses." And he went and encountered him at the mountain of God and kissed him. And Moses told Aaron all the words of Yahweh, who had sent him—and all the signs that he had commanded him. (Exod 4:27–28, LEB)

Operation Exodus was a go. As the intrepid brothers arrived in Egypt, they immediately set up a meeting with the elders of Israel.

> Then Moses and Aaron went and assembled all the elders of the Israelites. Aaron repeated everything the Lord had said to Moses and performed the signs before the people. The people believed, and when they heard that the Lord had paid attention to them and that he had seen their misery, they knelt low and worshiped. (Exod 4:29–31, CSB)

Excitement spread through the collective of God's allotted portion like a plague. All Israel worshiped their God with a fervor they hadn't felt in several centuries. God was not dead, and neither was His plan.

> And afterward, Moses and Aaron went, and they said to Pharaoh, "Thus says Yahweh the God of Israel, 'Release my people so that they may hold a festival for me in the desert.'" And Pharaoh said, "Who is Yahweh that I should listen to his voice to release Israel? I do not know Yahweh, and also I will not release Israel." And they said, "The God of the Hebrews has met with us. Please let us go on a three-day journey into the desert, and let us sacrifice to Yahweh our God, lest he strike us with plague or with sword." And the king of Egypt said, "Why, Moses and Aaron, do you take the people from their work? Go to your forced labor!" And Pharaoh said, "Look, the people of the land are now many, and you want to stop them from their forced labor." And on that day Pharaoh commanded the slave drivers over the people and his foremen, saying, "You must no longer give straw to the people to make the bricks like before. Let them go and gather straw for themselves. But the quota of the bricks that they were making before you must require of them. You must not reduce from it, because they are lazy. Therefore they are crying out, saying, 'Let us go and sacrifice to our God.' Let the work be heavier on the men so that they will do it and not pay attention to words of deception." (Exod 5:1–9, LEB)

Pharaoh's strong hand choked the life out of Israel's newfound optimism.

> And they met Moses and Aaron, who were waiting to meet them when they were going out from Pharaoh. And they said to them, "May Yahweh look upon you and judge because you have caused our fragrance to stink in the eyes of Pharaoh and in the eyes of his servants so as to put a sword into their hand to kill us." And Moses returned to Yahweh and said, "Lord, why have you brought trouble to this people? Why ever did you send me? And from the time I came to Pharaoh to speak in your name, he has brought trouble to this people, and you have certainly not delivered your people." (Exod 5:20–23, LEB)

With the people's belief destroyed, Moses's confidence was zapped to zilch. He doubted himself, and even worse, he was starting to doubt God.

> And Yahweh said to Moses, "Now you will see what I will do to Pharaoh, because with a strong hand he will release them, and with a strong hand he will drive them out from his land." And God spoke to Moses, and he said to him, "I am Yahweh. And I appeared to Abraham, to Isaac, and to Jacob as God Shaddai, but by my name Yahweh I was not known to them. And I not only established my covenant with them to give to them the land of Canaan, the land of their sojournings, in which they dwelt as aliens, but also I myself heard the groaning of the Israelites, whom the Egyptians are making to work, and I remembered my covenant. Therefore say to the Israelites, 'I am Yahweh, and I will bring you out from under the forced labor of Egypt, and I will deliver you from their slavery, and I will redeem you with an outstretched arm and with great punishments. And I will take you as my

> people, and I will be your God, and you will know that I am Yahweh your God, who brought you out from under the forced labor of Egypt. And I will bring you to the land that I swore to give to Abraham, to Isaac, and to Jacob, and I will give it to you as a possession. I am Yahweh." And Moses spoke thus to the Israelites, but they did not listen to Moses, because of discouragement and because of hard work. And Yahweh spoke to Moses, saying, "Go, speak to Pharaoh, the king of Egypt, and let him release the Israelites from his land." And Moses spoke before Yahweh, saying, "Look, the Israelites do not listen to me, and how will Pharaoh listen to me, since I am a poor speaker?" (Exod 6:1–12, LEB)

> And Yahweh said to Moses and to Aaron, saying, "When Pharaoh speaks to you, saying, 'Do a wonder for yourselves,' you will say to Aaron, 'Take your staff and throw it before Pharaoh, and it will become a snake.'" And Moses and Aaron came to Pharaoh, and they did so, as Yahweh had commanded. And Aaron threw his staff before Pharaoh and before his servants, and it became a snake. And Pharaoh also called the wise men and the sorcerers, and they also, the magicians of Egypt, did likewise with their secret arts. (Exod 7:8–11, LEB)

This magic battle royale was no illusion—it was a throwdown of the "gods" (*ʾelōhîm*) and "spirits" (*rûaḥôṯ*) of the invisible realm. The Lord was in Moses and Aaron's corner, and the malevolent gods of Egypt were empowering the magicians and sorcerers of Pharaoh.

> "Each one threw down their rod, and they became huge serpents; but Aaron's rod swallowed down their rods. But the heart of Pharaoh grew strong, and he did not listen to them, just as the Lord commanded them. (Exod 7:12–13, LES)

The casting down of staffs is very significant. In Egypt, the staff of the pharaoh was a symbol of status and rule. In his book, *Against the Gods*, Currid wrote,

> *The staff of Pharaoh in ancient Egypt was emblematic of royalty, power, and authority. The rod as a symbol of Pharaonic sovereignty began at the coronation of the king, when the crook was placed in his hand.*[1]

He then cites Pyramid Texts 196–203, which describes the scene of royal enthronement for new kings.

> *Stand (as king) over it, over this land which has come forth from Atum,*
> *The spittle which has come forth from the beetle.*
> *Be (king) over it; be high over it,*
> *That thy father may see thee,*
> *That he may see thee.*
> *He comes to thee, O father of his;*
> *He comes to thee, O Re ...*
> *Let him grasp the Heavens*
> *And receive the Horizon;*
> *Let him dominate the Nine Bows*
> *And equip (with offerings) the Ennead.*
> ***Give the crook into his hand.***
> ***So that the head of Lower and Upper Egypt shall be bowed.***[2]

Currid then reveals,

---

1 J. D. Currid, *Against the Gods: The Polemical Theology of the Old Testament* (Wheaton, IL: Crossway, 2013), 114.

2 Currid, *Against the Gods*, 114.

> *The rod was also the symbol of the authority and power of the gods (called the mdw nṯr, "rod of god"). In Egyptian reliefs and on statues the gods were pictured carrying staffs in their hands.*[3]

The pharaoh, however, wasn't the only person who held a rod imbued with magic and power from the gods. His magicians did as well.

> *The magicians of Egypt (hry-ḥbt) also carried staffs in order to perform their magical feats. It is recorded that when attacked by enemies, the magician-king Nectanebo II (c. 360–343 BC) turned wax figures of soldiers and ships into an animate force by means of a magical rod. Numerous scarabs attest to that practice by containing scenes of magicians holding rods in their hands that could instantly be turned into snakes. Wallis Budge claims that the practice of rod divination operated among the magicians of Egypt and refers to "from time immemorial ... a wonderful rod of which they worked wonders."27 Just as with the royal staffs, the Egyptians believed the magicians' rods to be charged with superhuman strength.* ***The magicians were thus invested with mysterious magical forces of the gods personified in the rods.*** *The crooks simply gave them divine ḥkȝ, "magical power."*[4]

God's decision to initiate the battle of dueling rods wasn't random—it was strategic signaling. When Aaron's rod swallowed up the rods of the magicians, it sent a powerful message and foreshadowed the fate of the pharaoh, the Egyptians, and their gods. Yahweh was about to swallow up their power.

---

3 Currid, *Against the Gods*, 115.

4 Currid, *Against the Gods*, 117.

> *In his book on Egyptian magic, Robert Ritner explains, "Consumption entails the absorption of an object and the acquisition of its benefits or traits. Alternatively, the act can serve a principally hostile function, whereby 'to devour' signifies 'to destroy'—though even here the concept of acquiring power may be retained."*[5],[6]

Professor Scott B. Noegel also commented on the symbolic message of the swallowing scene in Exodus 7, citing several lines from Egyptian texts.

> *In addition, priests generally viewed swallowing as a performative act that functioned either to destroy the thing swallowed or to acquire its power and knowledge:*
>
> *Pyramid Texts (ca. 2400 BCE): "(King) Unas is one who eats men and lives on the gods… Unas eats their ḥeka, swallows their spirits" (spell 273).*
>
> *Coffin Texts: "I have swallowed the seven uraei-serpents" (spell 612), and "I have eaten truth (lit. Maat), I have swallowed ḥeka" (spell 1017).*
>
> *Thus, we may see the devouring of the ḥarṭummīm's staffs by Aaron's "staff of God" (Exod 4:20) as depicting the destruction of their authority and absorption of their power.*[7]

Pharaoh and the gods of Egypt were about to experience a divinely ordered onslaught of disorder, destruction, and death on a scale that hadn't been seen since the flood. The swallowing of the magicians' staffs foreshadowed it.

---

5 Godawa, *When Watchers Ruled the Nations*, 184.

6 Robert Kriech Ritner, *The Mechanics of Ancient Egyptian Magical Practice* (Chicago, IL: The Oriental Institute of Chicago, 1993), 23.

7 Scott B. Noegel, "The Egyptian 'Magicians,'" *The Torah.com*, 2017, https://www.thetorah.com/article/the-egyptian-magicians.

> *The irony of the matter is that the two Hebrew leaders possessed a rod, a highly esteemed Egyptian emblem, in order to humiliate and defeat the Egyptians. That is to say, the very physical symbol that rendered glory to Egypt, authority to Egypt, power to Egypt, was the very object the Hebrews used to vanquish them. Hengstenberg comments, "Moses was furnished with power to perform that which the Egyptian magicians most especially gloried in, and by which they most of all supported their authority."*[8]

Their powers, though real, would prove to be no match for Yahweh. They would be swallowed up in ten sequential plagues. Each of the plagues was a polemic attack on their gods.

The first nine plagues pummeled the Egyptians' health, happiness, and economic state. Yet, Pharaoh's stubborn heart still wouldn't let the people of Israel go. Everything was about to change with plague number ten; it would be the straw that broke the camel's back. The mighty king of Egypt was about to be begging on his knees, supplicating to the "Lord, God of Hosts" (***Yhwh ʾĕlōhê ṣĕbāʾôt***).

> "And Yahweh said to Moses, "Still one plague I will bring upon Pharaoh and upon Egypt; afterward he will release you from here. At the moment of his releasing, he will certainly drive you completely out from here. Speak in the ears of the people, and let them ask, a man from his neighbor and a woman from her neighbor, for objects of silver and objects of gold." And Yahweh gave the people favor in the eyes of Egypt. Also the man Moses was very great in the land of Egypt, in the eyes of the servants of Pharaoh and in the eyes of the people. And Moses said, "Thus says Yahweh, 'About the

8 Currid, *Against the Gods*, 117.

middle of the night I will go out through the midst of Egypt, and every firstborn in the land of Egypt will die, from the firstborn of Pharaoh who sits on his throne to the firstborn of the slave woman who is behind the pair of millstones and every firstborn animal. And there will be a great cry of distress in all the land of Egypt, the like of which has not been nor will be again. But against all the Israelites, from a man to an animal, a dog will not even bark, so that you will know that Yahweh makes a distinction between Egypt and Israel.' And all of these your servants will come down to me and bow to me, saying, 'Go out, you and all the people who are at your feet.' And afterward I will go out." And he went out from Pharaoh in great anger. (Exod 11:1–8, LEB)

The Lord then spoke to Moses and Aaron and reiterated His plans for the populace of Egypt, including their gods.

Exodus 12:12 (ESV)	Exodus 12:12 (Brenton LXX En)
12 For I will pass through the land of Egypt that night, and I will strike all the firstborn in the land of Egypt, both man and beast; and **on all the gods of Egypt I will execute judgments:** I am the LORD.	12 And I will go through the land of Egypt in that night, and will smite every first-born in the land of Egypt both man and beast, and **on all the gods of Egypt will I execute vengeance:** I am the Lord.

In order for the Israelites to be spared from sharing the fate of the Egyptians and their gods, they would need to be covered by the blood of a spotless lamb.

"And Moses called all the elders of Israel, and he said to them, "Select and take for yourselves sheep for your clans and slaughter the Passover sacrifice. And take a bunch of

> hyssop and dip it into the blood that is in the basin and apply some of the blood that is in the basin to the lintel and the two doorposts. And you will not go out, anyone from the doorway of his house, until morning. And Yahweh will go through to strike Egypt, and **he will see the blood** on the lintel and on the two doorposts, and Yahweh will pass over the doorway and will not allow the destroyer to come to your houses to strike you. (Exod 12:21–23, LEB)
>
> And the Israelites went, and they did as Yahweh had commanded Moses and Aaron; so they did. And in the middle of the night, Yahweh struck all of the firstborn in the land of Egypt, from the firstborn of Pharaoh sitting on his throne to the firstborn of the captive who was in the prison house and every firstborn of an animal. And Pharaoh got up at night, he and all his servants and all Egypt, and a great cry of distress was in Egypt because there was not a house where there was no one dead. (Exod 12:28–30, LEB)

ANSWERING YOUR QUESTIONS

WHAT ABOUT MAGIC?

Many ages ago, the world was full of wonder and magic. All the civilizations dabbled in it.

> *Farber and Thomsen note that various Mesopotamian priests and physicians conducted magical rituals. Several overlapping forms of magic were common in ancient Mesopotamia.*
>
> - *Restorative magic, including healing magic and exorcism, involved the restoration of individuals and communities to states of health and security.*

- *Apotropaic, or prophylactic, magic focused on the protection of a person from harm caused by malevolent magic and spiritual forces (deities, ghosts, malevolent spirits).*
- *Sorcery (malevolent magic) may have been practiced, although it may have been an imagined practice used to explain misfortune.*[9]

Magic was especially utilized in ancient Egypt. The Egyptians were big proponents of a variety of magic that included items such as magic wands, spells, and amulets. The Lexham Bible Dictionary states,

> *Ancient Egyptian society intimately integrated magic into its religious traditions. Not only did Egyptian religion include a god of magic (Heka), but every Egyptian deity also had a capacity for magic. Magical practices were also common for priests of Egyptian religion*[10]

According to the book of Enoch, magic and sorcery were introduced to mankind by the fallen angels before the flood (1 Enoch 8:3). The dark arts continued to dominate the ancient world due to the heretical teaching of the gods over the nations. Even after the Lord defeated Egypt's magicians and their gods, He warned Israel not to seek the nations' conjurors, charmers, necromancers, fortune tellers, or sorcerers.

> 9 "When you enter the land the LORD your God is giving you, do not imitate the detestable **customs of those nations**. 10 No one among you is to **sacrifice his son or daughter in the fire, practice divination, tell fortunes, interpret omens, practice**

---

9 R. D. Roberts, "Magic," *The Lexham Bible Dictionary*.

10 Roberts, "Magic."

> **sorcery,** [11] **cast spells, consult a medium or a spiritist, or inquire of the dead.** [12] Everyone who does these acts is detestable to the LORD, and the LORD your God is driving out the nations before you because of these detestable acts. [13] You must be blameless before the LORD your God. [14] **Though these nations** you are about to drive out listen to **fortune-tellers and diviners**, the LORD your God has not permitted you to do this. (Deut 18:9–14, CSB)

> [19] And when they say to you, "Seek those who are mediums and wizards, who whisper and mutter," should not a people seek their God? Should they seek the dead on behalf of the living? [20] To the law and to the testimony! If they do not speak according to this word, it is because there is no light in them. (Isa 8:19–20, NKJV)

"Those nations" wielded their magical powers from the fallen angels, as was written in a fourth-century text titled *Recognitions of Clement*.

> *"Fallen angels taught men the use of magical incantations that would force demons to obey them. After the flood Ham the son of Noah unhappily discovered this and taught it to his sons. This became ingrained into the Egyptians, Persians, and Babylonians. Nimrod was handed this knowledge and by it caused men to go away from the worship of God and go into diverse and erratic superstitions and they began to be governed by the signs in the stars and motions of the planets."*[11]

Early church fathers Lactantius and Tertullian also attributed magic and divination to angels and demons. Tertullian (160–220 A.D.) wrote,

---

11 Ken Johnson, ed., *Recognitions of Clement*, vol. 4 of *Ancient Paganism, Biblefacts.org*, Kindle edition, 53–54.

> *"The arts of astrologers, soothsayers, augurs, and magicians were made known by the angels who sinned, and are forbidden by God." Tertullian Apology 35*[12]

Nearly one hundred years later, Lactantius (240–320 A.D.) wrote in *The Divine Institutes 2.17*,

> *These [fallen spirits] were the inventors of astrology, and soothsaying, and divination, and those productions which are called oracles, and necromancy, and the art of magic, and whatever evil practices besides these men exercise, either openly or in secret.* [13]

During Old Testament times, the Lord dared any magicians or witches to "hunt for the souls" of his chosen people, Israel.

> [18] and say, Thus says the Lord GOD: **Woe to the women who sew magic bands upon all wrists**, and make veils for the heads of persons of every stature, **in the hunt for souls**! Will you hunt down souls belonging to my people and keep your own souls alive? [19] You have profaned me among my people for handfuls of barley and for pieces of bread, putting to death souls who should not die and keeping alive souls who should not live, by your lying to my people, who listen to lies. [20] "Therefore thus says the Lord GOD: Behold, **I am against your magic bands with which you hunt the souls like birds, and I will tear them from your arms, and I will let the souls whom you hunt go free, the souls like birds**. (Ezek 13:18–20, ESV)

---

12 Johnson, *Ancient Paganism*, 67.

13 Lactantius, *The Divine Institutes*, 65.

In the New Testament, normal, everyday Christians were given various miraculous gifts and magic-like abilities as a means to rival occult practices and to confirm they were the disciples of the most powerful God, Yahweh (Mark 16:20; Heb 2:4). Early Christian writers often emphasized this. Irenaeus (130–203 A.D.) wrote in *Against Heresies 2.32*,

> *"The Church does not perform anything by means of angelic invocations, or incantations, or by any other wicked curious art; but, directing her prayers to the Lord."*[14]

In Origen's letter *Against Celsus 1.6*, he negated Celsus's claims that Christians' miraculous abilities were demonic or derivative of dark magic in any way, asserting they were of Christ and God's Word.

> *Celsus asserts that it is by the names of certain demons, and by the use of incantations, that the Christians appear to be possessed of (miraculous) power; hinting, I suppose, at the practices of those who expel evil spirits by incantations. And here he manifestly appears to malign the Gospel.* ***For it is not by incantations that Christians seem to prevail (over evil spirits), but by the name of Jesus, accompanied by the announcement of the narratives which relate to Him****; for the repetition of these has frequently been the means of driving demons out of men, especially when those who repeated them did so in a sound and genuinely believing spirit.* ***Such power, indeed, does the name of Jesus possess over evil spirits****, that there have been instances where it was effectual, when it was pronounced even by bad men, which Jesus Himself taught (would be the case), when He said: "Many shall say to Me*

14 Johnson, *Ancient Paganism*, 156.

> *in that day, In Thy name we have cast out devils, and done many wonderful works."*
>
> *...But even if it be impossible to show by what power Jesus wrought these miracles,* ***it is clear that Christians employ no spells or incantations, but the simple name of Jesus****, and certain other words in which they repose faith, according to the holy Scriptures.*[15]

The book of Acts provides a lot of insight into magic practices in the New Testament era.

- The apostle Paul performed an exorcism on a slave girl who worked as a mediumistic diviner (Acts 16:16–18).
- Paul rebuked and blinded a Jewish magician named Elymas (Acts 13:6–12).
- Luke writes of a great magician named Simon Magus who was converted to Christianity around 36 A.D. Formerly, he was known as "the great power of god," a title Paul later attributed to Jesus Christ (1 Cor 1:24).

> 9 But there was a certain man called Simon, who previously practiced sorcery in the city and astonished the people of Samaria, claiming that he was someone great, 10 to whom they all gave heed, from the least to the greatest, saying, "**This man is the great power of God**." 11 And they heeded him because he had astonished them with his sorceries for a long time. 12 But when they believed Philip as he preached the things concerning the kingdom of God and the name of Jesus Christ, both men and women were baptized. 13 Then Simon himself also believed; and when he was baptized he continued with Philip, and

15 Origen, *Origen Against Celsus*, 398–399 (Crombie).

> was amazed, seeing the miracles and signs which were done. (Acts 8:9–13, NKJV)

After his conversion, the apostle Peter rebuked the former magician for trying to buy the miraculous gifts of the Holy Spirit (Acts 8:18–24). Early Christian apologist Justin Martyr wrote of Simon and his former posse of fellow diviners.

> *In the third place [we wish to state] that, after the Ascension of Christ into Heaven, the demons produced certain men who claimed to be gods, who were not only not molested by you, but even showered with honors.* ***There was a certain Simon,2 a Samaritan****, from the village called Gitta, who, in the time of Emperor Claudius,* ***through the force of the demons working in him, performed mighty acts of magic in your royal city of Rome, and was reputed to be a god****. And as a god he was honored by you with a statue, which was erected [on an island] in the Tiber River, between the two bridges, with this Roman inscription: 'To Simon, the holy God.' Almost every Samaritan, and even a few from other regions, worship him and call him the first God. And they call a certain Helena, who was his traveling companion at that time, and had formerly been a prostitute, the first idea generated from him. And we know, too, that a certain* ***Menander,****4 also of Samaria, of the town of Capparetaea,* ***a disciple of Simon****, and* ***likewise inspired by the demons, deceived many by his tricks of magic while he was at Antioch****. He even convinced his followers that they would never die, and there are some alive today who, inspired by him, still believe this. Then there is a certain* ***Marcion of Pontus****, who even now still teaches his disciples to believe in another and greater god than the Creator.* ***Assisted by the demons, he has caused many men of every country to blaspheme, and to deny that God is the***

> ***Creator of the universe, and to proclaim another god to be greater and to have done greater deeds than He.***[16]

Yet another insightful passage in the book of Acts reveals the popularity of the magic arts during the New Testament era.

> [11] God was performing extraordinary miracles by Paul's hands, [12] so that even facecloths or aprons that had touched his skin were brought to the sick, and the diseases left them, and the evil spirits came out of them. [13] Now some of the itinerant Jewish exorcists also attempted to pronounce the name of the Lord Jesus over those who had evil spirits, saying, "I command you by the Jesus that Paul preaches!" [14] Seven sons of Sceva, a Jewish high priest, were doing this. [15] The evil spirit answered them, "I know Jesus, and I recognize Paul—but who are you?" [16] Then the man who had the evil spirit jumped on them, overpowered them all, and prevailed against them, so that they ran out of that house naked and wounded. [17] When this became known to everyone who lived in Ephesus, both Jews and Greeks, they became afraid, and the name of the Lord Jesus was held in high esteem. [18] And many who had become believers came confessing and disclosing their practices, [19] **while many of those who had practiced magic collected their books and burned them in front of everyone.** So they calculated their value and found it to be fifty thousand pieces of silver. [20] In this way the word of the Lord spread and prevailed. (Acts 19:11–20, CSB)

After the seven sons of Sceva failed to invoke the name of the Lord Jesus in order to cast out demons, many Christians from the church at

---

16 Martyr, *The First Apology, The Second Apology, Dialogue with Trypho, Exhortation to the Greeks, Discourse to the Greeks, The Monarchy or The Rule of God*, 61–63.

Ephesus confessed they were still dabbling in the dark arts and quickly decided to publicly burn their valued spell books. Letting go of the occult practices of witchcraft and wizardry was a real struggle for many of the first-century Christians. Jesus' followers couldn't serve the same demons whom He cast out during His earthly ministry. They had to renounce them and avoid the temptation of returning to the powers of darkness.

In 165 A.D., Justin Martyr wrote that demonic forces were always trying to coax back their former, faithful enchanters.

> *Indeed, we warn you to* ***be careful lest the demons****, previously accused by us,* ***should mislead you and turn you*** *from reading and understanding thoroughly what we have said. They strive to make you their slaves and servants.* ***They ensnare, now by apparitions in dreams, now by tricks of magic****, all those who do not labor with all their strength for their own salvation—even as we, also,* ***after our conversion by the Word have separated ourselves from those demons and have attached ourselves to the only unbegotten God****, through His Son. We who once reveled in impurities now cling to purity;* ***we who devoted ourselves to the arts of magic now consecrate ourselves to the good and unbegotten God;***[17]

The apostle John warned the church,

> 1 Beloved, do not believe every spirit, but test the spirits, whether they are of God; because many false prophets have gone out into the world. (1 John 4:1, NKJV)

---

17 Martyr, *The First Apology, The Second Apology, Dialogue with Trypho, Exhortation to the Greeks, Discourse to the Greeks, The Monarchy or The Rule of God*, 46–47.

Paul warned Timothy that these spirits would successfully bait Christians back to darkness.

> 1 Now the Spirit explicitly says that in later times some will depart from the faith, paying attention to deceitful spirits and the teachings of demons, 2 through the hypocrisy of liars whose consciences are seared. (1 Tim 4:1–2, CSB)

Lactantius (240–320 A.D.) warned the church hundreds of years later of the danger demons posed to the Truth.

> *Moreover, these impure and wandering spirits, that they may throw all things into confusion, and overspread the minds of men with errors, interweave and mingle false things with true.* [18]

The early church was tasked with exposing evil spirits. Tertullian (160–220 A.D.) informs us these "spirits" would, in fact, make truthful confessions as to their identity when commanded to do so by Christians.

> *"Moreover, if sorcerers call forth ghosts, and even make what seem the souls of the dead to appear; if they put boys to death, in order to get a response from the oracle; if, with their juggling illusions, they make a pretence of doing various miracles; if they put dreams into people's minds by the power of the angels and demons whose aid they have invited, by whose influence, too, goats and tables (ancient Ouija boards) are made to divine, how much more likely is this power of evil... The wicked spirit, bidden to speak by a follower of Christ, will as readily make the truthful confession that he is a demon." Tertullian Apology 23* [19]

---

18 Lactantius, *The Divine Institutes*, 65.

19 Johnson, *Ancient Paganism*, 72.

While modern magic is often seen as pulling a white rabbit out of a black hat—a sleight-of-hand, so to speak—ancient magic was very real. Magic was taught and powered by higher entities in a strategic effort to attract mankind to hell and its many gods.

CONNECTING THE GOSPEL

BLOOD & JUDGMENT

The catalyst for the ten plagues of Egypt wasn't Israel's long tenure in the land; it was their mistreatment by the Egyptians and their gods. Notice what Jethro, Moses's father-in-law, said when he was told of Israel's deliverance from Egyptian bondage.

> 10 Jethro said, "Blessed be the LORD, who has delivered you out of
> the hand of the Egyptians and out of the hand of Pharaoh and has
> delivered the people from under the hand of the Egyptians. 11 **Now I
> know that the** LORD **is greater than all gods, because in this affair
> they dealt arrogantly with the people**." (Exod 18:10–11, ESV)

The Egyptians and their gods were devoid of love and compassion for God's allotted portion, Israel. Abusing Israel was Egypt's undoing.

In Jesus' discourse on the subject of "love" and "compassion" (Matt 25), He reminded His disciples that hell was created for all uncompassionate beings in both the seen and unseen realms alike.

> 31 "When the Son of Man comes in his glory, and all the angels
> with him, then he will sit on his glorious throne. 32 **All the nations
> will be gathered before him**, and he will separate them one from
> another, just as a shepherd separates the sheep from the goats.
> 41 "Then he will also say to those on the left, 'Depart from me, you
> who are cursed, into the eternal fire **prepared for the devil and
> his angels!** 42 For I was hungry and you gave me nothing to eat; I

> was thirsty and you gave me nothing to drink; [43] I was a stranger and you didn't take me in; I was naked and you didn't clothe me, sick and in prison and you didn't take care of me.' [44] "Then they too will answer, 'Lord, when did we see you hungry, or thirsty, or a stranger, or without clothes, or sick, or in prison, and not help you?' [45] "Then he will answer them, 'Truly I tell you, whatever you did not do for one of the least of these, you did not do for me.' [46] "And they will go away into eternal punishment, but the righteous into eternal life." (Matt 25:31–32, 41–46, CSB)

Jesus' disciples would have, naturally, parsed His words in the context and frame of the Old Testament (Rom 15:4). Undoubtedly, they made the connection between the abuse Israel suffered at the hands of Egypt and her gods and Jesus' message of condemnation to the uncompassionate nations and their angels. As former Jews and students of the Old Testament, the disciples wouldn't have forgotten the Israelites were once "strangers" in the land of Egypt and were exploited as slaves "in prison" (i.e., they weren't properly fed, hydrated, or clothed). Informed with the ancient mind, the disciples knew exactly who the devil and "his angels" were—they were the small-G gods of "all the nations," including Egypt, that were "gathered before" the "enthroned," "seated" "Son of Man" in the final judgment (Matt 25:42).

The apostle Paul even seems to distantly be recycling ideas of the Exodus showdown to teach about the day of final judgment Jesus described to His disciples. Some common threads are (1) affliction, (2) destroying angels, (3) vengeance, (4) not knowing God, and (5) disobedience.

> [5] This is evidence of the righteous judgment of God, that you may be considered worthy of the kingdom of God, for which you are also suffering— [6] since indeed God considers it just to **repay with <u>affliction</u> those who afflict you,** [7] and to grant relief

to you who are afflicted as well as to us, when the Lord Jesus is
revealed from heaven with **his mighty angels** 8 **in flaming fire,
inflicting vengeance (*ĕkdikēsis*) on those who do not know
God** and on those who **do not obey** the gospel of our Lord
Jesus. 9 **They will suffer the punishment of eternal destruction**,
away from the presence of the Lord and from the glory of his
might, 10 when he comes on that day to be glorified in his saints,
and to be marveled at among all who have believed, because
our testimony to you was believed. (2 Thess 1:5–10, ESV)

Affliction **Exodus 3:7 (Brenton LXX En)**	***Destroying Angels*** **Psalm 78:43, 49 (ESV)**	***Vengeance*** **Exodus 12:12 (Brenton LXX En)**	***Not Knowing God*** **Exodus 5:2 (ESV)**	***Disobedience*** **Exodus 5:2 (ESV)**
7 And the Lord said to Moses, **I have surely seen the affliction of my people** that is in Egypt, and I have heard their cry caused by their taskmasters; for **I know their affliction**.	43 when he performed his signs in Egypt and his marvels in the fields of Zoan. 49 **He let loose on them** his burning anger, wrath, indignation, and distress, **a company of destroying angels**.	12 And I will go through the land of Egypt in that night, and will smite every first-born in the land of Egypt both man and beast, and **on all the gods of Egypt will I execute vengeance (*ĕkdikēsis*)**: I am the Lord.	2 But Pharaoh said, "Who is the LORD, that I should obey his voice and let Israel go? **I do not know the LORD,** and moreover, I will not let Israel go."	2 But Pharaoh said, **"Who is the LORD, that I should obey his voice and let Israel go**? I do not know the LORD, and moreover, **I will not let Israel go.**"

Both Jesus and Paul were trying to get a very important message across to their listeners: Be prepared for judgment! Final judgment is what I'm trying to help you prepare for. This is why it's vital to shed deception and reclaim the unfiltered gospel.

In Cyprian's third-century treatise, *To Demetrian*, he wrote,

> *For behold the day of the Lord shall come, a cruel day, and full of indignation, and of wrath, to lay the land desolate, and to destroy the sinners out of it.' And again: 'Behold the day of the Lord comes kindled as a furnace, and all the proud and all the wicked shall be as stubble; and the day coming shall set them on fire, says the Lord.'2 The Lord prophecies that aliens will be burned and consumed, that is,* ***aliens from the divine race, and the profane, those who have not been reborn spiritually and have not become sons of God.***[20]

Uncleansed human partakers of darkness will join their masters in eternal punishment, as Lactantius (240–320 A.D.), the Christian North African rhetorician, wrote in *The Divine Institutes*,

> *Whoever shall have worshipped and followed these most wicked spirits, will neither enjoy heaven nor the light, which are God's; but will fall into those things which we have spoken of as being assigned in the distribution of things to the prince of the evil ones himself,—namely, into darkness, and hell, and everlasting punishment.*[21]

We must be cleansed in the detergent of Christ's blood. As was previously stated, in order for the Israelites to be spared from sharing the

---

20 Cyprian, *To Demetrian*, 186–187 (Deferrari).

21 Lactantius, *The Divine Institutes*, 67.

fate of the Egyptians and their gods, they would need to be covered by the blood of a spotless lamb (Exod 12:23). God's offering you the same escape He offered them. Apply the blood of the Lamb, and you'll be saved (1 Pet 1:18–19).

Cyprian continued,

> *What preceded before in a figure in the slaying of a lamb is fulfilled in Christ the truth which followed later. Just as then, when Egypt was smitten, no one could escape except by the blood and sign of the lamb, so too when the world begins to be laid waste and smitten, he alone escapes who is found in the blood and sign of Christ.*[22]

In Justin Martyr's dialogue with Trypho in 155 A.D., Justin wrote,

> *And the blood of the Passover, which was smeared on the side posts and transoms of the doors, saved those fortunate ones in Egypt who escaped the death inflicted upon the first-born of the Egyptians. The Passover, indeed, was Christ, who was later sacrificed, as Isaias foretold when he said: "He was led as a sheep to the slaughter." It is also written that on the day of the Passover you seized Him, and that during the Passover you crucified Him. Now, just as the blood of the Passover saved those who were in Egypt, so also shall the blood of Christ rescue from death all those who have believed in Him. Would God have been mistaken, then, if this sign had not been made over the doors? That is not what I say, but I do say that He thus foretold that salvation was to come to mankind through the blood of Christ.*[23]

---

22 Cyprian, *To Demetrian*, 186–187.

23 Justin Martyr, *The First Apology, The Second Apology, Dialogue with Trypho, Exhortation to the Greeks, Discourse to the Greeks, The Monarchy or The Rule of God*, 319–320 (Falls).

In Paul's writing to the church at Rome, he reuses the framework of the Passover Lamb to relay the role Jesus' blood plays in our salvation. He writes,

> [23] For all have sinned and fall short of the glory of God; [24] they are justified freely by his grace through the redemption that is in Christ Jesus. [25] God presented him as the mercy seat **by his blood**, through faith, to demonstrate his righteousness, because in his restraint **God passed over the sins previously committed**. (Rom 3:23–25, CSB)

> [9] How much more then, since we have now been justified by his **blood**, will we be saved through him from wrath. (Rom 5:9, ESV)

The apostle John also interlaces ideas about the intrinsic quality of Christ's saving blood throughout the book of Revelation. Note the following verses:

> [5] and from Jesus Christ, the faithful witness, the firstborn from the dead and the ruler of the kings of the earth. To him who loves us and **has set us free from our sins by his blood**, (Rev 1:5, CSB)

> [9] And they sang a new song, saying, "Worthy are you to take the scroll and to open its seals, for you were slain, **and by your blood you ransomed people for God from every tribe and language and people and nation**, (Rev 5:9, ESV)

> [11] And they have conquered him **by the blood of the Lamb** and by the word of their testimony, for they loved not their lives even unto death. (Rev 12:11, ESV)

The Lamb's blood must be applied to the spiritual tabernacle of man: the soul. But how do we apply its purifying properties? As John records, we must be washed in the blood of the Lamb.

> [14] I said to him, "Sir, you know." And he said to me, "These are the ones coming out of the great tribulation. **They have washed their robes** and made them white **in the blood of the Lamb.** (Rev 7:14, ESV)

I cannot emphasize this enough—salvation is not the result of personal attainment, but of blood atonement. And by God's grace, it is available to all believers, as Victorinus of Pettau (martyred ca. 304 A.D.) reminds us:

> *"After this I beheld, and, lo, a great multitude, which no man was able to number, of every nation, tribe, and people, and tongue, clothed with white robes." What the great multitude out of every tribe implies, is to show the number of the elect out* ***of all believers****, who,* ***being cleansed by baptism in the blood of the Lamb****, have made their robes white, keeping the grace which they have received.*[24]

LOOKING AHEAD

After the Lord struck down all the firstborn in Egypt, Pharaoh was devastated.

> "And Pharaoh got up at night, he and all his servants and all Egypt, and a great cry of distress was in Egypt because there was not a house where there was no one dead. And he

24 Victorinus of Pettau, *Commentary on the Apocalypse of the Blessed John*, 352 (Wallis).

> called Moses and Aaron at night, and he said, "Get up, go out from the midst of my people, both you as well as the Israelites, and go, serve Yahweh, as you have said. Take both your sheep and goats as well as your cattle, and go, and bless also me." And the Egyptians urged the people in order to hurry their release from the land, because they said, "All of us will die!" And the people lifted up their dough before it had yeast; their kneading troughs were wrapped up in their cloaks on their shoulder. And the Israelites did according to the word of Moses, and they asked from the Egyptians for objects of silver and objects of gold and for clothing. And Yahweh gave the people favor in the eyes of the Egyptians, and they granted their requests, and they plundered the Egyptians. (Exod 12:30–36, LEB)

Israel's plundering of the people of Egypt symbolized they were the victors over the Egyptians and their gods. Yahweh defeated their gods with ten stifling plagues. In fact, on the very night Israel set out from the Egyptian city of Rameses, Yahweh punished his former angels, the rebellious gods of Egypt.

> "And they set out from Rameses in the first month, on the fifteenth day of the first month; on the day after the Passover the children of Israel went out boldly in the sight of all the Egyptians, while the Egyptians were burying all their firstborn, whom the LORD had struck down among them. **The LORD executed judgments even against their gods**. (Num 33:3–4, The Dead Sea Scrolls Bible)[25]

With this direct blow to Egypt's gods, the score increased to 11–0, Team Yahweh. But the match wasn't over just yet. There was one more

---

25 Wise, Abegg, Jr., and Cook, *The Dead Sea Scrolls*, Num 33:3–4.

point to be claimed in this supernatural showdown between the "gods" (*ʾ**elōhîm***) of the unseen realm. With the Egyptian gods neutralized, who would Yahweh face next? You will be shocked when you learn the rest of the story in the coming chapter.

CHAPTER 8

CROSSING OVER IN VICTORY

You divided the sea by your might; you broke the heads of the sea monsters on the waters. You crushed the heads of Leviathan; you gave him as food for the creatures of the wilderness. (Psalm 74:13–14, ESV)

READING THE STORY

PHASE 1 OF THE ABRAHAM PROMISE was now complete. Israel was a "great nation" (Acts 13:17), a free nation. The strong hand and uplifted arm of the Lord had defeated the mighty Egyptians and their gods (Ps 136:11–12), delivering Israel from the house of bondage (Mic 6:4). The only problem was they were a great nation without a home. As the Israelites set out from the Egyptian city of Rameses, they watched for that coveted land God had promised to give them (Gen 12:7).

> When Pharaoh let the people go, God did not lead them along the road to the land of the Philistines, even though it was nearby; for God said, "The people will change their minds and return to Egypt if they face war." So he led the people around toward the Red Sea along the road of the wilderness. And the Israelites left the land of Egypt in battle formation. (Exod 13:17–18, CSB)

The Israelites journeyed from Rameses to Sukkoth. There were about six hundred thousand men on foot, besides women and children. Many other people went up with them, and also large droves of livestock, both flocks and herds. (Exod 12:37–38, NIV)

> And they set out from Succoth, and they encamped at Etham on the edge of the desert. And Yahweh was going before them by day in a column of cloud to lead them on the way and by night in a column of fire to give light to them to go by day and night. (Exod 13:20–21, LEB)

Then, God gave the strangest command: Turn around!

Wait… what? Turn around? Yes, turn around.

> Then the LORD spoke to Moses: "Tell the Israelites to turn back and camp in front of Pi-hahiroth, between Migdol and the sea; **you must camp in front of Baal-zephon, facing it** by the sea. Pharaoh will say of the Israelites: They are wandering around the land in confusion; the wilderness has boxed them in. I will harden Pharaoh's heart so that he will pursue them. Then I will receive glory by means of Pharaoh and all his army, and the Egyptians will know that I am the LORD." So the Israelites did this. (Exod 14:1–4, CSB)

Was God a poor navigator? Was He bad with directions? No. As the passage reveals, there was a particular mountain He wanted His people to camp in front of. Strangely enough, He told them to face this mountain. It's as if he wanted them to stare it down. The mountain was called Baal-Zephon. The Dictionary of Demons and Deities sheds light on who ruled this "sacred space."

> *Baal-zaphon literally means the 'lord of (mount) →Zaphon' and it is a designation of the Ugaritic god →Baal.*[1]

This mountain was under the jurisdiction of none other than the infamous Baal, the primary antagonist of God's portion, Israel. Baal wore many masks in antiquity and was, seemingly, worshiped by all the nations of the world by one name or another. Jesus revealed his true identity in the New Testament.

> 20 Jesus entered a house, and the crowd gathered again so that
> they were not even able to eat. 21 When his family heard this,
> they set out to restrain him, because they said, "He's out of his
> mind." 22 The scribes who had come down from Jerusalem said,

1 H. Niehr, "Baal-Zaphon," *Dictionary of Deities and Demons in the Bible*, 2nd ed., 152.

> "He is possessed by **Beelzebul**," and, "**He drives out demons by the ruler of the demons.**" 23 So he summoned them and spoke to them in parables: "**How can Satan drive out Satan**? 24 If a kingdom is divided against itself, that kingdom cannot stand.
> 25 If a house is divided against itself, that house cannot stand.
> 26 And **if Satan opposes himself** and is divided, he cannot stand but is finished. 27 But no one can enter a strong man's house and plunder his possessions unless he first ties up the strong man. Then he can plunder his house. (Mark 3:20–27, CSB)

As Jesus clarified, Beelzebul, or Baal-zebul, is Satan, the slithering serpent who was cast out of the garden of Eden back in Genesis 3. Dr. Michael S. Heiser noted,

> *Baal was called "king of the gods" and "most high" at Ugarit and other places. In Ugaritic texts, Baal is "lord of Zaphon" (ba'al tsapanu). He is also called a "prince" (zbl in Ugaritic). Another of Baal's titles is "prince, lord of the underworld" (zbl ba'al 'arts). This connection to the realm of the dead of course dovetails with our discussion of the themes associated with the serpent figure from Genesis 3. It is no surprise that zbl ba'al becomes Baal Zebul (Beelzebul) and Baal Zebub, titles associated with Satan in later Jewish literature and the New Testament.*[2]

After the Lord drew the line of demarcation around the holy mountain of Eden and booted out all sinners, Satan found his new dwelling high in the skies at Mount Zaphon. There, he established his own kingdom and "holy" headquarters, where he, in the shadows, pulled the strings of all the disinherited nations and their rebellious gods. The prophet Isaiah outlined this in Isaiah 14.

---

2 Heiser, *The Unseen Realm*, 361.

Isaiah 14:12–14 (Brenton LXX En)	Isaiah 14:12–14 (NIV)
[12] How has Lucifer, that rose in the morning, fallen from heaven! **He that sent orders to all the nations** is crushed to the earth. [13] But thou saidst in thine heart, I will go up to heaven, I will set my throne above the stars of heaven: **I will sit on a lofty mount, on the lofty mountains towards the north *(tsaphon)*:** [14] I will go up above the clouds; I will be like the Most High.	[12] How you have fallen from heaven, morning star, son of the dawn! **You have been cast down to the earth, you who once laid low the nations**! [13] You said in your heart, "I will ascend to the heavens; I will raise my throne above the stars of God; **I will sit enthroned on the mount of assembly, on the utmost heights of Mount Zaphon.** [14] I will ascend above the tops of the clouds; I will make myself like the Most High."

Dr. Heiser went on to write,

> *Specifically, Baal's home was a mountain, now known as Jebel al-Aqra῾, situated to the north of Ugarit. In ancient times it was simply known as Tsaphon ("north"; Tsapanu in Ugaritic). It was a divine mountain, the place where Baal held council as he ruled the gods of the Canaanite pantheon. Baal's palace was thought to be on "the heights of Tsapanu/Zaphon."*[3]

The language used in Arslan Tash 1.9–14 (ancient Phoenician text) hints at Baal's council of gods.

> *9-10 Asshur has made with us and eternal covenant. He made (it)*
> *11 with us, and (with) all the sons of the* ***gods****,*
> *12 and the chiefs of the* ***council of all the holy ones***

3 Heiser, *The Unseen Realm*, 361.

13 with a covenant of heaven and earth
14 forever, by ***an oath of Baal,***[4]

Baal's home, Mount Zaphon, is roughly five hundred miles north of the Nile Delta. Later in the biblical narrative, the Psalmist has Mount Zion theologically displacing and replacing Mount Zaphon as the heavyweight champion of "the North" and emphasizes that Yahweh is the King of the gods in the ancient world.

Psalm 48:1–2 (NIV)	Psalm 48:1–2 (LEB)
Great is the Lord, and most worthy of praise, in the city of our God, **his holy mountain**. Beautiful in its loftiness, the joy of the whole earth, **like the heights of Zaphon is Mount Zion**, the city of the Great King.	**Yahweh is great and very worthy** of praise in the city of our God, in **his holy mountain**. Beautiful in elevation, the joy of the whole earth, is **Mount Zion**, in the **far north *(tsaphon)*,** the city of the great king.

But in our story, one of Baal's sacred satellite mountains, Baal-Zaphon, was being stared down by Israel, Moses, and the angel of the Lord.

> "When the king of Egypt was told that the people had fled, Pharaoh and his officials changed their minds about the people and said, "What have we done? We have released Israel from serving us." So he got his chariot ready and took his troops with him; he took six hundred of the best chariots and all the rest of the chariots of Egypt, with officers in each one. The Lord hardened the heart of Pharaoh king of Egypt, and he pursued the Israelites, who were going out defiantly. The Egyptians—all Pharaoh's horses and chariots, his horsemen, and his army—chased after them and caught

4 Michael S. Heiser, H. H. Hardy, and Charles Otte, *Hebrew and Canaanite Inscriptions in English Translation* (Bellingham, WA: Lexham Press, 2008).

> up with them as they camped by the sea beside Pi-hahiroth, in front of Baal-zephon. As Pharaoh approached, the Israelites looked up and there were the Egyptians coming after them! The Israelites were terrified and cried out to the LORD for help. They said to Moses, "Is it because there are no graves in Egypt that you have taken us away to die in the wilderness? What have you done to us by bringing us out of Egypt? Isn't this what we told you in Egypt: Leave us alone so that we may serve the Egyptians? It would have been better for us to serve the Egyptians than to die in the wilderness." But Moses said to the people, "Don't be afraid. Stand firm and see the LORD's salvation that he will accomplish for you today; for the Egyptians you see today, you will never see again. The LORD will fight for you, and you must be quiet." (Exod 14:5–14, CSB)

Israel's lack of faith was downright shameful and was considered an act of rebellion (Ps 106:7). Nevertheless, God wouldn't abandon His people now. His grace was too great, and His love was too deep to leave them pinned in at the Red Sea. God was there protecting them and fighting for them in one of His familiar forms, as the angel of the Lord. He wanted to be personally present for the final victory over the Egyptians and the cockiest small-G god of them all, Baal.

> "And Yahweh said to Moses, "Why do you cry out to me? Speak to the Israelites so that they set out. And you, lift up your staff and stretch out your hand over the sea and divide it so that the Israelites can go in the middle of the sea on the dry land. And as for me, look, I am about to harden the heart of the Egyptians so that they come after them, and I will display my glory through Pharaoh and through all of his army, through his chariots and through his charioteers. And the Egyptians will know that I am Yahweh when I display my glory through Pharaoh, through his chariots, and through his charioteers." (Exod 14:15–18, LEB)

In the last chapter, we learned about the significance of Aaron's rod swallowing up the magical powers of the gods of Egypt. God's insistence on Moses's continued use of a staff displayed His dominance over the gods of Egypt throughout the entire Exodus. Godawa wrote,

> *Moses also used that same staff raised or struck to turn the Nile to blood (7:20), draw forth the plagues of frogs (8:5), gnats (8:17), hail (9:23), locusts (10:13-14), and ultimately to split the sea for crossing (14:16). Though Yahweh did not need a magic item to accomplish his miracles, he clearly worked within the symbolic system of Egyptian magic to prove that he was God of gods, king of kings, and, one might add with tongue in cheek, "Magician of magicians."*[5]

Back to the story. The Lord commanded Moses to part the sea with his rod.

> "And the angel of God who was going before the camp of Israel set out and went behind them. And the column of cloud set out ahead of them, and it stood still behind them, so that it came between the camp of Egypt and the camp of Israel. And it was a dark cloud, but it gave light to the night, so that neither approached the other all night. And Moses stretched out his hand over the sea, and Yahweh moved the sea with a strong east wind all night, and he made the sea become dry ground, and the waters were divided. And the Israelites entered the middle of the sea on the dry land. The waters were a wall for them on their right and on their left. And the Egyptians gave chase and entered after them—all the horses of Pharaoh, his chariots, and his charioteers—into the middle of the sea. And during the morning watch, Yahweh looked down to the Egyptian camp from in the column of fire and cloud, and he threw the Egyptian camp into a

---

5 Godawa, *When Watchers Ruled the Nations*, 185.

> panic. And he removed the wheels of their chariots so that they drove them with difficulty, and the Egyptians said, "We must flee away from Israel because Yahweh is fighting for them against Egypt." And Yahweh said to Moses, "Stretch out your hand over the sea, and let the waters return over the Egyptians, over their chariots, and over their charioteers." And Moses stretched out his hand over the sea, and the sea returned at daybreak to its normal level, and the Egyptians were fleeing because of it, and Yahweh swept the Egyptians into the middle of the sea. And the waters returned and covered the chariots and the charioteers—all the army of Pharaoh coming after them into the sea. Not even one survived among them. But the Israelites walked on the dry land in the middle of the sea. The waters were a wall for them on their right and on their left. And Yahweh saved Israel on that day from the hand of Egypt, and Israel saw the Egyptians dead on the shore of the sea. And Israel saw the great hand that Yahweh displayed against Egypt, and the people feared Yahweh, and they believed in Yahweh and in Moses his servant. (Exod 14:19–31, LEB)

GAME. SET. MATCH.

The 430-year nightmare was all over. Through the lowly shepherd rod of Moses, Yahweh hit the reset button on history and shifted all power to the great rising nation of Israel. Currid noted,

> *Finally, it is ironic that Moses employed a simple shepherd's crook in the conflict with Egypt. He did not engage Pharaoh with a mighty, elaborate scepter of Egyptian royalty—the ḥkꜣt or the nḫḫw—but he came with the common mdw of the herder. According to the biblical author, the Egyptians clearly despised the lowly occupation of shepherding: Joseph is portrayed as separating the Hebrews from the Egyptians in Genesis 46 "because every shepherd is loathsome to the Egyptians" (v. 34b, AT). Moses's use of the mdw would have*

been insulting to Egyptian royalty and priesthood. How could a mere shepherd's staff match up with the royal staffs endowed with the power of Osiris? That idea underscores the theology of the Exodus writer that the real power of the universe was not in the staff but in the god. Yahweh was victorious, not because of the type of rod that was used, but by his great power and sovereignty. That is the main message of the Exodus account.[6]

The crossing of the Red Sea, however, was more than an escape from Egypt and their gods; it was also a victory over you-know-who, that ancient serpent and great dragon (Rev 12:9), the lord of Mount Zaphon. Both Asaph and Isaiah recognized the supernatural struggle at the Red Sea and emphasized both Egypt's and Satan's (Baal) defeat.

Psalm 73:13–15 (Brenton LXX En)	Psalm 74:13–15 (ESV)	Psalm 74:13–15 (ASV 1901)
13 **Thou didst establish the sea,** in thy might, thou didst break to pieces the heads of the dragons in the water. 14 **Thou didst break to pieces the heads of the dragon;** thou didst give him for meat to the Ethiopian nations. 15 **Thou didst cleave fountains and torrents; thou driedst up mighty rivers.**	13 **You divided the sea by your might;** you broke the heads of the sea monsters on the waters. 14 **You crushed the heads of Leviathan;** you gave him as food for the creatures of the wilderness. 15 **You split open springs and brooks; you dried up ever-flowing streams.**	13 **Thou didst divide the sea by thy strength:** Thou brakest the heads of the sea-monsters in the waters. 14 **Thou brakest the heads of leviathan in pieces;** Thou gavest him to be food to the people inhabiting the wilderness. 15 **Thou didst cleave fountain and flood: Thou driedst up mighty rivers.**

6 Currid, *Against the Gods*, 119.

Isaiah 51:9–10 (The Dead Sea Scrolls Bible)[7]	Isaiah 51:9–10 (LEB)	Isaiah 51:9–10 (KJV 1900)
9 Awake, awake, be clothed with strength, arm of the LORD! Awake, as in the days of old, ancient times. Was it not you who broke Rehob to pieces, **who pierced the sea monster**? 10 Was it not you who dried up Sea, the waters of the great deep, who made in the depths of the sea a path for the redeemed to pass over?	9 Awake! Awake; put on strength, O arm of Yahweh! Awake as in days of long ago, the generations of a long time back! Are you not the one who cut Rahab in pieces, the one who **pierced the sea-dragon?** 10 Are you not the one who dried up the sea, the waters of the great deep, the one who made the depths of the sea a way for those who are redeemed to cross over?	9 Awake, awake, put on strength, O arm of the Lord; Awake, as in the ancient days, in the generations of old. Art thou not it that hath cut Rahab, **and wounded the dragon?** 10 Art thou not it which hath dried the sea, the waters of the great deep; That hath made the depths of the sea a way for the ransomed to pass over?

CONNECTING THE GOSPEL

FLEEING EGYPT, FLEEING SIN

The most important thing in your life is for you to have your guilt expunged by Jesus, the Judge of the universe (John 5:22). To do that, your "sinner" status must be changed to "saved." The exodus out of Egypt serves as the perfect illustration of how the masses can escape their sin. No slave has ever escaped without running toward freedom. Israel's defiance against Egypt was their way out of the fortified city of

7 Wise, Abegg, Jr., and Cook, *The Dead Sea Scrolls*, Isa 51:9–10.

bondage. Similarly, unless you rebel against your Egypt, the taskmaster of sin, you will die as the devil's slave.

> 16 Do you not know that if you present yourselves to anyone as obedient slaves, you are slaves of the one whom you obey, either of sin, which leads to death, or of obedience, which leads to righteousness? (Rom 6:16, ESV)

Israel grew weary of obeying a master who ruled with hate. To earn their freedom, they needed to embrace the spirit of rebellion and cast off Egypt and her gods. Origen (185–254 A.D.) wrote extensively about Israel's Red Sea crossing. He likened Israel's flight out of Egypt to one's flight from sin. As he noted, fleeing "your Egypt" won't be easy.

> ***And, therefore, if you should depart from the Egyptians and flee the power of demons, see what great helps are prepared for you from heaven, see what great helpers you would enjoy.*** *This help is sufficient that you may remain strong in the faith, that the cavalry of the Egyptians and the fear of the four-horse chariots may not terrify you, that you may not cry out against Moses, the Law of God, and say as some of those said, "Were there not enough graves in Egypt? Have you thus brought us out that we might die in this wilderness? It were better for us to serve the Egyptians than to die in this wilderness." These are the words of a soul growing weak in temptation.*[8]
>
> ***If you flee Egypt, if you leave behind the darkness*** *of ignorance and follow Moses, the Law of God, should the sea hinder you and the waves of contradictions rush against you, strike the opposing waves with the rod of Moses, that is the word of the Law and by*

8 Origen, *Homilies on Genesis and Exodus*, 280–281.

> *vigilance in the Scriptures open a way for yourself by disputing with the adversaries. Immediately the waves will yield and the floods which surmounted will give place to the conquerors... For he who does not do "the works of darkness" destroys the Egyptian; he who lives not carnally but spiritually destroys the Egyptian; he who either casts out of his heart all sordid and impure thoughts or does not receive them at all destroys the Egyptian, as also the Apostle says, "Taking up the shield of faith that we may be able to extinguish all the fiery darts of the evil one." In this way, therefore, we can "see" even today "the Egyptians dead and lying on the shore," their four-horse chariots and cavalry drowned. We can even see Pharao himself drowned* ***if we live by such great faith that "God may quickly grind Satan under our feet" by Jesus Christ our Lord, "to whom belongs glory and sovereignty forever and ever. Amen.***[9]

As we will note next, you must flee into the water. There, you will gain your freedom.

BAPTIZED IN MOSES, BAPTIZED IN CHRIST

Israel's exodus from Egypt reached its climax at the water's edge. Trapped with nowhere to go, God did the unthinkable—He led His people through the heart of the Red Sea. Israel's deliverance "through water" is a typological picture of human salvation. Just like Israel, our tyrannical enemies will pursue us relentlessly to the bank of the sea. However, the sea is their undoing and our salvation. As we learned in chapter 3, the apostle Peter taught that the Noahic flood was a water template for baptism today (i.e., "eight souls saved by water," 1 Pet 3:18–22). Paul replicates Peter's pattern of using an Old Testament water template to assert his own teaching of spiritual deliverance.

---

9 Origen, *Homilies on Genesis and Exodus*, 284.

> [1] Now I do not want you to be unaware, brothers and sisters, that our ancestors were all under the cloud, **all passed through the sea**, 2 and **all were baptized into Moses in the cloud and in the sea**. (1 Cor 10:1–2, CSB)

What does Paul mean by, "all were baptized into Moses in the cloud and in the sea?" In Origen's *Exodum Homiliae*, he wrote,

> *What then are we taught by these words? We already mentioned above what the Apostle's understanding is in these matters.* ***He calls this "baptism in Moses consummated in the cloud and in the sea," that you also who are baptized in Christ, in water and the Holy Spirit****, might know that the Egyptians are following you and wish to recall you to their service. They are "****the rulers of this world****," of course, and "****the spiritual evils****" which you previously served.* ***These attempt to follow, but you descend into the water and come out unimpaired, the filth of sins having been washed away. You ascend "a new man" prepared to "sing a new song." But the Egyptians who follow you are drowned in the abyss*** *even if they appear to ask Jesus that he not send them into the abyss.*[10]

While Israel's baptism into Moses resulted in their physical deliverance, our baptism into Christ leads to our spiritual deliverance. Just as Moses led Israel, Christ Jesus leads us out of bondage, through saving water, to spiritual freedom.

In the fourth century, John Chrysostom likened baptism to the freedom the Israelites found in the Red Sea.

> *Now you shall see greater and much more brilliant [miracles] than those seen when the Jews went forth from Egypt.* ***You***

10 Origen, *Homilies on Genesis and Exodus*, 283–284.

> ***did not see the Pharaoh and his armies drowned, but you did see the drowning of the devil and his armies****. The Jews passed through the sea; you have passed through the sea of death. They were delivered from the Egyptians;* ***you are set free from the demon****. They put aside their servitude to barbarians; you have set aside the far more hazardous servitude to sin. (3.24)*[11]

With the Exodus story now in mind, notice Paul's language in Romans 6. He explains the process of how we escape the slavery of sin.

> 4 Therefore **we were buried with him by baptism** into death,
> in order that, just as Christ was raised from the dead by the
> glory of the Father, so we too may walk in newness of life. 5 For
> if we have been united with him in the likeness of his death, we
> will certainly also be in the likeness of his resurrection. 6 For we
> know that our old self was crucified with him **so that the body ruled by sin might be rendered powerless so that we may no longer be enslaved to sin**, (Rom 6:4–6, CSB)

No surprise, our freedom involves going through the waters of baptism, just as was the case when Israel gained their freedom. They were baptized into Moses; we are baptized into Christ. They gained physical freedom; we gain spiritual freedom. Both baptisms work by the power of God.

REJOICE: YOU ARE SAVED!

When the Israelites walked through the heart of the sea and were baptized into Moses, the enemy was finally defeated. It was an epic moment of jubilant celebration. They all sang what is called, "The Song of Moses."

---

11 Ferguson, *Baptism in the Early Church*, 549.

1 Then sang Moses and the children of Israel this song to
God, and spoke, saying, Let us sing to the Lord, for he is very
greatly glorified: horse and rider he has thrown into the sea.
2 He was to me a helper and protector for salvation: this is my
God, and I will glorify him; my father's God, and I will exalt him.
3 The Lord bringing wars to nought, the Lord is his name. **4 He**
has cast the chariots of Pharao and his host into the sea, the
chosen mounted captains: they were swallowed up in the Red
Sea. 5 He covered them with the sea: they sank to the deep like
a stone. 6 Thy right hand, O God, has been glorified in strength;
thy right hand, O God, has broken the enemies. 7 And in the
abundance of thy glory thou hast broken the adversaries to
pieces: thou sentest forth thy wrath, it devoured them as stubble.
8 And by the breath of thine anger the water parted asunder;
the waters were congealed as a wall, the waves were congealed
in the midst of the sea. 9 The enemy said, I will pursue, I will
overtake, I will divide the spoils; I will satisfy my soul, I will
destroy with my sword, my hand shall have dominion. 10 Thou
sentest forth thy wind, the sea covered them; they sank like
lead in the mighty water. 11 Who is like to thee among the gods,
O Lord? who is like to thee? glorified in holiness, marvellous
in glories, doing wonders. 12 Thou stretchedst forth thy right
hand, the earth swallowed them up. 13 Thou hast guided in thy
righteousness this thy people whom thou hast redeemed, by
thy strength thou hast called them into thy holy resting-place.
17 Bring them in and plant them in the mountain of their inheritance, in thy prepared habitation, which thou, O Lord, hast
prepared; the sanctuary, O Lord, which thine hands have made
ready. 18 The Lord reigns for ever and ever and ever. **19 For the**
horse of Pharao went in with the chariots and horsemen into
the sea, and the Lord brought upon them the water of the
sea, but the children of Israel walked through dry land in the

> **midst of the sea. [20] And Mariam the prophetess, the sister of Aaron, having taken a timbrel in her hand—then there went forth all the women after her with timbrels and dances. [21] And Mariam led them, saying, Let us sing to the Lord, for he has been very greatly glorified: the horse and rider has he cast into the sea.** (Exod 15:1–13, 17–21, Brenton LXX En)

The catchy lyric, "The horse and the rider, he has thrown into the sea," is pretty great. It rings with relief, and rightly so. Origen (185–254 A.D.) commented on this phrase and made an application about who the "riders" and "captains" are, who are in pursuit of our souls even now.

> *(2) "He cast forth horse and rider into the sea; he became my helper and protector in salvation." The men who pursue us are horses, and, so to speak, all who have been born in the flesh are figuratively horses. But these have their own riders. There are horses whom the Lord mounts and they go around all the earth, of whom it is said, "And your cavalry is salvation."* ***There are horses, however, who have the devil and his angels as riders.*** *Judas was a horse, but as long as he had the Lord as his rider he was part of the cavalry of salvation. Having been sent with the other apostles indeed, he gave health to the sick and wholeness to the weak. But when he surrendered himself to the devil—for "after the morsel, Satan entered him"—* ***Satan became his rider*** *and when he was guided by his reins he began to ride against our Lord and Savior. All, therefore, who persecute the saints are neighing horses, but* ***they have evil angels as riders by whom they are guided*** *and, therefore, are wild. If, then, you ever see your persecutor raging very much, know that he is being urged on by a demon as his rider and, therefore, is fierce and cruel.*
>
> *The Lord, therefore, "cast forth horse and rider into the sea and became my salvation..."The Lord who destroys wars, the*

> *Lord is his name." **I do not wish you to think that "the Lord destroys" only visible battles. He also "destroys" those battles which we have "not against flesh and blood, but against principalities and powers and against the rulers of the darkness of this world."** For "the Lord is his name" and there is no creature of which he is not Lord.*
>
> *...**Those "captains" therefore, are evil angels** from Pharao's army who stand in ways of this kind watching each of us to lead us into sin by these ways. **The Lord will drown these "captains" in the Red Sea** and deliver them to fiery turbulence on the day of judgment and cover them in the sea of punishments if you, following God, have removed yourself from their power.*[12]

Anyone who's ever been baptized into Christ knows firsthand the relief and excitement that follows. It's as breathtaking as when a newborn baby is born into the world. When a certain Ethiopian eunuch was born again of water and Spirit, of course he "rejoiced." Luke catalogued this very special moment between Philip, the evangelist, and the unnamed eunuch of Acts 8.

> [36] As they were traveling down the road, they came to some water. The eunuch said, "Look, there's **water**. What would keep me from being **baptized**?" [38] So he ordered the chariot to stop, and **both Philip and the eunuch went down into the water, and he baptized him.** [39] When they came up out of the water, the Spirit of the Lord carried Philip away, and the eunuch did not see him any longer but went on his way **rejoicing**. (Acts 8:36–39, CSB)

The book of Revelation paints a picture of all believers reenacting Israel's celebration after slaying the dragon of the sea. Together, the faithful

---

12 Origen, *Homilies on Genesis and Exodus*, 287–289.

hold the harps of God and sing the song of Moses and the Lamb, for we, too, have been delivered from the serpent through the heart of the saving sea.

> 2 I also saw something like a sea of glass mixed with fire, and those who had won the **victory over the beast**, its image, and the number of its name, were standing on the sea of glass **with harps from God**. 3 **They sang the song of God's servant Moses and the song of the Lamb**: Great and awe-inspiring are your works, Lord God, the Almighty; just and true are your ways, **King of the nations**. (Rev 15:2–3, CSB)

LOOKING AHEAD

As Israel's singing ceased, they gathered their belongings and slipped out of eyesight of Mount Baal-Zaphon. A brand-new beginning full of bright days was on the horizon for the young nation of Israel. But before they could officially move into their new home, Canaan, some ground rules would be etched in stone at the summit of another holy mountain, Mount Sinai. This ceremony would be so epochal, all the excellencies of heaven would be in attendance.

CHAPTER 9

HOLY, HOLY, HOLY

Then he said, "Yahweh came from Sinai, and he dawned upon them from Seir; he shone forth from Mount Paran, and he came with myriads of holy ones, at his right hand a fiery law for them." (Deuteronomy 33:2, LEB)

READING THE STORY

THE ISRAELITES WERE SINAI-BOUND. THERE, THEY would receive their Law that would govern them until the coming of Jesus Christ. But currently in our story, Israel had to trek through the parched desert full of fiery serpents and poisonous scorpions (Deut 8:15).

> Then Moses led Israel on from the Red Sea, and they went out to the Wilderness of Shur. They journeyed for three days in the wilderness without finding water. They came to Marah, but they could not drink the water at Marah because it was bitter—that is why it was named Marah. The people grumbled to Moses, "What are we going to drink?" So he cried out to the LORD, and the LORD showed him a tree. When he threw it into the water, the water became drinkable. The LORD made a statute and ordinance for them at Marah, and he tested them there. He said, "If you will carefully obey the LORD your God, do what is right in his sight, pay attention to his commands, and keep all his statutes, I will not inflict any illnesses on you that I inflicted on the Egyptians. For I am the LORD who heals you." Then they came to Elim, where there were twelve springs and seventy date palms, and they camped there by the water. The entire Israelite community departed from Elim and came to the Wilderness of Sin, which is between Elim and Sinai, on the fifteenth day of the second month after they had left the land of Egypt. (Exod 15:22–16:1, CSB)

The long, hot trip through the desert wore on their faith and patience. The people grumbled against Moses and Aaron, saying they had a better life back in Egypt because they had plenty of food to eat.

> And they tested God in their heart by asking food for their craving. And they spoke against God. They said, "Is

> God able to prepare a table in the wilderness? Yes, he struck the rock and water flowed and streams gushed out, but can he also give food or provide meat for his people?" Therefore Yahweh heard and he was very angry, and a fire was kindled against Jacob, and his anger also rose up against Israel, because they did not believe God, and they did not trust his salvation. (Ps 78:18–22, LEB)

> And at the moment of Aaron's speaking to all the community of the Israelites, they turned to the desert, and just then the glory of Yahweh appeared in the cloud. And Yahweh spoke to Moses, saying, "I have heard the grumblings of the Israelites. Speak to them, saying, 'At twilight you will eat meat, and in the morning you will be full with bread, and you will know that I am Yahweh your God.'" (Exod 16:10–12, LEB)

Just as was promised, God provided food for the hungry Israelites. It was the food of angels.

> "He gave a command to the clouds above and opened the doors of heaven. He rained manna for them to eat; he gave them grain from heaven. People ate the bread of angels. He sent them an abundant supply of food. He made the east wind blow in the skies and drove the south wind by his might. He rained meat on them like dust, and winged birds like the sand of the seas. He made them fall in the camp, all around the tents. The people ate and were completely satisfied, for he gave them what they craved. (Ps 78:23–29, CSB)

> The house of Israel named the substance manna. It resembled coriander seed, was white, and tasted like wafers made with honey. (Exod 16:31, CSB)

This wouldn't be the only time they ate manna. It would be the only thing on the menu for the next forty years (Exod 16:35). With full stomachs, they pressed on toward Sinai, the mountain of God. They stopped and camped at Dophkah, Alush, and Rephidim. Food was no longer a problem—it was water. They were thirsty again. The people despaired because there was no natural water source at Rephidim from which to drink.

> And the people quarreled with Moses, and they said, "Give us water so that we can drink." And Moses said to them, "Why do you quarrel with me? Why do you test Yahweh?" And the people thirsted for water, and the people grumbled against Moses and said, "Why ever did you bring us up from Egypt to kill me and my sons and my cattle with thirst?" And Moses cried out to Yahweh, saying, "What will I do with this people? A little longer and they will stone me." And Yahweh said to Moses, "Go on before the people and take with you some from the elders of Israel, and the staff with which you struck the Nile take in your hand, and go. Look, I will be standing before you there on the rock in Horeb, and you will strike the rock, and water will come out from it, and the people will drink." And Moses did so before the eyes of the elders of Israel. And he called the name of the place Massah and Meribah because of the quarrel of the Israelites and because of their testing Yahweh by saying, "Is Yahweh in our midst or not?" (Exod 17:2–7, LEB)

Suddenly, the Israelites came under attack by a group of aggressive seminomadic Amalekites (1 Sam 15:2), who struck down the stragglers of Israel's caravan from behind (Deut 25:17–18).

> Moses said to Joshua, "Select some men for us and go fight against Amalek. Tomorrow I will stand on the

> hilltop with God's staff in my hand." Joshua did as Moses had told him, and fought against Amalek, while Moses, Aaron, and Hur went up to the top of the hill. While Moses held up his hand, Israel prevailed, but whenever he put his hand down, Amalek prevailed. When Moses's hands grew heavy, they took a stone and put it under him, and he sat down on it. Then Aaron and Hur supported his hands, one on one side and one on the other so that his hands remained steady until the sun went down. So Joshua defeated Amalek and his army with the sword. (Exod 17:9–13, CSB)

Despite the unexpected ambush by the aggressive Amalekites, Israel survived the back-and-forth tussle. Was war a sign of things to come? Only time would tell. All they could do was mourn their dead and venture on toward Sinai.

Through faith and unbelief, through hunger and feasting, through drought and plenty, through war and peace, Israel finally arrived at the lofty landmark—Mount Sinai. The Israelites unpacked and settled in at the foot of the mountain while Moses climbed it to meet with God.

> "And Moses went up to the mount of God, and God called him out of the mountain, saying, These things shalt thou say to the house of Jacob, and thou shalt report them to the children of Israel. Ye have seen all that I have done to the Egyptians, and I took you up as upon eagles' wings, and I brought you near to myself. And now if ye will indeed hear my voice, and keep my covenant, ye shall be to me a peculiar people above all nations; for the whole earth is mine. And ye shall be to me a royal priesthood and a holy nation: these words shalt thou speak to the children of Israel. And Moses came and called the elders of the people, and he set before them all these words,

> which God appointed them. And all the people answered with one accord, and said, All things that God has spoken, we will do and hearken to: and Moses reported these words to God. (Exod 19:3–8, Brenton LXX En)

Up to this point, God has assumed their allegiance to Him as His allotted portion. Now, God seemingly gives them an option. If they were to stay as God's portion, they would have to do "all the things He commanded them." They quickly agreed. Yahweh chose them, and they chose Yahweh. The Lord then told Moses they would meet again in three days, including the people of Israel. There would be a special announcement from the Lord, and He wanted all Israel present to hear His voice. In the meantime, the people needed to cleanse themselves to approach God and His holy mountain (Exod 19:10–11).

> And on the third day, when it was morning, there was thunder and lightning, and a heavy cloud over the mountain and a very loud ram's horn sound, and all the people who were in the camp trembled. And Moses brought the people out from the camp to meet God, and they took their stand at the foot of the mountain. And Mount Sinai was all wrapped in smoke because Yahweh went down on it in the fire, and its smoke went up like the smoke of a smelting furnace, and the whole mountain trembled greatly. And the sound of the ram's horn became louder and louder, and Moses would speak, and God would answer him with a voice. And Yahweh went down on Mount Sinai, to the top of the mountain, and Yahweh called Moses to the top of the mountain, and Moses went up. And Yahweh said to Moses, "Go down, warn the people, lest they break through to Yahweh to see and many from them fall. And even the priests who come near Yahweh

must consecrate themselves, lest Yahweh break out against them." And Moses said to Yahweh, "The people are not able to go up to Mount Sinai, because you yourself warned us, saying, 'Set limits around the mountain and consecrate it.' " And Yahweh said to him, "Go, go down, and come up, you and Aaron with you and the priests, but the people must not break through to go up to Yahweh, lest he break out against them." And Moses went down to the people, and he told them. And God spoke all these words, saying, "I am Yahweh, your God, who brought you out from the land of Egypt, from the house of slaves. "There shall be for you no other gods before me. "You shall not make for yourself a divine image with any form that is in the heavens above or that is in the earth below or that is in the water below the earth. You will not bow down to them, and you will not serve them, because I am Yahweh your God, a jealous God, punishing the guilt of the parents on the children on the third and on the fourth generations of those hating me, and showing loyal love to thousands of generations of those loving me and of those keeping my commandments. "You shall not misuse the name of Yahweh your God, because Yahweh will not leave unpunished anyone who misuses his name. "Remember the day of the Sabbath, to consecrate it. Six days you will work, and you will do all your work. But the seventh day is a Sabbath for Yahweh your God; you will not do any work—you or your son or your daughter, your male slave or your female slave, or your animal, or your alien who is in your gates—because in six days Yahweh made the heavens and the earth, the sea and all that is in them, and on the seventh day he rested. Therefore Yahweh blessed the seventh day and consecrated it. "Honor your father and your mother, so that your days can be long on the land that Yahweh your God is giving you. "You shall not murder. "You

> shall not commit adultery. "You shall not steal. "You shall not testify against your neighbor with a false witness. "You shall not covet the house of your neighbor; you will not covet the wife of your neighbor or his male servant or his female servant or his ox or his donkey or anything that is your neighbor's." And all the people were seeing the thunder and the lightning and the sound of the ram's horn and the mountain smoking, and the people saw, and they trembled, and they stood at a distance. And they said to Moses, "You speak with us, and we will listen, but let not God speak with us, lest we die." And Moses said to the people, "Do not be afraid. God has come to test you so that his fear will be before you so that you do not sin." And the people stood at a distance, and Moses approached the very thick cloud where God was. And Yahweh said to Moses, "Thus you will say to the Israelites, 'You yourselves have seen that I have spoken to you from the heavens. (Exod 19:16–20:22, LEB)

Moses would climb the mountain a total of eight times to meet the Lord, and all His ascents were meaningful. He received two sets of written copies of the Ten Commandments (Exod 24:12; 34:1–4). He also received building specifications for constructing God's holy abode, the tabernacle of God. Additionally, Moses was given guidelines for the consecration of the tabernacle's ministers (the royal priesthood) and for their royal vestments (Exod 24:13–31:18). Each of these encounters with the Lord featured intense elements of nature (i.e., hard rain, lightning, earthquakes, etc.), apropos to His immense power, radiant magnificence, and par excellence over other gods (Ps 68:8).

Yahweh was not the only supernatural being at the great Sinai theophany. According to Moses, the holy mountain was filled with "holy angels" (***malākîm qôdeš***).

Deuteronomy 33:2–5 (CSB)	Deuteronomy 33:2–5 (Brenton LXX En)	Deuteronomy 33:2–5 (LEB)
[2] He said: **The LORD came from Sinai** and appeared to them from Seir; he shone on them from Mount Paran and came **with ten thousand holy ones**, with lightning from his right hand for them. [3] Indeed he loves the people. All your holy ones are in your hand, and they assemble at your feet. Each receives your words. [4] Moses gave us instruction, a possession for the assembly of Jacob. [5] So he became King in Jeshurun when the leaders of the people gathered with the tribes of Israel.	[2] And he said, **The Lord is come from Sina**, and has appeared from Seir to us, and has hasted out of the mount of Pharan, **with the ten thousands of Cades; on his right hand were his angels with him**. [3] And he spared his people, and all his sanctified ones are under thy hands; and they are under thee; and he received of his words [4] the law which Moses charged us, an inheritance to the assemblies of Jacob. [5] And he shall be prince with the beloved one, when the princes of the people are gathered together with the tribes of Israel.	[2] Then he said, "**Yahweh came from Sinai**, and he dawned upon them from Seir; he shone forth from Mount Paran, **and he came with myriads of holy ones, at his right hand a fiery law for them**. [3] Moreover, he loves his people, all the holy ones were in your hand, and they bowed down to your feet, each one accepted directions from you. [4] A law Moses instructed for us, as a possession for the assembly of Jacob. [5] And then a king arose in Jeshurun, at the gathering of the leaders of the people, united were the tribes of Israel.

Enoch appears to have foretold of this very event in the days of Noah. The apostle Jude also referenced Enoch's prophecy:

Jude 14–15 (ESV)	1 Enoch 1:9
14 It was also about these that **Enoch**, the seventh from Adam, **prophesied**, saying, "**Behold, the Lord comes with ten thousands of his holy ones,** 15 **to execute judgment on all and to convict all the ungodly of all their deeds of ungodliness…**	9. **And behold! He cometh with ten thousands of His holy ones To execute judgement upon all, And to destroy all the ungodly**:[1]

The New Testament writers reiterate Enoch's prophecy; God's holy angels were, in fact, on Mount Sinai. They weren't just there for moral support either—they played a pivotal role in this momentous and historic occasion. Their job was to deliver and declare the Law of Moses, thus rendering judgment by it upon all.

Galatians 3:19–20 (ESV)	Acts 7:38, 53 (ESV)	Hebrews 2:2 (ESV)
19 Why then the law? It was added because of transgressions, until the offspring should come to whom the promise had been made, **and it was put in place through angels** by an intermediary. 20 Now an intermediary implies more than one, but God is one.	38 This is the one who was in the congregation in the wilderness with **the angel who spoke to him at Mount Sinai**, and with our fathers. He received living oracles to give to us. 53 **you who received the law as delivered by angels and did not keep it**."	2 **For since the message declared by angels proved to be reliable**, and **every transgression or disobedience received a just retribution**,

1 Charles, *The Book of Enoch or 1 Enoch: Translation*, 7–8.

Josephus, the Jewish historian, also attested to the angels' role in delivering the holy Law of God.

> *...And for ourselves, we have learned from God the most excellent of our doctrines, and the most holy part of our law, by angels...*[2]

Before Moses's death on Mount Pisgah (Deut 34:1–7), he told a new generation of Israelites the story of how they came to possess the beloved commandments of God some forty years ago. He said to them,

> "When I went up the mountain to receive the stone tablets, the tablets of the covenant that Yahweh made with you, and remained on the mountain forty days and forty nights, I did not eat food and I did not drink water. And Yahweh gave me the two tablets of stone written with the finger of God, and on them was writing according to all the words that Yahweh spoke with you at the mountain, from the midst of the fire on the day of the assembly. And then at the end of forty days and forty nights, Yahweh gave me the two tablets of stone, the tablets of the covenant. And Yahweh said to me, 'Come now, go down quickly from this mountain because your people behave corruptly whom you brought out from Egypt, for they turned quickly from the way that I commanded them to follow; they have made for themselves a cast image.' And Yahweh spoke to me, saying, 'I have seen this people, and look! They are a stubborn people. Leave me alone, and let me destroy them, and let me blot out their name from under heaven, and let me make you into a nation mightier and more numerous than they!' "And I turned, and I went down the mountain, as the mountain was

2 Josephus, *The Works of Josephus*, 406.

> burning with fire, and the two tablets of the covenant were in my two hands. And I looked, and indeed you had sinned against Yahweh your God; you had made for yourselves an image of a calf of cast metal; you had turned quickly from the way that Yahweh had commanded for you. And I took hold of the two tablets, and I threw them out of my two hands and smashed them before your eyes. And then I lay prostrate before Yahweh, as earlier, forty days and forty nights; I did not eat food and I did not drink water because of all your sins that you committed, by doing evil in the eyes of Yahweh and so provoking him. For I was in dread from being in the presence of the anger and the wrath with which Yahweh was angry with you so as to destroy you, but Yahweh listened to me also at that time. And with Aaron Yahweh was angry enough to destroy him, and I prayed also for Aaron at that time. And your sinful thing that you had made, the molten calf, I took and I burned it with fire, and I crushed it, grinding it thoroughly until it was crushed to dust, and I threw its dust into the stream that flowed down the mountain. (Deut 9:9–21, LEB)

Since leaving Egypt, they had followed Moses through thick and thin, even being "baptized into Moses" and his leadership as they passed through the Red Sea. "The Law" became known as "the Law of Moses," largely due to his position as the mediator between man and God (Deut 5:5; Gal 3:19). He played that role pretty well, despite a handful of "hiccups" along the way.

CONNECTING THE GOSPEL

CHRIST & THE LAW

When the fullness of time had come, Jesus brought the Law of Moses to completion and read its last page, rendering "the end" of the Law of

Moses. This was by design. Many Jewish converts struggled to let go of the old Law. They often mixed and mingled it with "the faith" of Christ. This was a big mistake. Paul emphasized this to the church at Galatia in chapter three of his epistle.

> 10 For all who rely on the works of the law are under a curse,
> because it is written, Everyone who does not do everything
> written in the book of the law is cursed. 11 Now it is clear that
> no one is justified before God by the law, because the righteous
> will live by faith. 12 But the law is not based on faith; instead, the
> one who does these things will live by them. 13 Christ redeemed
> us from the curse of the law by becoming a curse for us, because
> it is written, Cursed is everyone who is hung on a tree. 14 The
> purpose was that the blessing of Abraham would come to the
> Gentiles by Christ Jesus, so that we could receive the promised
> Spirit through faith. (Gal 3:10–14, CSB)

If they continued to resurrect parts of Moses's law, they would be tethered to its curse and forfeit their spiritual life in Christ. Paul then illustrates that the Law of Moses simply acted as a "guardian" ***(παιδαγωγός, paidagōgŏs)*** to the children of Israel.

> *In classical times, a παιδαγωγός (paidagōgŏs) was a man, usually a slave, whose task it was to conduct a boy to and from school and to supervise and direct his general conduct. He was not a teacher.*[3]

This is precisely how Paul uses the word. Paul personifies the law as a slave who led the sons of Israel to Christ so that Christ could set

---

3 J. P. Louw and E. A. Nida, vol. 1 of *Greek-English Lexicon of the New Testament: Based on Semantic Domains*, 2nd ed. (New York: United Bible Societies, 1996), electronic edition, 465.

them free by redeeming them from the lord of the dead, cleansing them through baptism and adopting them as sons of God (Gal 4:5).

> [23] But before faith came, **we were detained** under the law, **imprisoned until the coming faith was revealed**. [24] So then, the law became our guardian (paidagōgŏs) until Christ, in order that we could be justified by faith. [25] But after faith has come, we are no longer under a guardian (paidagōgŏs). [26] For you are all sons of God through faith in Christ Jesus, [27] for as many of you as were baptized into Christ have put on Christ. [28] There is neither Jew nor Greek, there is neither slave nor free, there is neither male and female, for you are all one in Christ Jesus. [29] And if you are Christ's, then you are descendants of Abraham, heirs according to the promise. (Gal 3:23–29, LEB)

Simply put, the Law was a glorified babysitter for roughly 1,500 years, patiently waiting for the one to come who would bring it to completion. That someone was Jesus Christ.

ANSWERING YOUR QUESTIONS

DID CHRIST COME TO DESTROY THE LAW?

No. He came to fulfill it. Jesus addressed this question specifically.

> [17] Think not that I came to destroy the law or the prophets: I came not to destroy, but to fulfil. [18] For verily I say unto you, Till heaven and earth pass away, one jot or one tittle shall in no wise pass away from the law, till all things be accomplished. (Matt 5:17–18, ASV 1901)

He could say this because the entire Law of Moses pointed to one person—Jesus (Luke 24:27).

The whole point of the Law of Moses was for Christ to come and fulfill all of its promises (2 Cor 1:20). When He did that, He became "the end of the law for righteousness to everyone who believes" (Rom 10:4, ESV). This was the plan all along. We know this from explicit examples and statements.

First, consider the example of Moses when he descended from Sinai with the stone tablets in hand.

> [29] As Moses descended from Mount Sinai—with the two tablets
> of the testimony in his hands as he descended the mountain—
> he did not realize that the skin of his face shone as a result of his
> speaking with the Lord. [30] When Aaron and all the Israelites saw
> Moses, the skin of his face shone! They were afraid to come near
> him. [31] But Moses called out to them, so Aaron and all the leaders
> of the community returned to him, and Moses spoke to them.
> [32] Afterward all the Israelites came near, and he commanded
> them to do everything the Lord had told him on Mount Sinai.
> [33] When Moses had finished speaking with them, he put a veil
> over his face. 34 But whenever Moses went before the Lord to
> speak with him, he would remove the veil until he came out.
> After he came out, he would tell the Israelites what he had been
> commanded, 35 and the Israelites would see that Moses's face
> was radiant. Then Moses would put the veil over his face again
> until he went to speak with the Lord. (Exod 34:29–35, CSB)

This veil Moses put over his face is significant. It wasn't just to spare the people from fear. The apostle Paul notes it was to spare them, at least in that moment, from realizing the glorious Law of Moses they were receiving was going to vanish away. Moses's fading face was representative of Moses's fading Law.

> [1] Are we beginning to commend ourselves again? Or do we need,
> like some, letters of recommendation to you or from you? [2] You

> yourselves are our letter, written on our hearts, known and read by everyone. 3 You show that you are Christ's letter, delivered by us, not written with ink but with the Spirit of the living God—not on tablets of stone but on tablets of human hearts. 4 Such is the confidence we have through Christ before God. 5 It is not that we are competent in ourselves to claim anything as coming from ourselves, but our adequacy is from God. 6 He has made us competent to be ministers of a new covenant, not of the letter, but of the Spirit. For the letter kills, but the Spirit gives life. 7 Now if the ministry that brought death, chiseled in letters on stones, came with glory, so that the Israelites were not able to gaze steadily at Moses's face because of its glory, which was set aside, 8 how will the ministry of the Spirit not be more glorious? 9 For if the ministry that brought condemnation had glory, the ministry that brings righteousness overflows with even more glory. 10 In fact, what had been glorious is not glorious now by comparison because of the glory that surpasses it. 11 For if what was set aside was glorious, what endures will be even more glorious. 12 Since, then, we have such a hope, we act with great boldness. 13 We are not like Moses, who used to put a veil over his face to prevent the Israelites from gazing steadily until the end of the glory of what was being set aside, (2 Cor 3:1–13, CSB)

Second, consider this: We learn the Law was temporary because the Law itself claimed it was (Jer 31:31–34). The Hebrews writer quotes from Jeremiah 31:31–34 as he teaches about the superiority of Christ and His New Testament:

> 8 But finding fault with his people, he says: See, the days are coming, says the Lord, when **I will make a new covenant** with the house of Israel and with the house of Judah— 9 not like the covenant that I made with their ancestors on the day I took them

> by the hand to lead them out of the land of Egypt. I showed no
> concern for them, says the Lord, because they did not continue
> in my covenant. 10 **For this is the covenant that I will make**
> with the house of Israel after those days, says the Lord: I will
> put my laws into their minds and write them on their hearts.
> I will be their God, and they will be my people. 11 And each
> person will not teach his fellow citizen, and each his brother
> or sister, saying, "Know the Lord," because they will all know
> me, from the least to the greatest of them. 12 For I will forgive
> their wrongdoing, and I will never again remember their sins.
> 13 **By saying a new covenant, he has declared that the first is**
> **obsolete. And what is obsolete and growing old is about to**
> **pass away**. (Heb 8:8–13, CSB)

WHEN WAS THE LAW OF MOSES FULFILLED?

Jesus fulfilled the Old Law and rendered it obsolete upon His death on the cross; simultaneously, He established the new covenant by His blood, as the writer of Hebrews notes.

> 11 But Christ has arrived as a high priest of the good things to
> come. Through the greater and more perfect tent not made by
> hands, that is, not of this creation, 12 and not by the blood of
> goats and calves, but by his own blood, he entered once for all
> into the most holy place, obtaining eternal redemption. 13 For
> if the blood of goats and bulls and the ashes of a young cow
> sprinkled on those who are defiled sanctify them for the ritual
> purity of the flesh, 14 how much more will the blood of Christ,
> who through the eternal Spirit offered himself without blemish
> to God, cleanse our consciences from dead works to serve the
> living God? 15 And because of this, **he is the mediator of a new**
> **covenant**, in order that, **because a death has taken place** for

> the redemption of transgressions committed during the first
> covenant, those who are the called may receive the promise
> of the eternal inheritance. 16 **For where there is a will, it is**
> **a necessity for the death of the one who made the will to**
> **be established**. 17 For a will is in force concerning those who
> are dead, since it is never in force when the one who made
> the will is alive. 18 **Therefore not even the first covenant was**
> **ratified without blood**. 19 For when every commandment
> had been spoken by Moses to all the people according to the
> law, he took the blood of calves with water and scarlet wool
> and hyssop and sprinkled both the scroll itself and all the
> people, 20 saying, "This is the blood of the covenant that God
> has commanded for you." 21 And likewise he sprinkled both
> the tabernacle and all the utensils of service with the blood.
> 22 Indeed, nearly everything is purified with blood according
> to the law, and apart from the shedding of blood there is no
> forgiveness. (Heb 9:11–22, LEB)

ARE CHRISTIANS UNDER ANY LAW?

Yes—we are under the freeing law of grace. Let me explain. Consider what Paul wrote to the church at Rome.

> 14 For sin will have no dominion over you, since you are not
> under law but under grace. (Rom 6:14, ESV)

The law Paul referenced was the Law of Moses. He contrasts Moses's rigid Law with grace. Grace is such a beautiful thing in the eyes of believers. We stare into the eyes of God as wretched sinners who smell of putrid filth and shame. But what we find there is what Noah found—a glimmer of grace in God's loving eyes. I assure you; you won't be going to heaven on merit or moral perfection. You'll enter in on the coattails of Jesus' saving grace because you've been redeemed by His saving blood.

> [21] But now, apart from the law, the righteousness of God has been revealed, attested by the Law and the Prophets. 22 The righteousness of God is through faith in Jesus Christ to all who believe, since there is no distinction. 23 For all have sinned and fall short of the glory of God; 24 they are justified freely by his grace through the redemption that is in Christ Jesus. 25 God presented him as the mercy seat by his blood, through faith, to demonstrate his righteousness, because in his restraint God passed over the sins previously committed. (Rom 3:21–25, CSB)

All of us need "grace upon grace" (John 1:16), "his multiplied grace" (2 Pet 1:2). And this isn't only something we receive at baptism—it's ongoing. Every day, we need new measures of His grace for our new moments of guilt. But if grace teaches us anything (Titus 2:11–15), it's not to multiply our sin so we can maximize His grace; it's quite the opposite. Paul writes,

> [1] What should we say then? **Should we continue in sin so that grace may multiply**? [2] **Absolutely not**! How can we who died to sin still live in it? [3] Or are you unaware that all of us who were baptized into Christ Jesus were baptized into his death? [4] Therefore we were buried with him by baptism into death, in order that, just as Christ was raised from the dead by the glory of the Father, so we too may walk in newness of life. (Rom 6:1–4, CSB)

As born-again sons of God, our daily walk should be with Christ, not with Satan. It should be in light, not in darkness.

> 5 This is the message we have heard from him and declare to
> you: **God is light**, and there is absolutely **no darkness in him**.
> 6 If we say, "We have fellowship with him," **and yet we walk
> in darkness**, we are lying and are not practicing the truth.
> 7 **If we walk in the light** as he himself is in the light, we have
> fellowship with one another, and the blood of Jesus his Son
> cleanses us from all sin. 8 If we say, "We have no sin," we are
> deceiving ourselves, and the truth is not in us. 9 If we confess
> our sins, he is faithful and righteous to forgive us our sins and
> to cleanse us from all unrighteousness. 10 If we say, "We have
> not sinned," we make him a liar, and his word is not in us.
> (1 John 1:5–10, CSB)

Grace demands that we walk by the Spirit so as not to seek the satisfaction of the flesh (Gal 5:16). To do that, God has given us resources. We've already discovered one of them—the gift of His Spirit into our hearts (Gal 4:6). But He's also given us the sword of the Spirit, the written Word of God (Eph 6:17).

"Are we under any law?"

The answer is yes, we are. Imperfect Christians are to live righteously and walk gracefully in the perfect law of liberty, the New Testament of Jesus Christ. In other words, what's written in your New Testament is your law, and thankfully, it's a law of multiplied grace.

> 19 My dear brothers and sisters, understand this: Everyone should
> be quick to listen, slow to speak, and slow to anger, 20 for human
> anger does not accomplish God's righteousness. 21 Therefore,
> ridding yourselves of all moral filth and the evil that is so
> prevalent, humbly receive the implanted word, which is able
> to save your souls. 22 But be doers of the word and not hearers
> only, deceiving yourselves. 23 Because if anyone is a hearer of the
> word and not a doer, he is like someone looking at his own face

> in a mirror. [24] For he looks at himself, goes away, and immediately forgets what kind of person he was. [25] But the one who looks intently into the perfect law of freedom and perseveres in it, and is not a forgetful hearer but a doer who works—this person will be blessed in what he does. (Jas 1:19–25, CSB)

LOOKING AHEAD

Israel was Yahweh's pride and joy. His presentation of the Law at Sinai with myriads of angels was a huge testament to how much He loved His chosen people. Israel would spend the next year camped at Sinai as they built the portable tabernacle to His exact specifications (Exod 36:8–39:43). When completed, this would allow them to have a transportable place to atone for the sins of the people no matter where in the world they were. As you'll discover in the next chapter, God would set up the royal priesthood from the line of Aaron, Moses's brother. But what followed would provide an unforgettable lesson on sanctification, and it's all in the context of a jaw-dropping link back to Genesis 6, to the fallen angel who's under lock and key in the desert of Dûdâêl.

CHAPTER 10

AZAZEL, THE ROYAL PRIESTHOOD, AND ONE REALLY GUILTY GOAT

And Aaron shall cast lots over the two goats, one lot for the LORD and the other lot for Azazel. (Leviticus 16:8, ESV)

READING THE STORY

SINCE THEIR ARRIVAL TO THE HOLY mountain about a year ago, Israel has experienced the power of God, encountered the supernatural, and agreed to keep the whole Law. They were nearly ready to march and take the land of promise, but there were a few loose ends that needed to be tied up first.

> "In the first month of the second year, on the first of the month, the tabernacle was set up. And Moses raised the tabernacle, and he placed its bases, and he set up its frames, and he placed its bars, and he raised its pillars. And he spread the tent over the tabernacle; he placed the covering of the tent over it, above it, as Yahweh had commanded Moses. And he took and he put the testimony into the ark, and he placed the poles on the ark, and he put the atonement cover on the ark, above it. And he brought the ark into the tabernacle, and he set up the curtain of the screening, and he shielded the ark of the testimony, as Yahweh had commanded Moses. And he put the table in the tent of assembly on the north side of the tabernacle outside the curtain. And he arranged on it an arrangement of bread before Yahweh, as Yahweh had commanded Moses. And he placed the lampstand in the tent of assembly opposite the table on the south side of the tabernacle. And he set up the lamps before Yahweh, as Yahweh had commanded Moses. And he placed the gold altar in the tent of assembly before the curtain. And he turned fragrant incense into smoke on it, as Yahweh had commanded Moses. And he set up the entrance screen for the tabernacle. And the altar of burnt offering he placed at the entrance of the tabernacle of the tent of assembly, and he offered on it the burnt offering and the grain offering, as Yahweh had commanded Moses. And he placed the basin between the tent of assembly and the altar, and he put there water for washing. And Moses and Aaron and

> his sons washed their hands and their feet from it. At their going into the tent of assembly and at their approaching the altar, they washed, as Yahweh had commanded Moses. And he set up the courtyard all around the tabernacle and the altar, and he put up the screen of the gate of the courtyard, and Moses completed the work. (Exod 40:17–33, LEB)

Israel's hard work had finally paid off. They stood back and looked on with a sense of accomplishment and awe as the glory of the Lord descended and filled the tabernacle they had built (Exod 40:34–35). As they held their breath in anticipation, the voice of God suddenly crescendoed from the tent of meeting (Lev 1:1).

> The LORD spoke to Moses: "Take Aaron, his sons with him, the garments, the anointing oil, the bull of the sin offering, the two rams, and the basket of unleavened bread, and assemble the whole community at the entrance to the tent of meeting." (Lev 8:1–3, CSB)

Moses understood—his brother Aaron and his nephews were about to be ordained and initiated as the first class of the Levitical priesthood of God.

> So Moses did just as Yahweh commanded him, and the community gathered by the entrance to the tent of assembly. Then Moses said to the community, "This is the word that Yahweh has commanded to be done." So Moses brought Aaron and his sons near, and he washed them with water. Then he put the tunic on him and tied the sash around him; then he clothed him with the robe and put the ephod on him; then he tied the ephod's waistband around him and fastened the ephod to him with it. Then he placed the breastpiece on him

and put the Urim and the Thummim into the breastpiece; and he placed the turban on his head, and on the front of the turban he placed the gold rosette, the holy diadem, just as Yahweh had commanded Moses. Then Moses took the anointing oil and anointed the tabernacle and all that was in it, and he consecrated them. And he spattered part of it on the altar seven times—thus he anointed the altar and all of its utensils, and the basin and its stand, to consecrate them. Then he poured out part of the anointing oil on Aaron's head—thus he anointed him in order to consecrate him. Then Moses brought Aaron's sons near and clothed them with tunics and tied a sash around each one, and he bound headbands on them, just as Yahweh had commanded Moses. Then he brought forth the bull of the sin offering, and Aaron and his sons placed their hands on the head of the bull of the sin offering, and he slaughtered it, and Moses took the blood and put it with his finger on the altar's horns all around and purified the altar; then he poured the blood out on the altar's base—thus he consecrated it in order to make atonement for it. Then he took all the fat that was on the inner parts and the lobe on the liver and the two kidneys and their fat, and Moses turned them into smoke on the altar, but he burned the bull and its skin and its meat and its offal in the fire outside the camp, just as Yahweh had commanded Moses. Then he brought the ram of the burnt offering near, and Aaron and his sons placed their hands on the ram's head, and he slaughtered it. Then Moses sprinkled the blood on the altar all around. Then he cut the ram into pieces, and Moses turned into smoke the head and the pieces and the suet, but he washed the inner parts and the lower leg bones with water, and Moses turned into smoke all of the ram on the altar; it was a burnt offering as an appeasing fragrance, an offering made by fire for Yahweh, just as Yahweh had commanded Moses. Then he brought the second ram near, the ram of the consecration, and Aaron and his sons placed their hands on the ram's head, and he slaughtered it. Then Moses took some of its blood and put it on Aaron's right ear lobe and on his right hand's thumb and on his right foot's big toe. Then he brought Aaron's sons near, and Moses put some of the blood on their right ear lobe and on their right hand's thumb and on their right foot's big toe, and Moses sprinkled the blood on the altar all around. Then he took the fat and the fat tail and all of the fat that was on the inner parts and the lobe of the liver and the two kidneys and their fat and the right upper thigh; and from the basket of the unleavened bread that was before Yahweh he took one ring-shaped unleavened bread and one ring-shaped bread with oil and one wafer, and he placed them on the fat parts and on the right upper thigh. Then he put all of these on Aaron's palms and on his sons' palms, and he waved them as a wave offering before Yahweh. Then Moses took them from upon their palms, and he turned them into smoke upon the burnt offering on the altar; they were a consecration offering as an appeasing fragrance—it was an offering made by fire for Yahweh. Then Moses took the breast section, and he waved it as a wave offering before Yahweh from the ram of the consecration offering; it was Moses' share, just as Yahweh had commanded Moses. Then Moses took some of the anointing oil and some of the blood that was on the altar, and he spattered them on Aaron, on his garments, and on Aaron's sons and on his sons' garments with him—thus he consecrated Aaron, his garments, and his sons and his sons' garments with him. Then Moses said to Aaron and to his sons, "Boil the meat in the entrance to the tent of assembly, and there you must eat it and the bread that is in the basket of the consecration offering, just as I have commanded, saying, 'Aaron and his sons must eat it,' but the remainder of the meat and the bread you must burn in

> the fire. And you must not go out from the entrance to the tent of assembly for seven days, until the day of fulfilling the days of your consecration, because it will take seven days to ordain you. Just as was done on this day, Yahweh commanded to be done in order to make atonement for you. And you must stay at the entrance to the tent of assembly day and night for seven days, and you shall keep the obligation from Yahweh, so you might not die, for thus I have been commanded." (Lev 8:4–35, LEB)

Do this or you will die?! The gravity of their priestly duties couldn't be overstated. God made it crystal clear that any deviation, whatsoever, from His specific instructions would be deadly. As the story reads, Aaron and his sons did everything the Lord had commanded (Lev 8:36). After the seven days of isolated sanctification, Moses called Aaron, his sons, and the elders of Israel.

> "and he said to Aaron, "Take for yourself a bull calf as a sin offering and a ram as a burnt offering, without defect, and present them before Yahweh. Then you must speak to the Israelites, saying, 'Take a he-goat as a sin offering and a bull calf and a male sheep, yearlings without defect, as a burnt offering, and an ox and a ram as fellowship offerings to sacrifice before Yahweh, and a grain offering mixed with oil, because today Yahweh will appear to you." So they took what Moses had commanded to the front of the tent of assembly, and the whole community presented themselves, and they stood before Yahweh. Then Moses said, "This is the word that Yahweh commanded you to do so that the glory of Yahweh might appear to you." Then Moses said to Aaron, "Approach the altar and sacrifice your sin offering and your burnt offering, and make atonement for yourself and for the people. And sacrifice the people's offering and make atonement for them, just as

Yahweh has commanded." Then Aaron approached the altar, and he slaughtered the bull calf of the sin offering, which was for himself. Then Aaron's sons presented the blood to him, and he dipped his finger in the blood, and he put it on the altar's horns, and he poured out the blood on the altar's base. And the fat and the kidneys and the lobe from the sin offering's liver he turned into smoke on the altar, just as Yahweh had commanded Moses, but the meat and the skin he burned with fire outside the camp. Then he slaughtered the burnt offering, and Aaron's sons brought the blood to him, and he sprinkled it on the altar all around; and they brought the burnt offering to him by its pieces, as well as the head, and he turned them into smoke on the altar; and he washed the inner parts and the lower leg bones, then he turned them into smoke upon the burnt offering on the altar. Then he presented the people's offering, and he took the goat of the sin offering, which was for the people, and he slaughtered it and offered it as a sin offering like the first one. Then he presented the burnt offering, and he sacrificed it according to the regulation. Then he presented the grain offering, and he filled his palm with some of it, and he turned it into smoke on the altar besides the morning's burnt offering. Then he slaughtered the ox and the ram, the fellowship offerings that are for the people, and Aaron's sons brought the blood to him, and he sprinkled it on the altar all around. And as for the fat portions from the ox and from the ram (the fat tail and the layer of fat and the kidneys and the lobe of the liver), they placed the fat portions on the breast sections, and he turned the fat portions into smoke on the altar. Then Aaron waved the breast sections and the right upper thigh as a wave offering before Yahweh, just as Moses had commanded. Then Aaron lifted his hand toward the people, and he blessed them, and he came down after sacrificing the sin offering and the burnt offering and the fellowship

> offerings. Then Moses and Aaron entered the tent of assembly. When they came out, they blessed the people, and Yahweh's glory appeared to all the people. Then a fire went out from before Yahweh, and it consumed the burnt offering and the fat portions on the altar. And all the people saw it, so they shouted for joy, and they fell on their faces. **And Aaron's sons Nadab and Abihu** each took his censer, and they put fire in them and placed incense on it; then they **presented before Yahweh illegitimate fire, which he had not commanded them.** So fire went out from before Yahweh, and it consumed them so that they died before Yahweh. Therefore Moses said to Aaron, "This is what Yahweh spoke, saying, 'Among those who are close to me I will show myself holy, and in the presence of all the people I will display my glory.'" So Aaron was silent. (Lev 9:2–10:3, LEB)

The death of Nadab and Abihu was a big blow to the newly-ordained priesthood—that much is clear. However, it was especially heart-wrenching for Aaron. Can you imagine? He went from teeming with pride in the newfound family business to walking through the valley of the shadow of death twice.

Was God overly severe? No. God had been super specific every step of the way. As priests, they were to sanctify God by distinguishing between holy and common, clean and unclean (Lev 10:10). They did quite the opposite. They, in essence, spit in the face of the holiness of God in front of all of Israel. What Moses said to his brother Aaron is key in understanding why Yahweh lowered the hammer of destruction on the two clergymen, Nadab and Abihu. Echoing the Lord's words, Moses reminded his grieving brother what God had said: "Among those who are near me I will be sanctified" (Lev 10:3, ESV).

Yahweh is inviolable and set apart as sacred among His people. For Nadab and Abihu to commit such a flagrant foul by offering unauthorized fire before the Lord was unthinkable. Their negligence was an act of rebellion and put them in the same category as Nimrod, Pharaoh, and the fallen angels.

There is, however, a more grotesque lesson to be learned about sanctification, and it comes from a special ritual in the Jewish calendar—the Day of Atonement.

> Then Yahweh spoke to Moses after the death of Aaron's two sons, when they had come near before Yahweh and they died. And Yahweh said to Moses, "Tell your brother Aaron that he should not enter at any time into the sanctuary behind the curtain in front of the atonement cover that is on the ark, so that he might not die, because I appear in the cloud over the atonement cover. "Aaron must enter the sanctuary with this: a young bull as a sin offering and a ram as a burnt offering. He must put on a holy linen tunic, and linen undergarments must be on his body, and he must fasten himself with a linen sash, and he must wrap a linen turban around his head—they are holy garments, and he shall wash his body with water, then he shall put them on. And he must take from the Israelites' community two he-goats as a sin offering and one ram as a burnt offering. "And Aaron shall present the sin offering's bull, which is for himself, and so he shall make atonement for himself and for his family. (Lev 16:1–6, LEB)

Notice that after Aaron is to make atonement for his own sin and the sin of his family, Yahweh articulates a very strange command—send a goat to Azazel.

> And he shall take the two goats, and he shall present them before Yahweh at the tent of assembly's entrance. Then Aaron shall cast lots for the two goats: **one lot for Yahweh and one for Azazel**. And Aaron shall present the goat on which the

> lot for Yahweh fell, and he shall sacrifice it as a sin offering. But he must present alive before Yahweh the goat on which the lot for Azazel fell to make atonement for himself, **to send it away into the desert to Azazel**. (Lev 16:7–10, LEB)

This head-scratching revelation begs three questions: Who is Azazel? Why is he in the desert? And why does he get a goat?

There's no other text in the sixty-six books of your Bible that sheds any light on Azazel's identity. However, Moses and Aaron knew exactly who he was and why he was in the desert. Azazel was the ringleader of the angels who sinned with women in Genesis 6:1–4. This is precisely how he's described in *4Q180 Frag. 1:7–10* of the Dead Sea Scrolls.

> *7The prophetic interpretation concerning Azazel and the angels wh[o went in to the daughters of man,] 8[so that] they bore mighty men to them. And concerning Azazel [who taught them] 9[to love] iniquity and to pass on wickedness as an inheritance, all [...] 10[...] judgments, and the judgment of the council of [...]*[1]

This is also how he's described in the book of 1 Enoch (8:1; 9:6; 10:4–8; 13:1; 54:5–6; 55:4; 69:2). Azazel became enamored with this world and its many beautiful women. Interestingly enough, a Midrashic document written in 79–81 A.D. titled *The Apocalypse of Abraham* has Azazel being scolded by one of Yahweh's holy angels for his lewd, lascivious behavior.

> *"What is this, my lord?" And he said, "This is disgrace, this is Azazel!" 7 And he said to him, "Shame on you, Azazel! For Abraham's portion is in heaven, and yours is on earth, 8 for you have selected here, (and) become enamored of the dwelling place*

---

1 Wise, Abegg, Jr., and Cook, *The Dead Sea Scrolls*, 269.

> *of your blemish. Therefore the Eternal Ruler, the Mighty One, has given you a dwelling on earth. 9 Through you the all-evil spirit (is) a liar, and through you (are) wrath and trials on the generations of men who live impiously. (Apoc. Abraham 13.6-9)*[2]

If you recall from our chapter 3 journey into the prediluvian world of Enoch and Noah, the angel Azazel was punished for his Genesis 6 debacle by being bound and buried—you guessed it—in the desert.

> 4. And again the Lord said to Raphael: '**Bind Azâzêl hand and foot, and cast him into the darkness: and make an opening in the desert, which is in Dûdâêl, and cast him therein.** 5. And place upon him rough and jagged rocks, and cover him with darkness, and let him abide there for ever, and cover his face that he may not see light. 6. And on the day of the great judgement he shall be cast into the fire." (1 Enoch 10:4–6)[3]

Azazel symbolized the totality of sin and evil, and so did the desert. It was the perfect symbol of transporting the people's sin outside of God's holy camp, where sin belonged, and transferring it upon the one to whom sin belonged—on one of the key sinister angelic leaders of Satan's camp, Azazel.

Further down in Leviticus 16, Yahweh commands Aaron, the high priest, to place all guilt on the head of Azazel's goat and to send the guilty goat into the detestable desert.

> "And Aaron shall place his two hands on the living goat's head, and he shall confess over it all the Israelites' iniquities and all their transgressions for all their sins, and **he**

---

2 Charlesworth, *The Old Testament Pseudepigrapha*, 695.

3 Charles, *The Book of Enoch or 1 Enoch: Translation*, 22–25.

> **shall put them on the goat's head, and he shall send it away into the desert** with a man standing ready. **Thus the goat shall bear on it to a barren region all their guilt, and he shall send the goat away into the desert.** (Lev 16:21–22, LEB)

The Day of Atonement's inclusion of Azazel's goat was an annual lesson of contrast. While the Lord was sanctified for holiness and glory, Azazel and his rebel god cronies are set apart for guilt and punishment, destined to live eternally in the barren, hot, xerothermic pit of hell.

ANSWERING YOUR QUESTIONS

WHY DOES MY BIBLE SAY "SCAPEGOAT?"

Some translations (KJV, NKJV, NIV, NASB) omit the literal Hebrew word ʿăzāʾzēl and translate it as "scapegoat," while others simply carry over ʿăzāʾzēl as "Azazel" (ESV, ASV, NRSV, NLT, LEB, RSV). Heiser wrote about this subject,

> *The word "Azazel" in the Hebrew text can be translated "the goat that goes away."... The scapegoat, so the translator has it, symbolically carries the sins of the people away from the camp of Israel into the wilderness. Seems simple enough. However, "Azazel" is really a proper name. In Lev 16:8 one goat is "for Yahweh," while the other goat is "for Azazel." Since Yahweh is a proper name and the goats are described in the same way, Hebrew parallelism informs us that Azazel is also a proper name.*[4]

The Bible Background Commentary agrees with Heiser's conclusion, stating,

4 Heiser, *The Unseen Realm*, 176.

> *Since verse 8 identifies one goat as "for Yahweh" and the other goat as "for Azazel," it is most consistent to consider Azazel a proper name, probably of a demon. Early Jewish interpreters had this understanding, as is demonstrated in the book of Enoch...This goat is not sacrificed to Azazel (consistent with 17:7) but released "to Azazel" (v. 26).*[5]

This is further evidenced in Leviticus 16:26.

> 26 And he who lets the **goat go to Azazel** shall wash his clothes and bathe his body in water, and afterward he may come into the camp. (Lev 16:26, ESV)

Recovering the idea that Azazel is a supernatural being restores a very important and interesting link back to the angelic rebellion of Genesis 6. This is a prime example of an instance where many modern translations simply miss the boat.

WHAT DID "SENDING" AZAZEL'S GOAT INTO THE DESERT ENTAIL?

While the Bible gives no further details or descriptions about how the "guilty goat" was released into the desert, the Dead Sea Scrolls and Jewish oral tradition does. The Dead Sea Scroll *11Q19 Col. xxvi:3–13* notes the high priests' preparation of the guilty goat and an appointed "prepared man" who would lead the goat to Azazel.

> *Then] the [high pri]est [shall cast lots for] 4[the two goats,] o[ne] lot [designated "The LORD" and the other "Azazel."] 5He*

5 V. H. Matthews, M. W. Chavalas, and J. H. Walton, *The IVP Bible Background Commentary: Old Testament* (Downers Grove, IL: InterVarsity Press, 2000), electronic edition, Lev 16:8.

> *is to slaughter the goat [upon whom] fall[s the lot designated "The LORD," and receive] 6its blood in the golden bowl that he ho[lds...Then he shall wash the blood of the sin offering from his hands and feet and approach 11the living goat. He is to confess over its head all the iniquities of the children of Israel, as well as 12all their guilt and sins, thus putting them upon the goat's head. Then he shall send him away 13to Azazel in the wilderness led by a man prepared for the moment. The goat shall carry away all the iniquities*[6]

Yoma 6 of the Mishnah describes the goat's journey eastward, from Jerusalem to a ravine in the Judean Desert known as Beth Hadudo or [Ha] Duduael, the same place Azazel—a leader of the fallen angels—was held prisoner under jagged rocks. Since it was a long and hot journey, the priest who led the goat stopped at ten stations/booths (tents) to offer it food and water.

> *AT EACH BOOTH THEY SAY TO HIM, "LO, HERE IS FOOD, HERE IS WATER."*[7]

After the goat was taken to the tenth and final booth, it was led to the ravine at Duduael. The priest then divided a crimson thread.

> *Half of it he tied to a rock, and half of it he tied between its horns. He then pushed it over backward, and it rolled down the ravine. And it did not reach halfway down the mountain before it broke into pieces.*[8]

---

6 Wise, Abegg, Jr., and Cook, *The Dead Sea Scrolls*, 605.

7 J. Neusner, ed., *The Jerusalem Talmud: A Translation and Commentary* (Peabody, Massachusetts: Hendrickson Publishers, 2008), *Yoma 6:4*.

8 Neusner, *The Jerusalem Talmud*, Yoma 6:4, III.1.

Killing the goat of Azazel was a methodical and meticulous process. This is a testament to just how seriously the Israelites took this ritual. Ultimately, it all concluded with the violent death of Azazel's goat. Its tumble down the precipice, being broken into pieces by sharp rocks, was a reflection of the "violence" Azazel introduced to humanity before the flood and was a continual reminder of Azazel's past, present, and future punishment as a "goat-demon" of the desert (Lev 17:7).

OTHER PRIESTHOODS?

The Levitical priesthood was not the first. It was preceded by Melchizedek's priesthood. Still yet, there were many more priesthoods in the biblical world than priesthoods centered around Yahweh. I was taken aback when I first read many of the ancient religious texts from Gentile nations. While the Bible alludes to paganistic priesthoods, it was surreal to read their "sacred" texts and was unsettling to my modern ears.

While there are hundreds of texts to explore, I've provided a small sampling of them. First, notice this prayer from a coronation ritual during the reign of Assyrian King Tukulti-Ninurta I (reigned from 1244–1208 B.C.).

> *A PRAYER FROM A CORONATION RITUAL OF THE TIME OF TUKULTI-NINURTA I (1.140)*
>
> *(1) May Assur and Ninlil, the lords of your crown, set your crown on your head for a hundred years!*
>
> *(3) May your foot in Ekur and your hands stretched toward the breast of Assur, your god, be agreeable!*
>
> *(4) May your priesthood and the priesthood of your sons be agreeable to Assur, your god! With your straight scepter widen your land! May Assur give you authority, obedience, concord, justice and peace!*[9]

9 W. W. Hallo and K. L. Younger, *The Context of Scripture* (Leiden; New York: Brill, 1997), 471.

Another tablet of great interest is from Lagaš and dates back to 2025 B.C. It was carved in stone as a form of marital recordkeeping. In line 12, it reads that Puzur-Haya married Ubartum in the year that "En-amgalana, the high-priest of Inanna, was installed."

> *THE MARRIAGE OF PUZUR-HAYA AND UBARTUM (3.135B)*
>
> *This tablet and its envelope originate from Lagaš and date to the Ur III period (4th year of Ibbi-Sin, ca. 2025 BCE).*
>
> *(lines 1–4)*
>
> *Puzur-Haya took Ubartum as his wife.*
>
> *(lines 5–11)*
>
> *Before Ur-Damu, son of Ur-meme, (before) Ur-Dumuzi, (before) Bulali, (and before) Alduga, son of Ur-Dumuzi, the witnesses, before them, the oath by the name of the king was sworn.*
>
> *(line 12)*
>
> *Year that En-amgalana, the high-priest of Inanna, was installed.*[10]

High priest?! Yes. Israel was not the only nation to flaunt a royal priesthood and its high priest. When the angels were put over the nations at Babel, they rebelled and mimicked the things of heaven, such as the concepts of holiness and worship. This is evident in their implementation of royal priesthoods in their religious service. The powers of darkness continue to mimic the things of God, such as Christian baptism and the removal of shoes in their pagan temples, as Justyn Martyr (100–165 A.D.) explained in *First Apology 62.*

> *And the devils, hearing of this baptism which was taught by the prophet, instigate those who enter into their temples, and who*

10 W. W. Hallo and K. L. Younger, *The Context of Scripture* (Leiden; Boston: Brill, 2003), 302.

> *are about to come before them, paying drink offerings and burnt offerings, also to sprinkle themselves; and they cause men to go and wash their whole persons before they come to the temples where they are enshrined. Moreover, the command given by the priests to those who enter the temples and worship in them to put off their shoes the devils have learned and imitated from what happened to Moses, the prophet whom I have mentioned.*[11]

I'm no longer surprised or bothered by the similarities between godly worship and pagan worship. These other religions were run by fallen powers of heaven, venerated copycats who demanded to have God's glory and the praises of men.

CONNECTING THE GOSPEL

CHRIST AS HIGH PRIEST

Very rarely do Christians think of Jesus as a high priest, but that's what He is. In fact, that's why He came to Earth.

> [17] Therefore he had to be made like his brothers in every respect, so that he might become a merciful and faithful high priest in the service of God, to make propitiation for the sins of the people. (Heb 2:17, ESV)

As we learned in the last chapter, when Christ fulfilled the Law, He rendered it obsolete and established a new covenant by blood—His blood. He didn't abandon the priesthood, however; He acquired it. And His first order of business was to change from the Levitical requirements of the Law to a much earlier model: the priesthood of Melchizedek.

---

11 Jackson, *The Apostolic Fathers and the Apologists of the Second Century*, 174.

> 12 For when there is a change of the priesthood, there must be
> a change of law as well. 13 For the one these things are spoken
> about belonged to a different tribe. No one from it has served at
> the altar. 14 Now it is evident that our Lord came from Judah, and
> Moses said nothing about that tribe concerning priests. 15 And
> this becomes clearer if another priest like Melchizedek appears,
> 16 who did not become a priest based on a legal regulation about
> physical descent but based on the power of an indestructible
> life. 17 For it has been testified: You are a priest forever according
> to the order of Melchizedek. (Heb 7:12–17, CSB)

Christ's priesthood is like Melchizedek's in that both are called "kings" and have no beginning and no end, as described by the Hebrews writer.

> 1 For this Melchizedek, king of Salem, priest of God Most High,
> met Abraham and blessed him as he returned from defeating
> the kings, 2 and Abraham gave him a tenth of everything. First,
> his name means king of righteousness, then also, king of Salem,
> meaning king of peace. 3 Without father, mother, or genealogy,
> having neither beginning of days nor end of life, but resembling
> the Son of God, he remains a priest forever. 4 Now consider how
> great this man was: even Abraham the patriarch gave a tenth of
> the plunder to him. (Heb 7:1–4, CSB)

As the new high priest, Jesus has fulfilled all the requirements of the office, including making atonement for our sin.

> 17 Therefore he had to be made like his brothers in every respect,
> so that he might become a merciful and faithful high priest
> in the service of God, to make propitiation for the sins of the
> people. (Heb 2:17, ESV)

> [11] But when Christ appeared as a high priest of the good things that have come, then through the greater and more perfect tent (not made with hands, that is, not of this creation) [12] he entered once for all into the holy places, not by means of the blood of goats and calves but by means of his own blood, thus securing an eternal redemption. (Heb 9:11–12, ESV)

It's no surprise that Jesus' priesthood is described as a ministry in the holy places.

> [1] Now the point in what we are saying is this: we have such a high priest, one who is seated at the right hand of the throne of the Majesty in heaven, [2] a minister in the holy places, in the true tent that the Lord set up, not man. (Heb 8:1–2, ESV)

> [12] he entered once for all into the holy places, not by means of the blood of goats and calves but by means of his own blood, thus securing an eternal redemption. (Heb 9:12, ESV)

Due to the limited lifespans and sinfulness of elect members of the Levitical priesthood, the Jews were stuck in the revolving door of mediocre mediators. New Testament Christians don't have this problem and shouldn't be afraid of the storms of life or the floods of temptations; we have an anchor for the soul. His term as high priest is inexorable.

> [19] We have this as a sure and steadfast anchor of the soul, a hope that enters into the inner place behind the curtain,
> [20] where Jesus has gone as a forerunner on our behalf, having become a high priest forever after the order of Melchizedek. (Heb 6:19–20, ESV)

CHRIST AS THE GOAT(S)

Not only is Christ to be understood as the high priest—He's also described as playing the role of the two goats in the Day of Atonement ritual. His role as the sacrificial goat to Yahweh is most apparent, but what's often overlooked is His semblance to the second goat, the goat of Azazel. Recall that the goat of Azazel bore all the people's guilt in a barren region outside the camp as Israel wandered through the wilderness, the waterless home of the demonic world. This was the framework through which the New Testament writers parsed Jesus bearing our sins "outside the gate" and outside the holy city of Jerusalem (Matt 27:32–33).

Hebrews 13:12 (ESV)	1 Peter 2:24 (ESV)
So Jesus also suffered **outside the gate** in order to sanctify the people through his own blood.	**He himself bore our sins in his body** on the tree, that we might die to sin and live to righteousness. By his wounds you have been healed.

YOU AS PRIEST

No matter the system or law, Yahweh has always been set apart for holiness. The Levitical priesthood allowed the Israelites to draw near to God as His holy ministers. The prophet Ezekiel wrote,

> 15 "But the Levitical priests, the sons of Zadok, who kept the charge of my sanctuary when the people of Israel went astray from me, shall come near to me to minister to me. And they shall stand before me to offer me the fat and the blood, declares the Lord God. (Ezek 44:15, ESV)

While the Levitical priesthood is no more, Christ's priesthood is alive and well. Peter and John both illuminate their readers to this fact and couple it with the understanding that heaven considers the "called out" to be an entourage of priests.

> [9] But you are a chosen race, a royal priesthood, a holy nation, a people for his own possession, that you may proclaim the excellencies of him who called you out of darkness into his marvelous light. (1 Pet 2:9, ESV)

> [10] and you have made them a kingdom and priests to our God, and they shall reign on the earth." (Rev 5:10, ESV)

As born-again Gentiles, we should approach the Lord in full assurance, knowing our spiritual sacrifices are now warmly received and accepted by Yahweh, our God.

> [19] Therefore, brothers and sisters, since we have boldness to enter the sanctuary through the blood of Jesus—[20] he has inaugurated for us a new and living way through the curtain (that is, through his flesh)—[21] and since we have a great high priest over the house of God, [22] let us draw near with a true heart in full assurance of faith, with our hearts sprinkled clean from an evil conscience and our bodies washed in pure water. (Heb 10:19–22, CSB)

> [5] you yourselves like living stones are being built up as a spiritual house, to be a holy priesthood, to offer spiritual sacrifices acceptable to God through Jesus Christ. (1 Pet 2:5, ESV)

LOOKING AHEAD

With the holy Law guiding them toward righteousness and the royal priesthood tethering them to God's presence, the Israelites were battle-ready to recover the land of promise and fulfill their destiny in the land of milk and honey (Exod 3:8).

> “And so they set out from the mountain of Yahweh a journey of three days, with the ark of the covenant of Yahweh setting out ahead of them three days' journey to search out a resting place for them; and the cloud of Yahweh was over them by day when they set out from the camp. And whenever the ark was setting out Moses would say, “Rise up, Yahweh! May your enemies be scattered; may the ones that hate you flee from your presence.” (Num 10:33–35, LEB)

Little did Moses know, it would soon be Israel who fled from their enemies, filled with doubt and feeling like mere grasshoppers in their sight. Lurking in the shadows of Canaan was an old enemy, with bones like iron forged in the fires of hell. The giants were back and defiant as ever. What would this mean for God's promises and His portion, His pint-sized people? We'll find out in the next chapter.

CHAPTER 11

FEARFUL SPIES AND FAITHLESS SOLDIERS

And there we saw the Nephilim (the sons of Anak, who come from the Nephilim), and we seemed to ourselves like grasshoppers, and so we seemed to them. (Numbers 13:33, ESV)

READING THE STORY

AS THE FAÇADE OF HOME FADED at Sinai, the Israelites once again adopted the nomadic lifestyle of a desert dweller. This existence was palatable because it wasn't permanent. They knew where they were headed. They were headed home—their real home, that is—to the land of Canaan.

> "And they set out from the wilderness of Sinai and camped at Kibroth-hattaavah. And they set out from Kibroth-hattaavah and camped at Hazeroth. (Num 33:16–17, ESV)

After that, the people set out from Hazeroth and camped in the Wilderness of Paran. The LORD spoke to Moses: "Send men to scout out the land of Canaan I am giving to the Israelites. Send one man who is a leader among them from each of their ancestral tribes." Moses sent them from the Wilderness of Paran at the LORD's command. All the men were leaders in Israel. These were their names: Shammua son of Zaccur from the tribe of Reuben; Shaphat son of Hori from the tribe of Simeon; Caleb son of Jephunneh from the tribe of Judah; Igal son of Joseph from the tribe of Issachar; Hoshea son of Nun from the tribe of Ephraim; Palti son of Raphu from the tribe of Benjamin; Gaddiel son of Sodi from the tribe of Zebulun; Gaddi son of Susi from the tribe of Manasseh (from the tribe of Joseph); Ammiel son of Gemalli from the tribe of Dan; Sethur son of Michael from the tribe of Asher; Nahbi son of Vophsi from the tribe of Naphtali; Geuel son of Machi from the tribe of Gad. These were the names of the men Moses sent to scout out the land, and Moses renamed Hoshea son of Nun, Joshua. When Moses sent them to scout out the land of Canaan, he told them, "Go up this way to the Negev, then go up into the hill country. See what the land is like, and whether the people who live there are strong or weak, few or many. Is the land they live in good or bad? Are the cities they live in encampments or fortifications? Is the land fertile or unproductive? Are there trees in it or

> not? Be courageous. Bring back some fruit from the land." It was the season for the first ripe grapes. So they went up and scouted out the land from the Wilderness of Zin as far as Rehob near the entrance to Hamath. They went up through the Negev and came to Hebron, where Ahiman, Sheshai, and Talmai, the descendants of Anak, were living. Hebron was built seven years before Zoan in Egypt. When they came to Eshcol Valley, they cut down a branch with a single cluster of grapes, which was carried on a pole by two men. They also took some pomegranates and figs. That place was called Eshcol Valley of because of the cluster of grapes the Israelites cut there. At the end of forty days they returned from scouting out the land. (Num 12:16–13:25, CSB)

Undoubtedly, the forty days of waiting must have seemed like forty years. Can you imagine closing on a new house, being handed the keys to your new front door, and having to wait forty days to go in?

As the weeks passed, the anticipation grew as the tribes of Israel were forced to simply wait. Would they ever return? Would all twelve survive? If so, what news would they bring to God's people? On day forty, with eyes glued to the horizon, the waiting Israelites got a glimpse of the twelve glorious reconnaissance reporters. All of Israel exhaled a sigh of relief. The heroes returned and brought nutritious spoils: juicy grapes, ripe pomegranates, and sweet figs.

> "They came back to Moses and Aaron and the whole Israelite community at Kadesh in the Desert of Paran. There they reported to them and to the whole assembly and showed them the fruit of the land. They gave Moses this account: "We went into the land to which you sent us, and it does flow with milk and honey! Here is its fruit. (Num 13:26–27, NIV)

Israel's elation, however, was short-lived due to a surprising development and disturbing truth. The spies said,

> "But the people who live there are powerful, and the cities are fortified and very large. We even saw descendants of Anak there. The Amalekites live in the Negev; the Hittites, Jebusites and Amorites live in the hill country; and the Canaanites live near the sea and along the Jordan." (Num 13:28–29, NIV)

The spies' poison paralyzed God's people. Caleb, the son of Jephunneh, was in disbelief from the doom and gloom message he was hearing. While Caleb spent the last forty days scouting Canaan alongside his fellow spies, he didn't share their outlook or drink their fear-flavored Kool-Aid.

Numbers 13:30–33 (ESV)	Numbers 13:31–34 (Brenton LXX En)
But Caleb quieted the people before Moses and said, "Let us go up at once and occupy it, for we are well able to overcome it." Then the men who had gone up with him said, "**We are not able to go up against the people, for they are stronger than we are**." So they brought to the people of Israel a bad report of the land that they had spied out, saying, "The land, through which we have gone to spy it out, **is a land that devours its inhabitants, and all the people that we saw in it are of great height. And there we saw the Nephilim (the sons of Anak, who come from the Nephilim), and we seemed to ourselves like grasshoppers, and so we seemed to them**."	And Chaleb stayed the people from speaking before Moses, and said to him, Nay, but we will go up by all means, and will inherit it, for we shall surely prevail against them. But the men that went up together with him said, We will not go up, for we shall not by any means be able to go up against the nation, for **it is much stronger than we**. And they brought a horror of that land which they surveyed upon the children of Israel, saying, **The land which we passed by to survey it, is a land that eats up its inhabitants; and all the people whom we saw in it are men of extraordinary stature. And there we saw the giants; and we were before them as locusts, yea even so were we before them**.

The dialogue between Caleb and ten of the spies creates cognitive dissonance. Did they really just say the Nephilim giants were back, those mighty men of old who were the offspring born out of illicit unions between angels and women? Moses, the author of both Genesis 6 and Numbers 13, says so. Point-blank.

ANSWERING YOUR QUESTIONS

HOW DID THE GIANTS RETURN?

While the caravan of spies disagreed on their ability to overcome their enemy, they were all in agreement as to who their enemies were. The text in Numbers 13:33 says, "And there we saw the Nephilim (the sons of Anak, who come from the Nephilim)." Moses writes that the sons of Anak, typically called the "Anakim" elsewhere in Scripture, came from the Nephilim. This has caused many to scratch their heads. How could the Anakim have come from the Nephilim if the Nephilim giants were all wiped out in the flood? Some suggest a remnant of Nephilim must have survived the flood. There's even Talmudic and Midrashic tradition that has the biblical giant—Og of Bashan, the last of the Rephaim giants (Deut 3)—surviving the flood on top of Noah's ark. Furthermore,

> *In Peake's Commentary on the Bible (1962 Edition), N. H. Snaith states that the term Anak defined a strain of giants that survived the deluge and inhabited the hill country of Palestine before the conquest by Israel.*[1]

Others suggest the flood was regional, not global. Both of these explanations are highly problematic and, quite frankly, prove to be unnecessary. The biblical explanation seems to be given in Genesis 6:4.

---

1 Gary Wayne, *The Genesis 6 Conspiracy: How Secret Societies and the Descendants of Giants Plan to Enslave Humankind* (Trusted Books, 2014), Kindle edition, 51.

> *Genesis 6:4 tells us there were Nephilim on earth before the flood "and also afterward, when the sons of God went into the daughters of humankind." The "when" in the verse could be translated "whenever," thereby suggesting a repetition of these preflood events after the flood. In other words, since Genesis 6:4 points forward to the later giant clans, the phrasing could suggest that other sons of God fathered more Nephilim after the flood. As a result, there would be no survival of original Nephilim, and so the postflood dilemma would be resolved. A later appearance of other Nephilim occurred by the same means as before the flood.*[2]

The giants after the flood weren't fathered by the paternal angels of Genesis 6. Those angels were locked up until the great judgment (2 Pet 2:4–5; Jude 6–7). The postdiluvian giants were fathered by a different set of divine sons, presumably the angels that were set over the nations at Babel who eventually rebelled and followed the way of Eden's serpent.

WHAT DID THE GIANTS LOOK LIKE?

There was a visceral response to the returned spies' announcement. The size and appearance of the tribal giants were enough to spook Israel from charging Canaan. First-century Jewish historian Josephus wrote,

> *3(125) … There were till then left the race of giants, who had bodies so large, and countenances so entirely different from other men, that they were surprising to the sight, and terrible to the hearing. The bones of these men are still shown to this very day, unlike to any creditable relations of other men.*[3]

---

2 Heiser, *The Unseen Realm*, 190–191.

3 Josephus, *The Works of Josephus*, 135.

As Josephus pointed out, the bodies of the giants were a spectacle in the ancient world and were put on display. Clement of Rome attested to this as well and wrote in 96 A.D.,

> *"The giants [were] men of immense bodies, whose bones of enormous size are still shown in certain places for confirmation of their existence."*[4]

The biblical record is often considered outlandish by modern skeptics. Passages such as Amos 2:9 are often berated because they paint giants as being as tall as cedar trees and as strong as oaks. Other passages reveal they have twelve fingers and twelve toes (1 Chr 20:6–8). Of one fact I'm certain—the Bible is right, and the tomato-throwers are wrong. Extensive researcher Gary Wayne defends the biblical record and argues that it matches the historical records and legends from antiquity about the giants.

> *Nephilim were believed to have a frightening (snake-like) appearance, just as Josephus and others have stated. They were terrible to behold, just as emim translates as "inspiring fear," and rephaim translates as "causing one's heart to grow weak at a glance." To be specific, Josephus described the Anak as a famous race of giants that were of such tremendous size, and that their countenance was so completely different compared to humans, that the Anak were extraordinarily surprising, frightening, and terrible to both the senses of sight and hearing. Nephilim mirrored their fathers, fallen angels, for watchers possess the face of a viper—serpents identified as seraphim, employed as*

---

4 Clement of Rome, *Recognitions 1.29*, quoted in Adrienne Mayor, *The First Fossil Hunters: Dinosaurs, Mammoths, and Myth in Greek and Roman Times* (Princeton, NJ: Princeton University Press, 2011), Kindle edition.

> *liaisons between heaven and earth. Satan took the form of a seraph when he deceived Eve in the Garden of Eden. Serpent-like angels were recorded in the Gnostic gospel Origin of the World, possessing faces that were long and narrow, prominent cheekbones, elongated jawbones, thin lips, and slanted eyes (similar to aliens), while their offspring looked just like them. In fact, Nephilim and watchers were both referred to by the antediluvians as serpents. Unaccounted for long-headed skulls, dating back to the antediluvian epoch, have been unearthed in both Sumer and Egypt, lending further credence to the viper look of the Nephilim. Further, Nephilim eyes were said to have been glowing and solid gold or honey colored, while their skin was white and rough.*[5]

Gary's diligent research leaves no stone unturned. In his book, *The Genesis 6 Conspiracy*, he discusses the sheer size of the giants.

> *Their size was staggering. Goliath…was affirmed to be over nine feet tall. That would be four feet taller than the average height of a person of that time, or almost twice as tall! Iris Freelander, an ordained minister, who holds hold degrees in psychology and theology, notes that depending on which Bible scholar tells the Goliath narrative, he was anywhere from eight and a half feet to thirteen and a half feet tall. In antiquarian measurements, Goliath's height was six cubits and one span. A cubit was either a common eighteen inches or twenty-one royal inches, while a span was nine inches. This then tallied Goliath's height at nine feet, nine inches on the common measure, but because Goliath was of royal Nephilim bloodlines, one could argue Goliath's true height at eleven feet, three inches. That calculation would align perfectly with an account from the time of Alexander, where a conversation*

5 Wayne, *The Genesis 6 Conspiracy*, 56

between Midas and Silenus noted Titans grew to twice the size of humans and lived twice as long.

...We can only speculate as to what size some giants may have grown to or even how large the pure original offspring might have been, before they intermingled with humankind, diluting their size and strength throughout the generations. The Genesis giants must have been monsters.

We can only attempt to imagine beings that were nine feet tall or taller, with body weight ranging from 600 to 900 pounds of pure muscle. Nephilim were not just extraordinarily tall like the modern basketball player. Nephilim were built more like the modern football player or the modern WWF wrestler. Fallen ones recorded in Theogany by Hesiod (907 B.C.E.) were described as a monstrous race... They were bulked by muscle, gifted with strength. Og's height to breadth ratio, as a classic example, was an astonishing two to one, establishing Og as being incredibly broad, for the average human maintains a three to one ratio. Furthermore, Nephilim were fleet of foot and famous for their quickness, dexterity, and adeptness with their hands.

Nephilim inflicted terror with both their height and their breadth. They were powerful beasts, who dressed with armor and weaponry that would force the average man to collapse from the weight. This no doubt left the average man awestruck with amazement and fear, especially when they'd see such feats of strength and the giants sporting their armor into battle and then waging war from underneath it. They were known to have a company of menservants just to carry their armor behind them; the average man could only bear to carry one piece of their armor at a time, thus requiring a harem of servants. Nephilim were fearsome warriors, heroes of old.[6]

---

6 Wayne, *The Genesis 6 Conspiracy*, 52

The enormous size and frightening appearance of the biblical giants often defeated the hearts of men before the battle ever began (1 Sam 17:11). Only men of great faith could defeat the dreaded giants.

READING THE STORY

Despite Caleb's timely heroism and valiant speech, fear had set into the people.

> "Then all the community lifted up their voices, and the people wept during that night. And all the Israelites grumbled against Moses and Aaron, and all the community said to them, "If only we had died in the land of Egypt or in this desert! Why did Yahweh bring us into this land to fall by the sword? Our wives and our little children will become plunder; would it not be better for us to return to Egypt?" They said to each other, "Let us appoint a leader, and we will return to Egypt." Then Moses and Aaron fell on their faces before the assembly of the community of the Israelites. Joshua son of Nun and Caleb son of Jephunneh, from the explorers of the land, tore their garments. And they said to all the community of the Israelites, "The land that we went through to explore is an exceptionally good land. If Yahweh delights in us, then he will bring us into this land, and he will give it to us, a land that is flowing with milk and honey. Only do not rebel against Yahweh, and you will not fear the people of the land, because they will be our food. Their protection has been turned from them; Yahweh is with us. You should not fear them." And all the community said to stone them with stones, but the glory of Yahweh appeared in the tent of assembly among the Israelites. And Yahweh said to Moses, "How long until this people will despise me, and how long until they will not believe in me, and in all the signs that I have

> done in their midst? I will strike them with disease, and I will dispossess them; I will make you into a greater and stronger nation than them." (Num 14:1–12, LEB)

The same people who sang in victory at the bank of the Red Sea (Exod 15:1) now wept in defeat at the door to Canaan. The Lord was so disgusted with His people that He was ready to disinherit them, implying Moses would play the part of Abraham as Yahweh's new allotted portion.

> And Moses said to Yahweh, "Then the Egyptians will hear that you brought up this people from their midst in your power, and they will tell it to the inhabitants of this land. They heard that you, Yahweh, are in the midst of this people, that you are seen eye to eye, and your cloud is standing over them, and in a column of cloud you go before them by day and in a column of fire at night. But if you destroy this people all at once, the nations that will have heard your message will say, 'Yahweh was unable to bring this people in the land that he swore by an oath, and he slaughtered them in the desert.' But now, please, let the power of my Lord be great, just has you spoke, 'Yahweh is slow to anger and great of loyal love, forgiving sin and rebellion; but surely he leaves nothing unpunished, visiting the sin of the fathers on the sons to the third and fourth generations.' Please forgive the sin of this people according to the greatness of your loyal love, just as you forgave this people, from Egypt until now." (Num 14:13–19, LEB)

Moses's petition to the Lord was valid and sincere. He didn't want to be the new Abraham or start over—He wanted Israel to finish what they'd started. They had come too far and endured too much to be thrown into the hands of lesser gods.

"Yahweh said, "I have forgiven them according to your word; but as I am alive, the glory of Yahweh will fill all the earth. But because all the men who have seen my glory and my signs that I did in Egypt and in the desert yet tested me these ten times and did not listen to my voice, they will not see the land that I swore by oath to their ancestors, and all those who despised me will not see it. But my servant Caleb, because another spirit was with him, he remained true after me, and I will bring him into the land that he entered, and his offspring will take possession of it. And the Amalekites and the Canaanites live in the valleys; tomorrow turn and set out for the desert by way of the Red Sea." And Yahweh spoke to Moses and Aaron, saying, "How long will I bear this evil community who are grumbling against me? I have heard the grumbling of the Israelites which they are making against me. Say to them, 'Surely as I live,' declares Yahweh, 'just as you spoke in my hearing, so I will do to you; in this desert your corpses will fall, and all your counted ones, according to all your number, from twenty years old and above who grumbled against me. You yourselves will not come into the land that I swore by oath to make you to dwell in it, but Caleb son of Jephunneh and Joshua son of Nun. But your little children, whom you said would be plunder, I will bring them, and they will know the land that you rejected. But for you, all your corpses will fall in this desert. And your children will be shepherds in the desert forty years, and you will bear your unfaithfulness until all your corpses have fallen in the desert. According to the number of the days that you explored the land, forty days, a day for each year, you will bear your sins forty years, and you will know my opposition.' I, Yahweh, have spoken; I will surely do this to all this evil community who has banded together against me. In this desert they will

> come to an end, and there they will die." As for the men whom Moses sent to explore the land, who returned and made the community grumble against him by spreading a report over the land, the men who spread the evil report of the land died by the plague before Yahweh. But Joshua son of Nun and Caleb son of Jephunneh lived from among the men who went to explore the land. (Num 14:20–38, LEB)

CONNECTING THE GOSPEL

BRAVE & UNSTOPPABLE

While the early Christians and their contemporaries often wrote of the dreaded giants, their enemies were much more powerful and elusive. Paul concludes his letter to the church at Ephesus by writing,

> 10 Finally, be strengthened by the Lord and by his vast strength.
> 11 Put on the full armor of God so that you can stand against the
> schemes of the devil. 12 For our struggle is not against flesh and
> blood, but against the rulers, against the authorities, against the
> cosmic powers of this darkness, against evil, spiritual forces in
> the heavens. 13 For this reason take up the full armor of God, so
> that you may be able to resist in the evil day, and having prepared
> everything, to take your stand. 14 Stand, therefore, with truth
> like a belt around your waist, righteousness like armor on your
> chest, 15 and your feet sandaled with readiness for the gospel
> of peace. 16 In every situation take up the shield of faith with
> which you can extinguish all the flaming arrows of the evil one.
> 17 Take the helmet of salvation and the sword of the Spirit—
> which is the word of God. 18 Pray at all times in the Spirit with
> every prayer and request, and stay alert with all perseverance
> and intercession for all the saints. (Eph 6:10–18, CSB)

While I'm thankful we're not battling 900-pound Nephilim on a daily basis, we *are* battling their fathers, the fallen angels. Modern Christians give spiritual warfare very little thought in their daily lives, but early Christians didn't—they lived in constant awareness and stayed battle-ready, pressing on toward the heavenly land of promise (Heb 11:16). A second-century literary work titled *The Shepherd of Hermas* reminded early Christians not to get too attached to this world, but to stay focused on the one to come.

> *HE said to me, "You know that you, as the servants of God, are living in a strange country, for your city is far from this city. If then you know your city, in which you are going to dwell, why do you here prepare lands and costly establishments and buildings and vain dwellings? He therefore, who prepares these things for this city, is not able to return to his own city.*[7]

As Christians, "we have no lasting city, but we seek the city that is to come" (Heb 13:14, ESV). The Christian pursuit of the promised land of heaven is no less treacherous than Israel's. We're in a spiritual battle against the rulers, against the authorities, against the cosmic powers over this present darkness, against the spiritual forces of evil in the heavenly places. Are you fearful?

The paranormal has struck fear into the hearts of countless generations. Whether it's a floating hand that writes (Dan 5:5–9), a tribe of insatiable giants (Num 13:32), or a supernatural struggle with the demonic realm (Luke 8:35–37), men exude fear. Paul wrote extensively on fear and encouraged the churches to kill it. His argument in Romans 8 takes readers through the desert of doubt and lifts them to the pinnacle of Christian confidence.

---

7 K. Lake, ed., vol. 2 of *The Apostolic Fathers* (Cambridge, MA; London: Harvard University Press, 1912–1913), 139.

> 31 What then shall we say to these things? If God is for us, who can be against us? 32 He who did not spare his own Son but gave him up for us all, how will he not also with him graciously give us all things? 33 Who shall bring any charge against God's elect? It is God who justifies. 34 Who is to condemn? Christ Jesus is the one who died—more than that, who was raised—who is at the right hand of God, who indeed is interceding for us. 35 **Who shall separate us from the love of Christ**? Shall **tribulation, or distress, or persecution,** or famine, or nakedness, or danger, or sword? 36 As it is written, "For your sake we are being killed all the day long; we are regarded as sheep to be slaughtered." 37 No, in all these things we are more than conquerors through him who loved us. 38 **For I am sure that neither death nor life, nor angels nor rulers**, nor things present nor things to come, nor powers, 39 nor height nor depth, nor anything else in all creation, will be able to separate us from the love of God in Christ Jesus our Lord. (Rom 8:31–39, ESV)

Our supernatural enemies can't stop us. We are tethered to the unbreakable love of God. This doesn't stop them from trying, however. Hell's host uses other people to persecute us and distress us in our fight against them. Minucius Felix, a second-century Christian soldier, wrote,

> *"What happens is that they [power of darkness] slip into the minds of the ignorant; there they secretly implant hatred against us by means of fear; for it is only natural to hate and, if you can, to molest one who makes you afraid and terrified. This is how they take hold of men's thoughts and stop up their hearts,* ***so that they begin to hate us*** *even before they know us. For if men investigated us, they might then either be able to imitate us or be unable to condemn us.*[8]

---

8 Felix, *The Octavius of Marcus Minucius Felix*, 102–103.

In the striking words of Ignatius of Antioch (50–107 A.D.),

> *Fire and the cross, scattering of the bones and the array of the beasts, the mutilation of the limbs and the grinding of the whole body—hard torments of the devil!—let them come upon me, if only I may attain Jesus Christ.*[9]

While we're afflicted, we are not crushed. Our God has anointed us into the King's soldiers and sculpts us into fearless vessels. Paul writes,

> 7 Now we have this treasure in clay jars, so that this extraordinary power may be from God and not from us. 8 We are
> afflicted in every way but not crushed; we are perplexed but not
> in despair; 9 we are persecuted but not abandoned; we are struck
> down but not destroyed. 10 We always carry the death of Jesus
> in our body, so that the life of Jesus may also be displayed in our
> body. 11 For we who live are always being given over to death for
> Jesus' sake, so that Jesus' life may also be displayed in our mortal
> flesh. (2 Cor 4:7–11, CSB)

Perhaps Paul's greatest argument for disciples to be unashamed in life and unafraid in battle is the realization of who is fighting for you, with you, through you, and in you.

> 14 For this reason I kneel before the Father 15 from whom
> every family in heaven and on earth is named. 16 I pray that
> he may grant you, according to the riches of his glory, to be
> strengthened with power in your inner being through his
> Spirit, 17 and that Christ may dwell in your hearts through

9 Jackson, *The Apostolic Fathers and the Apologists of the Second Century*, 76.

> faith. I pray that you, being rooted and firmly established in love, [18] may be able to comprehend with all the saints what is the length and width, height and depth of God's love, [19] and to know Christ's love that surpasses knowledge, so that you may be filled with all the fullness of God. [20] Now to him who is able to do above and beyond all that we ask or think according to the power that works in us—[21] to him be glory in the church and in Christ Jesus to all generations, forever and ever. Amen. (Eph 3:14–21, CSB)

Paul served fearlessly in his apostleship and stood toe-to-toe with the dark forces of Satan, so much so that they knew him by name (Acts 19:15). I wonder—do they know your name? Are you storming their gates and pulling down their strongholds? Or are you paralyzed by fear and doubt? If you often doubt your purpose and shrink from the battle, remember who's fighting in you—it's Jesus, the captain of your salvation, and He's riding on His white horse, leading the armies of heaven. The apostle John writes,

> [11] Then I saw heaven opened, and there was a white horse. Its rider is called Faithful and True, and with justice he judges and makes war. [12] His eyes were like a fiery flame, and many crowns were on his head. He had a name written that no one knows except himself. [13] He wore a robe dipped in blood, and his name is called the Word of God. [14] The armies that were in heaven followed him on white horses, wearing pure white linen. [15] A sharp sword came from his mouth, so that he might strike the nations with it. He will rule them with an iron rod. He will also trample the winepress of the fierce anger of God, the Almighty. [16] And he has a name written on his robe and on his thigh: KING OF KINGS AND LORD OF LORDS. (Rev 19:11–16, CSB)

Also, let us not forget the beautiful words Paul penned in his epistle to the Philippians,

> 13 I can do all things through Christ who strengthens me. (Phil 4:13, NKJV)

Fear is for the faithless and from the devil. Regarding this, Paul told Timothy,

> 7 for God gave us a spirit not of fear but of power and love and self-control. (2 Tim 1:7, ESV)

The traits Paul notes are significant. Through Jesus, these three things (power, love, and self-control) will give you the upper hand and the high ground. Jesus' power will put you on the offensive. His love will overcome hate, and self-control will be your defense, protecting you during surprise attacks. For Christ's seeking soldiers, the trifecta of gifts to which Paul alludes can still be found at the foot of the cross. All who pick them up and put them on will be an unmovable force in the good fight of faith.

> 57 But thanks be to God, who gives us the victory through our Lord Jesus Christ. 58 Therefore, my beloved brothers, be steadfast, immovable, always abounding in the work of the Lord, knowing that in the Lord your labor is not in vain. (1 Cor 15:57–58, ESV)

LOOKING AHEAD

God's people were slapped with a stiff penalty because of their fear and unbelief. Everyone twenty-years-old and older would die after an unfathomable forty-year period of wandering through the unforgiving desert of demons.

> When Moses reported these words to all the Israelites, the people were overcome with grief. They got up early the next morning and went up the ridge of the hill country, saying, "Let's go to the place the LORD promised, for we were wrong." But Moses responded, "Why are you going against the LORD's command? It won't succeed. Don't go, because the LORD is not among you and you will be defeated by your enemies. The Amalekites and Canaanites are right in front of you, and you will fall by the sword. The LORD won't be with you, since you have turned from following him." But they dared to go up the ridge of the hill country, even though the ark of the LORD's covenant and Moses did not leave the camp. Then the Amalekites and Canaanites who lived in that part of the hill country came down, attacked them, and routed them as far as Hormah. (Num 14:39–45, CSB)

Their swift defeat by the Amalekites and the Canaanites was a humbling reminder that they couldn't thwart the plans of God. Whether they liked it or not, there was no escaping the path of punishment. For the next forty years, they would be forced to wander as nomadic desert dwellers, students in Yahweh's school of hard knocks and biting serpents.

While these tests were certainly predictable, God's means of teaching Israel about faith and healing were very unconventional.

CHAPTER 12

BITING SERPENTS & THE SIGN OF THE CROSS

"And as Moses lifted up the serpent in the wilderness, so must the Son of Man be lifted up," (John 3:14, ESV)

READING THE STORY

ISRAEL'S DEFEAT WAS EMBARRASSING AND HUMBLING. To make matters worse, they were slapped with a stiff penalty and shuddered at the notion of forty years of wandering. On the surface, this sequence of events promised to be a good first phase in recovering their softened hearts. That's what makes their next step so surprising. The story reads,

> "Now Korah son of Izhar, son of Kohath, son of Levi, with Dathan and Abiram, sons of Eliab, and On son of Peleth, sons of Reuben, took two hundred fifty prominent Israelite men who were leaders of the community and representatives in the assembly, and they rebelled against Moses. They came together against Moses and Aaron and told them, "You have gone too far! Everyone in the entire community is holy, and the LORD is among them. Why then do you exalt yourselves above the LORD's assembly?" When Moses heard this, he fell facedown. Then he said to Korah and all his followers, "Tomorrow morning the LORD will reveal who belongs to him, who is set apart, and the one he will let come near him. He will let the one he chooses come near him. Korah, you and all your followers are to do this: take firepans, and tomorrow place fire in them and put incense on them before the LORD. Then the man the LORD chooses will be the one who is set apart. It is you Levites who have gone too far!" Moses also told Korah, "Now listen, Levites! Isn't it enough for you that the God of Israel has separated you from the Israelite community to bring you near to himself, to perform the work at the LORD's tabernacle, and to stand before the community to minister to them? He has brought you near, and all your fellow Levites who are with you, but you are pursuing the priesthood as well. Therefore, it is you and all your followers who have conspired against the LORD! As for Aaron, who is he that you should complain about him?" (Num 16:1–11, CSB)

Korah, Dathan, and Abiram's uprising was centered around jealousy. They and 250 of Israel's top leaders didn't think it was fair for Moses and Aaron to hold such high positions. They demanded equality of status across the board in the Lord's covenant community. As Moses pointed out, this was the pot calling the kettle black. Korah and his fellow Levites should have been grateful they were selected to serve in the tabernacle. Then, Moses sought the Lord's direction. Yahweh would emphatically "decide" on the matter.

> And Moses said to Korah, "You and your entire company will be before Yahweh tomorrow, you and they and Aaron. Each one take his censer, and put incense on it and you will present it before Yahweh, and each of you bring his censer, two hundred and fifty censers, you and Aaron, each his censer." So each of them took his censer, and they put fire on them, and they placed incense on them; they stood at the doorway of the tent of the assembly of Moses and Aaron. And Korah summoned them, the entire community, by the doorway of the tent of assembly, and the glory of Yahweh appeared to all the community. (Num 16:16–19, LEB)

The congregation got exactly what they wanted—to be in close proximity to the Lord Himself. But their experience with the Lord wasn't what they had envisioned.

> And Yahweh spoke to Moses and Aaron, saying, "Separate yourselves from the midst of this community, that I can destroy them in a moment." And they fell on their faces, and they said, "God, God of the spirits of all flesh, will one man sin and you become angry toward the entire community?" Yahweh spoke to Moses, saying, "Speak to the community, saying, 'Move away from the dwelling of Korah, Dathan, and Abiram.'" (Num 16:20–24, LEB)

Moses rushed to the Israelites, who were about to be cut down in the crossfire.

> He warned the community, "Get away now from the tents of these wicked men. Don't touch anything that belongs to them, or you will be swept away because of all their sins." So they got away from the dwellings of Korah, Dathan, and Abiram. Meanwhile, Dathan and Abiram came out and stood at the entrance of their tents with their wives, children, and infants. Then Moses said, "This is how you will know that the LORD sent me to do all these things and that it was not of my own will: If these men die naturally as all people would, and suffer the fate of all, then the LORD has not sent me. But if the LORD brings about something unprecedented, and the ground opens its mouth and swallows them along with all that belongs to them so that they go down alive into Sheol, then you will know that these men have despised the LORD." (Num 16:26–30, CSB)

As Moses spoke his last syllable, the ground split open like the jaws of a gluttonous serpent.

> The land opened its mouth and swallowed them up with their houses and every person that belonged to Korah and all the property. They went down alive to Sheol, they and all that belonged to them, and the land covered over them, and they perished from the midst of the assembly. All Israel who were around them fled at their cry, because they said, "Lest the land swallow us up!" And fire went out from Yahweh, and it consumed the two hundred and fifty men presenting the incense. (Num 16:32–35, LEB)

Shock and awe filled the surviving witnesses. Their response wasn't repentance—it was retaliation. They were furious over the deaths of the uprisers. Now, they too grumbled against Moses and Aaron, hurling accusations and pointing fingers at God's chosen leaders.

> Then, when the community had gathered against Moses and Aaron, they turned to the tent of assembly, and behold, the cloud covered it, and the glory of Yahweh appeared. And Moses and Aaron came to the front of the tent of assembly, and Yahweh spoke to Moses, saying, "Get away from the midst of this community, and I will finish them in an instant," but they fell on their faces. And Moses and Aaron said, "Take the censer, and put fire on it from the altar. Place incense on it, and bring it quickly to the community, and make atonement for them, because wrath went out from the presence of Yahweh, and a plague has begun." And so Aaron took it just as Moses had spoken, and he ran into the midst of the assembly, for behold, the plague had begun among the people; so he gave the incense and made atonement for the people. He stood between the dead and between the living, and the plague was stopped. Those who died by the plague were fourteen thousand seven hundred, besides those who died on account of Korah. Then Aaron returned to Moses at the doorway of the tent of assembly, and the plague was stopped. (Num 16:42–50, LEB)

Moses and Aaron's timely heroics spared thousands of ungrateful grumblers.

As the years passed, Moses's siblings passed away. His sister, Miriam, died at Kadesh-barnea in the wilderness of Zin (Num 20:1), and Aaron's death soon followed at Mount Hor (Num 20:22–29). The loss of Aaron was a big blow to Moses and all the tribes of Israel. They wept for their beloved high priest thirty days. Their outlook was infectiously gloomy, and delirium was setting in. As Moses and his Israeli caravan of travelers set out from Mount Hor, the people's frustration boiled over yet again.

> The people spoke against God and Moses: "Why have you led us up from Egypt to die in the wilderness? There is no bread or water, and we detest this wretched food!" Then

> the LORD sent poisonous snakes among the people, and they bit them so that many Israelites died. The people then came to Moses and said, "We have sinned by speaking against the LORD and against you. Intercede with the LORD so that he will take the snakes away from us." And Moses interceded for the people. Then the LORD said to Moses, "Make a snake image and mount it on a pole. When anyone who is bitten looks at it, he will recover." So Moses made a bronze snake and mounted it on a pole. Whenever someone was bitten, and he looked at the bronze snake, he recovered. (Num 21:5–9, CSB)

ANSWERING YOUR QUESTIONS

WHY SEND SERPENTS?

Moses reminded the people in Deuteronomy 8:15 that God led them through "the great and terrifying wilderness, with its fiery serpents and scorpions" (ESV). These biting beasts were part of the local animal population that made their home in the dry, dusty desert. They were the obvious choice for Israel's punishment. But is it really that simple? Is that why God sent serpents? Truthfully, God could have sent any domestic or international animal to bite the people if that had been His only intent. He's all-powerful and not restricted to the local, convenient options. Yahweh was telegraphing a message. As modern readers, we often miss the message within the message. This is because we're not thinking like an ancient Israelite, but like a coffee-sipping, twenty-first-century Christian.

> *As evidenced in the Bible, Israelite culture viewed the snake in much the same manner as the surrounding Near Eastern environment: as an agent of blessing, healing, fertility, fear, danger, and chaos*[1]

1 J. L. Kelley, "Nehushtan," *The Lexham Bible Dictionary*.

This is why the snake is depicted as both the curse and the cure in Numbers 21:5–9. The poisonous serpents were sent as a means of curse and chaos. Yet, the hidden message was very apparent to the people. Through grumbling and faithlessness, they had sinfully aligned themselves with the twisted serpent of Genesis 3 who would strike the promised seed of Israel, killing Him on the cross.

Many Bible students are bewildered by God's command to build a bronze serpentine image as a means of healing the people, especially since one of the Ten Commandments forbids them from making graven images (Exod 20:4). While serpents often carried a negative connotation in antiquity, they also carried a positive one. The International Standard Bible Encyclopaedia points out,

> *Living serpents were kept in Bab (Babylonian) temples. So the cobra was the guardian of royalty in Egypt, symbolizing the kingly power of life and death. In mythology, the serpent was not always considered a bad demon, enemy of the Creator, but often appears as the emblem of wisdom, esp. in connection with health-giving and life-giving gods, such as Ea, savior of mankind from the flood, and special "god of the physicians" in Babylon; Thoth, the god of wisdom in Egypt, who healed the eye of Horus and brought Osiris to life again; Apollo, the embodiment of physical perfection, and his son, Aesculapius, most famous giver of physical and moral health and curer of disease among the Greeks.*[2]

As the God of gods, it was Yahweh who controlled the power of the serpent and was the true healer, both physically and spiritually. This episode was an unforgettable lesson on the supremacy of God, and interestingly enough, it relates to the gospel, as we'll soon discover.

---

2 C. M. Cobern, "Images," vol. 1–5 of *The International Standard Bible Encyclopaedia* 1455.

WHAT HAPPENED TO THE BRONZE SERPENT?

God's forbiddance of making "graven images" in the Ten Commandments was for good reason. While He made an exception in our story, it was not the norm, and Israel knew it. The surrounding Gentile nations manufactured "gods" as stand-ins for the supernatural powers they worshiped. Idol worship is defined as,

> *The adoration and expression of praise to a god (including the God of Israel) as represented in an idol.*[3]

Note how one of God's songwriters shames all heathen participants of idol worship:

Psalm 97:7, 9 (ESV)	Psalm 96:7, 9 (Brenton LXX En)
[7] All worshipers of images are put to shame, who make their boast in **worthless idols**; **worship him, all you gods**! [9] For you, O LORD, are most high over all the earth; you are exalted **far above all gods**.	[7] Let all that worship graven images be ashamed, who boast of their **idols**; **worship him, all ye his angels**. [9] For thou art Lord most high over all the earth; thou art greatly exalted **above all gods**.

As the Old Testament story unfolds, there isn't a single mention of Moses's bronze serpent anywhere else in the Pentateuch. Roughly seven hundred long years pass, and it seemed to be long forgotten about. That is, until an obscure verse brings it out of the shadows. What's revealed about the bronze serpent, and Judah's use of it, is shocking.

---

3 D. Witthoff, ed., *The Lexham Cultural Ontology Glossary* (Bellingham, WA: Lexham Press, 2014).

> 1 In the third year of Hoshea son of Elah, king of Israel,
> Hezekiah the son of Ahaz, king of Judah, began to reign. 2
> He was twenty-five years old when he began to reign, and he
> reigned twenty-nine years in Jerusalem. His mother's name was
> Abi the daughter of Zechariah. 3 And he did what was right in
> the eyes of the Lord, according to all that David his father had
> done. 4 He removed the high places and broke the pillars and
> cut down the Asherah. **And he broke in pieces the bronze
> serpent that Moses had made, for until those days the people
> of Israel had made offerings to it (it was called Nehushtan).**
> (2 Kgs 18:1–4, ESV)

In Hezekiah's effort to clean house of all the high places of idol worship that had crept into the kingdom of Judah, he smashed Moses's serpent to pieces, leaving no possibility that it might be repaired by anyone seeking its allure or to worship and praise it. Despite God's warning, His people were often mesmerized by the nations' gods and occasionally worshiped them through idols. It's unclear if the brazen serpent was being utilized as a stand-in for Jehovah God or one of the small-G gods of the nations. Either way, it was despicable. God prospered and blessed the righteous king of Judah for purging His land of demon worship and restoring purity, once again, among His allotted portion (2 Kgs 18:7).

CONNECTING THE GOSPEL

THE CURE OF THE CROSS

In Jesus' dialogue with a man named Nicodemus in John 3, Jesus hints at how He will die. Notice what is said:

> 5 Jesus answered, "Truly I tell you, unless someone is born of
> water and the Spirit, he cannot enter the kingdom of God.
> 6 Whatever is born of the flesh is flesh, and whatever is born of

> the Spirit is spirit. [7] Do not be amazed that I told you that you must be born again. [8] The wind blows where it pleases, and you hear its sound, but you don't know where it comes from or where it is going. So it is with everyone born of the Spirit." [9] "How can these things be?" asked Nicodemus. [10] "Are you a teacher of Israel and don't know these things?" Jesus replied. [11] "Truly I tell you, we speak what we know and we testify to what we have seen, but you do not accept our testimony. [12] If I have told you about earthly things and you don't believe, how will you believe if I tell you about heavenly things? [13] No one has ascended into heaven except the one who descended from heaven—the Son of Man. [14] "**Just as Moses lifted up the snake in the wilderness, so the Son of Man must be lifted up**, [15] so that everyone who believes in him may have eternal life. (John 3:5–15, CSB)

It's interesting that Jesus' prophecy of being lifted up on the cross is linked to the bronze serpent being lifted up in the wilderness. Both the cross and the bronze serpent saved, one physically and one spiritually. That much is clear. But could there be more to this connection that's evaded modern eyes?

Notice again what the Lord said to Moses.

> [8] And the Lord said to Moses, "Make a fiery serpent and **set it on a pole**, and everyone who is bitten, when he sees it, shall live." [9] So Moses made a bronze serpent and **set it on a pole**. And if a serpent bit anyone, he would look at the bronze serpent and live. (Num 21:8–9, ESV)

The Septuagint reads, "put it on a signal staff." A pole or a signal staff? What is this "signaling?" The belief held by many early Christians was the bronze serpent was in fact hung on a cruciform piece of wood to denote the cross of Christ, the future cure of sin. Justin Martyr (100–c. 165 A.D.) wrote in *Dialogue with Trypho 94*,

'Tell me, did not God, through Moses, forbid the making of an image or likeness of anything in the heavens or on earth, yet He Himself had Moses construct the brazen serpent in the desert and set it up as a sign by which those who had been bitten by the serpents were healed, and in doing so was He not free of any sin? By this, as I stated above, He announced a mystery by which ***He proclaimed that He would break the power of the serpent,*** *which prompted the sin of Adam, and that He would deliver from the bites of the serpent (that is, evil actions, idolatries, and other sins) all those who believe in Him who was to be put to death by this sign, namely, the cross.* ***If this is not the interpretation of the passage, give me one reason why Moses set up the brazen serpent on the sign [cross],*** *and commanded all who had been bitten to look upon it; and they were healed, and this, in spite of the fact that he himself had forbidden them to make an image of anything whatsoever.'*[4]

Basil of Caesarea (330–379 A.D.) also alluded to the bronze serpent being hung on a cross in *Letter 260.8*.

By a sign, we properly, understand in Scripture a cross. Moses, it is said, set the serpent "upon a pole." That is upon a cross.[5]

If, in fact, Moses put the serpent on a cross, Jesus' words in John 3 are not random and unexpected; they are a direct link back to Numbers 21:8–9. This sheds light on Jesus' expectation for Nicodemus to "understand these things." And what was Jesus signaling? He was signaling the very thing Moses was signaling when he put the bronze

---

4 Martyr, *The First Apology, The Second Apology, Dialogue with Trypho, Exhortation to the Greeks, Discourse to the Greeks, The Monarchy or The Rule of God*, 297.

5 Basil of Caesarea, *Letters*, 299 (Jackson).

serpent on a cross—defeat for the serpent and his cronies, the lesser gods, and a cure for those who look to Jesus by the power of the cross. In the words of Theodoret of Cyrus (393–458 A.D.), a desk theologian,

> *As for us who have believed in him, we turn our faces toward him [Chirst on the cross]. For as the Jews were able to neutralize the venom of the poisonous snake by looking at the bronze serpent (Num 21:9), so we are healed from the sting of sin by looking at him.*[6]

The end of Jesus' dialogue with Nicodemus in John 3 calls on those who seek the cure of eternal life to choose the power of light over the powers of darkness.

> [16] For God loved the world in this way: He gave his one and only Son, so that everyone who believes in him will not perish but have eternal life. [17] For God did not send his Son into the world to condemn the world, but to save the world through him. [18] Anyone who believes in him is not condemned, but anyone who does not believe is already condemned, because he has not believed in the name of the one and only Son of God. [19] This is the judgment: **The light has come into the world, and people loved darkness rather than the light** because their deeds were evil. [20] For everyone who does evil hates the light and avoids it, so that his deeds may not be exposed. [21] **But anyone who lives by the truth comes to the light**, so that his works may be shown to be accomplished by God." (John 3:16–21, CSB)

6 R. L. Wilken, A. R. Christman, and M. J. Hollerich, eds., *Isaiah: Interpreted by Early Christian and Medieval Commentators*, trans. R. L. Wilken, A. R. Christman, and M. J. Hollerich (Grand Rapids, MI; Cambridge, UK: William B. Eerdmans Publishing Company, 2007), 157.

As children of light, "we must not put Christ to the test, as some of them did and were destroyed by serpents" (1 Cor 10:9, ESV).

Additionally, there's another link between the Numbers 21:8–9 account and the gospel accounts. Showing His supernatural supremacy over Satan and the power of darkness, Jesus interlaces this admonition into the Great Commission:

> [17] And these signs will accompany those who believe: in my name they will cast out demons; they will speak in new tongues;
> [18] **they will pick up serpents with their hands; and if they drink any deadly poison, it will not hurt them**; they will lay their hands on the sick, and they will recover." [19] So then the Lord Jesus, after he had spoken to them, was taken up into heaven and sat down at the right hand of God. [20] And they went out and preached everywhere, while the Lord worked with them and confirmed the message by accompanying signs. (Mark 16:17–20, ESV)

As the disciples went out to preach the gospel, their message was simple: The serpent had been defeated by the power of the cross. To illustrate this point, they picked up venomous serpents and drank their poisonous venom and would walk away completely unharmed and unabated. While this may seem like a strange gift and admonition to us, it was a powerful testimony to first-century people. They took it as Jesus' disciples having power over "the serpent" of Genesis 3 and over evil spirits of darkness.

While on the island of Malta, Luke records that Paul was gathering some sticks to build a fire when a viper bit his hand.

> [4] When the native people saw the creature hanging from his hand, they said to one another, "No doubt this man is a murderer. Though he has escaped from the sea, Justice has not allowed

> him to live." [5] He, however, shook off the creature into the fire and **suffered no harm.** [6] They were waiting for him to swell up or suddenly fall down dead. But when they had waited a long time and saw no misfortune come to him, they changed their minds and said **that he was a god.** (Acts 28:4–6, ESV)

This miraculous ability was the perfect talking point to teach the Gentiles that Yahweh was superior to their gods and only Christ held the cure to the sting of sin and death. All they needed to do was look to Jesus and the cure of the cross.

> [2] **looking to Jesus**, the founder and perfecter of our faith, **who for the joy that was set before him endured the cross**, despising the shame, and is seated at the right hand of the throne of God. (Heb 12:2, ESV)

LOOKING AHEAD

Snake-bitten and humbled, Israel returned to their wilderness wandering, making many stops along the way (Num 21:10–20). Little did they know, they were about to, once again, come toe-to-toe with the giants. And not just any giants—the biggest and most powerful giant kings in all the land. Would Israel fearlessly battle the Titans, or would they shriek in terror? Would their faith stand strong, or would their trust in God completely crumble?

We'll find out in the next chapter.

CHAPTER 13

BATTLING THE TITANS

Thus the LORD gave to Israel all the land that he swore to give to their fathers. And they took possession of it, and they settled there. (Joshua 21:43, ESV)

READING THE STORY

AS MOSES LEAD HIS PEOPLE THROUGH the desert of thirst and war, they made camp in Oboth.

> They set out from Oboth and camped at Iye-abarim in the wilderness that borders Moab on the east. From there they went and camped at Zered Valley. They set out from there and camped on the other side of the Arnon River, in the wilderness that extends from the Amorite border, because the Arnon was the Moabite border between Moab and the Amorites. Therefore it is stated in the Book of the LORD's Wars: Waheb in Suphah and the ravines of the Arnon, even the slopes of the ravines that extend to the site of Ar and lie along the border of Moab. From there they went to Beer, the well the LORD told Moses about, "Gather the people so I may give them water." (Num 21:11–16, CSB)

The desert was physically draining. God's divine omniscience kept track of Israel's vitals, and right now, they were on the verge of dehydration and extinction. When Yahweh told Moses to gather the people, all of Israel broke into song with the following lyrics:

> "Spring up, O well!—Sing to it!— the well that the princes made, that the nobles of the people dug, with the scepter and with their staffs…" (Num 21:18, ESV)

Their stay in Beer was precisely what they needed to restore them to full strength. Proper hydration would be paramount because the percussive drums of war were beginning to roll. God's people were about to contend with the tall Amorite Titans and their legendary king, Sihon.

> Then Israel sent messengers to Sihon king of the Amorites, saying, "Let me pass through your land. We will not turn

> aside into field or vineyard. We will not drink the water of a well. We will go by the King's Highway until we have passed through your territory." (Num 21:21–22, ESV)

The prophet Amos shed light on the mysterious, sinister Amorites. He reveals they were as tall as cedars and as strong as oaks (Amos 2:9), leaving no doubt to their true identity. Israel would have understood the Amorites to be a clan of giants whose bulging veins ran with Nephilim blood. These were not just normal people. They were fathered by fallen angels and born through mortal women for the purpose of perpetuating a competing bloodline that would rival God's chosen portion and prevent the coming Messiah.

Recalling the encounter with Sihon years later, Moses wrote,

> But King Sihon of Heshbon would not let us travel through his land, for the Lord your God had made his spirit stubborn and his heart obstinate in order to hand him over to you, as has now taken place. "Then the Lord said to me, 'See, I have begun to give Sihon and his land to you. Begin to take possession of it.' (Deut 2:30–31, CSB)

Sihon's size and strength didn't matter. Yahweh fought for Israel and made quick work to end Sihon's reign in the Transjordan.

> Then Sihon and all his people came out to meet us for battle at Jahaz. And so Yahweh our God gave him over to us, and we struck him down, and his sons and all of his people. So we captured all of his cities at that time, and we destroyed each town of males and the women and the children; we did not leave behind a survivor. We took only the livestock as spoil for ourselves, and also the booty of the cities that we had captured. From Aroer, which is on the edge of the wadi of Arnon and the

> city that was in the wadi on up to Gilead, there was not a city that was inaccessible to us; Yahweh our God gave everything to us. Only the land of the Ammonites you did not approach, all along the whole upper region of the Jabbok River and the towns of the hill country, according to all that Yahweh our God had instructed. (Deut 2:32–37, LEB)

Slain in battle, the mighty Amorites from hell relinquished their precious land they once ruled.

> Thus Israel lived in the land of the Amorites. (Num 21:31, ESV)

This battle belonged to the Lord, and so would the next one. Waiting in the wings was the last of the original Rephaim giants, Og. His turf was the land of Bashan ("Bathan" in Ugaritic), the sinister home of Mount Hermon (Josh 12:4–6).

> *The linguistic note is intriguing since Bashan/Bathan both also mean "serpent," so that the region of Bashan was "the place of the serpent."*[1]

According to the book of Enoch, the first wave of fallen angels descended upon Hermon, the mighty mountain of Bashan. Wickedness had permeated from this baleful place ever since. The Psalmist understood the significance Mount Hermon played in the narrative of good versus evil. In Psalm 68, he emphasizes that the sinister servants of Bashan and Mount Hermon are thwarted by God's original holy mountain, Sinai, and are subservient to her "twice ten thousand" supernatural servants of light, God's holy angels.

---

1 Heiser, *The Unseen Realm*, 200.

> [15] A mountain of God is **the mountain of Bashan**; a mountain of many peaks is the mountain of Bashan. [16] Why do you look with hostility, O many-peaked mountains? This mountain God desires for his dwelling. Yes, Yahweh will abide in it forever. [17] The chariots of God are twice ten thousand, with thousands doubled. The Lord is among them at Sinai, distinctive in victory. (Ps 68:15–17, LEB)

And in our story, the king over the mountain brooded from its many peaks, bloodthirsty for war. In Moses's recollection of the battle at Edrei, he writes,

> "Then we turned and went up the road to Bashan, and King Og of Bashan came out against us with his whole army to do battle at Edrei. But the Lord said to me, 'Do not fear him, for I have handed him over to you along with his whole army and his land. Do to him as you did to King Sihon of the Amorites, who lived in Heshbon.' So the Lord our God also handed over King Og of Bashan and his whole army to us. We struck him until there was no survivor left. We captured all his cities at that time. There wasn't a city that we didn't take from them: sixty cities, the entire region of Argob, the kingdom of Og in Bashan. All these were fortified with high walls, gates, and bars, besides a large number of rural villages. We completely destroyed them, as we had done to King Sihon of Heshbon, destroying the men, women, and children of every city. But we took all the livestock and the spoil from the cities as plunder for ourselves. "At that time we took the land from the two Amorite kings across the Jordan, from the Arnon Valley as far as Mount Hermon, which the Sidonians call Sirion, but the Amorites call Senir, all the cities of the plateau, Gilead, and Bashan as far as Salecah and Edrei, cities of Og's kingdom in Bashan. (Only King

> Og of Bashan was left of the remnant of the Rephaim. His bed was made of iron. Isn't it in Rabbah of the Ammonites? It is 13½ feet long and 6 feet wide by a standard measure.) "At that time we took possession of this land. I gave to the Reubenites and Gadites the area extending from Aroer by the Arnon Valley, and half the hill country of Gilead along with its cities. I gave to half the tribe of Manasseh the rest of Gilead and all Bashan, the kingdom of Og. The entire region of Argob, the whole territory of Bashan, used to be called the land of the Rephaim. Jair, a descendant of Manasseh, took over the entire region of Argob as far as the border of the Geshurites and Maacathites. He called Bashan by his own name, Jair's Villages, as it is today. I gave Gilead to Machir, and I gave to the Reubenites and Gadites the area extending from Gilead to the Arnon Valley (the middle of the valley was the border) and up to the Jabbok River, the border of the Ammonites. The Arabah and Jordan are also borders from Chinnereth as far as the Sea of the Arabah, the Dead Sea, under the slopes of Pisgah on the east. (Deut 3:1–17, CSB)

ANSWERING YOUR QUESTIONS

WHY DID ISRAEL KILL THESE PEOPLE AND TAKE THEIR LAND?

Many critics of the Bible point to the totality of Israel's conquest of Canaan as abominable and cruel. They paint our God as a graceless, ruthless tyrant who's hellbent on raising His family in a specific ZIP code and is willing to slaughter innocent men, women, and children to do it. Are they right? Is the God of the Old Testament merciless and despotic? Is He guilty of killing innocent children for mere acreage? And how does this make sense in light of Christ's words about the innocence of children and their place as members of the kingdom of God?

Deuteronomy 3:6 (ESV)	Mark 10:13–14 (ESV)
[6] And we devoted them to destruction, as we did to Sihon the king of Heshbon, **devoting to destruction every city, men, women, and children**.	[13] And they were bringing children to him that he might touch them, and the disciples rebuked them. [14] But when Jesus saw it, he was indignant and said to them, "**Let the children come to me; do not hinder them, for to such belongs the kingdom of God**.

Before I understood the supernatural element of it all, I stood defenseless to these claims. My stomach churned as I read my Bible and imagined hearing God give the order of the mass murder of adolescent children. I often thought, "How is that a loving God?"

The truth is God was "devoting to destruction" (***Hebrew: kharam***) what the fallen angels corruptly produced—the abominable giant clans and their evil offspring. The original report the spies brought back when they observed the locals of Canaan was that all the people were of great height and were considered Nephilim (Num 13:32–33). These giants are specifically listed in Numbers 13:28–29 as among the Amorites, Amalekites, Hittites, Jebusites, and Canaanites. Similar passages reveal additional people groups where giants could be found: Anakim (Num 13:28–33; Deut 1:28; 2:10–11, 21; 9:2; Josh 14:12), Emim (Deut 2:10–11), Rephaim (Deut 2:10–11, 20; 3:11), Zamzummim (Deut 2:20), Zuzim (Gen 14:5), Perizzites (Gen 15:20; Josh 17:15), Philistines (2 Sam 21:18–22), Horites/Horim (Deut 2:21–22), Avvim (Deut 2:23), and the Caphtorim (Deut 2:23).

Furthermore, pockets of giants are listed as being in cities and regions such as Ashteroth-karnaim (Gen 14:5), Ham (Gen 14:5), Shaveh-kiriathaim (Gen 14:5), Hebron/Kiriath-arba (Num 13:22; Josh 14:15), Ar (Deut 2:9), Seir (Deut 2:21–22), Bashan (Deut 3:10–11), Debir/Kiriath-sepher (Josh 11:21–22), Anab (Josh 11:21–22), Gaza (Josh 11:21–22),

Gath (Josh 11:21–22), Ashdod (Josh 11:21–22), Valley of the Rephaim (Josh 15:8), Gob (2 Sam 21:18), and Moab (1 Chr 11:22). It's no surprise that Israel often found themselves battling in these cities.

In summation, the targeted people groups during the conquest weren't "innocent" human lives—they were an abomination of life who threatened humanity's very existence. They were a byproduct of angelic pollution to the human gene pool God so wonderfully engineered to bear His own image. God wasn't okay with humanity coexisting with human hybrids that were remade in the image of God's supernatural rivals and raised up to eradicate God's people. Yahweh was committed and devoted to destroying the Nephilim armies of Satan, and He did so first through the flood and then through various Israelite leaders such as Moses and Joshua, and later through David (1 Sam 17) and his mighty men of courage (2 Sam 21:15–22). Upon victory, the acreage of Canaan was divvied out to the tribes of Israel as they conquered the tribes of giants one by one (Neh 9:22; Ps 135:8–12).

WHY DID MOSES MENTION OG'S BED?

When Moses told the story of when he and the Israelites battled Og of Bashan, he detoured in thought and mentioned Og's bed, oddly enough.

> 11 (For only Og the king of Bashan was left of the remnant of the Rephaim. **Behold, his bed was a bed of iron. Is it not in Rabbah of the Ammonites? Nine cubits was its length, and four cubits its breadth, according to the common cubit.)** (Deut 3:11, ESV)

It's strange to mention a piece of furniture in a war story—unless there was an important connection. What exactly did Moses want his readers to know about his fallen nemesis? Certainly, the fact that it was made of iron speaks to the sheer weight and girth of Bashan's giant king. But could there be more to the story? Dr. Michael Heiser pointed out,

For an ancient Israelite reader with a command of Hebrew and a worldview that included the idea that supernatural opposition to Israel had something to do with preflood events in Mesopotamia, several things in this short passage would have jumped out immediately. None of them are obvious in English translation.

First, the most immediate link back to the Babylonian polemic is Og's bed (Hebrew: ʿeres). Its dimensions (9 × 4 cubits) are precisely those of the cultic bed in the ziggurat called Etemenanki—which is the ziggurat most archaeologists identify as the Tower of Babel referred to in the Bible. Ziggurats functioned as temples and divine abodes. The unusually large bed at Etemenanki was housed in "the house of the bed" (bit erši). It was the place where the god Marduk and his divine wife, Zarpanitu, met annually for ritual lovemaking, the purpose of which was divine blessing upon the land.

Scholars have been struck by the precise correlation. It's hard not to conclude that, as with Genesis 6:1–4, so with Deuteronomy 3, those who put the finishing touches on the Old Testament during the exile in Babylon were connecting Marduk and Og in some way. The most transparent path is in fact giant stature. Og is said to have been the last of the Rephaim—a term connected to the giant Anakim and other ancient giant clans in the Transjordan (Deut 2:11, 20). Marduk, like other deities in antiquity, was portrayed as superhuman in size. However, the real matrix of ideas in the mind of the biblical author may be derived from wordplay based on Babylonian mythology.[2]

The original readers would have considered Moses's details about Og's bed important and would have instantly picked up on the sinister undertones of the passage.

---

2 Heiser, *The Unseen Realm*, 198–199.

CONNECTING THE GOSPEL

TARTARUS & GREEK MYTHOLOGY

What if I told you that Greek demigods such as Hercules, Theseus, Perseus, and Achilles may not only be chalked up to imagination and myth? Early Christian writer Justin Martyr wrote in 125 A.D.,

> *"Whence also the poets and mythologists, not knowing that it was the angels and those demons who had been begotten by them that did these things to men, and women, and cities, and nations, which they related, ascribed them to god himself, and to those who were accounted to be his very offspring, and to the offspring of those who were called his brothers, Neptune and Pluto, and to the children again of these their offspring. For whatever name each of the angels had given to himself and his children, by that name they called them."*[3]

The context of New Testament times was, largely, Greek mythos. When Paul preached the gospel in Athens, Greece, he was met by curious Epicureans and Stoic philosophers who wanted to know more about Jesus and the resurrection, saying Paul seemed "to be a setter forth of strange gods" (Acts 17:18, KJV). Luke recorded what happened next.

> [19] They took him and brought him to the Areopagus, and said, "May we learn about this new teaching you are presenting? [20] Because what you say sounds strange to us, and we want to know what these things mean." [21] Now all the Athenians and the foreigners residing there spent their time on nothing else but

3 Justin Martyr, *The Second Apology of Justin Martyr*, quoted in A. Coxe, James Donaldson, and Alexander Roberts, eds., vol. 1 of *The Ante-Nicene Fathers: The Apostolic Fathers, Justin Martyr, Ireneaus* (New York: Christian Literature Publishing, 1885), 190.

telling or hearing something new. 22 Paul stood in the middle of the Areopagus and said, "People of Athens! I see that you are extremely religious in every respect. (Acts 17:19–22, CSB)

Greek religion counted a theoretically limitless number of heroes who range from godlike figures like →Herakles to ordinary dead humans.[4]

The Grecians' religious rolodex was a hodgepodge of hero-worship. They worshiped deities, mighty men, and heroes of old. In the Grecians' minds, their gods were the good guys, as Plato wrote in *Laws 906.*

For as we acknowledge the world to be full of many goods and also of evils, and of more evils than goods, there is, as we affirm, an ***immortal conflict going on among us****, which requires marvellous watchfulness; and in that conflict* ***the Gods and demigods are our allies****, and we are their property.*[5]

Stories from Greek mythology have become popularized in modern times. In beloved and classic films, the stories of Zeus hurling his thunderbolts from Mount Olympus as his demigod son, Hercules, pummels his enemies with strength and force are quite celebrated. These fantastic stories are truly fascinating and produce lucrative earnings at the box office for filmmakers. But could they actually be echoing ancient truths? Nineteenth-century preacher Robert Govett thought so. In 1841, Govett wrote,

"Lastly, it should be observed that the general view here taken is corroborated by Gentile records, and the traditions of profane

4 F. Graf, "Heroes," *Dictionary of Deities and Demons in the Bible*, 2nd ed., 412.

5 Plato, vol. 5 of *The Dialogues of Plato*, 3rd ed., 293 (Jowett).

> *writers. As the story of Deucalion, with other traditions, present manifest traces of the reality of the Scripture history of the deluge, so* ***the poetic fables and early historic traditions of the war of the giants or Titans against Saturn, the fables of the Cyclops, of Hercules, and other mystic heroes, manifest the truth of the Scripture declarations, respecting the fall of the angels****, their strength, their violence, their pride, their destruction. Their celestial origin was noticed in the tradition that represented them as sons of Ouranus. Their vastness, and their war against heaven, are celebrated by Homer, Hesiod, Ovid, Plato, Lucan, Seneca, and others."*[6]

Second-century Christian apologist Justin Martyr wrote,

> *When, indeed, we assert that the Word, our Teacher Jesus Christ, who is the first-begotten of God the Father, was not born as the result of sexual relations, and that He was crucified, died, arose from the dead, and ascended into Heaven,* ***we propose nothing new or different from that which you say about the so-called sons of Jupiter****. You know exactly the number of sons ascribed to Jupiter by your respected writers: Mercury, who was the interpretative word and teacher of all; Aesculapius, who, though himself a healer of diseases, was struck by a thunderbolt and ascended into heaven; Bacchus, who was torn to pieces; Hercules, who rushed into the flames of the funeral pyre to escape his sufferings; the Dioscuri, the sons of Leda; Perseus, the son of Danäe; and Bellerophon, who, though of human origin, rose to heaven on his horse Pegasus.2 And what can we say of*

6 Robert Govett, *Isaiah Unfulfilled: Being an Exposition of the Prophet, with New Version and Critical Notes*, quoted in Ryan Pitterson, *Judgment of the Nephilim* (Days of Noe Publishing, 2017), Kindle edition, 139.

Ariadne and those like her, who are said to be placed among the stars? And what about the emperors who die among you, whom you think worthy to be deified, and for whom you lead forth a false witness to swear that he saw the burning Caesar rise from the funeral pyre and ascend to heaven?4 Nor is it necessary to relate to you, who know them already, what kind of actions are imputed to those so-called sons of Jupiter, except to add that they have been recorded for the profit and instruction of young students; ***for everyone considers it a good thing to imitate the gods. But may such a thought concerning the gods be far from every sound mind****, as to believe that Jupiter himself, whom they consider the ruler and creator of all things, was a parricide and the son of a parricide, and that, seized by a lust of evil and shameful pleasures, he descended upon Ganymede and the many women whom he violated, and that his sons were guilty of similar actions.* ***But, as we stated above, the wicked demons have done these things****. We, however, have been taught that only they will have eternal bliss who live a holy and virtuous life close to God; we believe that they who live an evil life and do not repent will be punished in everlasting fire.*[7]

By now on our journey, you've learned the origin of the Old Testament giants. They were hybrid humans who were the culture heroes that ruled ancient times. What's stunning is there's actually a direct overlap between Greek mythology and the Bible.

First, let's consider the Titans. The general narrative of Greek mythos is summarized well by author Douglas Van Dorn in his book, *Giants: Sons of the Gods*.

---

7 Martyr, *The First Apology, The Second Apology, Dialogue with Trypho, Exhortation to the Greeks, Discourse to the Greeks, The Monarchy or The Rule of God*, 56–57.

In the Greek story, Gaia and Uranus get married and have children. It is at this point that the primeval creation turns into more recognizable history. Think about these children this way—they are the product of a marriage between heaven and earth. When we understand who these children are it is easily understood that they tell the Genesis 6:1-4 story. The sons of God (personified in Uranus) married the daughters of men (personified by Gaia) and begat children called the Nephilim. At this point, the story gets very interesting. There are several branches of children that are born from this unholy union. These branches take place at two different periods in history, and through two different means of generation. The first group of children all come from the union between Gaia and Uranus. These consist of the Cyclopes, the Hekatonkheires, and the Titans. One thing unites all of these groups. They are all giants...

The third group were the Titans and there were twelve of them. The youngest and most important is Cronus. His name is of unknown origin. The Romans called him Saturn. His is the sixth planet and we also remember him ever Satur day. Some have suggested that his name derives from a word meaning "to cut" (Gk: keirō). Others, thinking of the Latin equivalent Sadorn, suggest it means "martial" or "warlike." Both are reminiscent of this figure.[8]

Many scholars have made the connection between the biblical giant King Og and the mythological Ogygos (Cronus) of the Titans. The brilliant Estonian scholar Amar Annus wrote,

---

8 Douglas Van Dorn, *Giants: Sons of the Gods*, (Erie, CO: Waters of Creation, 2013), Kindle edition, 286–289.

> *In the Greek myth Ogygos is a son of Gaia Pelore, who is a well-known source of destructive forces represented by her gegenes sons, giants and Titans. They are all finally locked up in the Netherworld as punishment.*[9]

Locked up in the Netherworld? Sound familiar? Annus went on to write,

> *The chthonic nature of Titans, similar to that of the Rephaim, can also be demonstrated on the basis on the Greek texts. In Illiad 14:274-79 we find a very interesting passage, where Hypnos bids Hera to pray in the name of gods that are below with Kronos (who by that time had already been moved into Hades) and she failed not to hearken, but sware as he bade and invoked by name all the gods below* ***Tartarus****, that are called Titans. The description of Titans living in the Netherworld with Kronos, who is their king, closely parallel Rephaim (rpum) and Og as their King. It is of significance, that Greek Ogygos is also named the King of the Titans in some parts of the Greek tradition.*[10]

Shedding the deception and recovering the supernatural worldview of Scripture is eye-opening to the parallels of myth and truth. There are no coincidences—it's all connected. All civilizations share one world history. Naturally, there are crossovers among oral and written traditions of the ancient civilizations. Moses simply set the record straight about the king of Bashan, the last of the Rephaim (Deut 3:11). Cronus, who's lauded as the king of the twelve Titans and ruler of the cosmos

---

9 Amar Annus, "Are There Greek Rephaim? On the Etymology of Greek Meropes and Titanes," vol. 31 of *Ugarit Forschungen* (Kevelaer, Germany: Verlag Butzon & Bercker, 2000), 23.

10 Annus, "Are There Greek Rephaim?," 22.

in the Golden Age, met his doom, not at the hand of his son Zeus, but by Yahweh—the god of Gods—and the mortal soldiers of Israel.

The plot thickens, however. There are passages that explicitly connect the Old Testament giants to the Titans of Greek mythology. The Greek translation (LXX) of the Hebrew Scriptures calls the stomping grounds of the mighty "Rephaim" a "Valley of Titans" ***(Greek: Τιτάνων, Titanōn***) in two instances.

2 Samuel 5:18 (ESV)	2 Kingdoms 5:18 (Brenton LXX En)
[18] Now the Philistines had come and spread out in the Valley of Rephaim.	[18] And the Philistines came, and assembled in the valley of the giants ***(Greek: Τιτάνων, Titanōn).***
2 Samuel 5:22 (ESV)	**2 Kingdoms 5:22 (Brenton LXX En)**
[22] And the Philistines came up yet again and spread out in the Valley of Rephaim.	[22] And the Philistines came up yet again, and assembled in the valley of Giants ***(Greek: Τιτάνων, Titanōn).***

The LXX (Greek Septuagint) was the preferred form of the Old Testament Scriptures by the first-century church, and even Jesus Christ, Himself. Ancient Christians understood the sinister backstory of the Titans of Greek mythology. They knew they echoed back to the Old Testament giants of the world's past. These fallen warriors once walked in a place that ancient Jews and Christians called the "Valley of Titans."

There's a second important link between the Bible and Greek mythology. In the Genesis 6:1–4 account, the Greek text (LXX) uses the word "*gigantes, γίγαντες*" that translates as "giants," while the Hebrew calls them "Nephilim." The Lexham English Septuagint reads,

> [1] And Noah lived five hundred years, and Noah fathered three sons: Shem, Ham, and Japheth. And it happened,

> when humans began to become numerous upon the land, and they had daughters, [2] the angels of God, having seen the daughters of humans, that they were beautiful, took for themselves women from all whom they picked out. [3] The Lord God said, "My breath will not at all reside in these humans for very long because they are flesh, but their days will be one hundred and twenty years." [4] Now giants (gigantes, **γίγαντες**) were upon the land in those days, and after that, whenever the sons of God visited the daughters of humans, they fathered children for themselves; those were the giants (gigantes, **γίγαντες**) who were from long ago, the people of renown. (Gen 6:1–4, LES)

These "gigantes" also show up in Greek mythology. Van Dorn wrote,

> *It is through the blood (sometimes semen) of Uranus that is thrown into the sea that the second batch of children are born. These are the Meliae, the Erinyes, and most importantly, the Gigantes. The first two are female. The Meliae are nymph-spirits. The Erinyes are deities that dwell in the underworld to punish whoever has sworn a false oath. Underworld deities and spirits? Hmmm. The final group, the Gigantes, is where the LXX's translation of nephilim originates. Remember, the Nephilim are called gigantes in the Greek. Thus, the story of the children of Gaia and Uranus seems to be an interesting, albeit perverted memory of the events of antediluvian and early post-diluvian history where the world, full of giants, perished only to be replaced with wicked spirits and more giants that terrorized humanity all around the globe.*[11]

---

11 Van Dorn, *Giants: Sons of the Gods*, 246–250.

The Dictionary of Demons and Deities substantiates Van Dorn's claims:

> *In the strict sense the Gigantes in Greek mythology were the serpent-footed giants who were born from the blood-drops of the castration of Uranus (→Heaven) that had fallen on →Earth (Hesiod Theogony 183–186). The term gigantes occurs about 40 times in the LXX and refers there respectively to: a) the giant offspring of 'the sons of God' and 'the daughters of mankind' (Gen 6:1–4; Bar 3:26–28; Sir 16:7); b) strong and mighty men, like →Nimrod (Gen 10:8–9); c) several pre-Israelite peoples of tall stature in Canaan and Transjordania.*[12]

A third link between the Bible and Greek mythology is a place or "prison" known as "Tartarus." The apostle Peter states the angels who sinned in the days of Noah (Gen 6:1–4) are locked up, or imprisoned, in "Tartarus" (2 Pet 2:4–5).

2 Peter 2:4–5 (LEB)	**2 Peter 2:4–5 (ESV)**
[4] For if God did not spare the angels who sinned, **but held them captive in Tartarus with chains of darkness** and handed them over to be kept for judgment, [5] and did not spare the ancient world, but preserved Noah, a proclaimer of righteousness, and seven others when he brought a flood on the world of the ungodly,	[4] For if God did not spare angels when they sinned, but cast them into hell (**ταρταρωσας**) and committed them to chains of gloomy darkness to be kept until the judgment; [5] if he did not spare the ancient world, but preserved Noah, a herald of righteousness, with seven others, when he brought a flood upon the world of the ungodly;

12 G. Mussies, "Giants," *Dictionary of Deities and Demons in the Bible*, 2nd ed., 343.

Similar to the masking of the name "Azazel" as "scapegoat" by the English translators, "Tartarus" is often masked in translation as"hell."

> *Where or what is Tartarus (translated as "hell)? This word is only found in this verse in the New Testament… Tartarus was the name in classical mythology for the subterranean abyss in which rebellious gods and other such beings as the Titans were punished.*[13]

The idea of living beings/spirits being held in a subterranean abyss isn't foreign to Scripture. Paul says all beings under the earth will bow to the exalted Christ.

> 9 Therefore God has highly exalted him and bestowed on him the name that is above every name, 10 so that at the name of Jesus **every knee should bow**, in heaven and on earth and **under the earth**, (Phil 2:9–10, ESV)

In John's apocalypse, he reveals that four angels are imprisoned, presumably, under the great Euphrates River.

> 13 Then the sixth angel blew his trumpet, and I heard a voice from the four horns of the golden altar before God, 14 saying to the sixth angel who had the trumpet, "**Release the four angels who are bound at the great river Euphrates**." (Rev 9:13–14, ESV)

As strange as it sounds to our modern ears, it's possible Tartarus isn't in some alternate reality or spiritual dimension—it could actually be a fortified prison thousands of miles beneath the surface of the earth.

---

13 D. Walls, vol. 11 of *I & II Peter, I, II & III John, Jude*, ed. M. Anders (Nashville, TN: Broadman & Holman Publishers, 1999), 133.

A fourth and final link between the Bible and Greek mythology is Apollyon. John writes that "a fallen star" or "angel" called Apollyon, which means "the destroyer," will use a key to open an abyss inside the earth that will release demonic beings and creatures to torment those who are not marked with the seal of God on their foreheads.

> 1 The fifth angel blew his trumpet, and **I saw a star that had fallen from heaven to earth. The key for the shaft to the abyss was given to him**. 2 He opened the shaft to the abyss, and smoke came up out of the shaft like smoke from a great furnace so that the sun and the air were darkened by the smoke from the shaft. 3 Then locusts came out of the smoke on to the earth, and power was given to them like the power that scorpions have on the earth. 4 They were told not to harm the grass of the earth, or any green plant, or any tree, but only those people who do not have God's seal on their foreheads. 5 They were not permitted to kill them but were to torment them for five months; their torment is like the torment caused by a scorpion when it stings someone. 6 In those days people will seek death and will not find it; they will long to die, but death will flee from them. 7 The appearance of the locusts was like horses prepared for battle. Something like golden crowns was on their heads; their faces were like human faces; 8 they had hair like women's hair; their teeth were like lions' teeth; 9 they had chests like iron breastplates; the sound of their wings was like the sound of many chariots with horses rushing into battle; 10 and they had tails with stingers like scorpions, so that with their tails they had the power to harm people for five months. 11 **They had as their king the angel of the abyss**; his name in Hebrew is Abaddon, and **in Greek he has the name Apollyon**. (Rev 9:1–11, CSB)

Just who is this angel named Apollyon? The Anchor Yale Bible Dictionary notes,

> *In one manuscript (syrph), instead of Apollyon the text reads "Apollo," the Greek god of death and pestilence as well as of the sun, music, poetry, crops and herds, and medicine. Apollyon is no doubt the correct reading.*[14]

The Greek poem *The Iliad* discusses Apollo's destructive nature.

> *The beginning of the Iliad introduces Apollo as the frightening god who sends a deadly pestilence into the cattle and the army of the Achaeans.*
>
> *...But the author of the disease is also the one who can stop it; to that end one has to propitiate Apollo by means of sacrifices, hymns and prayers (NILSSON 1955:538–544), as was in fact done by the Achaeans (Iliad I:48–52, 450–456). In the second and third centuries CE, this way of propitiating the god to avert a plague was still advised by Apollo himself in several oracles given at Clarus and Didyma (R. LANE FOX, Pagans and Christians [New York 1987] 231–235). Similarly ambivalent gods, said to be both the cause of evil and of its disappearance, are found all over the world; in India, it is the god Rudra who shows a remarkable similarity to Apollo (LORENZ 1988:4, 8).*[15]

The evidence points to the Greek god Apollo, or Apollyon, as the god who, according to the apostle John, will open the subterranean pit under the earth.

---

14 H. J. Grether, "Apollyon," *The Anchor Yale Bible Dictionary* 1:301–302.

15 R. Van den Broek, "Apollo," *Dictionary of Deities and Demons in the Bible*, 2nd ed., 75.

The key players and places of Greek mythology dovetail closely with the Bible. Here is a side-by-side comparison of Hesiod's (Greek poet from 750–650 B.C.) explanation of how and where the "Titans" were punished versus Peter and Jude's explanation about how and where the angels were punished following their antediluvian rebellion. The similarities are undeniable.

2 Peter 2:4–5 (LEB)	Jude 6 (ESV)	Hesiod, Theogony 313–320
[4] For if God did not spare **the angels** who sinned, **but held them captive in Tartarus with chains of darkness** and handed them over to be kept for judgment, [5] and did not spare the ancient world, but preserved Noah, a proclaimer of righteousness, and seven others when he brought a flood on the world of the ungodly,	[6] And **the angels** who did not stay within their own position of authority, but left their proper dwelling, he has **kept in eternal chains under gloomy darkness** until the judgment of the great day	Among the foremost Cottus and Briareos and Gyes insatiate for war raised fierce fighting: three hundred rocks, one upon another, they launched from their strong hands and **overshadowed the Titans** with their missiles, and **buried them** beneath the wise-pathed earth, and **bound them in bitter chains** when they had conquered them by their strength for all their great spirit, as far **beneath the earth to Tartarus.**[16]

Why would the apostles use the underworld prison of Greek mythos and its gloomy chains to articulate where and how the rebel gods (angels) of

16 Van Dorn, *Giants: Sons of the Gods*, 225.

Genesis 6:1–4 are being held if Greek mythology were merely fairytale and fiction? The answer is simple—they wouldn't! While many details surrounding the Greek stories are embellished, the biblical writers make no efforts to debunk the nucleus of Greek mythology—a supernatural struggle between the gods and their metahuman sons, the Titans and giants. Just because something is "mythic" doesn't disqualify it from being historic. In fact, as is evidenced in this chapter, the prophets and apostles often embraced aspects of the Grecian worldview as biblical history.

LOOKING AHEAD

The victory over the two Amorite giant kings was the beginning of a long string of holy conquests in the land. When Moses retold the story about Sihon and Og in the Transjordan, he's recorded as saying,

> "And I charged you all at that time when I said, "Yahweh has given you—to all of you—this land to possess. All the warriors shall cross over, ready to fight, before your brothers, the Israelites. Only your wives and your little children and your livestock (I know that you have much livestock) must stay in your towns that I have given you, until Yahweh shall give rest to your brothers as he did to you, and also they take possession of the land that Yahweh your God is giving to them beyond the Jordan; then they may return, each one to his possession that I have given to them. And I commanded Joshua at that time, saying, 'Your eyes see all that Yahweh your God has done to these two kings; so Yahweh will do to all of the kingdoms where you are about to cross over to. You shall not fear them, for Yahweh your God is the one fighting for you. (Deut 3:18–22, LEB)

And that's exactly what the Lord did. He gave Israel superhuman strength to fight against the mighty Titans, the demigods akin to Greek mythology. As the biblical record plays out, Moses died at the doorstep of Canaan on Mount Nebo.

> Then Moses went up from the plains of Moab to Mount Nebo, to the top of Pisgah, which faces Jericho, and the LORD showed him all the land: Gilead as far as Dan, all of Naphtali, the land of Ephraim and Manasseh, all the land of Judah as far as the Mediterranean Sea, the Negev, and the plain in the Valley of Jericho, the City of Palms, as far as Zoar. The LORD then said to him, "This is the land I promised Abraham, Isaac, and Jacob, 'I will give it to your descendants.' I have let you see it with your own eyes, but you will not cross into it." So Moses the servant of the LORD died there in the land of Moab, according to the LORD's word. He buried him in the valley in the land of Moab facing Beth-peor, and no one to this day knows where his grave is. Moses was one hundred twenty years old when he died; his eyes were not weak, and his vitality had not left him. (Deut 34:1–7, CSB)

After mourning his death (Deut 34:8), his apprentice, Joshua, rallied the troops and charged Canaan with the Israelite army. With full force, they slit the throats of the serpent's sinister giants, whom the Lord devoted to destruction.

> At that time Joshua proceeded to exterminate the Anakim from the hill country—Hebron, Debir, Anab—all the hill country of Judah and of Israel. Joshua completely destroyed them with their cities. No Anakim were left in the land of the Israelites, except for some remaining in Gaza, Gath, and Ashdod. So Joshua took the entire land, in keeping with all that the LORD had told Moses. Joshua then gave it as an inheritance to Israel according to their tribal allotments. After this, the land had rest from war. (Josh 11:21–23, CSB)

Despite their early and often successes in the land, there were a few of the Canaanites that they simply, by choice, didn't destroy or drive out from the land (Judg 1). The unwillingness to finish what they'd started was a catastrophic mistake with generational effects. Over the next five hundred years, God's people were ruled by flawed judges and wicked kings. These so-called "leaders" repeatedly led Israel to the altars of Satan and the nations' gods (Judg 2:3). Over and over, Israel repeated the vicious cycle of sin, oppression, repentance, deliverance, and peace. But on the horizon was a faithful prophet, who in one of the most surreal and epic showdowns in all of human history, would battle 450 of Satan's most loyal servants to a fiery death. Many amazing and paranormal details surrounding this biblical scene will be uncovered in the next chapter.

CHAPTER 14

DESPERATE PROPHETS, DYING GODS, AND THE DIVINE COUNCIL

But the prophet who presumes to speak a word in my name that I have not commanded him to speak, or who speaks in the name of other gods, that same prophet shall die.' (Deuteronomy 18:20, ESV)

READING THE STORY

AFTER THE PERIOD KNOWN AS "THE Judges" passed, God's chosen portion demanded to have a king like the nations around them (1 Sam 8:5, 20). Despite Yahweh's frequent warnings to be separate and holy, they were insistent. So God let them be driven by the desires of their misguided hearts straight into King Saul's poor leadership.

Saul's reign was, well… disastrous. His refusal to utterly destroy the Amalekites cost him his crown. David, the famed giant slayer, was selected next. Despite his mistakes, Yahweh loved David, and David loved the Lord. David's son, Solomon, was the next to rule the twelve tribes at Mount Zion in the holy city of Jerusalem. Solomon built Yahweh's 207-foot temple as a permanent replacement for Moses's now tattered tent of meeting (i.e., the tabernacle), just as David had asked him to do. But the back end of his term as king was filled with treachery and illicit sex. His love for women and worldly power led him to marry many beautiful pagan women. 1 Kings 11:1–8 states,

> "King Solomon loved many foreign women: the daughter of Pharaoh, Moabite, Ammonite, Edomite, Sidonian, Hittite; from the nations which Yahweh had said to the Israelites, "You shall not marry them, and they shall not marry you. They will certainly turn your heart after their gods." But Solomon clung to them to love. He had seven hundred princesses and three hundred concubines, and his wives turned his heart. It happened at the time of Solomon's old age that his wives guided his heart after other gods, and his heart was not fully with Yahweh his God as the heart of David his father had been. Solomon went after Ashtoreth the god of the Sidonians and after Milcom the abhorrence of the Ammonites. So Solomon did evil in the eyes of Yahweh and did not fully follow after Yahweh as David his father. At that time, Solomon built a high place for Chemosh, the abomination of Moab, on the mountain

> which faces Jerusalem and for Molech, the abomination of the Ammonites. Thus he did for all of his foreign wives, offering incense and sacrificing to their gods. (1 Kgs 11:1–8, LEB)

Solomon's life is an ugly reminder of just how quickly one's loyalty can shift from Yahweh to Satan in the battlefield of the heart. Rehoboam, Solomon's son, was a carbon copy of his father's wickedness and ruled terribly on his father's throne (931–913 B.C.). His greedy heart caused a national divide among the Lord's people. The tribes of Israel split into two separate kingdoms. The southern kingdom consisted of the descendants of David and became known as Judah. Their capital was still the holy city of Jerusalem. The new northern kingdom who pulled out under Rehoboam's reign became known as Israel, and their capital cities were Shechem, Tirzah, and Samaria.

> "...they made Jeroboam the son of Nebat king. And Jeroboam drove Israel from following the LORD and made them commit great sin. The people of Israel walked in all the sins that Jeroboam did. They did not depart from them, (2 Kgs 17:21–22, ESV)

Long story short, both kingdoms had roughly twenty kings apiece (931–715 B.C.), and only eight—all from the southern kingdom of Judah—out of the forty ruled righteously in the sight of God.

But the central focus of our story takes place six kings beyond Jeroboam. King Ahab is now on the throne in the northern kingdom of Israel.

> "But Ahab son of Omri did evil in the eyes of Yahweh more than all who were before him. If it wasn't enough that he went after the sins of Jeroboam the son of Nebat, he also took as wife Jezebel the daughter of Ethbaal the king of the Sidonians. He

> went and served Baal and bowed down to him. And he built an altar to Baal in the house of Baal which he had built in Samaria. Ahab also made the sacred pole, and he continued to provoke Yahweh the God of Israel more than all the kings of Israel who were before him. (1 Kgs 16:30–33, LEB)

Ahab's allegiance was to Baal, whom Jesus clarified to be none other than the insidious serpent called Satan. It's as despicable as it sounds; Ahab built a temple so he, Jezebel, and Israel could worship the devil instead of Yahweh. He also set up Asherah poles, or stylized Asherah trees, to honor Asherah, the Canaanite goddess and sexual consort of the supreme god El.

> *Allegiance to the Asherah cult was proscribed (Exod. 34:13–14; Deut. 7:5), and various attempts were made to eradicate the practice (e.g., Gideon, Judg. 6:25–30). Maacah the queen mother had placed an "image" of Asherah in Judah which her grandson Asa destroyed in the Wadi Kidron (1 Kgs. 15:13; cf. 2 Chr. 15:16). King Josiah of Judah burned the "vessels" and the woven "hangings" of Asherah (2 Kgs. 23:4, 7; 2 Chr. 34:3, 7) which his predecessor Manasseh had erected in the temple at Jerusalem (2 Kgs. 21:7; cf. 2 Chr. 33:3, 19); earlier reforms were carried out by Jehoshaphat (2 Chr. 19:3) and Hezekiah (2 Kgs. 18:4). Prophetic judgments include references to continued devotion to the "sacred poles" (Isa. 27:9; Jer. 17:1 ff.; Mic. 5:14).*[1]

But not everyone in the land bowed to Baal. There was a devoted man named Elijah whose loyalty to the Lord never wavered.

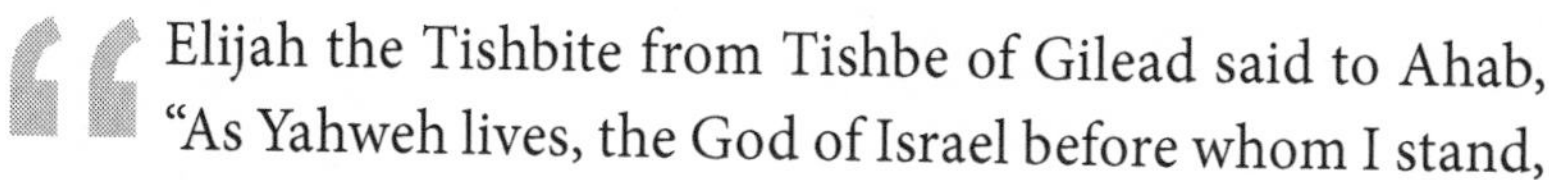

> Elijah the Tishbite from Tishbe of Gilead said to Ahab, "As Yahweh lives, the God of Israel before whom I stand,

1 A. C. Myers, "Asherah," *Eerdmans Dictionary of the Bible* 113.

> there shall surely not be dew nor rain these years except by my command." Then the word of Yahweh came to him, saying, "Go from this place and turn to the east; you must hide yourself in the Wadi Kerith which faces the Jordan. It shall be that you shall drink from the wadi, and I have commanded the crows to sustain you there." So he went and did according to the word of Yahweh. He went and stayed in the Wadi Kerith which faces the Jordan. The crows were bringing bread and meat in the morning for him and bread and meat in the evening, and he drank from the wadi. It happened after a while that the wadi dried up, because there was no rain in the land. (1 Kgs 17:1–7, LEB)

Yahweh's decision to bring a drought to Ahab's kingdom was meaningful and filled with sarcasm. Baal was paraded as the "storm god" of the ancient world; the Jews knew Yahweh really commanded the rains and wielded the storms (Jer 14:22). Archaeologists have recovered a hymn from Ugarit that was sung to Baal. The following lyrics are from the text *KTU 1.101–9.*

> *1–4 1.101 R 1 Baal sits like the base of a mountain; Hadd se[ttles] as the ocean, in the midst of his divine mountain, Saphon, in [the midst of] the mountain of victory. Seven lightning-flashes [ ], eight bundles of thunder, a tree-of-lightning [in his] ri[ght hand].*
>
> *5–9 1.101 R 5 His head is magnificent, His brow is dew-drenched. his feet are eloquent in (his) wrath. [His] horn is [exal]ted; his head is in the snows in heaven, [with] the god there is abounding water. His mouth is like two clouds [ ], [his lips] like wine from jars, his heart [ ]*[2]

---

2 N. Wyatt, *Religious Texts from Ugarit*, 2nd ed. (London; New York: Sheffield Academic Press, 2002), 388–390.

Satan, or Baal, the acclaimed god of "much water," is about to be exposed as powerless against the God of heaven in the very land that now worships his unholy name.

> It happened many days later that the word of Yahweh came to Elijah in the third year, saying, "Go, present yourself to Ahab so that I may give rain on the surface of the earth." So Elijah went to present himself to Ahab. Now the famine was severe in Samaria. Ahab summoned Obadiah who was over the house. (Now Obadiah was fearing Yahweh greatly. It had happened that when Jezebel killed the prophets of Yahweh, Obadiah took a hundred prophets and hid them by fifties in the cave and sustained them with food and water.) Ahab said to Obadiah, "Go through the land to all the springs of water and to all the wadis. Perhaps we may find green grass that we may keep horses and mules alive and that we might not lose any of the animals." So they divided the land for themselves in order to pass through it; Ahab went one way by himself, and Obadiah went another way by himself. It happened that Obadiah was on the way, and suddenly Elijah was there to meet him. When he recognized him, he fell on his face and said, "Is this you, my lord Elijah?" He said to him, "I am. Go, say to your lord, 'Elijah is here.'" He said, "How have I sinned that you are giving your servant into the hand of Ahab to kill me? As Yahweh your God lives, surely there is not a nation or a kingdom to which my lord has not sent me to seek you. If they would say, 'He is not here,' then he would make the kingdom or the nation swear that it could not find you. Now you are saying, 'Go, say to your lord: "Elijah is here."' And it will happen that I will go from you and the Spirit of Yahweh will carry you up to where I do not know. Then I will come to tell Ahab, but he will not find you, and then he will kill me, even though your servant has feared Yahweh from my youth. Has it not been told to my lord what I did

> when Jezebel killed the prophets of Yahweh? I hid a hundred men of the prophets of Yahweh by fifties in the cave, and I sustained them with food and water. Now you are saying, 'Go, say to your lord: "Elijah is here,"' and he will kill me." Elijah said, "As Yahweh of hosts lives, before whom I stand, I will certainly show myself to him today." So Obadiah went to meet Ahab, and he told him, so Ahab went to meet Elijah. When Ahab saw Elijah, Ahab said to him, "Is this you who throws Israel into confusion?" He said, "I did not throw Israel into confusion; rather you and the house of your father have by forsaking the commands of Yahweh when you went after the Baals! So then, send word and assemble all of Israel to me on Mount Carmel, with the four hundred and fifty prophets of Baal and the four hundred prophets of Asherah, who eat at the table of Jezebel." (1 Kgs 18:1–19, LEB)

Elijah didn't stutter. He fiercely stared Ahab square in the eyes and demanded him to gather all 850 of Satan and Asherah's henchmen for an epic showdown of the prophets and gods.

> "So Ahab sent word among the Israelites, and he assembled the prophets to Mount Carmel. Elijah approached to all the people and said, "How long will you go limping over two opinions? If Yahweh is God, go after him; but if Baal, go after him." But the people did not answer him a word. Then Elijah said to the people, "I alone am left a prophet of Yahweh, but the prophets of Baal are four hundred and fifty men. Let them give us two bulls, and let them choose for themselves one bull, cut him in pieces, and put it on the wood, but don't let them start a fire on it. I will prepare the other bull and set it on the wood, but I will put no fire on it. Then you call on the name of your god, and I will call on the name of Yahweh, and it shall be that the god who answers by fire, he is God." Then all the people answered and said, "The word

> is good!" Then Elijah said to the prophets of Baal, "Choose for yourselves one bull and prepare it first, for you are the majority, and call on the name of your god, but don't set fire under it." So they took the bull that he allowed to them, prepared it, and called upon the name of Baal from morning until noon, saying, "O Baal, answer us!" But there was no voice and there was no answer, so they limped about the altar which they had made. It happened at noon that Elijah mocked them and said, "Call out with a loud voice, for he is a god! Perhaps he is meditating, or is using the bathroom, or is on a journey. Perhaps he is asleep and must wake up!" So they called out with a loud voice, and they cut themselves with swords and with spears as was their custom, until the blood poured out over them. It happened as noon passed, they raged until the time of the evening offering, but there was no voice, there was no answer, and no one paid attention. (1 Kgs 18:20–29, LEB)

The dialogue between Elijah and Baal's prophets carries a much deeper meaning than most realize. The ongoing discoveries of ancient documents and tablets have provided tremendous insight into the religions of Israel's neighboring rivals.

> *In terms of religion, the importance of the Baal Cycle cannot be overstated. Prior to its discovery, the only source of information regarding religion in ancient Syro-Palestine, or Canaan, was what little could be gleaned from the Old Testament itself... There was simply no way of accessing information about the religious world of the Canaanites. Once the Baal Cycle was discovered and interpreted, it opened the doors for a more complicated and nuanced understanding of ancient Israelite religion and the God of Israel, Yahweh.*[3]

---

3 A. L. Balogh and D. Mangum, "Baal Cycle," *The Lexham Bible Dictionary*.

Studying the ancient liturgical text from Ugarit titled The Baal Cycle supplies much-needed context to this conversation. Undoubtedly, Elijah was familiar with the dramatized and poetic stories that were often told about Baal, such as is found in The Baal Cycle. Prolific author Brian Godawa wrote,

> *In the Baal epic from Ugarit, El was the supreme father of the gods who lived on a cosmic mountain. A divine council of gods called Sons of El surrounded him, vying for position and power. When the god Sea (Yam) is coronated by El and given a palace, Baal rises up and kills Sea, taking Sea's place as Most High over the other gods (excepting El). A temple is built and a feast celebrated. Mot (Death) then insults Baal, who goes down to the underworld, only to be defeated by Mot. Anat, Baal's violent sister, seeks Death and cuts him up into pieces, then brings Baal's body back up to earth, where he is brought back to life, only to fight Mot to a stalemate. This return of the storm and vegetation god is a common mythical representation of the annual death of winter and new life of spring and autumn. The temporary loss of Baal to the underworld is also reflected in Jezebel's name, which in Canaanite means "Where is the Prince?" a liturgical call that Canaanites proclaimed every harvest.*[4]

"The journey" Elijah alludes to seems to echo back to the narrative of The Baal Cycle, when Baal traveled to the underworld and was absent from his loyalists, who asked,

> *Where is Valiant Baal?*
> *Where is the Prince, Lord of the earth?"*[5]

---

4 Brian Godawa, *The Spiritual World of Jezebel and Elijah: Biblical Background to the Novel Jezebel: Harlot Queen of Israel* (Los Angeles, CA: Embedded Pictures Publishing, 2019), Kindle edition.

5 Wyatt, *Religious Texts from Ugarit*, 139.

The prophet Elijah suggested maybe Baal was "asleep" or "dead" and needed to be "awakened" or "made alive," just like the story from ancient Ugarit in CTA 6:3:1–9.

> *[For dead is Valiant Baal,]*
> *for perished is the Prin[ce, Lord of the earth!]*
> *But if V[aliant Baal] should be alive,*
> *and if the Prince, Lo[rd of the earth] should exist*
> *in a dream of the Wise One, the perceptive god,*
> *in a vision of the Creator of Creatures,*
> *let the skies rain oil,*
> *let the wadis run with honey!*
> *And I shall know that Valiant Baal is alive,*
> *that the Prince, Lord of the earth, exists!*[6]

Then, according to The Baal Cycle, Anat began cutting and mutilating her own body in sorrow, pain, and desperation.

> *Her skin with a stone she scored,*
> *her side-locks [with a razor],*
> *she gashed cheeks and chin.*
> *She [ploughed] her collar-bones,*
> *she turned over like a garden her chest,*
> *like a valley she ploughed her breast.*[7]

In our story, amazingly, Elijah's articulate mockery provoked the 450 prophets of Baal so much that they, in total desperation, mimicked Anat by cutting themselves profusely to "resurrect" Baal's presence so

---

6 Wyatt, *Religious Texts from Ugarit*, 136–137.

7 Wyatt, *Religious Texts from Ugarit*, 128–129.

he could rain down lightning from the heavens and consume the sacrificial bull. But Baal simply did nothing.

No response. No appearance. No nothing.

> Then Elijah said to all the people, "Come near to me," so all the people came closer to him. He repaired the altar of Yahweh that had been destroyed. Elijah took twelve stones according to the number of the tribes of the sons of Jacob, to whom the word of God came, saying, "Israel shall be your name." With them, he built an altar in the name of Yahweh, and he made a trench which would have held about two seahs of seed, all around the altar. And he arranged the wood, cut the bull into pieces, and placed it on the wood. Then he said, "Fill four jars with water, and pour it on the burnt offering and on the wood." He said, "Do it again!" They did it again. He said, "Do it a third time!" So they did it a third time. The water went all around the altar, and the trench also was filled with water. It happened at the offering of the evening oblation, Elijah the prophet went near, and he said, "O Yahweh, God of Abraham, Isaac, and Israel; let it be known today that you are God in Israel and that I am your servant and that I have done all of these things by your words. Answer me, O Yahweh, answer me; that this people may know that you, O Yahweh, are God and that you have turned their hearts back again." Then the fire of Yahweh fell, and it consumed the burnt offering, and the wood, and the stones, and the dust; and the water which was in the trench it licked up! When all the people saw, they fell on their faces and said, "Yahweh, he is God! Yahweh, he is God!" Then Elijah said to them, "Seize the prophets of Baal; don't let any man of them escape!" So they seized them, and Elijah brought them down to the wadi of Kishon and killed them there. (1 Kgs 18:30–40, LEB)

Baal's silence spoke volumes. He simply didn't care what happened to his faithful followers on Mount Carmel. Their deaths meant 450 more lost souls would be his to claim forever in the fires of hell. So how does this story end for Satan's biggest puppet, King Ahab? Well—spoiler alert—it ends with King Ahab being fatally shot by a "random" arrow in battle, with his blood pooling in the bottom of his chariot at the battle of Ramoth-gilead four chapters later.

> But a man drew his bow without taking special aim and struck the king of Israel through the joints of his armor. So he said to his charioteer, "Turn around and take me out of the battle, for I am badly wounded!" The battle raged throughout that day, and the king was propped up in his chariot facing the Arameans. He died that evening, and blood from his wound flowed into the bottom of the chariot. Then the cry rang out in the army as the sun set, declaring: Each man to his own city, and each man to his own land! So the king died and was brought to Samaria. They buried the king in Samaria. Then someone washed the chariot at the pool of Samaria. The dogs licked up his blood, and the prostitutes bathed in it, according to the word of the LORD that he had spoken. The rest of the events of Ahab's reign, along with all his accomplishments, including the ivory palace he built, and all the cities he built, are written in the Historical Record of Israel's Kings. Ahab rested with his ancestors, and his son Ahaziah became king in his place. (1 Kgs 22:34–40, CSB)

But where things get interesting is the divine steps that led to Ahab's decision to fight. Micaiah, a true prophet of God, was summoned at the request of Ahab's newfound ally, Jehoshaphat, king of Judah. Apparently, the southern and northern kingdoms were willing to hug it out and put aside their differences to defeat a common enemy—Syria.

> And he [Ahab] said to Jehoshaphat, "Will you go with me to battle at Ramoth-gilead?" And Jehoshaphat said to the king of Israel, "I am as you are, my people as your people, my horses as your horses." (1 Kgs 22:4, ESV)

Before Micaiah was called in to utter his prophecy concerning the pending battle with the Syrians, Ahab called on his four hundred prophets—his yes-men—for their "divine" wisdom.

> ...And they said, "Go up, for the Lord will give it into the hand of the king." (1 Kgs 22:6, ESV)

What's said next is extremely important.

> Then the messenger who had gone to summon Micaiah said to him, "Please now, the words of the prophets are unanimously favorable to the king. Please let your words be as one word with them, and speak favorably." Then Micaiah said, "As Yahweh lives, surely only as Yahweh speaks to me, that will I speak." When he came to the king, the king asked him, "Micaiah, shall we go to Ramoth-Gilead to the battle, or shall we refrain?" He said to him, "Go up and triumph, and Yahweh will give it into the hand of the king." Then the king said to him, "How many times must I make you swear that you shall not tell me anything but truth in the name of Yahweh?" So he said, "I saw all of Israel scattering to the mountains, like the sheep without a shepherd. Yahweh also said, 'There are no masters for these, let them return in peace, each to his house.'" Then the king of Israel said to Jehoshaphat, "Did I not say to you that he would not prophesy good concerning me, but disaster?" And he said, "Therefore, hear the word of Yahweh. **I saw Yahweh sitting on his throne with all the hosts of heaven standing**

> **beside him** from his right hand and from his left hand. **And Yahweh said, 'Who will entice Ahab so that he will go up and fall at Ramoth-Gilead?' Then this one was saying one thing and the other one was saying another. Then a spirit came out and stood before Yahweh and said, 'I will entice him,'** and Yahweh said to him, 'How?' He said, 'I will go out and I will be a false spirit in the mouth of all his prophets.' And he said, 'You shall entice and succeed, go out and do so.' So then, see that Yahweh has placed a false spirit in the mouth of all of these your prophets, and Yahweh has spoken disaster concerning you." (1 Kgs 22:13–23, LEB)

As modern Bible students, Micaiah's vision prompts many puzzling questions. Who are the hosts of heaven standing at the Lord's left and right hand? And why is Yahweh asking for their input? Did these spiritual beings really just decide Ahab's fate? At this point in our ancient journey, it's time you finally learned about what the Psalmist called, "the Divine Council."

ANSWERING YOUR QUESTIONS

WHAT IS THE DIVINE COUNCIL?

Psalm 82 is a compelling chapter in the Bible. It provides incredible insight into the hierarchy and function of some of Yahweh's heavenly hosts.

> 1 **God has taken his place in the divine council; in the midst of the gods he holds judgment:** 2 "How long will you judge unjustly and show partiality to the wicked? Selah
> 3 Give justice to the weak and the fatherless; maintain the right of the afflicted and the destitute. 4 Rescue the weak and the needy; deliver them from the hand of the wicked."

> 5 They have neither knowledge nor understanding, they walk about in darkness; all the foundations of the earth are shaken.
> 6 I said, "You are gods, sons of the Most High, all of you;
> 7 nevertheless, like men you shall die, and fall like any prince."
> 8 Arise, O God, judge the earth; for you shall inherit all the nations! (Ps 82:1–8, ESV)

There's a lot to unpack here. Let's start by identifying this mysterious "divine council." The reality of the gods doesn't need to be rehashed here since we've already established this in previous chapters. The Psalmist said God [***elohim***] takes His place in the divine council in the midst of the gods [***elohim***] and holds judgment. *Elohim* is a Hebrew word that can be singular or plural based on the context of its usage. Just remember, the biblical writers' use of the,

> *...word Elohim was more of a reference to a plane of existence than to a substance of being. In this way, Yahweh was Elohim, but no other elohim was Yahweh. Yahweh is incomparably THE Elohim of Elohim*[8]

Psalm 82 paints the picture of Yahweh entering His divine courtroom in the midst of a council of lesser gods. It makes a lot of sense that this council is "in the skies," or the heavenlies.

> 6 For who in the skies can be compared to the LORD? Who among the heavenly beings is like the LORD, 7 a God greatly to be feared in the council of the holy ones, and awesome above all who are around him? (Ps 89:6–7, ESV)

---

8 Brian Godawa, *Psalm 82: The Divine Council of the Gods, the Judgment of the Watchers and the Inheritance of the Nations* (Los Angeles, CA: Embedded Pictures Publishing, 2018), Kindle edition, 7.

This is exactly what Micaiah's prophecy revealed in 1 Kings 22. Yahweh and these angelic council members were holding a meeting to decide the fate of Ahab. Council members made various motions as to how to deal with Ahab until it was decided that one of them would be a lying spirit in the mouths of all his prophets. This is the role the divine council plays throughout Scripture. They decide fates and carry out judgments with the approval of the Most High, of course. Simply put, the divine council is Yahweh's organized celestial judicial system, which consists of appointed participatory spirits who determine how, when, and where to intervene in the affairs of men and how, when, and where to punish the wicked from all realms.

WHAT AUTHORITY DO THESE ELOHIM HAVE?

There's another instance where a biblical writer pulls back the curtain and gives his readers VIP access to how the divine council operates. One of those passages is Daniel 4:4–27. The text begins with the Babylonian king, Nebuchadnezzar, revealing he's had a very mysterious dream. He says,

> 5 And I saw a dream and a revelation on my bed and it frightened
> me, and the visions of my head terrified me. 6 And a decree was
> sent out, ordering that all the wise men of Babylon were to be
> brought in before me so that they may make known to me the
> explanation of the dream. 7 Then the magicians, the conjurers,
> the astrologers and the diviners came in and I told them the
> dream, but they could not make known to me its explanation.
> 8 Then at last Daniel came before me whose name was Belte-
> shazzar, according to the name of my god, and in whom was
> the spirit of the holy gods, and I related the dream to him.
> 9 "'O Belteshazzar, chief of the magicians, I myself know that the
> spirit of the holy gods is in you, and no mystery is too difficult
> for you. Now tell me the visions of my dream that I saw, and its

> explanation. 10 Now these were the visions of my head as I was
> lying on my bed: I was gazing and, look, a tree was in the midst
> of the earth, and its height was exalted. 11 The tree grew and
> it became strong, and its height reached to heaven, and it was
> visible to the end of the whole earth. 12 Its foliage was beautiful,
> and its fruit abundant, and in it was provision for all. Under it
> the animals of the field sought shade, and in its branches the
> birds of heaven nested, and from it all the living beings were fed.
> 13 "'I was looking in the vision of my head as I lay on my bed,
> and look, **a watcher**, and **a holy one**, **came down from heaven**.
> 14 He cried aloud and so he said: "Cut down the tree and chop
> off its branches; shake off its foliage and scatter its fruit. Let the
> animals flee from under it, and the birds from its branches.
> 15 But the stump of its roots leave in the earth, along with a band
> of iron and bronze; leave it in the grass of the field. And in the
> dew of heaven let it be watered, and with the animals let his lot
> be in the grass of the earth. 16 Let his mind be changed from that
> of a human, and let the mind of an animal be given to him, and
> let seven times pass over him. 17 **The sentence is by the decree
> of the watchers, and the decision by the command of the holy
> ones**, in order that the living will know that the Most High is
> sovereign over the kingdom of humankind, and to whomever
> he wills he gives it, and he even sets the humblest of men over
> it." 18 "'This is the dream that I, Nebuchadnezzar the king, saw.
> Now you, Belteshazzar, declare its explanation, for all of the
> wise men of my kingdom were not able to make the explanation
> known to me, but you are able because **the spirit of holy gods is
> in you**.' (Dan 4:5–18, LEB)

You can tell Nebuchadnezzar was well-acquainted with the small-G gods of the nations by his frequent allusions to the "spirit of the holy gods" he mistakenly claimed was in Daniel. He's correct, however, in that this sentence was by the decree of "the watchers." We were first introduced to this term back in chapters 2 and 3 of our literary journey, where we learned the fallen angels of Genesis 6 were "the watchers" (1 Enoch 6) who descended upon Mount Hermon and made oaths of rebellion, bound by a curse to corrupt humanity. The "watchers" is a common title for fallen angels in what scholars call "second temple literature," or Jewish writings written from 539 B.C.E.–70 C.E. (e.g., Jubilees 4:15, 22; 5:1–10; 7:20–25; 8:1–4; 10:1–11; T. Reu. 5:6–7; T. Naph. 3:5; CD 2:18).

But the watchers of Nebuchadnezzar's vision aren't rebellious; they are holy members of God's council.

> [19] Then Daniel, whose name was Belteshazzar, was dismayed
> for a while, and his thoughts alarmed him. The king answered
> and said, "Belteshazzar, let not the dream or the interpretation
> alarm you." Belteshazzar answered and said, "My lord, may the
> dream be for those who hate you and its interpretation for your
> enemies! [20] The tree you saw, which grew and became strong,
> so that its top reached to heaven, and it was visible to the end
> of the whole earth, [21] whose leaves were beautiful and its fruit
> abundant, and in which was food for all, under which beasts of
> the field found shade, and in whose branches the birds of the
> heavens lived— [22] it is you, O king, who have grown and become
> strong. Your greatness has grown and reaches to heaven, and
> your dominion to the ends of the earth. [23] And because **the king
> saw a watcher, a holy one, coming down from heaven** and
> saying, 'Chop down the tree and destroy it, but leave the stump
> of its roots in the earth, bound with a band of iron and bronze,
> in the tender grass of the field, and let him be wet with the dew
> of heaven, and let his portion be with the beasts of the field,
> till seven periods of time pass over him,' [24] **this is the inter-
> pretation, O king: It is a decree of the Most High, which has**

> **come upon my lord the king,** [25] that you shall be driven from among men, and your dwelling shall be with the beasts of the field. You shall be made to eat grass like an ox, and you shall be wet with the dew of heaven, and seven periods of time shall pass over you, till you know that the Most High rules the kingdom of men and gives it to whom he will. [26] And as it was commanded to leave the stump of the roots of the tree, your kingdom shall be confirmed for you from the time that you know that Heaven rules. (Dan 4:19–26, ESV)

Daniel's interpretation is telling. The judicial ruling by the holy watchers (v. 17) carries the same weight as a decree from the Most High God, Yahweh. Why? Because they've been given authority in heaven by the head of the council, the Lord, to carry out judicial rulings on the earth. This is why the book of Zechariah frames the watchers in zoomorphic terms, calling them horses sent out to *patrol* the earth.

> [8] "I saw in the night, and behold, a man riding on a red horse! He was standing among the myrtle trees in the glen, and behind him were red, sorrel, and white horses. [9] Then I said, 'What are these, my lord?' The angel who talked with me said to me, 'I will show you what they are.' [10] So the man who was standing among the myrtle trees answered, 'These are **they** whom the LORD has sent to **patrol the earth**.' [11] And they answered **the angel** of the LORD who was standing among the myrtle trees, and **said**, '**We have patrolled the earth, and behold, all the earth remains at rest**.' (Zech 1:8–11, ESV)

Three chapters later, Daniel has a vision of Yahweh, the Ancient of Days, taking His seat among the other thrones of the heavenly court. Once again, the divine council is hard at work judging important affairs.

> [9] "As I looked, **thrones were placed**, and the Ancient of Days
> took his seat; his clothing was white as snow, and the hair of his
> head like pure wool; his throne was fiery flames; its wheels were
> burning fire. [10] A stream of fire issued and came out from before
> him; a thousand thousands served him, and ten thousand times
> ten thousand stood before him; **the court sat in judgment**, and
> the books were opened. (Dan 7:9–10, ESV).

WHO'S BEING JUDGED IN PSALM 82?

Let's read Psalm 82 again.

> [1] God has taken his place in the divine council; in the midst
> of the gods he holds judgment: [2] **"How long will you judge
> unjustly and show partiality to the wicked? Selah** [3] **Give
> justice to the weak and the fatherless; maintain the right
> of the afflicted and the destitute.** [4] **Rescue the weak and the
> needy; deliver them from the hand of the wicked."** [5] **They
> have neither knowledge nor understanding, they walk about
> in darkness; all the foundations of the earth are shaken.**
> [6] **I said, "You are gods, sons of the Most High, all of you;**
> [7] nevertheless, like men you shall die, and fall like any prince."
> [8] Arise, O God, judge the earth; for you shall inherit all the
> nations! (Ps 82:1–8, ESV)

Now that we understand the members and role of the divine council, we need to dig deeper into who is being judged by the council in Psalm 82. Yahweh starts speaking to the guilty parties in verse 2. The guilty are accused of ruling or "judging" unjustly and being partial to the wicked. Yahweh, the Lord, then preaches to them about what they should be doing: giving justice and helping the weak and afflicted. The people over which they (i.e., the guilty) are ruling are walking in darkness in all parts of the earth (i.e., the foundations of the earth) and are ignorant of real knowledge.

Who could this be? Who could be so guilty? In verse 6, we learn the true identity of who is on trial. The Lord says, "You are gods, sons of the Most High, all of you." The convicted parties of Psalm 82 are none other than the fallen sons of God of Deuteronomy 32:8–9. They're the gods whom Yahweh set over the nations, who have ruled unjustly. They're the angelic spirits who led the Gentiles into darkness and ignorant worship. Here's a comparison of Deuteronomy 32:8–9 and Psalm 82:6–7. The Psalmist draws on Moses's former use of the "Most High" (*'elyôn*) language because he wants his readers' minds to go back to Babel and Deuteronomy 32:8–9.

Deuteronomy 32:8–9 (ESV)	Deuteronomy 32:8–9 (Brenton LXX En)	Psalm 82:6–7 (ESV)
8 When the **Most High** gave to the nations their inheritance, when he divided mankind, he fixed the borders of the peoples according to the number of the **sons of God**. 9 But the LORD's portion is his people, Jacob his allotted heritage.	8 When the **Most High** divided the nations, when he separated the sons of Adam, he set the bounds of the nations according to the number of the **angels of God**. 9 And his people Jacob became the portion of the Lord, Israel was the line of his inheritance.	6 I said, "You are **gods**, **sons** of the **Most High**, all of you; 7 nevertheless, like men you shall die, and fall like any prince."

The Dead Sea Scrolls emphasize in 11QMelchizedek 2.10–16 that the "gods" of Psalm 82 are Satan's loyal spirits who rebelled, implicitly following the allotment at the Tower of Babel.

And as for that which he s[aid, How long will you] judge unjustly and show partiality to the wicked? Selah [Ps 82:2], its interpretation concerns Satan and the spirits of his lot [who] rebelled by turning away from the precepts of God[9]

Tyrannius Rufinus of Aquileia (345–411 A.D.) reiterates that the angels deviated from their role as guidance officers of truth:

"When the Most High divided the nations, He appointed the bounds of the nations according to the number of the angels of God." But some of these, as he who is called the Prince of this world, ***did not exercise the power which God had committed to them*** *according to the laws by which they had received it,* ***nor did they teach mankind to obey*** *God's commandments,* ***but taught them rather to follow their own perverse guidance.***[10]

So those rulers, whom God had appointed over mankind, turning stubborn and tyrannical, did their best to wage war on the human beings committed to their charge and to rout them in their conflict with sin.[11]

Origen also echoed this sentiment in his *Homilies on Genesis and Exodus*, calling these angels' actions a "violation of duty."

Whence also the Lord said to the angels who did not preserve their preeminence: "I said, 'You are gods and are all sons of the Most High. But you shall die like men and shall fall like one of the princes,'" imitating, of course, the devil who became the leader

---

9 J. C. VanderKam, *The Dead Sea Scrolls Today* (Grand Rapids, MI: Eerdmans, 1994), 53.

10 Rufinus, *A Commentary on the Apostles' Creed*, 549 (Fremantle).

11 Rufinus, *Rufinus: A Commentary on the Apostles' Creed*, 49 (Kelly).

> *of all to ruin. Whence it is evident that* ***violation of duty****, not nature, made those accursed*[12]

The nations' gods were malevolent guides who were devoid of the love of Yahweh. This is shown by the way they ruled the children of man. Earlier in Psalms, David writes,

> [1] Do you indeed decree what is right, you gods? Do you judge the children of man uprightly? [2] No, in your hearts you devise wrongs; your hands deal out violence on earth. (Ps 58:1–2, ESV)

Their violence spilled over in Daniel 10:12–14 when Gabriel, one of Yahweh's angelic princes, was attacked by the "Prince of Persia" (fallen angelic prince) and was stalemated from seeing Daniel for twenty-one days. He finally managed to get free from the Persian god when Michael, one of the Lord's chief princes, came to his assistance. After explaining his tardiness to Daniel, he said,

> [20] … "Do you know why I have come to you? But now I will return to fight against the prince of Persia; and when I go out, behold, the prince of Greece will come. [21] But I will tell you what is inscribed in the book of truth: there is none who contends by my side against these except Michael, your prince. (Dan 10:20–21, ESV)

Whether it's the prince of Persia, the prince of Greece, or Satan—the prince of the power of the air (Eph 2:1–2)—the gods were deemed guilty as charged by Yahweh and His divine council. The question is, what punishment will they receive?

---

12 Origen, *Homilies on Genesis and Exodus*, 319–320.

WHAT WILL BE THEIR PUNISHMENT?

The rebel gods of Babel were guilty. Now what?

> 1 God has taken his place in the divine council; in the midst of the gods he holds judgment: 2 "How long will you judge unjustly and show partiality to the wicked? Selah 3 Give justice to the weak and the fatherless; maintain the right of the afflicted and the destitute. 4 Rescue the weak and the needy; deliver them from the hand of the wicked." 5 They have neither knowledge nor understanding, they walk about in darkness; all the foundations of the earth are shaken. 6 I said, "You are gods, sons of the Most High, all of you; 7 **nevertheless, like men you shall die, and fall like any prince."** 8 Arise, O God, judge the earth; for you shall inherit all the nations! (Ps 82:1–8, ESV)

The former divine sons of God will die like mortal men and lose their divine nature and immortality. They are "doomed" to pass away, as Paul put it.

> 6 Yet among the mature we do impart wisdom, although it is not a wisdom of this age or of the rulers of this age, who are doomed to pass away. (1 Cor 2:6, ESV)

The prophet Isaiah has the fallen hosts of heaven and their loyal nationalists, fittingly, being slain together. The stench of their rotting corpses will rise in the very mountains that flow with their traitorous blood.

> 1 Come near, nations, to hear; and peoples, listen attentively! Let the earth hear, and that which fills it; the world and all its offspring. 2 For the anger of Yahweh is against all the nations, and his wrath is against all their host; he has put them under a ban, he has given them up for slaughter. 3 And their slain shall

> be cast out; as for their corpses, their stench shall go up. And the mountains shall melt with their blood, [4] and all the host of heaven shall rot. And the skies shall roll up like a scroll, and all their host shall wither like the withering of a leaf from a vine, or like the withering from a fig tree. (Isa 34:1–4, LEB)

Isaiah also writes,

> [21] On that day the LORD will punish the host of heaven, in heaven, and the kings of the earth, on the earth. [22] They will be gathered together as prisoners in a pit; they will be shut up in a prison, and after many days they will be punished. [23] Then the moon will be confounded and the sun ashamed, for the LORD of hosts reigns on Mount Zion and in Jerusalem, and his glory will be before his elders. (Isa 24:21–23, ESV)

Here, Isaiah has the rebel hosts being taken captive, led to a pit, and shut up in a prison, while Yahweh is glorified from His holy mountain of Zion. The fallen hosts of heaven are often described in additional astral terms such as stars, moon, or sun, such as in Isaiah 24:21–23 and other passages. First Enoch 90:20–27 tells a similar story of a, yet still, future punishment of the fallen stars and spirit shepherds who were placed over the nations.

> [20.] And I saw till a throne was erected in the pleasant land, and the Lord of the sheep sat Himself thereon, and the other took the sealed books and opened those books before the Lord of the sheep. [21.] And the Lord called those men the seven first white ones, and commanded that they should bring before Him, beginning with the first star which led the way, all the stars whose privy members were like those of horses, and they brought them all before Him. [22.] And He said to that man who wrote

> before Him, being one of those seven white ones, and said unto him: "**Take those seventy shepherds to whom I delivered the sheep**, and who taking them on their own authority slew more than I commanded them." 23. And behold they were all bound, I saw, and they all stood before Him. 24. And the judgement was held first over the stars, and they were judged and found guilty, and went to the place of condemnation, and they were cast into an abyss, full of fire and flaming, and full of pillars of fire. 25. And those seventy shepherds were judged and found guilty, and they were cast into that fiery abyss. 26. And I saw at that time how a like abyss was opened in the midst of the earth, full of fire, and they brought those blinded sheep, and they were all judged and found guilty and cast into this fiery abyss, and they burned; now this abyss was to the right of that house. 27. And I saw those sheep burning and their bones burning.[13]

The seventy "shepherds" who were allotted the seventy nations at Babel will indeed die like men, as the Psalmist promised his readers. The original preservers of the Dead Sea Scrolls depict in the War Scroll (1Q33 Col. I:9–15) the gods' final undoing in an epic battle of the Sons of Darkness and the Sons of Light.

> *On the day when the Kittim fall there shall be a battle and horrible carnage before the God of 10Israel, for it is a day appointed by Him from ancient times as a battle of annihilation for the Sons of Darkness. On that day the congregation of the gods and the congregation of men shall engage one another, resulting in great carnage. 11The Sons of Light and the forces of Darkness shall fight together to show the strength of God with the roar of a great multitude and the shout of gods and men; a day of disaster. It is*

13 Charles, *The Book of Enoch or 1 Enoch: Translation*, 212–213.

> *a time of 12distress fo[r al]l the people who are redeemed by God. In all their afflictions none exists that is like it, hastening to its completion as an eternal redemption. On the day of their battle against the Kittim, 13they shall g[o forth for] carnage in battle. In three lots the Sons of Light shall stand firm so as to strike a blow at wickedness, and in three the army of Belial shall strengthen themselves so as to force the retreat of the forces 14[of Light. And when the] banners of the infantry cause their hearts to melt, then the might of God will strengthen the he[arts of the Sons of Light.] In the seventh lot the great hand of God shall overcome 15[Belial and al]l the angels of his dominion, and all the men of [his forces shall be destroyed forever.]*[14]

While the details of the eschaton are highly debated in the Christian community, the Bible is clear—judgment is coming for all of Jesus' created imagers, divine and mortal alike.

CONNECTING THE GOSPEL

JESUS' DEFENSE & PSALM 82

It's no secret that Jesus, the good Shepherd, came to save the lost sheep of the house of Israel. Jesus told the Jews in John 10 that He was the only door available through which the Jews could find good pastures and salvation.

> [9] I am the door. If anyone enters through me, he will be saved, and will come in and will go out and will find pasture. [10] The thief comes only so that he can steal and kill and destroy; I have come so that they may have life, and have it abundantly. [11] "I am the good shepherd. The good shepherd lays down his life for the

14 Wise, Abegg, Jr., and Cook, *The Dead Sea Scrolls*, 148.

> sheep. [12] The hired hand, who is not the shepherd, whose own the sheep are not, sees the wolf approaching and abandons the sheep and runs away—and the wolf seizes them and scatters them—[13] because he is a hired hand and he is not concerned about the sheep. [14] "I am the good shepherd, and I know my own, and my own know me, [15] just as the Father knows me and I know the Father, and I lay down my life for the sheep. [16] And I have other sheep which are not from this fold. I must bring these also, and they will hear my voice, and they will become one flock—one shepherd. (John 10:9–16, LEB)

The other sheep that weren't of "this fold" (i.e., the Jews) that Jesus mentioned were the Gentiles—all the other nations of the world. Origen (185–254 A.D.), in his *Commentary on the Song of Songs 2.4*, wrote,

> *So perhaps the flocks of the Bridegroom's companions may be* ***all those nations that are divided up like herds under angel shepherds; but those are to be called the Bridegroom's flock****, of whom He Himself says in the Gospel: My sheep hear my voice. For look and note carefully that He says 'my sheep,' as though there may be others beside which are not His; even as He Himself says in another passage: Ye are not of my sheep.*[15]

So, Jesus didn't only come to Earth to be the good Shepherd for the Jews; He came to be the good Shepherd the nations never had (Ps 49:14). The only way He could unite the two flocks into one was by being the sacrificial lamb that united both into His one body (Eph 4:4). Jesus alludes to this idea in the very next verse of our John 10 passage—verse 17.

---

15 Rufinus, *The Commentary*, 122 (Lawson).

> [17] For this reason the Father loves me, because I lay down my life that I may take it up again. [18] No one takes it from me, but I lay it down of my own accord. I have authority to lay it down, and I have authority to take it up again. This charge I have received from my Father." (John 10:17–18, ESV)

Well, guess what? The Jews didn't like what Jesus said. His claim to be the authoritative divine Son of God caused division among the Jews. Some even barked that Jesus was a demon. Their outrage centered around His acclaimed divine status. A few verses later, another set of Jews demanded Jesus to tell them plainly if He was truly the Christ, the sent Messiah.

> [25] Jesus answered them, "I told you, and you do not believe. The works that I do in my Father's name bear witness about me, [26] but you do not believe because you are not among my sheep. [27] My sheep hear my voice, and I know them, and they follow me. [28] I give them eternal life, and they will never perish, and no one will snatch them out of my hand. [29] My Father, who has given them to me, is greater than all, and no one is able to snatch them out of the Father's hand. [30] I and the Father are one." (John 10:25–30, ESV)

Their frustration with Jesus didn't stem from His ambiguity about who He was; their repeated questions were a result of their recurrent rejection of His divinity, His royal sonship, and His claim to be one with the Father (v. 30) and to be God (v. 33). The text says,

> [31] The Jews picked up stones again to stone him. [32] Jesus answered them, "I have shown you many good works from the Father; for which of them are you going to stone me?" [33] The Jews answered him, "It is not for a good work that we are going to stone you but for blasphemy, because you, being a man, make yourself God." (John 10:31–33, ESV)

What Jesus says next will solidify and substantiate His claim to be "one with the Father" and the uniquely divine, one-of-a-kind Son of God.

> [34] Jesus answered them, "Is it not written in your Law, **'I said, you are gods'**? [35] If he called them gods to whom the word of God came—and Scripture cannot be broken— [36] do you say of him whom the Father consecrated and sent into the world, 'You are blaspheming,' because I said, 'I am the Son of God'? [37] If I am not doing the works of my Father, then do not believe me; [38] but if I do them, even though you do not believe me, believe the works, that you may know and understand that the Father is in me and I am in the Father." (John 10:34–38, ESV)

Jesus' best argument for His divinity and identity as the consecrated Son whom the Father sent links back to Psalm 82. The phrase, "I said you are gods" is unmistakable. Outside of John 10, it only occurs once in the entire Bible—Psalm 82. Jesus said in verses 35–36, "If he called them gods to whom the word of God came—and Scripture cannot be broken—do you say of him whom the Father consecrated and sent into the world, 'You are blaspheming,' because I said, 'I am the Son of God'?" (ESV). The gods to whom the word of God came in Psalm 82 were the rebel gods who were being judged by the head of the council. If these Jews could accept there were other *elohim*, or other divine sons, then why couldn't they accept the one standing in front of them? And if these other gods, though rebellious, were still called "sons" by God, then why wouldn't they accept Jesus, the Son who was always doing the works of His Father?

> *In John 10:36–38, Jesus asserts that his high status as the Son is based on Him doing the works of His Father: the Father is "in him." This phrase parallels Exod 23:20–21, where the Name—Yahweh's*

> *Presence—was in the angel of Yahweh. In John 10:36–38, Jesus claims that the Presence is in Him.*[16]

We discovered in previous chapters that the angel of the Lord throughout the Old Testament was God himself. Many scholars believe that a pre-incarnate Jesus played that role. So If Yahweh's presence was in Him as the angel of the Lord, then it was certainly still in Him in His earthly form as Jesus, the Son. Their eternal oneness cannot be denied, even by the stubborn Jews in John 10. Again, Jesus used Psalm 82 because it verifies not that He is just another *elohim*, but that in both His heavenly and earthly forms, He was one with the Father, even having served with Yahweh as the head of the divine council. His divinity and oneness with the Father never stopped, even when He was a mortal man.

LOOKING AHEAD

As time pressed on, the days of Elijah battling Baal and false prophets stopped. God finally called home His faithful follower and gave him a royal escort up to heaven in what's described as a whirlwind and chariots of fire (2 Kgs 2:11). Over the next eight hundred years, God's people would be picked apart, conquered, and carried off by the Assyrian, Babylonian, and Persian empires because of their idolatry and incessant veneration of the gods.

> They rejected his [Yahweh] statutes, his covenant which he made with their ancestors, and his warnings which he gave to them; and they went after the idols, became vain, and went after all the nations which were all around them, which Yahweh had commanded them not to do as they did. They abandoned all the commands of Yahweh their God and made for themselves two molten calf-shaped idols; they made

16 M. S. Heiser, "Divine Council," *The Lexham Bible Dictionary*.

> a pole of Asherah worship and **bowed down to the army of the heavens and served Baal**. (2 Kgs 17:15–16, LEB)

Satan's army of gods ruled over all the earth, even enslaving the Lord's own precious people. With all human hope completely dead, a baby boy would soon be born in the quaint and inconspicuous town of Bethlehem. And this child would be no ordinary child—He's the promised messenger of the great divine council.

> [6] Because a child was born to us; a son was given to us whose leadership came upon his shoulder; and his name is called "**Messenger of the Great Council**," for I will bring peace upon the rulers and health to him. (Isa 9:6, LES)

As Isaiah foreshadowed, the Chosen One was coming, and He was coming to reclaim His own!

CHAPTER 15

THE VIRGIN BIRTH, THE HUNT FOR THE CHILD, AND THE WAR IN HEAVEN

"Behold, the virgin shall conceive and bear a son, and they shall call his name Immanuel" (which means, God with us). (Matthew 1:23, ESV)

READING THE STORY

OVER THE YEARS, SOME OF THE Jews eventually came out of exile and returned to Zion, the coveted Promised Land of their forefathers. Men such as Zerubbabel, Ezra, and Nehemiah led large groups back to Zion. However, most of the Jews never made it back home—the diaspora Jews were "swallowed up" (Hos 8:8) and assimilated into many different cultures across the biblical landscape.

Our story now picks up around 6 B.C., when Caesar Augustus of Rome ruled supremely among the kingdoms of men. The Roman Empire appointed leaders in all their controlled provinces. In the summer of 37 B.C., the Roman senate crowned Herod the Great as the regional king over all Judea.

> *Herod was born in the late 70s B.C.E. into an aristocratic Idumean family that had converted to Judaism a half century earlier, in the reign of John Hyrcanus I.*[1]

While Herod identified with Judaism, make no mistake—his loyalty to Rome was unwavering.

However, as loyal as Herod was to Judea, a baby named John would soon grow into a much more important role: the loyal proclaimer of the promised Messiah.

> "In the days of King Herod of Judea, there was a priest of Abijah's division named Zechariah. His wife was from the daughters of Aaron, and her name was Elizabeth. Both were righteous in God's sight, living without blame according to all the commands and requirements of the Lord. But they had no children because Elizabeth could not conceive, and both of them were well along in years. When

---

1 L. I. Levine, "Herod the Great (Person)," *The Anchor Yale Bible Dictionary* 3:161.

> his division was on duty and he was serving as priest before God, it happened that he was chosen by lot, according to the custom of the priesthood, to enter the sanctuary of the Lord and burn incense. At the hour of incense the whole assembly of the people was praying outside. An angel of the Lord appeared to him, standing to the right of the altar of incense. When Zechariah saw him, he was terrified and overcome with fear. But the angel said to him, "Do not be afraid, Zechariah, because your prayer has been heard. Your wife Elizabeth will bear you a son, and you will name him John. There will be joy and delight for you, and many will rejoice at his birth. For he will be great in the sight of the Lord and will never drink wine or beer. He will be filled with the Holy Spirit while still in his mother's womb. He will turn many of the children of Israel to the Lord their God. And he will go before him in the spirit and power of Elijah, to turn the hearts of fathers to their children, and the disobedient to the understanding of the righteous, to make ready for the Lord a prepared people." (Luke 1:5–17, CSB)

As the angel Gabriel announced, this boy, John, would help turn Israel back to Yahweh by prepping their hearts for repentance. Interestingly, Gabriel also says John would do this in the spirit and power of Elijah—the courageous prophet who defied Baal and defeated 450 of his prophets on top of Mount Carmel.

> "How can I know this?" Zechariah asked the angel. "For I am an old man, and my wife is well along in years." The angel answered him, "I am Gabriel, who stands in the presence of God, and I was sent to speak to you and tell you this good news. Now listen. You will become silent and unable to speak until the day these things take place, because you did

> not believe my words, which will be fulfilled in their proper time." Meanwhile, the people were waiting for Zechariah, amazed that he stayed so long in the sanctuary. When he did come out, he could not speak to them. Then they realized that he had seen a vision in the sanctuary. He was making signs to them and remained speechless. When the days of his ministry were completed, he went back home. After these days his wife Elizabeth conceived and kept herself in seclusion for five months. She said, "The Lord has done this for me. He has looked with favor in these days to take away my disgrace among the people." (Luke 1:18–25, CSB)

Zechariah's concern was reminiscent of Abraham, in that both men were old and well beyond the prime age for having children. But just as Yahweh miraculously helped Abraham and Sarah conceive, He also helped Zechariah and Elizabeth do the same.

The angel Gabriel isn't quite done playing his role as Yahweh's divine birth announcer, though.

> "In the sixth month, the angel Gabriel was sent by God to a town in Galilee called Nazareth, to a virgin engaged to a man named Joseph, of the house of David. The virgin's name was Mary. And the angel came to her and said, "Greetings, favored woman! The Lord is with you." But she was deeply troubled by this statement, wondering what kind of greeting this could be. Then the angel told her, "Do not be afraid, Mary, for you have found favor with God. Now listen: You will conceive and give birth to a son, and you will name him Jesus. He will be great and will be called the Son of the Most High, and the Lord God will give him the throne of his father David. He will reign over the house of Jacob forever, and his kingdom will have no end." (Luke 1:26–33, CSB)

Mary was shocked! Her question centered around the fact that she was an unmarried virgin. How could she possibly be pregnant?

> Mary asked the angel, "How can this be, since I have not had sexual relations with a man?" The angel replied to her, "The Holy Spirit will come upon you, and the power of the Most High will overshadow you. Therefore, the holy one to be born will be called the Son of God. And consider your relative Elizabeth—even she has conceived a son in her old age, and this is the sixth month for her who was called childless. For nothing will be impossible with God." "See, I am the Lord's servant," said Mary. "May it happen to me as you have said." Then the angel left her. (Luke 1:34–38, CSB)

Choosing the mother of the Son of God was a big decision. Of all the women in the land, Yahweh's selection was the virgin Mary. She and Joseph met the prophesied pedigree that linked back to the house of David. Equally important, they served the Lord.

> In those days Mary set out and hurried to a town in the hill country of Judah where she entered Zechariah's house and greeted Elizabeth. When Elizabeth heard Mary's greeting, the baby leaped inside her, and Elizabeth was filled with the Holy Spirit. Then she exclaimed with a loud cry, "Blessed are you among women, and your child will be blessed! How could this happen to me, that the mother of my Lord should come to me? For you see, when the sound of your greeting reached my ears, the baby leaped for joy inside me. (Luke 1:39–44, CSB)

The motherly connection Mary and Elizabeth shared was special. Each was pregnant with a son who would help turn the tide against man's battle with sin and Yahweh's war with the fallen angels. John would "prepare the way" for Jesus to become "the Way" to eternal life

(John 14:6). His message would be Christ-centered: "Repent, for the kingdom of heaven is at hand" (Matt 3:2, ESV).

Mary and Elizabeth spent three months together (Luke 1:56), undoubtedly planning for the arrivals of John and Jesus. At full term, Elizabeth gave birth to her precious baby boy, John (Luke 1:57–58).

> "In those days a decree went out from Caesar Augustus that the whole empire should be registered. This first registration took place while Quirinius was governing Syria. So everyone went to be registered, each to his own town. Joseph also went up from the town of Nazareth in Galilee, to Judea, to the city of David, which is called Bethlehem, because he was of the house and family line of David, to be registered along with Mary, who was engaged to him and was pregnant. While they were there, the time came for her to give birth. Then she gave birth to her firstborn son, and she wrapped him tightly in cloth and laid him in a manger, because there was no guest room available for them. In the same region, shepherds were staying out in the fields and keeping watch at night over their flock. Then an angel of the Lord stood before them, and the glory of the Lord shone around them, and they were terrified. But the angel said to them, "Don't be afraid, for look, I proclaim to you good news of great joy that will be for all the people: Today in the city of David a Savior was born for you, who is the Messiah, the Lord. This will be the sign for you: You will find a baby wrapped tightly in cloth and lying in a manger." Suddenly there was a multitude of the heavenly host with the angel, praising God and saying: Glory to God in the highest heaven, and peace on earth to people he favors! When the angels had left them and returned to heaven, the shepherds said to one another, "Let's go straight to Bethlehem and see what has happened, which the Lord has made known to us." They hurried off and found both Mary and Joseph, and the baby who was lying in the manger. After

> seeing them, they reported the message they were told about this child, and all who heard it were amazed at what the shepherds said to them. But Mary was treasuring up all these things in her heart and meditating on them. The shepherds returned, glorifying and praising God for all the things they had seen and heard, which were just as they had been told. When the eight days were completed for his circumcision, he was named Jesus—the name given by the angel before he was conceived. (Luke 2:1–21, CSB)

Jesus' arrival also garnered the attention of some mysterious "wise men" (i.e., Magi) of the east, who were alerted by a signaling star in the night sky. They traveled to Jerusalem and met with Herod, the king of the Jews.

> After Jesus was born in Bethlehem in Judea, during the time of King Herod, Magi from the east came to Jerusalem and asked, "Where is the one who has been born king of the Jews? We saw his star when it rose and have come to worship him." When King Herod heard this he was disturbed, and all Jerusalem with him. When he had called together all the people's chief priests and teachers of the law, he asked them where the Messiah was to be born. "In Bethlehem in Judea," they replied, "for this is what the prophet has written: "'But you, Bethlehem, in the land of Judah, are by no means least among the rulers of Judah; for out of you will come a ruler who will shepherd my people Israel.'" Then Herod called the Magi secretly and found out from them the exact time the star had appeared. He sent them to Bethlehem and said, "Go and search carefully for the child. As soon as you find him, report to me, so that I too may go and worship him." After they had heard the king, they went on their way, and the star they had seen when it rose went ahead of them until it stopped over the place where the child was. When they saw the star, they were overjoyed. On coming to the house, they saw the child with his mother Mary,

> and they bowed down and worshiped him. Then they opened their treasures and presented him with gifts of gold, frankincense and myrrh. And having been warned in a dream not to go back to Herod, they returned to their country by another route. When they had gone, an angel of the Lord appeared to Joseph in a dream. "Get up," he said, "take the child and his mother and escape to Egypt. Stay there until I tell you, for Herod is going to search for the child to kill him." (Matt 2:1–13, NIV)

When Herod's ruse of wanting to worship the Christ child tanked due to Yahweh warning the wise worshipers, his desperation festered into a spineless plan of mass murder. His paranoia of being usurped by a Davidic heir to the throne consumed Herod and dismantled his judgment. God acted quickly, deploying one of His angels to expose Herod's plan to Joseph. The angel's message was for Joseph to take Jesus and Mary far away to the land of Egypt—there was about to be a manhunt for the boy who lived.

> "... Rise, take the child and his mother, and flee to Egypt, and remain there until I tell you, for Herod is about to search for the child, to destroy him." (Matt 2:13, ESV)

As Joseph and Mary fled to Egypt, Herod stewed in his fear and malice.

> When Herod realized that he had been outwitted by the Magi, he was furious, and he gave orders to kill all the boys in Bethlehem and its vicinity who were two years old and under, in accordance with the time he had learned from the Magi. Then what was said through the prophet Jeremiah was fulfilled: "A voice is heard in Ramah, weeping and great mourning, Rachel weeping for her children and refusing to be comforted, because they are no more." (Matt 2:16–18, NIV)

Herod's obsession with retaining his power as king over Judea drove him mad. So mad that he slaughtered every Jewish boy two-years-old and younger in Bethlehem. Countless mothers wept at the senseless slaughter of their baby boys. Matthew's citation of Jeremiah 31:15 is important.

> 15 This is what the LORD says: A voice was heard in Ramah, a lament with bitter weeping— Rachel weeping for her children, refusing to be comforted for her children because they are no more. (Jer 31:15, CSB)

Verse 15 captures the deep sorrow of these hurting mothers. But Matthew wants his readers to know that, despite this wicked act, there is still hope for the world.

> “After Herod died, an angel of the Lord appeared in a dream to Joseph in Egypt, saying, “Get up, take the child and his mother, and go to the land of Israel, because those who intended to kill the child are dead.” So he got up, took the child and his mother, and entered the land of Israel. (Matt 2:19–21, CSB)

Herod's death in 4 B.C. was undoubtedly a relief to Mary and Joseph. As the angel said, this meant they could finally return home, just like Jeremiah promised his weepers in the follow-up verse, Jeremiah 31:16.

> “Thus says the LORD: “Keep your voice from weeping, and your eyes from tears, for there is a reward for your work, declares the LORD, and they shall come back from the land of the enemy. There is hope for your future, declares the LORD, and your children shall come back to their own country. (Jer 31:16–17, ESV)

ANSWERING YOUR QUESTIONS

WHAT IS REPENTANCE?

Matthew 2 closes with the death of King Herod and the return of the future King, Jesus, from Egypt. Matthew 3 picks up around 26 A.D., some thirty-plus years after Jesus and John were born. Matthew writes,

> [1] In those days John the Baptist came preaching in the wilderness
> of Judea, [2] "Repent, for the kingdom of heaven is at hand." [3] For
> this is he who was spoken of by the prophet Isaiah when he said,
> "The voice of one crying in the wilderness: 'Prepare the way of
> the Lord; make his paths straight.'" (Matt 3:1–3, ESV)

John has obviously embraced his divinely appointed role to prepare the way for Jesus. Matthew even includes the line about his dress attire and diet, which again links him to preaching in the same spirit as Elijah the prophet.

Matthew 3:4 (ESV)	2 Kings 1:8 (ESV)
[4] Now John wore a garment of camel's hair and a leather belt around his waist, and his food was locusts and wild honey.	[8] They answered him, "He wore a garment of hair, with a belt of leather about his waist." And he said, "It is Elijah the Tishbite."

John's message was simple—repent. Repentance is a "churchy" word, meaning it's not a word Christians typically use outside of the church setting. Most believers are probably familiar with the word, but what does it actually mean?

> *Repentance is an act of acknowledging past wrongdoing, expressing regret or contrition, and committing to right behavior*

> *and obedience to God. It is a transformative process that involves turning away from sin or transgression and turning back to God.*[2]

Repentance is at the heart of the original gospel. The message of the kingdom was for the world to demonstrate a regret for their sin and servitude from following other gods. With that regret, they must wholeheartedly turn away from these taskmasters and cling to Christ. Like John the Baptizer, Jesus and His apostles also preached repentance (Matt 4:17).

> *The apostles carry on this ministry of preaching repentance even after his resurrection (Acts 2:38; 3:19; 8:22; 26:20). Paul refers to repentance as leading to salvation (2 Cor 7:9–10) and mourns over sinners who do not repent (2 Cor 12:21). In the book of Revelation, Christ calls seven churches to repent of wrongdoings (e.g., Rev 2:5); the book also declares destruction for those who do not repent (e.g., Rev 9:20–21).*[3]

Matthew notes that when John was baptizing penitent Jews of Jerusalem and Judea, he used the Jordan River (Matt 3:6). His insistence on baptizing in the Jordan River may link back to Elisha, Elijah's protégé, when he commanded Naaman to dip seven times in the Jordan to cleanse his leprosy. You may recall this story back from chapter 6 in our discussion on sacred space. As the Bible reveals, when Naaman was cleansed of his leprosy, he pledged his loyalty to Yahweh before Elisha (2 Kgs 5:16). His cleansing from physical leprosy is parallel to John's water baptism of repentance—it's a pledge of loyalty, a switching of sides in spiritual warfare from the gods to the Most High God, Yahweh.

---

2 L. DiFransico, "Repentance," *Lexham Theological Wordbook.*

3 DiFransico, "Repentance."

Baptism's importance makes John's response to the Pharisees and Sadducees who sought baptism glaringly suspicious. Matthew notes,

> [7] But when he [John] saw many of the Pharisees and Sadducees coming to his baptism, he said to them, "You brood of vipers! Who warned you to flee from the wrath to come? [8] Bear fruit in keeping with repentance. (Matt 3:7–8, ESV)

In other words, John is saying, "I'm not baptizing you guys because you're not penitent of your sin. Your sin doesn't bother you. Your hearts are hardened by your self-righteousness. You're not serious about changing." John's refusal to baptize them seems harsh on the surface. However, it wasn't. He knew repentance must precede baptism. Another way of saying it is that the desire to change has to precede the change itself. Repentance is a prerequisite to being born again. These guys bore no fruit of true repentance, and John knew it.

A positive case study of repentance is in Acts 2. On Pentecost, Peter preached to the Jews by saying,

> [36] Let all the house of Israel therefore know for certain that God has made him both Lord and Christ, this Jesus whom you crucified." [37] Now when they heard this **they were cut to the heart**, and said to Peter and the rest of the apostles, "Brothers, what shall we do?" [38] And Peter said to them, "**Repent and be baptized** every one of you in the name of Jesus Christ **for the forgiveness of your sins, and you will receive the gift of the Holy Spirit**. [39] For the promise is for you and for your children and for all who are far off, everyone whom the Lord our God calls to himself." [40] And with many other words he bore witness and continued to exhort them, saying, "Save yourselves from

> this crooked generation." [41] **So those who received his word were baptized, and there were added that day about three thousand souls.** (Acts 2:36–41, ESV)

The Pentecost believers were cut to the heart. The realization of their sin moved them to a state of godly sorrow, which led to true repentance. Paul writes,

> [10] For grief according to the will of God brings about a repentance leading to salvation, not to be regretted, but worldly grief brings about death. (2 Cor 7:10, LEB)

While John's ministry was vital, he wasn't the main event; he was the opening act. When Jesus kickstarted His ministry with His disciples, John emphasized he was not the Christ and that his role as the preparer was now complete. He simply decreased while Jesus increased. Note John 3:22–36.

> [22] After this, Jesus and his disciples went to the Judean countryside, where he spent time with them and baptized.
> [23] John also was baptizing in Aenon near Salim, because there was plenty of water there. People were coming and being baptized, [24] since John had not yet been thrown into prison.
> [25] Then a dispute arose between John's disciples and a Jew about purification. [26] So they came to John and told him, "Rabbi, the one you testified about, and who was with you across the Jordan, is baptizing—and everyone is going to him." [27] John responded, "No one can receive anything unless it has been given to him from heaven. [28] You yourselves can testify that I said, 'I am not the Messiah, but I've been sent ahead of him.' [29] He who has the bride is the groom. But the groom's friend, who stands by and listens for him, rejoices greatly at the groom's voice. So this joy

> of mine is complete. 30 He must increase, but I must decrease."
> 31 The one who comes from above is above all. The one who
> is from the earth is earthly and speaks in earthly terms. The
> one who comes from heaven is above all. 32 He testifies to what
> he has seen and heard, and yet no one accepts his testimony.
> 33 The one who has accepted his testimony has affirmed that
> God is true. 34 For the one whom God sent speaks God's words,
> since he gives the Spirit without measure. 35 The Father loves
> the Son and has given all things into his hands. 36 The one who
> believes in the Son has eternal life, but the one who rejects the
> Son will not see life; instead, the wrath of God remains on him.
> (John 3:22–36, CSB)

WHY PICK A VIRGIN?

The virgin birth of Christ is widely known, even among the unchurched of society. But why did God pick a virgin? Have you ever really considered what this is supposed to telegraph? Many people today would say it shows Mary's overall purity, which was of course apropos in mothering the pure Son of God. Others have suggested the virgin birth simply displays the miraculous power of God. Both of these things are certainly true; however, I suggest that first-century people would have interpreted the virgin birth with a totally different understanding.

The idea of the sexual mixture of human seed with the divine was commonplace in antiquity. First-century pagans and Jews both would have parsed the virgin birth as antipodal to what the fallen angels did in Genesis 6 and what the stories of Greek mythology entailed. In both instances, higher entities took human wives, had sex with them, and as a result, produced an offspring that was both heavenly and earthly. In God's plan to reverse the effects of sin and the Watchers' actions, in stark contrast, He too would father a son who was the product of two realms. Yet, Jesus wasn't formed by a sexual union between fallen spirits and mortal women; He was born from a nonsexual union between the Holy Spirit and a mortal woman. Mary never had sex with a celestial being or a mortal man. Her virginity status wasn't revoked until after the birth of Jesus.

> *In fact, effort is made to expunge the possibility of any sexual relations whatsoever between Mary and Joseph while Mary is pregnant. Joseph "did as the angel of the Lord commanded him; he took her as his wife, but had no marital relations with her" (οὐκ ἐγινωσκεν αὐτὴν) until after the child is born (Matt 1:25 NRSV).*[4]

Irenaeus (130–203 A.D.), a student of Polycarp (69–155 A.D.)—who was discipled by the apostle John (died in 100 A.D.)—makes several other significant remarks on Mary's virginal status and the importance of the angel's visit.

> *As Eve was seduced by the word of a [fallen] angel to flee from God, having rebelled against his word, so Mary by the word of an angel received the glad tidings that she would bear God by obeying his word. The former was seduced to disobey God [and so fell], but the latter was persuaded to obey God, so that the Virgin Mary might become the advocate of the virgin Eve. As the human race was subjected to death through the act of a virgin, so was it saved by a virgin, and thus the disobedience of one virgin was precisely balanced by the obedience of another. AGAINST HERESIES 5.19.1.*[5]

---

4 Amy Elizabeth Richter, "The Enochic Watchers' Template and the Gospel of Matthew" (PhD diss., Marquette University, 2010), http://epublications.marquette.edu/dissertations_mu/45, 155–156.

5 Louth and Conti, *Genesis 1–11*, 78–79.

In Paul's letter to the church at Galatia, he alludes to Jesus' birth and, in contrast, links it to the elemental spirits (***stoicheion***) that once enslaved them.

> [1] Now I say, for as long a time as the heir is a child, he is no
> different from a slave, although he is master of everything, [2] but
> he is under guardians and managers until the time set by his
> father. [3] So also we, when we were children, **we were enslaved
> under the elemental spirits of the world**. [4] But when the
> fullness of time came, God sent out his Son, **born of a woman**,
> born under the law, (Gal 4:1–4, LEB)

These are the same spirits (***stoicheion***) by which Paul said the brethren at Colossae had died (Col 2:20), and they're the same spirits by which Paul warned the church not to be deceived or taken captive.

> [8] See to it that no one takes you captive by philosophy and empty deceit, according to human tradition, **according to the elemental spirits of the world**, and not according to Christ. (Col 2:8, ESV)

Their predecessors, the sons of God of Genesis 6, were the first to enslave humanity. Stewart wrote,

> *Paul's reference to Jesus' birth in Galatians 4:4 is illuminated by the Watchers narrative. Jesus' divine mission is contrasted with the angelic rebellion. The Sons of God in the BW [Book of the Watcher] rebel in heaven (1 Enoch 6:1–6) and "enter" human women on earth (7:1). In Galatians, however, when the "fullness of time has come" God sends his Son to be born "from a woman" (Gal 4:5), thus Jesus' divinely ordained mission, accomplished birth from a woman is contrasted with the rebellion of Angels entering women.*

> *Both texts bring heaven and earth together through divine sons involved with human women.*[6]

Jesus' paranormal birth was the first of many subtle messages meant to telegraph the beginning of the end for the devil and his angels.

WHY SEND MAGI (WISE MEN) FROM THE EAST?

Nativity scenes often include three wise men who offer gifts to baby Jesus. The funny thing is the Bible never mentions the number of how many Magi were actually there. The real crime is that little thought is usually given to the significance of their westerly visit. Just who are these wise men and why is their visit important?

> *Extrabiblical evidence offers various clues that shed light on the place of origin and positions held by the "wise men" of Matthew 2. The historian Herodotus mentions "magi" as a priestly caste of Media, or Persia, and, as the religion in Persia at the time was Zoroastrianism, Herodotus' magi were probably Zoroastrian priests. Herodotus, together with Plutarch and Strabo, suggests that magi were partly responsible for ritual and cultic life (supervising sacrifices and prayers) and partly responsible as royal advisers to the courts of the East. Believing the affairs of history were reflected in the movements of the stars and other phenomena, Herodotus suggests the rulers of the East commonly utilized the magi's knowledge of astrology and dream interpretation to determine affairs of state. The magi were therefore concerned with what the movement of the stars (as sign and portents) might signify for the future affairs of history. Such an interest could account not only*

---

6 Tyler A. Stewart, "Fallen Angels, Bastard Spirits, and the Birth of God's Son: An Enochic Etiology of Evil in Galatians 3:19–4:11" (paper presented at the annual meeting of the Society of Biblical Literature, 2014), 15–16.

> *for the wise men's association with the star in Matthew 2, but also their conclusion, shared with Herod, that the nova's appearance signified the birth of a new ruler of great importance (2:2).*[7]

The Holman Bible Dictionary states the Magi are,

> *Eastern wise men, priests, and astrologers expert in interpreting dreams and other "magic arts."*[8]

Furthermore, Minucius Felix (second century), a defender of Christ, emphasized that Magi ran with demons.

> *The Magi, too, are acquainted with demons; but more than that, all their magical tricks they perform through demons; it is filled with their inspiration that they produce their feats of legerdemain, making appear things that do not exist and disappear things that do.*[9]

What's the significance of a group of pagan priests, astrologers, and conjurers of magic visiting and worshiping the Christ child? It seems odd, doesn't it? Many times, what seems odd in the Bible is actually really important.

You may recall reading 1 Enoch 6–9 back in chapter 3 of our journey. The Watchers taught humanity multiple categories of forbidden knowledge and heavenly secrets, including the skillset of the Matthean Magi that visited Jesus. The following chart from Richter is a good overview of the types of forbidden knowledge the Watchers taught humanity in 1 Enoch 6–9.

---

7 W. A. Elwell and B. J. Beitzel, "Wise Men," *Baker Encyclopedia of the Bible* 2:2153–54.

8 C. Brand, C. Draper, A. England, S. Bond, E. R. Clendenen, and T. C. Butler, eds., "Magi," *Holman Illustrated Bible Dictionary* 1066.

9 Felix, *The Octavius of Marcus Minucius Felix*, 100.

Knowledge	***Teacher***	***Recipient***	***Reference***
Sorcery, spells, cutting of roots and plants	Watchers	Watchers' wives	7:1cd
Metalworking for making weaponry [materials of war: attack and defense]	Asael [Azazel]	Men	8:1a
Metalwork for the adornment of women [bracelets, decora-tions]; cosmetic adornment; precious stones and dyes	Asael [Azazel]	Men [who use them for themselves and women, "their daughters"]	8:1b–2
Incantation and the cutting of roots	Shemihazah	Watchers' wives	8:3a
The undoing of spells, magic, and skill	Hermani	Watchers' wives	8:3b
Cosmological or heavenly augury Astrological skill	Baraqel, Kokabel, Ziqel, Arteqoph, Shamsiel, Sahriel	Watchers' wives	8:3c–h
(Summary of the subjects taught) iniquity and eternal heavenly secrets	Asael [Azazel]	Humans ("the sons of men")	9:6
(Summary) All sins	Shemihazah and the Watchers	Women	9:8[10]

10 Richter, "The Enochic Watchers' Template and the Gospel of Matthew," 42.

Just like the virgin birth, the visit of the "skilled" Magi echoed back to the sin of the Watchers. Their skillset of reading the stars reeked of Genesis 6. What once was victory for the Watchers now signaled their defeat.

The Magi's exodus from the east foreshadowed a great spiritual pilgrimage of the Gentile nations, who would also soon come to the King of kings, abandon their gods, and shed the deception of false teaching. People from all nations would soon seek Jesus and become true worshipers of Yahweh, the God of gods and the Lord of lords (Deut 10:17).

CONNECTING THE GOSPEL

REVELATION 12 & THE SIGN IN THE SKY

The apostle Matthew revealed that Jesus' arrival sparked hostility on Earth. Herod felt threatened by the arrival of the King of the Jews, so he launched a war on the baby boys of Bethlehem. But what's often overlooked by believers is the war that broke out in heaven at the birth of Christ. The apostle John writes,

> 1 And a great sign appeared in heaven: a woman clothed with
> the sun, with the moon under her feet, and on her head a crown
> of twelve stars. 2 She was pregnant and was crying out in birth
> pains and the agony of giving birth. 3 And another sign appeared
> in heaven: behold, a great red dragon, with seven heads and ten
> horns, and on his heads seven diadems. 4 His tail swept down
> a third of the stars of heaven and cast them to the earth. And the
> dragon stood before the woman who was about to give birth, so
> that when she bore her child he might devour it. 5 She gave birth
> to a male child, one who is to rule all the nations with a rod
> of iron, but her child was caught up to God and to his throne,
> 6 and the woman fled into the wilderness, where she has a place
> prepared by God, in which she is to be nourished for 1,260 days.
> (Rev 12:1–6, ESV)

What usually gets the attention in the passage is the great red dragon (Satan) who swept a third of the "stars," or angels, down to the earth. Many have suggested this supernatural struggle fits into the timeline near creation. That interpretation is wrong; it totally ignores what's actually being said in the text. In his book titled *Reversing Hermon*, Michael Heiser argues that what's really being described in Revelation 12 is an astro-theological story. Simply put, constellations in the sky signified what was happening in heaven and on Earth, hence the "great sign." What could the heavens be signifying? According to what's often called the first commentary book written on Revelation, its author, Oecumenius (sixth century)—a count of Isauria—said it describes Satan's attempt to kill the Christ child. Oecumenius noted,

> *"And the dragon stood before the woman who was about to bear a child, that he might devour her child when she brought it forth." He is speaking of events in the Lord's life. Since he who was to destroy his [i.e., Satan's] dominion was going to be born, [Satan] watched with close attention, so that when the Virgin gave birth, he might kill the child. And so, too, he took no chances but incited Herod, a lascivious man with a harem of women, to destroy the male and manly child. For Isaiah proclaims to us, "Before the child knows how to cry 'father' or 'mother,' he will take the power of Damascus and the spoils of Samaria before the king of Assyria."*[11]

Let's break down the passage, starting with the astronomical woman. Revelation 12:1 has the woman clothed with the sun with twelve stars around her head and the moon at her feet. Heiser argues the woman in the sky is the constellation called "Virgo," or the Virgin.

---

11 W. C. Weinrich, ed., *Revelation* (Downers Grove, IL: InterVarsity Press, 2005), 180.

The idea that the woman is a constellation is made plausible when one looks closely at the text. The description that the woman was "clothed" with the sun is stock astronomical language for the sun being in the midst of a constellation. While the sun is in the woman, the moon is at her feet. For this situation to occur, the constellation of the woman must be, in astronomical language, on the ecliptic, the imaginary line in the sky that the sun and moon follow in their journey through the zodiac constellations. Martin writes:

The apostle John saw the scene when the Sun was "clothing" or "adorning" the woman. This surely indicates that the position of the Sun in the vision was located somewhere mid-bodied to the woman, between the neck and the knees. The Sun could hardly be said to clothe her if it were situated in her face or near her feet. The only time in the year that the Sun could be in a position to "clothe" the celestial woman called Virgo (that is, to be mid-bodied to her, in the region where a pregnant woman carries a child) is when the Sun is located between about 150 and 170 degrees along the ecliptic. This "clothing" of the woman by the Sun occurs for a 20-day period each year. This 20 degree spread could indicate the general time when Jesus was born.

The constellation of the Virgin giving birth to the Messiah would of course been viewed as quite coherent by the Magi, especially if they knew about Isaiah 7:14. But even if they were ignorant of this prophecy, this astro-theological linkage would still make sense to them since the sign we know as Virgo has strong associations with other ancient "mother goddess" figures who would produce divine kings.

The detail that the moon was located under the feet of the woman (Virgo) must not be forgotten in all this. The sun must be in the Virgin constellation while the moon is simultaneously at her feet for John's vision to be accurately interpreted astronomically.

> *Because of the moon's "behavior" relative to the ecliptic and Virgo in any given year, the twenty-day window narrows to a roughly ninety-minute period in which to astronomically pinpoint the birth of the child.*[12]

The virgin in the sky represents Mary, the virgin mother of Jesus who "cried out in birth pains" at the "agony of giving birth." This becomes even clearer when you consider what's said of her son. Her male child was destined to "rule the nations with an iron rod." This is an explicit statement that echoes back to Psalm 2:7–9.

> 7 I will tell of the decree: The LORD said to me, "You are my Son; today I have begotten you. 8 Ask of me, and I will make the nations your heritage, and the ends of the earth your possession. 9 You shall break them with a rod of iron and dash them in pieces like a potter's vessel." (Ps 2:7–9, ESV)

The born son would defeat the evil spirit rulers of the nations, allowing the earthly kings to then "kiss the son" and "take refuge in him."

> 10 Now therefore, O kings, be wise; be warned, O rulers of the earth. 11 Serve the LORD with fear, and rejoice with trembling. 12 Kiss the Son, lest he be angry, and you perish in the way, for his wrath is quickly kindled. Blessed are all who take refuge in him. (Ps 2:10–12, ESV)

Then, there is the great red dragon—a clear reference to Satan. Scholars have suggested the dragon in the sky is either the constellation Hydra or Scorpio. Dr. Heiser suggested,

---

12 Heiser, *Reversing Hermon*, 60–61.

> *Hydra has the advantage of matching the description of the seven heads atop the Dragon in Revelation 12:3 (cf. 13:1; 17:3, 7, 9). Hydra was also conceived as a sea serpent, imagery that matches descriptions in Revelation (13:1), which in turn come from the Leviathan material of the Old Testament (Isaiah 27:1). However, Hydra is not precisely on the ecliptic; it is adjacent and only slightly below the woman. In other words, Hydra is not positioned directly under the feet of the woman, waiting to devour the child as soon as it emerges from the woman. The ecliptic problem is resolved if ancient Scorpio is John's referent, but that said, the text of Revelation 12 only has the Dragon present ("stood before the woman"), not directly under her feet. Both options are possible correlations.*[13]

The arrival of baby Jesus didn't only trigger a manhunt for the Christ child—it caused a multidimensional war where a third of the angels were swept down to the earth by the tail of the dragon. Herod wasn't the only one who felt threatened by the arrival of baby Jesus; Satan was nervously enraged. To his horror, the promised seed of Genesis 3:15 was just birthed into reality.

LOOKING AHEAD

By the divine protection of His heavenly Father, the promised child escaped the war of the worlds. Mary and Joseph built a simple life for Jesus in the unusually plain town of Nazareth. As Jesus increased in wisdom and stature (Luke 2:43), it was all leading to one inevitable meeting—Jesus would soon come face-to-face with the rebel cherub who, for thousands of years, deceived the whole world. The next chapter will take Jesus and Satan to the pinnacle of spiritual warfare, where they, for the first time, will battle it out for authority over the

---

13 Heiser, *Reversing Hermon*, 63.

nations. The stakes have never been higher, and our journey has never been more intense.

Buckle up. The battle of all battles is about to begin.

CHAPTER 16

THE SANCTIFIED SON, THE WAR IN THE DESERT, AND PSALM 91

For he will command his angels concerning you to guard you in all your ways. On their hands they will bear you up, lest you strike your foot against a stone. (Psalm 91:11–12, ESV)

READING THE STORY

OUR STORY NOW PICKS UP IN the fall of 26 A.D., some thirty years after "the dragon" (Satan) tried to kill and "devour" the child. John the Baptizer was well-established in his ministry, and it was time for Jesus to begin His mission. Step one was to seek out John.

> Then Jesus came from Galilee to John at the Jordan, to be baptized by him. But John tried to stop him, saying, "I need to be baptized by you, and yet you come to me?" Jesus answered him, "Allow it for now, because this is the way for us to fulfill all righteousness." Then John allowed him to be baptized. When Jesus was baptized, he went up immediately from the water. The heavens suddenly opened for him, and he saw the Spirit of God descending like a dove and coming down on him. And a voice from heaven said, "This is my beloved Son, with whom I am well-pleased." (Matt 3:13–17, CSB)

Immediately after coming up out of the water, the heavens ripped open, and the Spirit of God descended and rested on Jesus. What followed was a voice from heaven proclaiming Jesus was the consecrated Son. This marked the commencement of His task to save the nations. Yahweh's auditory and visible identification of His Son now officially began Jesus' role as the Savior in the methodical scheme of redemption.

The visual sign of Christ being anointed with the Spirit was prophesied in the book of Isaiah.

Isaiah 42:1 (ESV)	Isaiah 11:2 (ESV)
[1] Behold my servant, whom I uphold, my chosen, in whom my soul delights; I have **put my Spirit upon him**; he will bring forth **justice to the nations**.	[2] And **the Spirit of the Lord shall rest upon him**, the Spirit of wisdom and understanding, the Spirit of counsel and might, the Spirit of knowledge and the fear of the Lord.

His auditory sign echoed back to Psalm 2:7.

> [7] I will tell of the decree: The LORD said to me, "You are my Son; today I have begotten you. (Ps 2:7, ESV)

What John witnessed at Jesus' baptism was truly heavenly. He recognized he was "outranked" by the glorified Son. The apostle John records,

> "The next day John saw Jesus coming toward him and said, "Look, the Lamb of God, who takes away the sin of the world! This is the one I told you about: 'After me comes a man who ranks ahead of me, because he existed before me.' I didn't know him, but I came baptizing with water so that he might be revealed to Israel." And John testified, "I saw the Spirit descending from heaven like a dove, and he rested on him. I didn't know him, but he who sent me to baptize with water told me, 'The one you see the Spirit descending and resting on—he is the one who baptizes with the Holy Spirit.' I have seen and testified that this is the Son of God." (John 1:29–34, CSB)

Matthew, Mark, and Luke then reveal Jesus was led by the Spirit out of the Jordan River and into the Judean desert, a place haunted with wild beasts and evil spirits (Lev 16:10; Isa 13:21; 34:14). The sequence of events that follows is unequivocally the closest we get to actual dialogue between the Savior from heaven and the serpent from Eden. Luke writes,

> "Then Jesus left the Jordan, full of the Holy Spirit, and was led by the Spirit in the wilderness for forty days to be tempted by the devil. He ate nothing during those days, and when they were over, he was hungry. The devil said to him, "If

> you are the Son of God, tell this stone to become bread." But Jesus answered him, "It is written: Man must not live on bread alone." (Luke 4:1–4, CSB)

Satan's first temptation focused on Jesus' physical needs. Jesus had been fasting for forty days and forty nights and was physically famished. However, His fasting strengthened His devotion and connection with His Father. This is evidenced by His constant use of the Word of God to respond to all three of Satan's alluring temptations. Satan was hoping he could appeal to Jesus' weakened humanity first. The temptation was for a starving Jesus to physically sustain Himself. To become self-sufficient. To act like a grownup who's independent and not in need of Daddy to put food on the table. To rebel and become like Satan. Jesus rejected independence and denied His hunger by quoting Deuteronomy 8:3.

> 3 And he humbled you and let you hunger and fed you with manna, which you did not know, nor did your fathers know, that he might make you know that man does not live by bread alone, **but man lives by every word that comes from the mouth of the** LORD. (Deut 8:3, ESV)

The Bible Knowledge Commentary notes,

> *Jesus countered this temptation by quoting Deuteronomy 8:3, in which Moses had reminded the people of the manna which God had given them. Though the manna was on the ground, it still was a test of faith for the people. They had to believe that God's Word was trustworthy for their existence. If it was not God's will for them to live they certainly would have died; therefore they did not live by bread alone. Likewise Jesus, knowing God's Word, knew of the plan which was before Him and was trusting in the Father*

and His Word for sustenance. Jesus knew He would not die in the wilderness.[1]

When Jesus refused to turn stones into bread, Satan changed tactics. His second approach was to tempt Jesus in the arenas of authority and dominion.

> And the devil took him up and showed him all the kingdoms of the world in a moment of time, and said to him, "To you I will give all this authority and their glory, for it has been delivered to me, and I give it to whom I will. If you, then, will worship me, it will all be yours." (Luke 4:5–7, ESV)

Satan's offer is telling. It shows he's well aware of Jesus' mission to rescue all nations. Since the allotment at Babel (Deut 32:8–9), the devil and his angels have ruled all the kingdoms of the world. This was no bluff. Satan wasn't offering something that didn't belong to him; it was "delivered" to him. He's offering Christ what He was sent to Earth to retrieve—all the nations. The only caveat was Jesus must bow down to the ruler of this world (John 12:31; 14:30; 16:11); He must worship Satan. In response, Jesus quotes Deuteronomy 6:13.

> "You shall fear Yahweh your God, and you shall serve him, and by his name you shall swear. (Deut 6:13, LEB)

While Yahweh's plan was certainly for Christ to redeem the nations, it didn't involve Jesus being deferential to Satan, but defeating him. Jesus

---

1 J. A. Martin, "Luke," in vol. 2 of *The Bible Knowledge Commentary: An Exposition of the Scriptures*, eds. J. F. Walvoord and R. B. Zuck (Wheaton, IL: Victor Books, 1985), 213.

would, on His Father's timetable, regain ground in all the kingdoms of the world, stripping Satan and his supernatural cronies of their longstanding authority.

In a last-ditch effort to corrupt Christ, Satan changed his approach yet again. He now tempts Jesus to test the loyalty of His Father and angels in heaven.

> "And he took him to Jerusalem and set him on the pinnacle of the temple and said to him, "If you are the Son of God, throw yourself down from here, for it is written, "'He will command his angels concerning you, to guard you,' and "'On their hands they will bear you up, lest you strike your foot against a stone.'" (Luke 4:9–11, ESV)

Jesus' repeated use of Scripture is now parroted by the devil. What's interesting is of all the passages in the Old Testament, Satan quotes from Psalm 91, a chapter addressed to those who "dwell in the shelter of the Most High."

Luke 4:10–11 (ESV)	Psalm 91:11–12 (ESV)
10 for it is written, "'He will command his angels concerning you, to guard you,' 11 and "'On their hands they will bear you up, lest you strike your foot against a stone.'"	11 For he will command his angels concerning you to guard you in all your ways. 12 On their hands they will bear you up, lest you strike your foot against a stone.

Satan conveniently stops short of verse 13, which foreshadows his defeat as the trampled "serpent" and "young lion."

> 13 You will tread on the lion and the adder; the young lion and the serpent you will trample underfoot. (Ps 91:13, ESV)

The Jews considered Psalm 91 an exorcistic psalm—a psalm for exorcising demons and defeating the powers of darkness. The Dead Sea Scroll Bible notes,

> *One of the most interesting Psalms scrolls was found in Cave 11 at Qumran. Known as 11QApocryphal Psalms (or 11QPsApa or 11QApPs), this manuscript is dated about 50–70 CE and contains four Psalms for use in exorcisms against demons. Many scholars believe these to be the Four Songs for Playing over the Stricken that are mentioned in David's Compositions, which is part of the large Psalms scroll from Cave 11 (11QPsa col. 16:9–10). The first three of these Psalms were unknown until the discovery of the Dead Sea Scrolls, but the fourth is found in modern Bibles as Psalm 91.*[2]

Biblical scholar Evans wrote,

> *Commentators have long suspected that this psalm was understood as offering assurance against demonic affliction… However, the discovery at Qumran of Psalm 91 in combination with exorcism psalms has pretty well settled the matter once and for all: Psalm 91 apparently was understood in the time of Jesus as offering divine assurances of protection against demonic powers.*[3]

The fact that Psalm 91 was bundled with three other psalms of exorcism is very telling of its antidemonic properties. It's a song of protection from evil entities. It functioned much like when David expelled an evil spirit from Saul when playing his melodic lyre (1 Sam 16:23).

---

2 M. Abegg, Jr., P. Flint, and E. Ulrich, trans. *The Dead Sea Scrolls Bible: The Oldest Known Bible Translated for the First Time into English* (New York: HarperOne, 1999), 539.

3 *Celebrating the Dead Sea Scrolls: A Canadian Contribution*, eds. Peter W. Flint, Jean Duhaime, and Kyung S. Baek, vol. 30 of *Early Judaism and Its Literature*. Atlanta: Society of Biblical Literature, 2011.

In our story, Satan, the Darth Vader of the Bible, is the epitome of evil. He's the most sinister player of them all. Satan now tempts Jesus to test that theory—to put Himself in harm's way and see if Yahweh will send out His angels to protect Jesus from striking His foot against a stone should He throw Himself off the pinnacle of the temple.

Jesus doesn't take the bait. He responds by quoting Deuteronomy 6:16.

> And Jesus answered him, "It is said, 'You shall not put the Lord your God to the test.'" (Luke 4:12, ESV)

This is now the third time Jesus quoted from Deuteronomy 6–8. Coincidence? Not a chance! In the New International Commentary on the Gospel of Matthew, R. T. France wrote,

> *The most significant key to the understanding of this story is to be found in Jesus' three scriptural quotations. All come from Deut 6–8, the part of Moses' address to the Israelites before their entry into Canaan in which he reminds them of their forty years of wilderness experiences. It has been a time of preparation and of proving the faithfulness of their God. He has deliberately put them through a time of privation as an educative process. They have been learning, or should have been learning, what it means to live in trusting obedience to God: "As a father disciplines his son, so the Lord your God disciplines you" (Deut 8:5; for Israel as God's son cf. Exod 4:22; Jer 31:9; Hos 11:1–4). Among the lessons they should now have learned are not to depend on bread alone but rather on God's word (8:3), not to put God to the test (6:16), and to make God the exclusive object of their worship and obedience (6:13). Now another "Son of God" is in the wilderness, this time for forty days rather than forty years, as a preparation for entering into his divine calling. There in the wilderness he too*

faces those same tests, and he has learned the lessons which Israel had so imperfectly grasped. His Father is testing him in the school of privation, and his triumphant rebuttal of the devil's suggestions will ensure that the filial bond can survive in spite of the conflict that lies ahead. Israel's occupation of the promised land was at best a flawed fulfillment of the hopes with which they came to the Jordan, but this new "Son of God" will not fail and the new Exodus (to which we have seen a number of allusions in ch. 2) will succeed. "Where Israel of old stumbled and fell, Christ the new Israel stood firm." It is probably also significant that the passage of Deuteronomy from which Jesus' responses are drawn begins with the Šemaʿ, the text from Deut 6:4–5 recited daily in Jewish worship which requires Israel to "love the Lord your God with all your heart, and with all your soul, and with all your strength;" it is precisely that total commitment to God that this wilderness experience is designed to test.

The story of the testing in the wilderness is thus an elaborate typological presentation of Jesus as himself the true Israel, the "Son of God" through whom God's redemptive purpose for his people is now at last to reach its fulfillment.13[4]

The weakened Christ stood spiritually strong against his archnemesis in the desert—the "waterless" compound of demonic spirits (Luke 11:24–26).

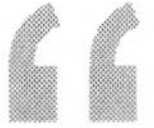

And when the devil had ended every temptation, he departed from him **until an opportune time**. (Luke 4:13, ESV)

4 R. T. France, *The Gospel of Matthew* (Grand Rapids, MI: Wm. B. Eerdmans Publication Co., 2007), 127–128.

ANSWERING YOUR QUESTIONS

WHY WAS JESUS BAPTIZED?

Many have wondered why Jesus was baptized. There is an answer given: "to fulfill all righteousness." However, that reason is somewhat vague to outsiders looking in. What does it mean to "fulfill all righteousness?" There was no Old Testament passage that demanded Christ be baptized by John. Some have suggested Jesus' baptism was designed to link Him to John's ministry of repentance. France wrote,

> *The most obvious way in which Jesus' baptism prepares for his mission is by indicating his solidarity with John's call to repentance in view of the arrival of God's kingship. By first identifying with John's proclamation Jesus lays the foundation for his own mission to take on where John has left off*[5]

There's an additional element to the explanation. In the fourth century, Chromatius of Aquileia preached a lesson titled "On the Epiphany of the Lord." In that sermon, he suggested that Jesus' baptism sanctified water baptism for all believers.

> *Our Lord came to give a new baptism for the salvation of the human race and forgiveness of all sins. First he considered it appropriate for himself to be baptized, not to put away sins, since he had done no sin, but he sanctified the waters of baptism in order to destroy the sins of all believers by the baptism of the reborn. He was baptized in water so that we by baptism might be washed from all sins....*
>
> *[Gal. 3:27 and Rom. 6:4 quoted.] Thus by baptism we die to sin, but we live with Christ; we bury our old life, but we are raised*

5 France, *The Gospel of Matthew*, 120.

> *to a new life; we take off the error of the old person, but we take on the clothing of the new person. Therefore, the Lord in baptism fulfilled all righteousness. He wanted to be baptized so that we might be baptized; he received this "washing of regeneration" [Titus 3:5] so that we might be reborn in life. (Sermon 34.3)*[6]

First-century witnesses would have understood that the Christological baptism linked Jesus to John; it served as a visual signal. The transition from John to Jesus had begun, and all future believers must embrace repentance and baptism in the era of Christ's new kingdom.

WHERE ARE THE DEMONS IN PSALM 91?

Psalm 91 reads,

> 1 He who dwells in the shelter of the Most High will abide in the shadow of the Almighty. 2 I will say to the LORD, "My refuge and my fortress, my God, in whom I trust." 3 For he will deliver you from the snare of the fowler and from the deadly pestilence. 4 He will cover you with his pinions, and under his wings you will find refuge; his faithfulness is a shield and buckler. 5 You will not fear the terror of the night, nor the arrow that flies by day, 6 nor the pestilence that stalks in darkness, nor the destruction that wastes at noonday. 7 A thousand may fall at your side, ten thousand at your right hand, but it will not come near you. 8 You will only look with your eyes and see the recompense of the wicked. 9 Because you have made the LORD your dwelling place— the Most High, who is my refuge— 10 no evil shall be allowed to befall you, no plague come near your tent. 11 For he will command his angels concerning you to guard you in all your ways. 12 On their hands they will bear you up, lest

6 Ferguson, *Baptism in the Early Church*, 659.

> you strike your foot against a stone. [13] You will tread on the lion and the adder; the young lion and the serpent you will trample underfoot. [14] "Because he holds fast to me in love, I will deliver him; I will protect him, because he knows my name. [15] When he calls to me, I will answer him; I will be with him in trouble; I will rescue him and honor him. [16] With long life I will satisfy him and show him my salvation." (Ps 91:1–16, ESV)

Skimming the chapter sets the tone for divine protection, but it also leaves the modern reader in the dark when looking for traces of the demonic. It leaves us wondering why Psalm 91 is a psalm for exorcising demons, seeing as there are no demons mentioned in the chapter. Grammatically, they are listed, but they're masked by our English translations in an attempt to demythologize the Bible. Not surprising.

David actually lists specific demons or evil spirits from which Yahweh will deliver His children.

Psalm 91:3–6 (ESV)	Psalm 90:3–6 (LES)
[3] For he will deliver you from the snare of the fowler and from the deadly **pestilence** [*deber*]. [4] He will cover you with his pinions, and under his wings you will find refuge; his faithfulness is a shield and buckler. [5] You will not fear the **terror of the night** [*paḥad laylâ*], nor **the arrow that flies** [ḥēṣ yā ʿûp] by day, 6 nor **the pestilence** [*deber*] that stalks in darkness, nor **the destruction** [qeṭeb] that wastes at noonday.	[3] because he will rescue from the trap of hunters and from a terrifying word. [4] With his shoulders he will overshadow you, and under his wings you will have hope; with a shield his truth will surround you. [5] That one will not be afraid from fear by night, from the arrow flying by day, 6 from the deed carried out in darkness, from mishap and **demon** [*daimonou*] **at midday**.

King David starts by addressing a demon called Deber. Deber, or "the pestilence," is an evil nocturnal deity in Canaanite religions who was viewed as the master of epidemics. Deber is listed twice in Psalm 91 (vv. 3, 6). The DDD notes,

> *Deber is one of the three proverbial causes of death on a wide scale. It is attested some 50 times in the Bible along with war (sword, blood) and famine (mainly in Jer and Ez). Besides this empirical meaning, it seems to be used a number of times in a personified sense as a demon or evil deity (Hab 3:5; Ps 91:3, 6; cf. Hos 13:14).*[7]

Secondly, David lists "the terror of the night," or *paḥad laylâ* in Hebrew. The DDD notes,

> *There have been some attempts to relate laylâ etymologically to →Lilith (Is 34:14), Akk (Ardat) lilî, a night demon (DE FRAINE 1959:375). But this is no more than a folk etymology (HALAT 502b). Functionally, however, the demon paḥad laylâ reveals traits similar to those of the Mesopotamian lilû and ardat lilî...*
>
> *Among the host of Mesopotamian demons, Lilû (Sum lú.líl.lá 'wind-man') and Lilītu/Ardat lilî most resemble the biblical paḥad laylâ. These demons seem to have been attached particularly to pregnant women and new-borns whom they harmed (FARBER, RLA 7 [1987–90] 23–24). A similar role is ascribed in cuneiform sources to the demon Lamashtu. In later texts, they are conceived as harmful to brides and grooms, whom they attack on their wedding night and prevent the consummation of the marriage (S. LACKENBACHER, RA 65 [1971] 119–154; M. MALUL, JEOL 32 [1991/1992: 78–85]). Lilītu survived a long time and occupies a central place in later Jewish demonology, whence she passed even into Arab demonology. Here, she seems to have retained*

7 del O. G. Lete, "Deber," *Dictionary of Deities and Demons in the Bible*, 2nd ed., 231–232.

> *her ancient character as a baby-killer, though she also appears (in Jewish Qabbala) as a stealer of men's semen (G. SCHOLEM, EncJud Vol 11, 245–249). As an attacker of brides and grooms she comes close to the incubus and succubus demons known all over the world.*[8]

David balances out the list of night demons with his mention of Qeteb, a daytime demon of destruction.

> *The parallelism of the verses twice balances a night and a daytime →Evil, each of which was understood by rabbinic interpreters to refer to a demonic spirit: the day-time Qeteb is balanced by the →night →demon, Pestilence, Deber... Thus the Qeteb is the personified destruction or disease, riding the hot desert wind (cf. Isa 28:2 and the wind demons of Mesopotamia).*[9]

In the Ugaritic text *KTU 1.5 ii:24*, Qeteb is listed as a kinsman, or accomplice, of Mot, the Canaanite deity of death. Qeteb's appearance is described as the stuff of nightmares. The Midrash *Tehillim* notes,

> *"the poisonous Qeteb is covered with scales and with hair, and sees only out of one eye, the other is in the middle of his heart"*[10]

In Psalm 91:5, David is likely alluding to the feared demonic archer of antiquity—Resheph (i.e., the "arrow" that flies by day). The Bible mentions this deity seven times in the Old Testament (Deut 32:24; 1 Chr 7:25; Job 5:7; Ps 76:3; 78:48; Song 8:6; Hab 3:5). Like other demons and deities, Resheph is masked in English translations by

---

8 M. Malul, "Terror of the Night," *Dictionary of Deities and Demons in the Bible*, 2nd ed., 852.
9 G. J. Riley, "Midday Demon," *Dictionary of Deities and Demons in the Bible*, 2nd ed., 572.
10 Riley, "Midday Demon," 573.

words apropos to his nature, such as "arrows," "fiery," "flame," "fire-bolt," "pestilence," and "plague."

In Psalm 76:3, Yahweh puts an end to war by breaking the "arrows of Resheph," a god of war.[11]

[1] In Judah God is known; his name is great in Israel. [2] His abode has been established in Salem, his dwelling place in Zion. [3] There he broke the **flashing** (*resheph*) **arrows**, the shield, the sword, and the weapons of war. Selah (Ps 76:1–3, ESV)

Resheph is very frequently mentioned in the Ugaritic ritual texts in the capacity of a chthonic deity, gatekeeper of the Netherworld. He is the lord of battle and of diseases, which he spreads through his bow and arrows.[12]

Furthermore,

Resheph was a chthonic god of war in the literature and iconography of the Levant and Egypt... Resheph became popular in Egypt during the Eighteenth Dynasty (1550–1295 BC), during which Egypt ruled the land of Canaan...

In the Iron Age II (ca. eighth century BC), references to Resheph appear among the Hittites, the Phoenicians, and the Israelites...

Literature from Cyprus dating to the seventh—fourth centuries BC contains several references to Resheph as an archer deity... A fourth-century inscription from Kition (KAI 32) mentions "Resheph of the Arrow" (rshp hs),[13]

---

11 J. L. Kelley, "Resheph," *The Lexham Bible Dictionary.*

12 P. Xella, "Resheph," *Dictionary of Deities and Demons in the Bible*, 2nd ed., 701.

13 Kelley, "Resheph."

Though evil, Habakkuk 3:5 portrays both Resheph and Deber as participants in God's military entourage against the very nations that worship them.

> [3] God came from Teman, and the Holy One from Mount Paran. Selah His splendor covered the heavens, and the earth was full of his praise. [4] His brightness was like the light; rays flashed from his hand; and there he veiled his power. [5] Before him went **pestilence** (*deber*), and **plague** (*resheph*) followed at his heels. 6 He stood and measured the earth; he looked and shook the nations; then the eternal mountains were scattered; the everlasting hills sank low. His were the everlasting ways. (Hab 3:3–6, ESV)

> *The eschatological hymn in Hab 3 presents Deber and Resheph marching at →Yahweh's side as His helpers. This follows the ancient Mesopotamian tradition according to which 'plague' and 'pestilence' are present in the entourage of the great god →Marduk (DE MOOR 1990:134)*[14]

In Moses's farewell speech to the Israelites in Deuteronomy 32, he reminds the new generation of Israelites how Yahweh once punished their ancestors for worshiping demons (v. 17) and idols (v. 21). They were not to follow in their steps. The Lord said,

> [22] For a fire is kindled by my anger, and it burns to the depths of Sheol, devours the earth and its increase, and sets on fire the foundations of the mountains. [23] "'And I will heap disasters upon them; I will spend **my arrows** on them; [24] they shall be wasted with hunger, and devoured by **plague** (resheph) and

14 Lete, "Deber," 232.

> poisonous **pestilence** (*qeteb*); I will send the teeth of beasts against them, with the venom of things that crawl in the dust. (Deut 32:22–24, ESV)

Fittingly, the very demons Israel once served were used to punish them. Their gods became their suffering. Israel was brought low by the power of Resheph and Qeteb.

The language of the biblical writers is clear—while demons are rebellious and vile entities, Yahweh is still Lord over every single one of them. None of the powers of darkness can usurp or undercut the God of heaven. They are wielded by the finger of God whenever He chooses.

You really get the full flavor of the supernatural tone of Psalm 91 by reading an Aramaic targum from the fourth to sixth century C.E.

> 1 He who has made his residence in the secret place of the Most High will abide in the shade of clouds of the glory of the Almighty. 2 David said, "I will say to the Lord, 'My security and my strong fortress, my God!' I will trust in his Memra. 3 For he will deliver you, Solomon my son, from the trap and the snare, from death and tumult. 4 With the shade of his Shekinah he will cover you, and beneath the shade of his glory you will be secure; his faithfulness is a shield and buckler. 5 **You will not be afraid of the terror of the demons that go about in the night, nor of the arrow of the angel of death that he shoots in the daytime,** 6 **nor of the death that goes about in the darkness, nor of the company of demons that destroy at noon.** 7 You will call to remembrance the Holy Name, and a thousand will fall at your left side, and ten thousand at your right hand; but they will not come near to you to do harm. 8 You will only look with your eyes, and you will see how the wicked are being destroyed." 9 Solomon answered, and this is what he said: "Because you,

> O LORD, are my refuge, in the most high dwelling place you have set the house of your Shekinah." [10] The Lord of the World responded, and this is what he said: **"No evil shall befall you, and no plague or demons shall come near your tent.** [11] For he will give his angels charge over you, to guard you in all your ways. [12] In their strength they will lift you up, lest your foot stumbles through your evil inclination, which may be compared to a stone. [13] You will tread upon the lion cub and the adder; you will trample the lion and the basilisk. [14] Because he delights in my Memra, I will rescue him; I will set him on high, because he knows my name. [15] He will pray before me, and I will answer him; I will be with him in distress; I will deliver him and honor him.16 With length of days I will satisfy him, and show him my deliverance." (Psalm 91, The Aramaic Bible, Volume 16: The Targum of Psalms)

It's no wonder Psalm 91 has brought comfort to children of the Most High for countless generations; it promises protection against demonic spirits and key players in the powers of darkness.

WHAT'S IN THE OTHER THREE PSALMS OF EXORCISM?

The discovery of the Dead Sea Scrolls introduced us to never before seen psalms, psalms that were lost to humanity. However, scroll 11Q5 reveals that David wrote a bevy of psalms that we simply still don't have in our possession. He's said to have written a total of 4,050 songs/psalms. That's thousands more than the 150 we have in the canonized psalter. Dead Sea Scroll 11Q5 Col. xxvii states,

> *Col. 27* ***2 Now David the son of Jesse*** *was wise and shone like the light of the sun, a scribe 3 and man of discernment, blameless in all his ways before God and humankind. The* LORD *gave 4 him*

> *a brilliant and discerning spirit, so that he wrote: psalms, three thousand six hundred; 5 songs to sing before the altar accompanying the daily 6 perpetual burnt offering for all the days of the year, three hundred and sixty-four; 7 for the Sabbath offerings, fifty-two songs; and for the new moon offerings, 8 all the festival days, and the Day of Atonement, thirty songs.*
>
> *9 The total of all the songs that he composed was four hundred and forty-six, not including 10* ***four songs for charming the demon-possessed with music. The sum total of everything, psalms and songs, was four thousand and fifty****.*
>
> *11 All these he composed through prophecy given him by the Most High.*[15]

Together, the playlist of the four psalms mentioned in line 10 of 11Q5 Col. xxvii was used to rescue the possessed from illness and dark bondage. Thankfully, the four psalms of exorcism were recovered at Qumran in scroll 11Q11.

Like many of the Dead Sea Scrolls, the exorcism psalms are very fragmented due to deterioration from time and natural elements. The first exorcism psalm is highly fragmentary and brief, but key words such as curse, dragon, exorcising, and demon are identifiable. It reads,

> *Col. 1:1 [... 2 ...] and the one who weeps for him 3 [...] the curse 4 [...] by the* Lord *5 [...] dragon 6 [...] the ear[th ... 7 ...] exor[cis]ing [... 8 ...] to [... 9 ...] this [... 10 ...] to the demon [... 11 ...] he will dwe[ll....]*[16]

The second exorcism psalm is attributed to Solomon, David's son. It calls on holy angels to combat demonic powers. It reads,

---

15 Wise, Abegg, Jr., and Cook, *The Dead Sea Scrolls*, 576–577.

16 Abegg, Jr., Flint, and Ulrich, *The Dead Sea Scrolls Bible*, 539.

Col. 2: 1–2 [... of] Solomon. He will invo[ke ... 3 ... the spi] rits and the demons [... 4 ...] These are [the de]mons. And the p[rince of enmi]ty [... 5 ... I]srael [...] the a[byss ... 6 ...] the gre[at ... 7 ...] his people [...] healing 8 [...] leans [upon] your name, and calls [... 9 ... He says to Is]rael, "Hold fast 10 [to the Lord, *... who made] the heavens [11 and the earth, and all that is in them, w]ho separated [12 light from darkness ...]"*

Col. 3:1 [...] the depth[s] 2 the earth and [...] the earth. Who m[ade these signs] 3 and won[ders on the] earth? The Lord, *it is he [who] 4 made the[se through] his [power], who summons all [his] an[gels] 5 [and] all the [holy] offspri[ng] to st[a]nd before [him, ... 6 all the hea]vens and [all] the earth [...] who committe[d] sin against 7 [all humani]ty, and [evil] against all pe[ople. But] they know 8 his [wonder]ful [...] which they do not [...]. If they do not 9 [desist] out of fear of the* Lord *from [... and] from killing the soul of 10 [...] the* Lord, *and [th]ey will fear tha[t] great [spell]. 11 "One of you [puts to flight] a thou[sand." ...] servants of the* Lor[d *... 12 ... g]reat and [...]*

Col. 4:1 [... and] great is [...] adjuring [you ...] 2 and the great [...] the mighty and [...] 3 all the earth [...] the heavens and [...] 4 May the Lord *smite you with a [migh]ty bl[ow] in order to destroy you [...], 5 and in his fierce wrath [may he send] against you a powerful angel [to carry out] 6 his [entire com] mand, who [will show no] mercy to you, wh[o ... 7 ...] against all these who [will send] you [down] into the great abyss 8 [and to] deepest [Sheol], and who [..., and there] you shall lie, and darkness 9 [...] very much [...]. [No lon]ger on the earth 10 [...] forever and [...] by the curse of des[truction ... 11 ...] the fierce anger of the* Lor[d *... in] darkness for a [ll 12 ...] affliction [...] your gift [...]*

> *Col. 5:1 [...] 2 which [...] and those possessed by [demons ...] 3 those crushed [by.... Ra]phael has healed [them. Amen, Amen, Selah].*[17]

The discovery of an exorcistic psalm written by Solomon isn't surprising. According to the Jewish historian Josephus, Solomon wrote 1,005 songs and was given the gift to cast out demons by God. In his book *Antiquities of the Jews 8.41–19*, Josephus wrote,

> *42)* ***Now the sagacity and wisdom which God had bestowed upon Solomon was so great, that he exceeded the ancients****, insomuch that he was no way inferior to the Egyptians, who are said to have been beyond all men in understanding; nay, indeed, it is evident that their sagacity was very much inferior to that of the king's. (43) He also excelled and distinguished himself in wisdom above those who were most eminent among the Hebrews at that time for shrewdness: those I mean were Ethan, and Heman, and Chalcol, and Darda, the sons of Mahol. (44)* ***He also composed books of odes and songs, a thousand and five****; of parables and similitudes, three thousand; for he spake a parable upon every sort of tree, from the hyssop to the cedar; and in like manner also about beasts, about all sorts of living creatures, whether upon the earth, or in the seas, or in the air; for he was not unacquainted with any of their natures, nor omitted inquiries about them, but described them all like a philosopher, and demonstrated his exquisite knowledge of their several properties. (45)* ***God also enabled him to learn that skill which expels demons****, which is a science useful and Sanative to men.* **He composed such incantations also by which distempers are alleviated. And he left behind him the manner**

17 Abegg, Jr., Flint, and Ulrich, *The Dead Sea Scrolls Bible*, 539–540.

> ***of using exorcisms, by which they drive away demons, so that they never return,*** *(46) and this method of cure is of great force unto this day; for I have seen a certain man of my own country whose name was Eleazar, releasing people that were demoniacal in the presence of Vespasian, and his sons, and his captains, and the whole multitude of his soldiers. The manner of the cure was this:—(47) He put a ring that had a root of one of those sorts mentioned by Solomon to the nostrils of the demoniac, after which he drew out the demon through his nostrils; and when the man fell down immediately, he abjured him to return into him no more, making still mention of Solomon, and reciting the incantations which he composed. (48) And when Eleazar would persuade and demonstrate to the spectators that he had such a power, he set a little way off a cup or basin full of water, and commanded the demon, as he went out of the man, to overturn it, and thereby to let the spectators know that he had left the man; (49) and when this was done, the skill and wisdom of Solomon was shown very manifestly; for which reason it is, that all men may know the vastness of Solomon's abilities, and how he was beloved of God, and that the extraordinary virtues of every kind with which this king was endowed may not be unknown to any people under the sun; for this reason, I say, it is that we have proceeded to speak so largely of these matters.*[18]

As Josephus testified, it appears this learned skill was being utilized by some in the first century who were not of the "following" of Christ.

> [38] John said to him, "Teacher, we saw someone casting out demons in your name, and we tried to stop him, because he was not following us." (Mark 9:38, ESV)

---

18 Josephus, *The Works of Josephus*, 214.

The third psalm praises the Lord for His ability to strike down "horned" demons, an image that's often connected with the devil.

> *Col. 5: 4 A Psalm of David. Again[st ... An incanta]tion in the name of the LOR[D. To be invoked at an]y time 5 to the heav[ens. For] he will come to you at nig[ht], and you will [say] to him: 6 "Who are you? [Withdraw from] humanity and from the offspring of the ho[ly one]s! For your appearance is one of 7 [vani]ty, and your horns are horns of illu[si]on. You are darkness, not light, 8 [wicked]ness, not righteousness [...] the commander of the army, the* Lord*, [will bring] you [down 9 into] deepest [Sheo]l, [... the] two bronze [ga]tes th[rough which n]o 10 light [can enter], and [the] sun [will] not [shine for you] tha[t rises 11 upon the] righteous to [..." And] then you will say, ["... 12 ... the right]eous, to come [...] for a de[mon to] harm him, [... 13 ... of tr]uth from [... because] he has [righ] teousness [... 14 ...] and ..."*[19]

The fourth and final psalm of exorcism is Psalm 91. Together, these psalms have a Messianic tone that forecast and framed Jewish expectations of the Christ, the son of David, to dominate the demonic as the King of kings, the messianic exorcist, the great physician, and the deliverer of humanity (Matt 12:23–28).

CONNECTING THE GOSPEL

TEMPTATION & THE ARMOR OF GOD

Every temptation you face is an act of war. A misunderstanding of much of the information we've discovered in this book has caused many modern disciples to mentally check out in the day-to-day

---

19 Abegg, Jr., Flint, and Ulrich, *The Dead Sea Scrolls Bible*, 540–541.

happenings of spiritual warfare. And yes, we're at war every single day. Who exactly are we fighting? If we're being completely honest, our knee-jerk reaction might prompt us to say other people—other countries, other regimes, other agendas, or other religions. People aren't the enemy. Sure, many people are opposed to our efforts because of their spiritual blindness.

> *However, people through whom Satan opposes and interferes with the work of God on earth are to be compassionately loved and prayed for (Matt. 5:43–48), for it is this very tactic which works toward the defeat of satanic schemes while avoiding the struggle against "flesh and blood."*[20]

Every sinner is a victim, a casualty of spiritual warfare. Everyone needs rescuing. If we abandon this mindset, we abandon the love of Christ.

Paul writes,

> 12 For we do not wrestle against flesh and blood, but against the rulers, against the authorities, against the cosmic powers over this present darkness, against the spiritual forces of evil in the heavenly places. (Eph 6:12, ESV)

Our fight is against fallen angels, against cosmic entities and dark demons. As Paul put it in Ephesians 6, "against rulers [archē], against the authorities [exousia], against the world rulers [kosmokratōr] of this darkness, against the spiritual forces [pneumatikos] of wickedness in the heavenly places." The powers of darkness to which Paul referred are the real enemy. Understand, they are well-organized and highly-trained assassins in the discipline of spiritual

---

20 R. J. Erickson, *Ephesians*, vol. 3 of *Evangelical Commentary on the Bible*, ed. Walter Elwell (Grand Rapids, MI: Baker Book House, 1995), 1032.

warfare. They've had thousands of years to perfect their craft and have slain countless souls. In light of this, here's a question: How then do modern humans, particularly laymen, stand a chance against them?

Studying Jesus' forty-day temptation teaches us a lot about the Satanic profile. We learn the pattern of temptation,

> *is brought to fulfillment by three stages: suggestion, delight, consent. And we in temptation generally fall through delight, and then through consent;*[21]

Satan had hoped he could lead Jesus through these stages to consent, but he left disappointed. Jesus' wilderness temptation shows us Satan can be defeated, that we don't have to consent to our desires and Satan's allurements. This scene also exposes Satan's strategy to weaken our assurance in our identity as a child of God. Some forty days after Jesus heard His Father say at His baptism, "This is my beloved Son, with whom I am well pleased" (Matt 3:17), Satan tried to get Jesus to doubt His sonship. He tried put a wedge between Christ and the Father with the snarky comment, "If you are the Son of God…" (Luke 4:3). The inclusion of this small detail is huge. France commented on this subject,

> *The special relationship with God which has just been authoritatively declared at the Jordan is now under scrutiny. The following clauses do not cast doubt on this filial relationship, but explore its possible implications: what is the appropriate way for God's Son to behave in relation to his Father? In what ways might he exploit this relationship*

---

21 T. C. Oden and C. A. Hall, eds., *Mark*, rev. edition (Downers Grove, IL: InterVarsity Press, 1998), 16.

> *to his own advantage? The actions suggested are ones which might be expected to put that relationship under strain. The devil is trying to drive a wedge between the newly-declared Son and his Father.*[22]

Doubt is one of many wedges Satan tries to sandwich between you and your heavenly Father. Hell's armory of weapons is most impressive. If you charge into battle defenseless, your carcass will likely rot in the desert of temptation. You must suit up for battle!

Paul concludes his letter to the church at Ephesus by admonishing them to be strong in the Lord by putting on the armor of God. The NIV reads,

> [10] Finally, be strong in the Lord and in his mighty power. [11] Put on the full armor of God, so that you can take your stand against the devil's schemes. [12] For our struggle is not against flesh and blood, but against the rulers, against the authorities, against the powers of this dark world and against the spiritual forces of evil in the heavenly realms. [13] Therefore put on the full armor of God, so that when the day of evil comes, you may be able to stand your ground, and after you have done everything, to stand. [14] Stand firm then, with the belt of truth buckled around your waist, with the breastplate of righteousness in place, [15] and with your feet fitted with the readiness that comes from the gospel of peace. [16] In addition to all this, take up the shield of faith, with which you can extinguish all the flaming arrows of the evil one. [17] Take the helmet of salvation and the sword of the Spirit, which is the word of God. [18] And pray in the Spirit on all occasions with all kinds of prayers and requests. With

22 France, *The Gospel of Matthew*, 127.

> this in mind, be alert and always keep on praying for all the Lord's people. (Eph 6:10–18, NIV)

Paul's words demonstrate that every soldier, even inexperienced ones, can stand strong against temptation. But without the armor of God, you're toast. Your weak spots are exposed. Cyril of Alexandria (375–444 A.D.) likened Satan's attacks to a skilled and wise general.

> *When a skilled general lays siege to a city, he spares no effort to quickly attack the weakest parts of the wall with his battering rams, knowing that in such areas the capture will be easy. I believe that Satan employs an identical strategy when laying siege to the human heart, attacking at its weakest point, thinking that he will easily bring it into subjection especially when he sees it unfortified by those reinforcements that would likely repel the attack...*[23]

Soldiers of the cross who fully dress in the armor of light are fortified, protecting their weaknesses. Each piece of armor plays an integral part in your success: the belt of truth (v. 14), the breastplate of righteousness (v. 14), shoes shod with the gospel of peace (v. 15), the shield of faith (v. 16), the helmet of salvation (v. 17), and the sword of the Spirit (v. 17).

These are all items you would expect any soldier to wear, but where does Paul conjure up the idea of spiritual armor? Commentators are quick to make parallels to the battle gear of Roman soldiers, and while this comparison may have partially been on Paul's mind, he's drawing on Old Testament passages and ideas to dress Christian soldiers, primarily the book of Isaiah.

---

23 J. C. Elowsky, ed., *John 11–21* (Downers Grove, IL: InterVarsity Press, 2007), 105–106.

Isaiah 59:17 (ESV)	Isaiah 52:7 (ESV)	Isaiah 11:5 (LES)
17 He put on righteousness as a **breastplate**, and a **helmet of salvation** on his head; he put on garments of vengeance for clothing, and wrapped himself in zeal as a cloak.	7 How beautiful upon the mountains are the **feet of him who brings good news**, who publishes peace, who brings good news of happiness, who publishes salvation, who says to Zion, "Your God reigns."	5 And he will be **girded at the waist with righteousness** and enclosed with **truth at his sides**.

Paul obviously alludes to passages in the Old Testament such as these out of Isaiah. The mention of the breastplate of righteousness is particularly meaningful. It seems to allude back to the breastplate—or the breastplate of judgment (Exod 28:15, 29)—the high priest wore as a holy and sacred vestment (Exod 28:4). Nestled in the breastplate (Lev 8:8) was the Urim and Thummim, two stones through which the will of Yahweh could be discerned (Num 27:21; 1 Sam 14:41; Neh 7:65; Ezra 2:63). The names "Urim" and "Thummim" are significant.

> *The LXX translates Urim and Thummim with delosis and aletheia, "revelation" and "truth."*[24]

According to Jewish tradition, in times of war, the high priest would use the breastplate as a strategic compass of sorts. God's revelation or truth would be revealed through the stones. Josephus (ca. 38–100 C. E.) wrote,

---

24 B. Embry, R. Herms, and A. T. Wright, eds., vol. 1 of *Early Jewish Literature: An Anthology* (Grand Rapids, MI: William B. Eerdmans Publishing Company, 2018), 722.

> *(311) Moses taught them also by what means their sacrifices might be the most acceptable to God; and how they should go forth to war, making use of the stones (in the high priest's breast-plate) for their direction,*[25]

We learned back in chapter 10 of our journey that all Christians are functioning priests in the royal priesthood of God (1 Pet 2:9). So, in a sense, we are warrior priests who put on this breastplate as we charge enemy lines, dressed in righteousness. The breastplate of judgment will certainly protect us from harm, but it also emboldens us; we know that we, too, have the blessing and backing of our God. We have the green light to go, fight, and conquer. And when we are unsure about what our next move should be in the battle, we have the Urim and Thummim of prayer. Ask the Lord to guide your steps and secure your heart. God is faithful—He will answer.

There's another intriguing phrase in Ephesians 6. Paul's admonition to take up the shield of faith against the "flaming arrows" of the evil one (v. 10), in context, may reference Satan's quiver of fiery demons of the air, sent out to plague and tempt mankind—demons such as Resheph (a.k.a., "the arrow"), the demonic archer of antiquity. Satan is not running low on arrows; he's well-stocked with innumerable fallen beings.

The powers of darkness fire shots at you every day. You're tempted at school, work, on vacation, or even around your brothers and sisters in Christ. It doesn't matter to them where you are or who's around you. To them, no setting is off limits. Being fully dressed in the armor of God at all times not only prevents you from being fatally wounded, as we'll soon see in upcoming chapters, but it also allows you to take the fight to Satan and his minions, to be on the offensive, to fire back, to gain ground in your temptations. Don't worry. Your lack of experience

---

25 Josephus, *The Works of Josephus*, 124.

and training is to be expected. God anticipated that. That's why He's given you something stronger than mithril to wear in battle. Your armor has been forged to withstand the boiling flares of hell's fire and the poisonous arrows of Resheph himself. Please, like Jesus, put on the whole armor of God so you can endure the episodes of temptation. In the words of a fifth-century Latin commentary on the book of Matthew called *Opus Imperfectum*,

> *If you endure, shattering your heart, or rather shattering the devil in your heart, he will depart from you because he has not been able to conquer you. When, as the sinful longing recedes, your heart begins to exult because you have escaped that evil attack and a certain spirit rejoices in you quietly, as it were, and gives thanks to God, know that the devil has withdrawn from you*[26]

LOOKING AHEAD

Jesus' forty days of desert dwelling were now over. Victory belonged to the Son of God. But the battle of heaven and earth would rage on. His fasting and victory over Satan had physically drained Him. Yahweh saw His fatigued Son and immediately sent out holy angels to minister unto the Messiah (Matt 4:11), thus fulfilling the promise of angelic aid cited in Psalm 91:11. In the next chapter, Jesus is going to ground zero, where He'll turn it up a notch and stir the pot at the gates of hell. He's going to provoke the powers of darkness on the lonely mountain, that baleful place of Bashan that birthed the angelic rebellion ages ago. What Jesus says and does there will render you completely speechless.

---

26 T. C. Oden and G. L. Bray, eds., vol. 1 and 2 of *Incomplete Commentary on Matthew (Opus Imperfectum)*, trans. J. A. Kellerman (Downers Grove, IL: IVP Academic: An Imprint of InterVarsity Press, 2010), 73.

CHAPTER 17

THE GATES OF HELL, THE MALEFICENT MOUNTAIN, AND THE FELLOWSHIP OF THE KING

And I tell you, you are Peter, and on this rock I will build my church, and the gates of hell shall not prevail against it. (Matthew 16:18, ESV)

READING THE STORY

JESUS' LONG-AWAITED MEETING WITH THE DEVIL wa over, but the war had just begun. Right now, outside of John and hi disciples, the human army of God was pretty thin. Jesus knew that ha to change. In 29 A.D., the Messiah started recruiting troops to enlist i the army of God. These were not highly-trained assassins; they wer minutemen, simpletons who had skills in things like fishing and taxes They certainly weren't the type of warriors you would expect to riva the armies of hell, but Jesus' approach wasn't normal or earthly. H was looking to collect students whom He could teach. Men who wer imperfect, but pliable. Disciples who, despite their ugly sins, would b dedicated to the cause of redeeming the nations and who would die o the battlefield doing it.

The selection process was, undoubtedly, one of the most critica chapters of Jesus' entire ministry. If He got it wrong, His entire mission would be compromised. With the weight of the world on His shoulders, He ascended a Galilean mountain and prayed all night to His Father (Luke 6:12).

> "Jesus went up the mountain and summoned those he wanted, and they came to him. He appointed twelve, whom he also named apostles, to be with him, to send them out to preach, and to have authority to drive out demons. He appointed the Twelve: To Simon, he gave the name Peter; and to James the son of Zebedee, and to his brother John, he gave the name "Boanerges" (that is, "Sons of Thunder"); Andrew; Philip and Bartholomew; Matthew and Thomas; James the son of Alphaeus, and Thaddaeus; Simon the Zealot, and Judas Iscariot, who also betrayed him. (Mark 3:13–19, CSB)

Together, this ragtag team of men formed a fellowship of the king known as the twelve apostles. His first lesson wasn't how to drive a tank or wield a sword—it was how to strengthen their hearts for battle and how to love people. Always. Jesus taught them, saying,

> "Blessed are the poor in spirit, for the kingdom of heaven is theirs. Blessed are those who mourn, for they will be comforted. Blessed are the humble, for they will inherit the earth. Blessed are those who hunger and thirst for righteousness, for they will be filled. Blessed are the merciful, for they will be shown mercy. Blessed are the pure in heart, for they will see God. Blessed are the peacemakers, for they will be called sons of God. Blessed are those who are persecuted because of righteousness, for the kingdom of heaven is theirs. "You are blessed when they insult you and persecute you and falsely say every kind of evil against you because of me. Be glad and rejoice, because your reward is great in heaven. For that is how they persecuted the prophets who were before you. "You are the salt of the earth. But if the salt should lose its taste, how can it be made salty? It's no longer good for anything but to be thrown out and trampled under people's feet. "You are the light of the world. A city situated on a hill cannot be hidden. No one lights a lamp and puts it under a basket, but rather on a lampstand, and it gives light for all who are in the house. In the same way, let your light shine before others, so that they may see your good works and give glory to your Father in heaven. (Matt 5:3–16, CSB)

These disciples would learn the ways of the Father—His love, His grace, His forgiveness. Over many months, they came to know the power of the light side of the forces of heaven as they shadowed Jesus, marveled by His every move. They witnessed miracles such as the healing of the centurion's servant (Matt 8:5–13) and the resurrection of the widow's son (Luke 7:11–17). They sat through many sermons, listening to Jesus teach unforgettable parables about things like soils (Mark 4:2–9) and weeds (Matt 13:36–43), all of which spoke to the very people they were trying to help save. They witnessed Jesus conquer the chaos of the stormy seas (Mark 4:35–41) and battle legions of demons (Matt 8:28–32). When they were ready, they too were given the power to heal the sick and authority over unclean spirits (Matt 10:1; Mark 6:7; Luke 9:1–2). They witnessed Jesus feed 5,000 (John 6:1–14) and walk on water (Matt 14:24–33). These experiences helped solidify their faith in their teacher, their mission, and their God.

As Jesus concluded His ministry in Galilee, He turned his attention northward.

> “Now when Jesus came into **the district of Caesarea Philippi**, he asked his disciples, “Who do people say that the Son of Man is?” And they said, “Some say John the Baptist, others say Elijah, and others Jeremiah or one of the prophets.” He said to them, “But who do you say that I am?” Simon Peter replied, “You are the Christ, the Son of the living God.” And Jesus answered him, “Blessed are you, Simon Bar-Jonah! For flesh and blood has not revealed this to you, but my Father who is in heaven. And I tell you, you are Peter, and on this rock I will build my church, and the gates of hell shall not prevail against it. I will give you the keys of the kingdom of heaven, and whatever you bind on earth shall be bound in heaven, and whatever you loose on earth shall be loosed in heaven.” Then he strictly charged the disciples to tell no one that he was the Christ. (Matt 16:13–20, ESV)

In his book *Reversing Hermon*, Michael Heiser wrote at length about the supernatural significance of this famous scene in Scripture.

> *The “gates of hell” incident (Matthew 16:13–20) in Jesus’ ministry is familiar to most Bible students. However, the geography is*

unfortunately ignored, an oversight that prevents us from understanding the impact of what Jesus said and did in a region theologically tethered to the Watchers.

The events of Matthew 16:13–20 took place at Caesarea Philippi, a city located in the northern part of what had been called Bashan, at the foot of Mount Hermon. Jesus asked the disciples a famous question, "Who do people say that I am?" Peter answered, "You are the Christ, the Son of the living God." Then Jesus followed with this:

Blessed are you, Simon Bar-Jonah! For flesh and blood has not revealed this to you, but my Father who is in heaven. And I tell you, you are Peter, and on this rock I will build my church, and the gates of hell shall not be able to withstand it. (Matthew 16:17–18)

This passage is among the most controversial in the Bible, as it is a focal point of debate between Roman Catholics and Protestants. The former argue that Peter is the rock upon which the church is established and thus the passage makes Peter the leader of the original church (and the first pope). Protestants insist the rock is a reference to God on analogy of passages like 1 Corinthians 10:4.

Both of these traditional understandings are incorrect. The reference to the rock is the place where they are standing—Caesarea Philippi at the foot of Mount Hermon. The apostate King Jereboam built an idolatrous worship center there (1 Kings 12) and the city adopted the worship of Baal practiced by the Canaanites since the days of Joshua in their city Baal-Gad (Joshua 11:17; cp. Judges 3:3). In Jesus' day, Caesarea Philippi was also called Panias, having been dedicated to the worship of Pan.

When viewed from this perspective, the scene takes place on geography considered the gates of hell in Old Testament times, the domain of Baal, the lord of the dead, and at the mountain where

> *the plot of the Watchers was hatched. Hell, of course, wouldn't be complete without the devil. It is well known to scholars that Baal is the Old Testament counterpart to the devil. In Ugaritic, one of Baal's titles is ba'al zebul 'arṣ ("Prince Baal of the Underworld"), from which the New Testament Beelzebul and Beelzebub derive. This isn't about who gets to be pope (or not). It's a cosmic confrontation, with Jesus challenging the authority of the lord of the dead.*
>
> *The theological messaging couldn't be more dramatic. Jesus says the "gates of hell" will not prevail against the church. We often think of this phrase as though God's people are in a posture of having to bravely fend off Satan and his demons. This simply isn't correct. Gates are defensive structures, not offensive weapons. The kingdom of God is the aggressor. Jesus goes to ground zero in biblical demonic geography to announce that Bashan will be defeated. It is the gates of hell that are under assault—and they will not hold up against the church. Hell has no claim on those who align themselves with Jesus. He will reverse the curse of death and His own will rise on account of Him.*[1]

Jesus' fieldtrip to the gates of hell served as the biggest teaching moment yet for His class of twelve. They learned their mentor wasn't going to supplicate to Satan. They witnessed Jesus provoke the dark lord himself at the maleficent mountain, Mount Hermon, the place sacrificially dedicated to the gods of angelic rebellion. Mount Hermon is littered with a rich history of "sacred" cult centers to the gods. The Anchor Yale Bible Dictionary notes,

> *More than twenty temples have been surveyed on Mt. Hermon and its environs. This is an unprecedented number in comparison*

---

1 Heiser, *Reversing Hermon*, 94–96.

> *with other regions of the Phoenician coast. They appear to be the ancient cult sites of the Mt. Hermon population and represent the Canaanite/Phoenician concept of open-air cult centers dedicated, evidently, to the celestial gods.*[2]

It's no coincidence that, for the first time, Jesus spoke openly with His disciples about His future suffering, death, and resurrection. He knew there would be angelic retaliation for stirring the pot in Bashan, the place of the serpent.

> "From that time Jesus began to show his disciples that he must go to Jerusalem and suffer many things from the elders and chief priests and scribes, and be killed, and on the third day be raised. And Peter took him aside and began to rebuke him, saying, "Far be it from you, Lord! This shall never happen to you." But he turned and said to Peter, "Get behind me, **Satan**! You are a hindrance to me. For you are not setting your mind on the things of God, but on the things of man." (Matt 16:21–23, ESV)
>
> Truly, I say to you, there are some standing here who will not taste death until they see the Son of Man coming in his kingdom." (Matt 16:28, ESV)

Jesus' mention of Satan is strategically timed. The Twelve needed to understand that Jesus must die so all could live, and He needed the powers of darkness to do it. If the Twelve were to remain loyal to the Son of Man and the scheme of redemption, they couldn't get in the way. However, His prediction of death was immediately followed by a promise of retribution. Despite dying, He would one day return to

---

2 R. Arav, "Hermon, Mount (Place)," *The Anchor Yale Bible Dictionary* 3:159.

Earth with His own angels and repay justice to the ungodly loyalists of the rebellion.

> For the Son of Man is going to come with his angels in the glory of his Father, and then he will repay each person according to what he has done. (Matt 16:27, ESV)

But Jesus isn't done provoking the powers of darkness. He's going to climb Mount Hermon and be transfigured on top of the enemies' sacred mountain.

> After six days Jesus took Peter, James, and his brother John and led them up on a high mountain by themselves. He was transfigured in front of them, and his face shone like the sun; his clothes became as white as the light. Suddenly, Moses and Elijah appeared to them, talking with him. Then Peter said to Jesus, "Lord, it's good for us to be here. If you want, I will set up three shelters here: one for you, one for Moses, and one for Elijah." While he was still speaking, suddenly a bright cloud covered them, and a voice from the cloud said, "This is my beloved Son, with whom I am well-pleased. Listen to him!" When the disciples heard this, they fell facedown and were terrified. Jesus came up, touched them, and said, "Get up; don't be afraid." When they looked up they saw no one except Jesus alone. (Matt 17:1–8, CSB)

Dr. Michael Heiser wrote,

> *The imagery is striking. Jesus picks Mount Hermon to reveal to Peter, James, and John exactly who He is—the embodied glory-essence of God, the divine Name made visible by incarnation. The meaning is just as transparent: I'm putting the hostile powers of*

> *the unseen world on notice. I've come to earth to take back what is mine. The kingdom of God is at hand.*[3]

Heiser added,

> *When Jesus chose to go to Mount Hermon to be transfigured, He was claiming it for the Kingdom of God. As the Gospel chronologies tell us, these events provoked His death, the linchpin event for reversing the human predicament and ensuring the defeat of the powers of darkness.*[4]

Everything Jesus had said and done thus far was so perfectly planned. He knew it would provoke hell, so much so that they would move swiftly to put Him to death. But that's exactly what heaven wanted. Only the disciples knew Jesus' big secret—His death would bring humanity's salvation. For the plan to work, the disciples couldn't tell anyone. They had to keep it secret, keep it safe—at least until the proper time.

> "As they were coming down the mountain, Jesus commanded them, "Don't tell anyone about the vision until the Son of Man is raised from the dead." So the disciples asked him, "Why then do the scribes say that Elijah must come first?" "Elijah is coming and will restore everything," he replied. "But I tell you: Elijah has already come, and they didn't recognize him. On the contrary, they did whatever they pleased to him. In the same way the Son of Man is going to suffer at their hands." Then the disciples understood that he had spoken to them about John the Baptist. When they reached the crowd, a man approached and knelt down before him. "Lord,"

3 Heiser, *Reversing Hermon*, 97.

4 Heiser, *Reversing Hermon*, 99.

> he said, "have mercy on my son, because he has seizures and suffers terribly. He often falls into the fire and often into the water. I brought him to your disciples, but they couldn't heal him." Jesus replied, "You unbelieving and perverse generation, how long will I be with you? How long must I put up with you? Bring him here to me." Then Jesus rebuked the demon, and it came out of him, and from that moment the boy was healed. Then the disciples approached Jesus privately and said, "Why couldn't we drive it out?" "Because of your little faith," he told them. "For truly I tell you, if you have faith the size of a mustard seed, **you will tell this mountain**, 'Move from here to there,' and it will move. Nothing will be impossible for you." As they were gathering together in Galilee, Jesus told them, "The Son of Man is about to be betrayed into the hands of men. (Matt 17:9–22, CSB)

What a perfect way to end the scene—Christ casting out a demon at the base of Mount Hermon. Jesus would *not* be bested. Everyone who witnessed it knew Jesus was their only hope. If the disciples could only put to bed all their doubts and have complete faith, they too could move this mountain, Mount Hermon—that diabolical rock of rebellion. For Christ's sake, for the world's sake, Jesus prayed they would.

ANSWERING YOUR QUESTIONS

WHAT DOES BINDING AND LOOSING REALLY MEAN?

In Jesus' dialogue with Peter and the other disciples, Jesus said to Peter,

> [19] I will give you the keys of the kingdom of heaven, and whatever you bind on earth shall be bound in heaven, and

whatever you loose on earth shall be loosed in heaven." (Matt 16:19, ESV)

For millennia, Christians have wrestled with the meaning behind the "binding" and "loosing" terminology. What does it all mean? In a 1985 article published in *The Journal of Biblical Literature* titled "Binding and Loosing," Richard Hiers does a good job exploring the possibilities. He noted a familiar interpretation of the Catholic church:

> *The sayings about binding and loosing reported in Matt 16:19 and 18:18 have given rise to a wide range of interpretations. Catholic scholars often have read them to mean that Jesus thereby authorized the establishment of the Roman Catholic Church, the primacy of Peter in its government, and the apostolic power of excommunication. Protestant commentators, on the other hand, tend to argue that the sayings either are inauthentic, since found only in Matthew, or else must surely mean something other than that Jesus bestowed sacerdotal authority on Peter or other apostles.*[5]

Other common interpretations relate to the binding and loosing vows, the authority to withhold and extend forgiveness, or final judgment based on apostolic teachings. Could it be that none of the common interpretations are correct? Could we be missing the forest for the trees? I believe so. None of the aforementioned explanations take into account the context and supernatural significance of the scene. That's an egregious error of interpretation. All of these peripheral things matter—the use of "binding" and

5 R. H. Hiers, "'Binding' and 'Loosing': The Matthean Authorizations," *JBL* 104 (1985): 233.

loosing" elsewhere in the NT and intertestamental period writings the sinister geography of Bashan, the angelic rebellion at Mount Hermon, and the other words of Jesus in the passage must also be taken into consideration. These things framed the context of the passage.

I argue that "binding" and "loosing" in Matthew 16:19 are in reference to the binding and loosing associated with demons and their victims. Hiers wrote,

> *Most commonly, however, in intertestamental writings and in the NT the terms "binding" and "loosing" refer to the binding of Satan or satanic beings (e.g., demons) and the loosing of such beings or their erstwhile victims.*[6]

Let's first consider how extrabiblical literature used these terms prior to the first century. Hiers wrote at length,

> *A familiar example is in the story of Tobit, where the angel Raphael has the task of binding (dein) the demon Asmodeus, which had been afflicting the virtuous Sarah, who was thereby delivered or released (lyein) from the demon and her affliction (Tob 3:17; 8:3). The cognate verb apolyein is used with respect to freeing of persons from demons in Josephus's description of exorcistic cures he claims to have witnessed (Ant. 8:2:5 §46).*
>
> *Several instances of such terminology occur in 1 Enoch, Jubilees, and the Testaments of the Twelve Patriarchs, mainly in connection with accounts of the previous "binding" of evil spirits in the days of Noah and of the prospective binding of Satan or Belial at the end of the age. Certain of the "watchers,"*

6 Hiers, "'Binding' and 'Loosing': The Matthean Authorizations," 235.

notably Azazel and Shemyaza, had corrupted the world of human beings. Consequently, God commanded Raphael, "Bind Azazel hand and foot, and cast him into the darkness ... and let him abide there forever.... And on the day of the great Judgment he shall be cast into the fire" (1 Enoch, chaps. 6–9; 10:4, 11–13). In 1 Enoch 88 we read that the "fallen" angels, described as "stars" and "beasts"—evidently the "sons of God" from Gen 6:1–4—"were bound hand and foot and cast into an abyss of the earth," apparently by the angels Michael, Gabriel, Raphael, and Phanuel. Such also was to be the fate of sinners who had not experienced judgment during their life on earth.

Perhaps the most significant intertestamental references to the binding or overpowering of Satan and the demons are found in the Testaments of the Twelve Patriarchs. The classic passage in T. Levi 18:10–12 refers to the activities of the "new priest" whom God would raise up as king in the era to come:

And he shall open the gates of paradise,
And he shall remove the threatening sword against Adam.
And he shall give to the saints to eat from the tree of life,
And the Holy Spirit shall be on them.
And Beliar shall be bound by him,
And he shall give power to his children to tread
upon the evil spirits.[7]

Second, we need to explore how the NT uses the idea of "binding" and "loosing." Let's first consider two parallel accounts of the "binding of the strong man."

---

7 Hiers, "'Binding' and 'Loosing': The Matthean Authorizations," 235–237.

Matthew 12:25–29 (ESV)	Mark 3:22–27 (ESV)
25 Knowing their thoughts, he said to them, "Every kingdom divided against itself is laid waste, and no city or house divided against itself will stand. 26 And if **Satan casts out Satan**, he is divided against himself. How then will his kingdom stand? 27 And **if I cast out demons by Beelzebul, by whom do your sons cast them out**? Therefore they will be your judges. 28 But if it is by the Spirit of God that I **cast out demons**, then the kingdom of God has come upon you. 29 Or how can someone enter a strong man's house and plunder his goods, unless he first **binds the strong man**? Then indeed he may plunder his house.	22 And the scribes who came down from Jerusalem were saying, "He is possessed by Beelzebul," and "by **the prince of demons he casts out the demons**." 23 And he called them to him and said to them in parables, "**How can Satan cast out Satan**? 24 If a kingdom is divided against itself, that kingdom cannot stand. 25 And if a house is divided against itself, that house will not be able to stand. 26 And if **Satan** has risen up against himself and is divided, he cannot stand, but is coming to an end. 27 But no one can enter a strong man's house and plunder his goods, unless he first **binds the strong man**. Then indeed he may plunder his house.

Hiers commented on these passages,

> *The context makes it clear that the strong man represents Satan and/or his demons. In many of the reported exorcisms, the demon is ordered or thrown out; to "cast out" evidently means much the same thing as to "bind" a demon. Matthew follows Mark in describing Jesus' exorcism of demons in terms of "binding" (Matt 12:29). Through exorcism or binding, the demon is brought under control by one who has superior power. The sense of Mark 3:27 is that by binding the demon the erstwhile demoniac is liberated from his afflicting demon. Thus binding*

> *and loosing occur simultaneously: the demon is bound while its victim is loosed.*[8]

In John's apocalypse, he has visions of Satan being bound for a thousand years then eventually loosed.

> [1] And I saw an angel coming down out of heaven, having the
> key of the abyss and a great chain in his hand. [2] And he laid
> hold on the dragon, the old serpent, which is the Devil and
> Satan, and **bound** him for a thousand years, [3] and cast him into
> the abyss, and shut it, and sealed it over him, that he should
> deceive the nations no more, until the thousand years should
> be finished: after this he must be **loosed** for a little time.
> (Rev 20:1–3, ASV 1901)

Sometimes in Scripture, however, the ones being loosed are the victims of demon possession. Such is the case with Luke 13:10–17. Notice that the Jewish woman was being loosed from the binding of Satan.

> [10] Now he was teaching in one of the synagogues on the Sabbath.
> [11] And behold, there was a woman who had had a disabling
> spirit for eighteen years. She was bent over and could not fully
> straighten herself. [12] When Jesus saw her, he called her over
> and said to her, "Woman, you are freed from your disability."
> [13] And he laid his hands on her, and immediately she was
> made straight, and she glorified God. [14] But the ruler of the
> synagogue, indignant because Jesus had healed on the Sabbath,
> said to the people, "There are six days in which work ought to
> be done. Come on those days and be healed, and not on the
> Sabbath day." [15] Then the Lord answered him, "You hypocrites!

---

8 Hiers, "'Binding' and 'Loosing': The Matthean Authorizations," 237–238.

> Does not each of you on the Sabbath untie his ox or his donkey
> from the manger and lead it away to water it? [16] And ought not
> this woman, a daughter of Abraham **whom Satan bound** for
> eighteen years, **be loosed** from this **bond** on the Sabbath day?"
> [17] As he said these things, all his adversaries were put to shame,
> and all the people rejoiced at all the glorious things that were
> done by him. (Luke 13:10–17, ESV)

Jesus said, as a daughter of Abraham, she had the right to be loosed from her demonic master. You see,

> *The term "to bind" is used, then, both with respect to the affliction of a person by Satan (or by demons) and to the binding of a demon (or of Satan) by an exorcist who thereby frees or looses the erstwhile victim.*[9]

You may be wondering that if "bind" and "loose" refer to exorcising demons, how do these terms affect the gist of the passage? Let's read the passage one more time.

> [18] And I tell you, you are Peter, and on this rock I will build my
> church, and the gates of hell shall not prevail against it. [19] I will
> give you the keys of the kingdom of heaven, and whatever you
> bind on earth shall be bound in heaven, and whatever you loose
> on earth shall be loosed in heaven." (Matt 16:18–19, ESV)

Essentially, Satan's defeat in the seen realm meant his defeat in the unseen realm—what was bound and loosed on Earth would be bound and loosed in heaven. This is exactly how it's spelled out when Jesus sends out seventy—yes, seventy—disciples in Luke 10. They were to go

---

9 Hiers, "'Binding' and 'Loosing': The Matthean Authorizations," 239.

as forerunners in every city Jesus would visit. Jesus chose seventy because it signaled the reclaiming of the seventy nations from the seventy gods allotted at Babel. Don't miss what Jesus said when they returned:

> 17 And the seventy returned with joy, saying, **Lord, even the demons are subject unto us in thy name.** 18 And he said
> unto them, **I beheld Satan fallen as lightning from heaven**.
> 19 Behold, I have given you authority to tread upon serpents and scorpions, and over all the power of the enemy: and nothing shall in any wise hurt you. 20 Nevertheless in this rejoice not, that the spirits are subject unto you; but rejoice that your names are written in heaven. (Luke 10:17–20, ASV 1901)

The seventy's ability to cast out demons on Earth meant the process of Satan's defeat had begun in heaven. Morris wrote,

> *...in the mission of the seventy Jesus saw the defeat of Satan (his verb means 'I was watching', imperfect tense), a defeat as sudden and unexpected (to the forces of evil) as a flash of lightning. To the casual observer all that had happened was that a few mendicant preachers had spoken in a few small towns and healed a few sick folk. But in that gospel triumph Satan had suffered a notable defeat.*[10]

As the Bible Knowledge Commentary points out,

> *Jesus was not speaking of Satan being cast out at that precise moment, but that his power had been broken and that he was subject to Jesus' authority.*[11]

---

10 L. Morris, vol. 3 of *Luke: An Introduction and Commentary* (Downers Grove, IL: Inter-Varsity Press, 1988), 203–204.

11 Martin, "Luke," 233.

WHAT IS A DEMON?

The ancient understanding of who or what demons are is, for the most part, pretty well-defined. The consensus view up until the fourth century was that demons were the departed spirits of the giants. Their understanding was, in large part, due to the explanation of demonic origin explained in the book of 1 Enoch.

> 8 And now the giants who are born from the spirits, even the strong spirits of flesh upon the earth, their dwelling will be on the earth. 9 Evil spirits went out from their body, for they came from the higher places, and the beginning of their creation and foundation is from the watchful holy ones. They will be called evil spirits. 10 And so for the spirits of heaven, their dwelling will be in heaven, and the spirits that are born upon the earth, their dwelling will be upon the earth. 11 "The spirits of the giants were doing unjustly, destroying, attacking, and wrestling with each other and thrown together upon the earth, the hard spirits of the giants. They are making courses and no one is eating, but they are fasting and thirsting and stumbling spirits. 12 These will rise up against the children of men and women because they have gone forth from them. (1 Enoch 15:8–12, LES)

In 177 A.D., Athenagoras wrote,

> *"These angels, then, who have fallen from heaven, and haunt the air, and the earth, and are no longer able to rise to heavenly things, and* ***the souls of the giants, which are the demons*** *who wander about the world, perform actions similar, the one (that is the demons) to the natures they have received, the other (that is the angels) to the appetites they have indulged."*[12]

---

12 Athenagoras, quoted in Pitterson, *Judgment of The Nephilim*, 415.

Tertullian (160–220 A.D.) wrote,

> *"We are instructed, moreover, by our sacred books how from certain angels, who fell of their own free-will, there sprang a more wicked* ***demon-brood****, condemned of God along with the authors of their race, and that chief we have referred to. It will for the present be enough, however, that some account is given of their work.* ***Their great business is the ruin of mankind****. So, from the very first, spiritual wickedness sought our destruction.* ***They inflict****, accordingly, upon our* ***bodies diseases and other grievous calamities****, while by violent assaults they hurry the soul into sudden and extraordinary excesses."*[13]

Justin Martyr (c. 100–c. 165 A.D.) wrote in *The Second Apology*,

> *But the angels violated their charge, fell into sin with women and begot children who are called demons.*[14]

Origen also understood wicked demons to be the souls of the Greek Titans or biblical giants. He wrote in *Against Celsus 4.92*,

> *In my opinion, however, it is certain wicked demons, and, so to speak, of the race of Titans or Giants, who have been guilty of impiety towards the true God, and towards the angels in heaven, and who have fallen from it, and who haunt the denser parts of bodies, and frequent unclean places upon earth, and who, possessing some power of distinguishing future events, because they*

---

13 Tertullian, *The Apology of Tertullian for the Christians*, quoted in Pitterson, *Judgment of The Nephilim*, 46–48.

14 Martyr, *The First Apology, The Second Apology, Dialogue with Trypho, Exhortation to the Greeks, Discourse to the Greeks, The Monarchy or The Rule of God*, 124.

are without bodies of earthly material, engage in an employment of this kind, and desiring to lead the human race away from the true God...[15]

The origin of demons is also well-catalogued in various ancient Judeo-Christian fanciful writings. For example, in a folkloric-style text from the first to third century titled *The Testament of Solomon*, an evil demon named Asmodeus admits to Solomon that he is the son of a human woman and an angel.

5 1 (21) I commanded another demon be brought to me; and he (Beelzeboul) brought me the evil demon Asmodeus, bound. 2 I asked him, "Who are you?" He scowled at me and said, "And who are you?" 3* I said to him, "You (dare to) answer (so arrogantly) when you have been punished like this?" He continued to give forth the same look and said to me, "How should I answer you? You are the son of a man, but* ***although I was born of a human mother, I (am the son) of an angel***[16]

This wasn't only the view of Jews and Christians, however; it was also the belief of popularized pagans such as Hesiod, the famous Greek poet. In 700 B.C., he wrote in *Works and Days* about the afterlife of the Titans and giants. He noted,

When they died, it was as though they were overcome with sleep, and they had all good things; for the fruitful earth unforced bare them fruit abundantly and without stint. They dwelt in ease and peace upon their lands with many good things, rich in flocks and loved by the blessed gods. But after earth had covered this

15 Origen, *Origen Against Celsus*, 538.

16 Charlesworth, *The Old Testament Pseudepigrapha*, 965.

> *generation—**they are called Pure Spirits (daimones hagnoi) dwelling on the earth**, and are kindly, delivering from harm, and guardians of mortal men; for they roam everywhere over the earth, clothed in mist and keep watch on judgements and cruel deeds, givers of wealth; for this royal right also they received. (Emphasis added)*[17]

The notion of the souls of the Titans being "pure" is not surprising coming from the Grecians. They loved, worshiped, and celebrated the tall uprisers. The New Testament writers paint a different picture of demonic spirits, however. They often call them "unclean spirits," a term which has implications of a forbidden mixture. This forbidden mixture is in reference to the mingled seed of women and angels, and they are called both "bastard spirits" and "unclean spirits" within the same sentence in 4Q444 Frag. 1:8 of the Dead Sea Scrolls. Lactantius (240–320 A.D.), the Christian rhetorician from North Africa, spoke of the demons' "mixed" nature in his work, *The Divine Institutes*.

> *Therefore, while they [angels] abode among men, that most deceitful ruler of the earth, by his very association, gradually enticed them to vices, and polluted them by intercourse with women. Then, not being admitted into heaven on account of the sins into which they had plunged themselves, they fell to the earth. Thus from angels the devil makes them to become his satellites and attendants. **But they who were born from these, because they were neither angels nor men, but bearing a kind of mixed nature**, were not admitted into hell, as their fathers were not into heaven. Thus there came to be two kinds of demons; one of heaven,*

---

17 Hesiod, *Works and Days*, quoted in Derek P. Gilbert, *Last Clash of the Titans: The Second Coming of Hercules, Leviathan, and the Prophesied War Between Jesus Christ and the Gods of Antiquity* (Crane, MO: Defender Publishing, 2018), Kindle edition.

> *the other of the earth. The latter are the wicked spirits, the authors of all the evils which are done, and the same devil is their prince.*[18]

But does the NT ever corroborate the claim that demons are the spirits of giants? Yes. It implicitly does during Jesus' encounter with Legion, a possessed man who has been driven out to dwell in the desert by demons. Together, Matthew, Mark, and Luke's narratives of Jesus and Legion leave a trail of breadcrumbs that leads back to the giants and flood of Genesis 6.

Let's start with the Gospel of Matthew. Matthew's account includes the demons asking if Jesus has come to torment them "before the time."

> 29 And, behold, they cried out, saying, What have we to do with thee, Jesus, thou Son of God? art thou come hither to torment us **before the time**? (Matt 8:29, KJV 1900)

The time they're referring to is the final judgment. Recall what Jude wrote of the angelic sons of God who sinned in Genesis 6.

> 6 And the angels who did not stay within their own position of authority, but left their proper dwelling, he has kept in eternal chains under gloomy darkness **until the judgment** of the great day— (Jude 6, ESV)

These demons are fully aware of God's plans to punish them alongside their paternal fathers, the sons of God. Second, notice what Luke writes in his Gospel.

> 30 Jesus then asked him, "What is your name?" And he said, "Legion," for many demons had entered him. 31 And they

18 Lactantius, *The Divine Institutes*, 64.

> begged him not to command them to depart into **the abyss.** (Luke 8:30–31, ESV)

Pitterson commented on this subject,

> *The angelic fathers of the antediluvian Nephilim were of course bound with chains in the abyss where they remain today until the judgment of the great day… The demons are not only aware of the existence of the abyss but beg Jesus not to send them to the prison of their angelic forefathers.*[19]

Third, Mark's account has the demons addressing Jesus as "Son of the Most High God" (Mark 5:7), a title that shows up in key passages that deal with Yahweh's war with the gods (Deut 32:8; Ps 82:6; Ps 91:1). Now, here's the biggest context clue that links the demons to the giants—in Mark's Gospel, Jesus doesn't send the demons into the abyss, per their request. Instead, He orders them into pigs that drown in the sea, oddly enough.

> 7 and crying out with a loud voice, he saith, What have I to do
> with thee, Jesus, thou Son of the Most High God? I adjure thee
> by God, torment me not. 8 For he said unto him, Come forth,
> thou unclean spirit, out of the man. 9 And he asked him, What
> is thy name? And he saith unto him, My name is Legion; for
> we are many. 10 And he besought him much that he would not
> send them away out of the country. 11 Now there was there on
> the mountain side a great herd of swine feeding. 12 And they
> besought him, saying, Send us into the swine, that we may enter
> into them. 13 And he gave them leave. And the unclean spirits
> came out, and entered into the swine: and the herd rushed down

19 Pitterson, *Judgment of The Nephilim*, 433–434.

> the steep into the sea, in number about two thousand; and they were drowned in the sea. (Mark 5:7–13, ASV 1901)

Pitterson noted,

> *In stunning fashion, Jesus permitted the demons to enter into the bodies of pigs (ritually unclean animals that God forbade the Israelites from eating or even touching in some instances). The herd charged "violently" into a deep portion of the sea and drowned. This was a reenactment of the flood judgment. The giants who once ruled the earth were wiped out by choking on the waters of the Flood. This passage provides some of the most compelling evidence of the link between the demons of the New Testament and the giants of the Old Testament.*[20]

Worldly Gentiles, ancient Jews, and early Christians overwhelmingly believed demons were the spirits of the tyrannical giants. Jesus' dominance over these entities is not unimportant. It forecast His victory by echoing back to OT victories, as Van Dorn noted:

> *Jesus vs. the demons is the NT equivalent of Israel vs. the giants. It is the beginning of the final battle, as it were, between the Eve's Seed and the serpent's seed. In this battle, Jesus shows the demons his power, authority, and ultimate victory.*[21]

WHAT ABOUT MOUNT TABOR?

Some have suggested Mount Tabor is the mountain of Jesus' transfiguration. However, this notion carries little to no evidence. Mount

---

20 Pitterson, *Judgment of The Nephilim*, 434.

21 Van Dorn, *Giants: Sons of the Gods*, 242.

Hermon is a much better fit in terms of geography and context. As Matthew clarifies, they were in Caesarea Philippi, also known as Banias/Panias. The Lexham Bible Dictionary states,

> *Banias was a major site for worship of the Roman deity Pan as well as the emperor. The city is the setting for two Gospel accounts of Peter's confession of Christ (Matt 16:18; Mark 8:29;). The contrast between the fulfillment of messianic hope in Jesus and the rituals of imperial and hedonistic cults would have been striking (Baly, Geography, 195; Wright, Greatness, 140).*
>
> *Mount Hermon is a strong contender for the location of Jesus' transfiguration. In all three Synoptic Gospels, the transfiguration occurs shortly after Peter's confession, and both Matthew and Mark specify a "high mountain" (while Luke refers to "the mountain"). If these sections are to be taken chronologically, then Mount Hermon is the closest location that fits.*[22]

Without a doubt, the high mountain Jesus visited in our story was Mount Hermon (9,230 ft.), not Mount Tabor (1,843 ft.).

CONNECTING THE GOSPEL

THE ARMY OF THE CHURCH

In Matthew 16:8, Jesus said, "I will build my church." Hmm. What does the word "church" really mean, though?

> *The English word church (and the cognate form kirk) are derived from the Greek word kyriakon, which means "belonging to the Lord." The only two uses of that word in the New Testament occur in 1 Corinthians 11:20 (referring to the Lord's Supper) and*

22 B. Ridley, "Hermon, Mount," *The Lexham Bible Dictionary.*

> *Revelation 1:10 (referring to the Lord's Day). The word came to be used to refer to other things such as the place or people or denomination or country related to the group that belong to the Lord.*[23]

While the idea of *kyriakon*, or "belonging to the Lord," is certainly biblical, it's not the word used in Matthew 16:18. The word that's hidden behind the cloak of translation is *ekklēsia*.

> [18] And I say also unto thee, That thou art Peter, and upon this rock I will build my church (ekklēsia); and the gates of hell shall not prevail against it. (Matt 16:18, KJV 1900)

We really should be asking, "What does the word *ekklēsia* mean?"

> *In Greek usage, ekklēsia means the process of gathering of the dēmos, the people of the city or the citizenry.*[24]

This is a Greek term. No surprise. The majority of the New Testament was written in Koine Greek. However, the idea of *ekklēsia*, or the gathering of citizens, has roots in Old Testament Hebrew. Malina and Pilch noted,

> *There are two Hebrew equivalents. The word ʿēdâ is the community as such, the body assembled; qāhāl is the action of gathering, convening, or "assembly-ing." In the Septuagint qāhāl is translated by synagōgē or ekklēsia in the first four books of Moses. However, from Deut. 5:22 onward (except for 2 Chron. 5:4, 6),*

---

23 C. C. Ryrie, *Basic Theology: A Popular Systematic Guide to Understanding Biblical Truth* (Chicago, IL: Moody Press, 1999), 454–455.

24 B. J. Malina and J. J. Pilch, *Social-Science Commentary on the Deutero-Pauline Letters* (Minneapolis, MN: Fortress Press, 2013), 239.

> *the Septuagint translators followed this pattern: qāhāl = ekklēsia; ʿēdâ = synagōgē.*
>
> *The New Testament usage is rooted in the Hebrew Bible, wherein the people of God were convoked in assembly in the desert. This idea and motif run throughout the entire Hebrew Bible. It is this desert gathering of the exodus that forms the qāhāl of God, Israel.*[25]

As we've discovered throughout our journey together, Israel's insistence on worshiping other gods cost them their relationship and status with Yahweh. The New Dictionary of Biblical Theology discusses Israel's implosion and replacement.

> *Whilst God's intention had been that Israel should be a theocracy, a holy nation set apart for and governed only by himself, the persistent sin of the people and their leaders eventually caused the division of the kingdom, the punishment of the Exile and the refining of the people of God. Consequently, some prophets posited a theology of a remnant who were faithful to God (Is. 10:20–22; 37:31–32; Mic. 2:12; 5:7–8; Zeph. 3:12–13; Zech. 8:11–12) and in whom Israel's future lay.*
>
> *Paul adopted this vision when he asserted that 'not all who are descended from Israel are Israel' (Rom. 9:6) and claimed that* ***the church is the true Israel of God and comprises the real descendants of Abraham****, the man of faith (Gal. 6:16). There are many other allusions to the church as the true successor of Israel (W. S. Campbell, in DLNTD, p. 212) (Matt. 3:9–10; 19:28; John 15:1–8; Eph. 2:11–22; Jas. 1:1; 1 Pet. 1:1).*[26]

---

25 Malina and Pilch, *Social-Science Commentary on the Deutero-Pauline Letters*, 239–240.

26 D. J. Tidball, "Church," *New Dictionary of Biblical Theology* 408.

So, the *ekklēsia* should be thought of as the new universal covenant community of Yahweh. Christians are the new Israelites, and the *ekklēsia* is the new Israel.

> *The church has entered a new covenant with God (2 Cor. 3:4–18), also initiated by divine grace (Eph. 1:3–14; 2:1–10). This covenant is sealed by the blood of Jesus (1 Cor. 11:25) and instituted by his sacrifice as a great high priest (Heb. 8–10).*[27]

As we learned in chapter 10, this is why,

> *The calling to be 'a royal priesthood' (1 Pet. 2:9) has passed to the church of Christ where the concept of 'the priesthood of all believers' has assumed a richer significance. All believers may now enter the presence of God without the need for any human mediator; the purifying effect of the blood of Christ qualifies them to do so (Heb. 9:14; 10:19–22; 1 Tim. 2:5).*[28]

Ekklēsia also became a term applied to individual congregations, too. Malina and Pilch noted,

> *As the Jesus movement spread and new assemblies arose, it was necessary to give a name to the different gatherings. The name given to each gathering was* ekklēsia *or church (e.g., 1 Thess. 1:1; Gal. 1:2; etc.). Thus, the one new qāhāl of God was divided into different local churches, which in their turn were qualified as churches of God (e.g., 1 Cor. 1:1), or churches in God and in Jesus Christ (e.g., 1 Thess. 1:1).* [29]

---

27 Tidball, "Church," *New Dictionary of Biblical Theology* 408.
28 Tidball, "Church," *New Dictionary of Biblical Theology*.
29 Malina and Pilch, *Social-Science Commentary on the Deutero-Pauline Letters*, 240.

The question remains: What was Jesus angling for in Matthew 16:18? Was Jesus telling Peter He was going to put together an amazing worship event, construct a beautiful church building, or start His own religion? No. While the church does in fact often worship in church buildings, and Christianity is considered a religion, Jesus wasn't hinting at any of these things in this particular passage. He was telling Peter that He was going to "build" or "assemble" an army!

Think about it. He's in Bashan, the home of Mount Hermon. He reveals to the twelve apostles that He's going to die, and yet somehow, the gates of hell won't withstand the surge of attacks the church, or the *ekklēsia*, is going to shell out. Clearly, the tone and context of the passage reveal what Jesus had in mind for this newly-amassed *ekklēsia*. Christ wanted the Twelve to know that when He died, they weren't alone in the fight against the armies of hell. They would have help, and lots of it. Men and women from all nations would soon be drawn to the power of the cross and join the ranks of the twelve freedom fighters. Together, the soldiers of the cross would storm the gates of hell and overwhelm the enemy.

Two thousand years later, the church's role hasn't shifted. We're still an army, and Christ is still our captain. We're the church, the *ekklēsia*, the fellowship of the King. As such, we take our marching orders from Him, and only Him.

> *It is his church (Matt. 16:18). The church of the new covenant is entered by faith in him (Gal. 3:1–14; Eph. 2:1–10) and, consequently, is international in membership and allows no ethnic, gender or social divisions (Gal. 3:28; Eph. 2:11–22; Col. 3:11). The church is his body on earth, and he is the head (Rom. 12:5; 1 Cor. 12:12–31; Col. 1:18). The church takes its alignment from him as a building takes its alignment from the cornerstone (Eph. 2:20–21). It derives its unity and growth from him (Eph. 2:19–22; 4:15–16). The life of the church is maintained by*

> *its vital union with him (Rom. 6:1–4; Eph. 2:21–22; 4:15–16, and by contrast, Col. 2:19) and exists only insofar as it is 'in him'. The person and work of Christ, then, are at the heart of the NT view of the ekklēsia.*[30]

LOOKING AHEAD

The happenings at Hermon was Jesus orchestrating His big move. The boldness with which He spoke and the glory surrounding Him would provoke the powers of darkness to retaliate. In the next chapter, you will experience the bleeding Savior trudge His way to Golgotha. There, the many "bulls" of Bashan will strike back, surrounding Him as the quivering Savior suffers upon His cross.

---

30 Tidball, "Church," *New Dictionary of Biblical Theology*, 408.

CHAPTER 18

THE KISS OF SATAN, THE CROSS OF CHRIST, AND THE BULLS OF BASHAN

When Jesus had received the sour wine, he said, "It is finished," and he bowed his head and gave up his spirit. (John 19:30, ESV)

READING THE STORY

THE "HOUR" OF JESUS' DEPARTURE WAS at hand. But so was th betrayal—Satan's "opportune time" of temptation (Luke 4:13).

> "Now the Feast of Unleavened Bread drew near, which is called Passover. And the chief priests and the scribes sought how they might kill Him, for they feared the people. **Then Satan entered Judas**, surnamed Iscariot, who was numbered among the twelve. So he went his way and conferred with the chief priests and captains, how he might betray Him to them. And they were glad, and agreed to give him money. So he promised and sought opportunity to betray Him to them in the absence of the multitude. Then came the Day of Unleavened Bread, when the Passover must be killed. And He sent Peter and John, saying, "Go and prepare the Passover for us, that we may eat." So they said to Him, "Where do You want us to prepare?" And He said to them, "Behold, when you have entered the city, a man will meet you carrying a pitcher of water; follow him into the house which he enters. Then you shall say to the master of the house, 'The Teacher says to you, "Where is the guest room where I may eat the Passover with My disciples?" ' Then he will show you a large, furnished upper room; there make ready." So they went and found it just as He had said to them, and they prepared the Passover. When the hour had come, He sat down, and the twelve apostles with Him. Then He said to them, "With fervent desire I have desired to eat this Passover with you before I suffer; for I say to you, I will no longer eat of it until it is fulfilled in the kingdom of God." Then He took the cup, and gave thanks, and said, "Take this and divide it among yourselves; for I say to you, I will not drink of the fruit of the vine until the kingdom of God comes." And He took bread,

> gave thanks and broke it, and gave it to them, saying, "This is My body which is given for you; do this in remembrance of Me." Likewise He also took the cup after supper, saying, "This cup is the new covenant in My blood, which is shed for you. **But behold, the hand of My betrayer is with Me on the table**. And truly the Son of Man goes as it has been determined, but woe to that man by whom He is betrayed!" Then they began to question among themselves, which of them it was who would do this thing. (Luke 22:1–23, NKJV)

The news that one of the Twelve had betrayed Jesus stunned them. *Who among the fellowship could do such a treacherous thing?* A great heaviness now filled the deflated upper room.

> "Then the disciples looked at one another, perplexed about whom He spoke. Now there was leaning on Jesus' bosom one of His disciples, whom Jesus loved. Simon Peter therefore motioned to him to ask who it was of whom He spoke. Then, leaning back on Jesus' breast, he said to Him, "Lord, who is it?" Jesus answered, "It is he to whom I shall give a piece of bread when I have dipped it." And having dipped the bread, He gave it to Judas Iscariot, the son of Simon. **Now after the piece of bread, Satan entered him**. Then Jesus said to him, "**What you do, do quickly**." But no one at the table knew for what reason He said this to him. For some thought, because Judas had the money box, that Jesus had said to him, "Buy those things we need for the feast," or that he should give something to the poor. Having received the piece of bread, he then went out immediately. And it was night. So, when he had gone out, Jesus said, "Now the Son of Man is glorified, and God is glorified in Him. If God is glorified in Him, God will also glorify Him in Himself, and glorify Him immediately.

> Little children, I shall be with you a little while longer. You will seek Me; and as I said to the Jews, 'Where I am going, you cannot come,' so now I say to you. **A new commandment I give to you, that you love one another; as I have loved you, that you also love one another. By this all will know that you are My disciples, if you have love for one another**." (John 13:22–35, NKJV)

The façade of Judas's faithfulness had faded away. He was now a human host for the dark side; he had become the tempter's tabernacle. The serpent's poisonous lies and unspeakable plans now resided in the heart of Judas Iscariot. Baal was finally going to kill Jesus, erasing the prophecy of Genesis 3:15, which for millennia, boasted of his defeat. But he wouldn't pierce Christ with a sword. No. Yahweh would never allow it (Job 1:12). In a conception of twisted evil, he would use the Jews and Jesus' own disciples to pierce His hands and feet, nailing Him to a bloody cross.

Then, Jesus turned to Peter.

> "And the Lord said, "Simon, Simon! Indeed, **Satan has asked for you, that he may sift you as wheat**. But I have prayed for you, that your faith should not fail; and when you have returned to Me, strengthen your brethren." But he said to Him, "Lord, I am ready to go with You, both to prison and to death." Then He said, "I tell you, Peter, the rooster shall not crow this day before you will deny three times that you know Me." (Luke 22:31–34, NKJV)

They concluded the dreary supper with a song on their lips and a burden on their hearts (Matt 26:30–35). Everything was about to change; they all felt it. Jesus and the eleven then climbed the Mount of Olives, where He dropped yet another disturbing bombshell on the disciples.

> Then Jesus said to them, "Tonight all of you will fall away because of me, for it is written: I will strike the shepherd, and the sheep of the flock will be scattered. But after I have risen, I will go ahead of you to Galilee." Peter told him, "Even if everyone falls away because of you, I will never fall away." "Truly I tell you," Jesus said to him, "tonight, before the rooster crows, you will deny me three times." "Even if I have to die with you," Peter told him, "I will never deny you," and all the disciples said the same thing. (Matt 26:31–35, CSB)

Despite their assurance, there was no escaping their destiny. Jesus had spoken. Christ and the eleven then ventured to the garden of Gethsemane.

> And when he was at the place, he said unto them, **Pray that ye enter not into temptation**. And he was parted from them about a stone's cast; and he kneeled down and prayed, saying, Father, if thou be willing, remove this cup from me; nevertheless not my will, but thine, be done. **And there appeared unto him an angel from heaven, strengthening him**. And being in an agony he prayed more earnestly; and his sweat became as it were great drops of blood falling down upon the ground. (Luke 22:40–44, ASV 1901)

Then he came to the disciples and found them sleeping. He asked Peter, "So, couldn't you stay awake with me one hour? **Stay awake and pray, so that you won't enter into temptation**. The spirit is willing, but the flesh is weak." Again, a second time, he went away and prayed, "My Father, if this cannot pass unless I drink it, your will be done." And he came again and found them sleeping, because they could not keep their eyes open. After leaving them, he went away again and prayed a third time, saying the same thing once more. Then he came to the disciples and said to them, "Are you still sleeping and resting? See, the time is near. The Son of Man is betrayed into the hands of sinners. Get up; let's go. See, **my betrayer is near**." (Matt 26:40–46, CSB)

Judas, who betrayed him, also knew the place, because Jesus often met there with his disciples. So Judas took a company of soldiers and some officials from the chief priests and the Pharisees and came there with lanterns, torches, and weapons. (John 18:2–3, CSB)

Then Jesus, knowing everything that was about to happen to him, went out and said to them, "Who is it that you're seeking?" "Jesus of Nazareth," they answered. "I am he," Jesus told them. Judas, who betrayed him, was also standing with them. When Jesus told them, "I am he," they stepped back and fell to the ground. Then he asked them again, "Who is it that you're seeking?" "Jesus of Nazareth," they said. "I told you I am he," Jesus replied. "So if you're looking for me, let these men go." (John 18:4–8, CSB)

His betrayer had given them a signal. "The one I kiss," he said, "he's the one; arrest him and take him away under guard." So when he came, immediately he went up to Jesus and said, "Rabbi!" and **kissed him**. They took hold of him and arrested him. (Mark 14:44–46, CSB)

And when those who were around him saw what would follow, they said, "Lord, shall we strike with the sword?" And one of them struck the servant of the high priest and cut off his right ear. But Jesus said, "No more of this!" And he touched his ear and healed him. (Luke 22:49–51, ESV)

> Then Jesus told him, "Put your sword back in its place because all who take up the sword will perish by the sword. Or do you think that I cannot call on my Father, and he will provide me here and now with more than twelve legions of angels? How, then, would the Scriptures be fulfilled that say it must happen this way?" (Matt 26:52–54, CSB)

> Then Jesus said to the chief priests and officers of the temple and elders, who had come out against him, "Have you come out as against a robber, with swords and clubs? When I was with you day after day in the temple, you did not lay hands on me. **But this is your hour, and the power of darkness**." (Luke 22:52–53, ESV)

> So the band of soldiers and their captain and the officers of the Jews arrested Jesus and **bound him**. (John 18:12, ESV)

> Then **everyone deserted him and fled**. (Mark 14:50, NIV)

As we studied in the last chapter, all throughout Jesus' ministry, Jesus bound the demonic realm. Now, in a swift turn of events, those roles have reversed. Jesus is now the bound one. The powers of darkness must have smiled smugly in celebration as the Roman soldiers and Jewish officials led Jesus straight to Annas, a former high priest from 6–15 A.D., and his son-in-law Caiaphas, the current high priest. Meanwhile, Peter and a second disciple trailed behind the mob and the shackled Messiah.

> Simon Peter and another disciple were following Jesus. Because this disciple was known to the high priest, he went with Jesus into the high priest's courtyard, but Peter had to wait outside at the door. The other disciple, who was known

> to the high priest, came back, spoke to the servant girl on duty there and brought Peter in. "You aren't one of this man's disciples too, are you?" she asked Peter. He replied, "I am not." (John 18:15–17, NIV)

> Then he went out to the gateway, where another servant girl saw him and said to the people there, "This fellow was with Jesus of Nazareth." He denied it again, with an oath: "I don't know the man!" (Matt 26:71–72, NIV)

> About an hour later, another kept insisting, "This man was certainly with him, since he's also a Galilean." But Peter said, "Man, I don't know what you're talking about!" Immediately, while he was still speaking, a rooster crowed. Then the Lord turned and looked at Peter. So Peter remembered the word of the Lord, how he had said to him, "Before the rooster crows today, you will deny me three times." And he went outside and wept bitterly. (Luke 22:59–62, CSB)

Jesus was right. The once-brazen Peter was now truly afraid.

> The men who were guarding Jesus began mocking and beating him. They blindfolded him and demanded, "Prophesy! Who hit you?" And they said many other insulting things to him. At daybreak the council of the elders of the people, both the chief priests and the teachers of the law, met together, and Jesus was led before them. "If you are the Messiah," they said, "tell us." Jesus answered, "If I tell you, you will not believe me, and if I asked you, you would not answer. But from now on, the Son of Man will be seated at the right hand of the mighty God." They all asked, "Are you then the Son of God?" He replied, "You say that I am." Then they said, "Why do we need any more

testimony? We have heard it from his own lips." Then the whole assembly rose and led him off to Pilate. And they began to accuse him, saying, "We have found this man subverting our nation. He opposes payment of taxes to Caesar and claims to be Messiah, a king." So Pilate asked Jesus, "Are you the king of the Jews?" "You have said so," Jesus replied. Then Pilate announced to the chief priests and the crowd, "I find no basis for a charge against this man." But they insisted, "He stirs up the people all over Judea by his teaching. He started in Galilee and has come all the way here." On hearing this, Pilate asked if the man was a Galilean. When he learned that Jesus was under Herod's jurisdiction, he sent him to Herod, who was also in Jerusalem at that time. When Herod saw Jesus, he was greatly pleased, because for a long time he had been wanting to see him. From what he had heard about him, he hoped to see him perform a sign of some sort. He plied him with many questions, but Jesus gave him no answer. The chief priests and the teachers of the law were standing there, vehemently accusing him. Then Herod and his soldiers ridiculed and mocked him. Dressing him in an elegant robe, they sent him back to Pilate. That day Herod and Pilate became friends—before this they had been enemies. Pilate called together the chief priests, the rulers and the people, and said to them, "You brought me this man as one who was inciting the people to rebellion. I have examined him in your presence and have found no basis for your charges against him. Neither has Herod, for he sent him back to us; as you can see, he has done nothing to deserve death. Therefore, I will punish him and then release him." But the whole crowd shouted, "Away with this man! Release Barabbas to us!" (Barabbas had been thrown into prison for an insurrection in the city, and for murder.) Wanting to release Jesus, Pilate appealed to them again. But they kept shouting, "Crucify him! Crucify him!" For the third time

> he spoke to them: "Why? What crime has this man committed? I have found in him no grounds for the death penalty. Therefore I will have him punished and then release him." But with loud shouts they insistently demanded that he be crucified, and their shouts prevailed. So Pilate decided to grant their demand. He released the man who had been thrown into prison for insurrection and murder, the one they asked for, and surrendered Jesus to their will. (Luke 22:63–23:25, NIV)

Pilate's hesitance was overcome by their strong emotion. The crowd of insatiable death had successfully rallied to murder the King of kings.

> Then the governor's soldiers took Jesus into the Praetorium and gathered the whole company of soldiers around him. They stripped him and put a scarlet robe on him, and then twisted together a crown of thorns and set it on his head. They put a staff in his right hand. Then they knelt in front of him and mocked him. "Hail, king of the Jews!" they said. They spit on him, and took the staff and struck him on the head again and again. After they had mocked him, they took off the robe and put his own clothes on him. Then they led him away to crucify him. (Matt 27:27–31, NIV)
>
> As the soldiers led him away, they seized Simon from Cyrene, who was on his way in from the country, and put the cross on him and made him carry it behind Jesus. A large number of people followed him, including women who mourned and wailed for him. Jesus turned and said to them, "Daughters of Jerusalem, do not weep for me; weep for yourselves and for your children. For the time will come when you will say, 'Blessed are the childless women, the wombs that never bore and the breasts that never nursed!' Then "'they will say to the mountains, "Fall on us!"

and to the hills, "Cover us!"' For if people do these things when the tree is green, what will happen when it is dry?" Two other men, both criminals, were also led out with him to be executed. When they came to the place called the Skull, they crucified him there, along with the criminals—one on his right, the other on his left. Jesus said, "Father, forgive them, for they do not know what they are doing." And they divided up his clothes by casting lots. The people stood watching, and the rulers even sneered at him. They said, "He saved others; let him save himself if he is God's Messiah, the Chosen One." The soldiers also came up and mocked him. They offered him wine vinegar and said, "If you are the king of the Jews, save yourself." There was a written notice above him, which read: THIS IS THE KING OF THE JEWS. One of the criminals who hung there hurled insults at him: "Aren't you the Messiah? Save yourself and us!" But the other criminal rebuked him. "Don't you fear God," he said, "since you are under the same sentence? We are punished justly, for we are getting what our deeds deserve. But this man has done nothing wrong." Then he said, "Jesus, remember me when you come into your kingdom." Jesus answered him, "Truly I tell you, today you will be with me in paradise." (Luke 23:26–43, NIV)

Near the cross of Jesus stood his mother, his mother's sister, Mary the wife of Clopas, and Mary Magdalene. When Jesus saw his mother there, and the disciple whom he loved standing nearby, he said to her, "Woman, here is your son," and to the disciple, "Here is your mother." From that time on, this disciple took her into his home. (John 19:25–27, NIV)

From noon until three in the afternoon **darkness came over all the land**. About three in the afternoon Jesus cried out in a loud voice, "Eli, Eli, lema sabachthani?" (which means "**My God,**

> **my God, why have you forsaken me?**"). When some of those standing there heard this, they said, "He's calling Elijah." Immediately one of them ran and got a sponge. He filled it with wine vinegar, put it on a staff, and offered it to Jesus to drink. The rest said, "Now leave him alone. Let's see if Elijah comes to save him." (Matt 27:45–49, NIV)

As David prophesied in Psalm 22, it was in this pivotal moment when all the powers of darkness—the "bulls of Bashan," as he calls them—surrounded the weakened King, watching, hungering, and roaring alongside their encircling Jewish accomplices. This psalm reads,

> 1 My God, my God, why have you forsaken me? Why are you so far from saving me, from the words of my groaning?... 12 **Many bulls encompass me; strong bulls of Bashan surround me**; 13 they open wide their mouths at me, **like a ravening and roaring lion**. 14 I am poured out like water, and all my bones are out of joint; my heart is like wax; it is melted within my breast; 15 my strength is dried up like a potsherd, and my tongue sticks to my jaws; you lay me in the dust of death. 16 **For dogs encompass me; a company of evildoers encircles me; they have pierced my hands and feet**— (Ps 22:1, 12–16, ESV)

Suspended in the black sky, He held the resolute attention of heaven and hell. With a final, shallow breath,

> … He said, "It is finished!" And bowing His head, He gave up His spirit. (John 19:30, NKJV)

> At that moment the curtain of the temple was torn in two from top to bottom. The earth shook, the rocks split and the tombs broke open. The bodies of many holy people who had

> died were raised to life. They came out of the tombs after Jesus' resurrection and went into the holy city and appeared to many people. When the centurion and those with him who were guarding Jesus saw the earthquake and all that had happened, they were terrified, and exclaimed, "Surely he was the Son of God!" (Matt 27:51–54, NIV)

ANSWERING YOUR QUESTIONS

WHAT ARE THE BULLS OF BASHAN?

By now, you are familiar with "Bashan," which, for all intents and purposes, is the gates of hell. David, the penman of Psalm 22, was fully aware of the supernatural stench of this place. His prophecy about Christ on the cross involved "the bulls of Bashan" encircling Him with open mouths like those of roaring lions.

> [12] Many bulls encompass me; strong bulls of Bashan surround
> me; [13] they open wide their mouths at me, like a ravening and
> roaring lion. (Ps 22:12–13, ESV)

Many commentators typically see this is as a reference to the people surrounding the cross. However, they're mistaken; they're totally missing the significance of the passage. Granted, the gang of "evildoers," or the "dogs" (Ps 22:16), who have pierced Jesus' hands and feet are clear references to the Jews. However, the "bulls of Bashan" term references the nations' gods—angels and demons.

Eerdmans Dictionary of the Bible notes,

> ***The bull is a very common figure in the religions of the ancient Near East.*** *In Egypt the Apis bull, a personification of the Nile, was the sacred animal of Osiris...The* ***Bull of Heaven***

> *appears in Mesopotamian mythology as* ***a vehicle for the gods' judgment.***[1]

Other texts depict this "vehicle" more literally. Gregorio del Olmo wrote,

> *In the glyptic arts, the storm god is portrayed mounted on a bull or in his chariot drawn by two bulls (a motif in the Hurrian and Hittite tradition), alongside other emblems special to him, such as the bolt of lightning...*[2]

However, bulls were associated with much more than only transportation and sacrifices. They became associated with the deities themselves.

> *In Canaanite religious practice* ***the bull was often used as a symbol for either Baal*** *or El. In Hazor a pair of bulls has been found with feet on their backs, interpreted as a representation of* ***Baal****. Similar depictions exist of Adad, often seen as a Mesopotamian representation of* ***Baal.***[3]

Bulls were symbolic of Satan and other gods because of their sheer power and strength. This is why people often worshiped their gods through bovine images such as the "golden calf," which Israel made and Moses destroyed at Sinai (Exod 32:4). Some gods, like the Canaanite god El, were even nicknamed "the bull" by their worshipers. Cobern noted,

---

1 M. A. Thomas, "Bull," *Eerdmans Dictionary of the Bible* 202.

2 Gregorio del Olmo, "From Baal to Yahweh," *The Bull in the Mediterranean World* (2004), https://www.academia.edu/4887401/2004_From_Baal_to_Yahweh_The_Bull_in_the_Mediterranean_World

3 Thomas, "Bull," 202–203.

> *...the Babylonians revered the bull as the symbol of their greatest gods, Anu and Sin and Marduk...*[4]

However, bovine terminology is also applied to underling gods, too, not only the big shots. Fleming wrote,

> *The Mesopotamian evidence indicates that the younger generation of gods with bull-like power may be portrayed as either calves or adult bulls, depending on the desired nuance.*[5]

Cobern added,

> *Few hymns in Egypt or Babylon express higher spiritual knowledge and aspiration than those addressed to the bull gods or to others honored with this title*[6]

So, in Psalm 22:12–13, David wasn't thinking of literal bulls from Bashan walking in circles around the foot of the cross; he prophesied that the nations' bullish gods would be personally present at the scene of the crucifixion.

Interestingly, an Aramaic targum of Psalm 22 has "the nations" and "the mighty ones of Bashan" encircling Jesus, rather than the "bulls" and "strong bulls of Bashan."

> 13 **The nations**, who may be compared to many oxen, have surrounded me; **mighty ones of Bashan have encircled me**.

---

4 C. M. Cobern, "Calf, Golden," vol. 1–5 *The International Standard Bible Encyclopaedia* 543.

5 Daniel Fleming, "If El Is a Bull, Who Is a Calf? Reflections on Religion in Second Millennium Syria-Palestine," quoted in *Frank Moore Cross Volume*, ed. Baruch A. Levine, et al.; ErIsr 26; (Jerusalem: Israel Exploration Society, 1999), 23–27.

6 Cobern, "Calf, Golden," 543.

> [14] They have opened their mouths at me, like a tearing and roaring lion. (Ps 22:13–14, The Aramaic Bible, Volume 16: The Targum of Psalms)

The inclusion of "the nations" terminology is quite telling. The targum seems to be highlighting a Deuteronomy 32 worldview, where lesser gods were placed over "the nations." The translation, "mighty ones" of Bashan more clearly bridges the gap to the supernatural. When we dig into the Hebrew language, yet another meaningful layer is revealed. The text reads,

> [12] Many **bulls** (pâr) encompass me; **strong bulls** (ʾabbîyr) of Bashan surround me; [13] they open wide their mouths at me, like a ravening and roaring lion. (Ps 22:12–13, ESV)

The Hebrew word translated "strong bulls" in verse 13 is the word ʾ***abbîyr*** in Hebrew. It is often translated as "bull" or "mighty," or sometimes as a combination of these ideas (i.e., "strong bull"). According to lexicons, this word can also be translated as "angel," too. This means the passage could translate, "Many bulls encompass me, angels of Bashan surround me." No matter the translation, the graphic imagery of Jesus' crucifixion in Psalm 22 includes the encircling presence of the bullish powers of darkness, celebrating and salivating at the foot of the cross.

WHY DID THE POWERS OF DARKNESS KILL JESUS IF IT LED TO THEIR DEFEAT?

The nations and their gods were flying totally blind when it came to the plans of Yahweh. The prophet Micah writes,

> [11] And now many nations have gathered together against you, who are saying, 'We will rejoice, and our eyes will look upon

> Zion.' [12] They did not know the reasoning of the Lord, and they did not understand his will, that he gathered them like sheaves of a threshing floor. (Mic 4:11–12, LES)

While messianic threads are interwoven into the Old Testament, the full tapestry of how God would save man was still very much hidden. Paul explains that if the demonic "rulers" (Gk: *archon*) of this world would have understood that killing Jesus meant their defeat and not their victory, they wouldn't have done it.

> [7] But we impart a secret and hidden wisdom of God, which God decreed before the ages for our glory. [8] None of the **rulers** (archon) of this age understood this, **for if they had, they would not have crucified the Lord of glory**. (1 Cor 2:7–8, ESV)

Ignorance and hatred left the door wide open for the Lord to disarm and triumph over the nations' spirit rulers and authorities through the inconspicuous power of the cross.

> [14] by canceling the record of debt that stood against us with its legal demands. This he set aside, nailing it to the cross. [15] **He disarmed the rulers** (archon) **and authorities** (ĕxŏusia) and put them to open shame, by triumphing over them in him. (Col 2:14–15, ESV)

Christ's pain led to His power of forgiving joy, as Cyril of Alexandria (378–444 A.D.) pointed out:

> *For God the Father wishes to take away from the pain of his soul (53:11); he wishes to transform the pain of Christ on the cross into joy by showing him those who were in darkness—that is, those who had wandered after other gods—changed into light. To these*

> *people the all-wise Paul wrote, For once you were darkness, but now you are light in the Lord (Eph 5:8).*[7]

An early church apologist named Athanasius the Great of Alexandri (296–373 A.D.) wrote at length concerning how Christ's work on th cross set the stage to overthrow the gods and liberate the Gentile nations

> *But if any one from among us asks, not as a lover of contention but as a lover of learning, why he endured the cross rather than some other way, then let him hear that in no other way than this was it beneficial for us, and that* ***it was good that the Lord endured this for us****. For if* ***he came himself to bear the curse which lay upon us****, how else could he have "become a curse" (Gal 3:13) if he had not accepted the death occasioned by the curse? And that is the cross, for thus it is written, "cursed is he who hangs from the tree" (Deut 21:23). Moreover, if the death of the Lord is a ransom for all and by his death "the wall of partition" (Eph 2:14) is broken down, and* ***the call of the Gentiles effected, how would he have called us if he had not been crucified?*** *For only upon the cross does one die with hands stretched out. Therefore it was fitting for the Lord to endure this, and to stretch out his hands,* ***that with the one he might draw the ancient people and with the other those from the Gentiles, and join both together in himself****. This he himself said when he indicated by what manner of death he was going to redeem all, "When I am lifted up, I shall draw all to myself" (Jn 12:32). And again, if the enemy of our race, the devil, having fallen from heaven, wanders around these lower airs and, lording it here over the demons with him, similar in disobedience, through them works illusions in those who are deceived and attempts to prevent them*

7 Wilken, Christman, and Hollerich, eds., *Isaiah*, 421.

> *rising upwards—about this the Apostle also says, "Following the prince of the power of the air, who is now at work in the sons of disobedience" (Eph 2:2)—* ***yet Christ came that he might overthrow the devil, purify the air, and open up for us the way to heaven****, as the Apostle said, "through the veil, that is, his flesh" (Heb 10:20), this must have been by death, and by what other death would these things have happened except that which takes place in the air, I mean the cross? For only he that completes his life on the cross dies in the air. Therefore it was right that the Lord endured it.* ***For being thus lifted up, he purified the air from the diabolical plots of all demons****, saying "I saw Satan falling as lightning" (Lk 10:18), and blazing the trail he made anew the way up to heaven, saying again, "Lift up your gates, O princes of yours, and be raised up, everlasting gates" (Ps 23:7). For it was not the Word himself who needed the gates to be opened, since he is the Lord of all, nor was any made thing closed to its Maker; but we were those who needed it, whom he himself carried up through his own body. For* ***as he offered to death on behalf of all, so through it he opened up again the way to heaven.***[8]

One of his contemporaries, Tyrannius Rufinus of Aquileia (345–411 A.D.), also explained the pivotal role the cross played in flipping the script on the fallen angels from Babel.

> ***Those rulers, then, whom God had set over mankind****, having become contumacious and tyrannical, took in hand to assail the men who had been committed to their charge and to rout them utterly in the conflicts of sin, as the Prophet Ezekiel mystically intimates when he says, "In that day angels shall come forth*

8 Athanasius the Great of Alexandria, vol. 44a of *On the Incarnation: Translation*, 103–105 (Behr).

> *hastening to exterminate Ethiopia, and there shall he perturbation among them in the day of Egypt; for behold He comes." 37 Having stript them then of their almighty power, Christ is said to have triumphed, and to have delivered to men the power which was taken from them, as also Himself saith to His disciples in the Gospel, "Behold I have given you power to tread upon serpents and scorpions, and upon all the might of the enemy."* ***The Cross of Christ, then, brought those who had wrongfully abused the authority which they had received into subjection to those who had before been in subjection to them.*** *But us, that is, mankind, it teaches first of all to resist sin even unto death, and willingly to die for the sake of religion. Next, this same Cross sets before us an example of obedience, in like manner as it hath* ***punished the contumacy of those who were once our rulers.***[9]

WHAT'S THE MEANING OF THE FOUR PHENOMENA?

At the passing of Jesus, Matthew 27:45–54 reveals there were four paranormal events that occurred.

1. The darkness came over the earth (v. 45).
2. The curtain of the temple was torn in two (v. 51).
3. The earth shook (v. 51).
4. The graves were opened (v. 52).

Each of these four anomalies telegraphed a powerful message.

First, the physical darkness that overshadowed the land from noon until 3 PM mirrored the encircling presence of the spiritual forces of darkness at Calvary and Yahweh's displeasure with them (Amos 8:9–10). Second, the meaning of the tearing of the "veil" or "curtain" is a little challenging to parse because we aren't told which

---

9 Rufinus, *A Commentary on the Apostles' Creed*, 549.

urtain was torn. It was either the great outer curtain that covered the ntry to the sanctuary or the inner curtain that hung between the Holy Place and the Most Holy Place. In his commentary on Matthew, France isted commonly proposed implications of the event.

> *Interpreters suggest various more specific symbolic meanings, including especially: (1) a sign that God no longer needs the temple and its rituals; (2) a sign of its coming destruction34 as predicted by Jesus (and so a divine riposte to the mockery of Jesus' threat to the temple in v. 40); (3) a symbol of mourning (as in 2 Kgs 2:12) either for the death of Jesus or for the approaching end of the temple; (4) a sign of the opening of the way into God's presence, hitherto closed by the cultic exclusion symbolized by the curtain (the symbolism developed by Hebrews);36 (5) an apocalyptic sign of "divine revelation triggered by the death of Jesus."*[10]

France concluded,

> *the tearing of the curtain suggests that as Jesus dies the transfer of authority from the old temple-focused régime (which has been responsible for his death) to the shortly-to-be-vindicated Son of Man is already taking place. The result will be that access to God will no longer be through the old, discredited cultic system but through Jesus himself, and more specifically through his death as a ransom for many.*[11]

Third, the earthquake at Golgotha is especially meaningful in Christ's mission to take back the nations. You may recall that the earth shook

---

10 France, *The Gospel of Matthew*, 1080.

11 France, *The Gospel of Matthew*, 1081.

at Mount Sinai when Israel was inaugurated into the Law of Mose (Exod 19:18). Haggai prophesied that "once more," God would shak the heavens and the earth and "fill" His house with glory.

> [6] For thus says Yahweh of hosts: 'Once again, in a little while, **I will shake the heavens and the earth and the sea and dry land.** [7] **I will shake all the nations so that the treasure of all the nations will come, and I will fill this house with glory**,' says Yahweh of hosts. (Hag 2:6–7, LEB)

Looking back on these two events, the Hebrews writer acknowledge the fulfillment of Haggai's prophecy—the "once more" reenactmen of the great Sinai earthquake was fulfilled by the newly-established unshakable kingdom, the church of Christ.

> [26] whose voice then shook the earth; but now He has promised, saying, "**Yet once more I shake not only the earth, but also heaven.**" [27] Now this, "Yet once more," indicates the removal of those things that are being shaken, as of things that are made, that the things which cannot be shaken may remain. [28] Therefore, since **we are receiving a kingdom which cannot be shaken,** let us have grace, by which we may serve God acceptably with reverence and godly fear. [29] For our God is a consuming fire. (Heb 12:26–29, NKJV)

The earthquake at the death (Matt 27:51) and resurrection of Christ (Matt 28:2) signaled that Haggai's prophecy of God filling His house with the "treasure of all the nations" was now officially underway. And lastly, the resurrected saints who came out of their graves and appeared to many were linked to Christ's victory over death and the grave and foreshadowed the day in which "the dead in Christ will rise" at the, still pending, return of the King (1 Thess 4:16).

CONNECTING THE GOSPEL

THE LOVE OF GOD

The story of the cross demonstrates the deep well of God's endless love. The authenticity of Christ's love is unmatched, even by the nations' gods. This isn't to say the nations' gods never convinced the world they truly loved them, because they had. We've found plenty of evidence of that in archaeological discoveries, such as in the Amarna Letters of Egypt (fourteenth century B.C.E.).

> *76 so may Teššup, Šauška, Amanu, 77 Šimige, Ea-šarri and all 78* ***the gods love us in their hearts very, very much.***[12]

The Greek pagan philosopher Plato (428–348 B.C.) framed the question,

> *And do not all human things share in soul, and is not man the most religious of animals and the possession of the Gods? And the Gods, who are the best of owners, will surely take care of their property, small or great.* [13]

Despite all the years of worshiping the gods, the nations never really experienced true love. To the gods, people were nothing more than meaningless servants and expendable pawns in their chess match with Yahweh. Jesus stepped into a world that was anemic and deprived of love. His strategy to rescue all nations was simply to be Himself, to embody the love of God in human form.

Perhaps there is no greater chapter in all the Bible that speaks of God's unbiased love than John 3. In John 3:16–18, Jesus taught

---

12 W. L. Moran, ed., *The Amarna Letters*, trans. W. L. Moran (Baltimore: Johns Hopkins University Press, 1992), 64.

13 Plato, vol. 5 of *The Dialogues of Plato*, 179.

Nicodemus, a secret disciple of Christ in the Jewish Sanhedrin, that He was born to love every nation under heaven, not just Israel.

> [16] **For God so loved the world**, that he gave his only begotten Son, **that whosoever** believeth in him should not perish, but have everlasting life. [17] For God sent not his Son into the world to condemn the world; but that the world through him might be saved. [18] He that believeth on him is not condemned: but he that believeth not is condemned already, because he hath not believed in the name of the only begotten Son of God. (John 3:16–18, KJV 1900)

Through His ministry and death, the world experienced firsthand the pure, selfless, and soothing nature of our God, no strings attached. It was beautiful. John testified to the breathtaking love he and many others came to know through the power of the gospel.

> [14] And we have seen and testify that **the Father has sent the Son as Savior of the world**. [15] Whoever confesses that Jesus is the Son of God, God abides in him, and he in God. 16 And **we have known and believed the love that God has for us. God is love,** and he who abides in love abides in God, and God in him. (1 John 4:14–16, NKJV)

As twenty-first-century Christians who have come to feel this same love through God's Holy Spirit, we intrinsically carry on the Lord's earthly ministry of sharing His loving-kindness with every creature (Rom 5:5). Rest assured, the devil's angels and demons are against the ministry of God's love because it destroys their false happiness, through which they deceive many—this deception exposes them as nothing more than selfish deities. They work tirelessly to terminate our efforts and intercept our opportunities, stopping at nothing to stunt the spread of God's love throughout he whole world. They turn brother against brother, sister against sister, ace against race, church against church, and nation against nation. The evel of their success is sickening. Our world is so full of their hate, yet ecause of you, there is hope. While it may seem like an insurmountable ask to reverse their hate, it's not. Good will always overcome evil (Rom 2:21). We must rival their hate with love. It starts by letting go of personal rudges and sinful attitudes. Paul wrote to the church at Ephesus,

> [31] **Let all bitterness and wrath and anger and clamor and**
> **slander be put away from you, along with all malice.** [32] Be kind
> to one another, tenderhearted, forgiving one another, as God
> in Christ forgave you. [1] **Therefore be imitators of God, as**
> **beloved children.** [2] And **walk in love, as Christ loved us** and
> gave himself up for us, a fragrant offering and sacrifice to God.
> (Eph 4:31–5:2, ESV)

Again, John writes,

> [7] Dear friends, **let us love one another, because love is from**
> **God**, and everyone who loves has been born of God and knows
> God. [8] The one who does not love does not know God, because
> God is love. [9] God's love was revealed among us in this way: God
> sent his one and only Son into the world so that we might live
> through him. [10] Love consists in this: not that we loved God, but
> that he loved us and sent his Son to be the atoning sacrifice for
> our sins. [11] Dear friends, **if God loved us in this way, we also**
> **must love one another.** [12] No one has ever seen God. If we love
> one another, God remains in us and his love is made complete
> in us. (1 John 4:7–12, CSB)

The gods were convinced they could rid the world of the Father's love by hanging His Son on a cross. Boy, were they wrong! They underestimated the lasting impact Jesus' sacrificial death would hav on His disciples. It increased their faith, supported their hope, an awakened their love. It lit a fire beneath them that burned hotte than the fires of hell. They stopped at nothing, even in the face o martyrdom, to spread the love of God. They understood that n matter what, the powers of darkness could not separate them from the love of God. The apostle Paul writes,

> [31] What then shall we say to these things? **If God is for us, who
> can be against us**? [32] He who did not spare his own Son but
> gave him up for us all, how will he not also with him graciously
> give us all things? [33] Who shall bring any charge against God's
> elect? It is God who justifies. [34] Who is to condemn? Christ
> Jesus is the one who died—more than that, who was raised—
> who is at the right hand of God, who indeed is interceding
> for us. [35] **Who shall separate us from the love of Christ**?
> Shall tribulation, or distress, or persecution, or famine, or
> nakedness, or danger, or sword? [36] As it is written, "For your
> sake we are being killed all the day long; we are regarded as
> sheep to be slaughtered." [37] No, in all these things **we are more
> than conquerors through him who loved us**. [38] For I am
> sure that neither death nor life, **nor angels nor rulers**, nor
> things present nor things to come, **nor powers**, [39] nor height
> nor depth, **nor anything else in all creation, will be able to
> separate us from the love of God in Christ Jesus our Lord**.
> (Rom 8:31–39, ESV)

Satan's hate is no match for God's love. God will never stop loving people. God is love—He cannot be anything else. The good news of the cross forever demonstrates His eternal love for all nations. Red, yellow, black, or white, people's values are no longer defined by where they're from or even which god they serve; every man, woman, and child is so oved by their Creator. Ultimately, the story of the cross teaches us this truth more than anything else.

LOOKING AHEAD

esus' suffering was now over. The King was dead. John narrates,

> Since it was the preparation day, the Jews did not want the bodies to remain on the cross on the Sabbath (for that Sabbath was a special day). They requested that Pilate have the men's legs broken and that their bodies be taken away. So the soldiers came and broke the legs of the first man and of the other one who had been crucified with him. When they came to Jesus, they did not break his legs since they saw that he was already dead. But one of the soldiers pierced his side with a spear, and at once blood and water came out. He who saw this has testified so that you also may believe. His testimony is true, and he knows he is telling the truth. For these things happened so that the Scripture would be fulfilled: Not one of his bones will be broken. Also, another Scripture says: They will look at the one they pierced. (John 19:31–37, CSB)

In our final visit to the earth's ancient past, the battle for heaven and earth will take a shocking turn that no one saw coming. In death, Christ would soon fight back, resisting Sheol and the power of Mot, the god of death. The outcome of this struggle would soon seal the fate of the gods and their nations forever. What will it all mean? No secrets are safe. All will be revealed in the final chapter of this spellbinding and supernatural journey back into the world of the ancient gospel. Buckle up!

CHAPTER 1

THE RISE OF THE SAVIOR, THE DEFEAT OF THE GODS, AND THE GREAT COMMISSION

And Jesus came and said to them,
"All authority in heaven and on earth
has been given to me. Go therefore
and make disciples of all nations,
baptizing them in the name of the
Father and of the Son and of the
Holy Spirit," (Matthew 28:18–19, ESV)

READING THE STORY

N OUR STORY, GOD IN THE flesh is dead. The powers of darkness .ave successfully killed their archrival in the most torturous of ways—y death on a cross. With all His public disciples scattered like scared heep, it seemed the corpse of Christ would now rot—along with the novement and following He had built. But, providentially, from the hadows of shame, emerged a secret disciple of our Lord (John 19:38) vho wouldn't be silenced. He was a rich man (Matt 27:57) who was good and righteous (Luke 23:51). He had served as one of the seventy on he Jewish council (Sanhedrin), which was responsible for carrying out esus' death sentence. Yet, he opposed their ruling and never consented o their unspeakable crime (Luke 23:51). The Bible tells us,

> When it was already evening, because it was the day of preparation (that is, the day before the Sabbath), Joseph of Arimathea, a prominent member of the Sanhedrin who was himself looking forward to the kingdom of God, came and boldly went to Pilate and asked for Jesus' body. Pilate was surprised that he was already dead. Summoning the centurion, he asked him whether he had already died. When he found out from the centurion, he gave the corpse to Joseph. (Mark 15:42–45, CSB)

Joseph's timely courage reclaimed the body of Jesus from the cross (Acts 13:29) and inspired Nicodemus, another timid council member who admired Jesus, to come forward and assist in honoring Christ in His death. The apostle John writes,

> Nicodemus (who had previously come to him at night) also came, **bringing a mixture of about seventy-five pounds of myrrh and aloes**. They took Jesus' body and wrapped it in linen cloths with the fragrant spices, according to the burial custom of the Jews. **There was a garden in the place**

> **where he was crucified. A new tomb was in the garden**; no one had yet been placed in it. They placed Jesus there because of the Jewish day of preparation and since the tomb was nearby. (John 19:39–42, CSB)

In order to seal the tomb that housed the body of our Lord in th botanical garden, they rolled a dense stone in front of it as heavy a their godly sorrow and walked away, depressed.

> "The next day, which followed the preparation day, the chief priests and the Pharisees gathered before Pilate and said, "Sir, we remember that while this deceiver was still alive he said, 'After three days I will rise again.' So give orders that the tomb be made secure until the third day. Otherwise, his disciples may come, steal him, and tell the people, 'He has been raised from the dead,' and the last deception will be worse than the first." "You have a guard of soldiers," Pilate told them. "Go and make it as secure as you know how." They went and secured the tomb by setting a seal on the stone and placing the guards. After the Sabbath, as the first day of the week was dawning, Mary Magdalene and the other Mary went to view the tomb. There was a violent earthquake, because **an angel of the Lord descended from heaven and approached the tomb**. He rolled back the stone and was sitting on it. His appearance was like lightning, and his clothing was as white as snow. The guards were so shaken by fear of him that they became like dead men. **The angel told the women, "Don't be afraid, because I know you are looking for Jesus who was crucified. He is not here. For he has risen**, just as he said. Come and see the place where he lay. Then go quickly and tell his disciples, 'He has risen from the dead and indeed he is going ahead of you to Galilee; you will see him there.' Listen, I have told you." So, departing

quickly from the tomb with fear and great joy, they ran to tell his disciples the news. (Matt 27:62–28:8, CSB)

> "When they came back from the tomb, they told all these things to the Eleven and to all the others. It was Mary Magdalene, Joanna, Mary the mother of James, and the others with them who told this to the apostles. But they did not believe the women, because their words seemed to them like nonsense. (Luke 24:9–11, NIV)

The tale of the women sounded a little too unbelievable. Their story about visions of angels (Luke 24:23) and an empty tomb, quite frankly, sounded too hopeful to the disciples' critical ears. Nevertheless, their curiosity was piqued.

> "Then Peter and the other disciple went out and were going to the tomb. And the two were running together, and the other disciple ran ahead, faster than Peter, and came to the tomb first. And bending over to look, he saw the strips of linen cloth lying there, though he did not go in. Then Simon Peter also came following him, and he went into the tomb and saw the strips of linen cloth lying there, and the facecloth that was on his head—not lying with the strips of linen cloth, but folded up separately in one place. So then the other disciple who had come to the tomb first also went in, and he saw and believed. (For they did not yet know the scripture that it was necessary for him to rise from the dead.) Then the disciples went away again to their own homes. (John 20:3–10, LEB)

The women couldn't bring themselves to abandon the empty tomb of Jesus. Their sorrow drove them back to it. Mary Magdalene soon split off from the group.

> "...But Mary stood outside the tomb, crying. As she was crying, she stooped to look into the tomb. **She saw two angels in white sitting where Jesus' body had been lying**, one at the head and the other at the feet. They said to her, "Woman, why are you crying?" "Because they've taken away my Lord," she told them, "and I don't know where they've put him." Having said this, she turned around and saw Jesus standing there, but she did not know it was Jesus. "Woman," Jesus said to her, "why are you crying? Who is it that you're seeking?" **Supposing he was the gardener**, she replied, "Sir, if you've carried him away, tell me where you've put him, and I will take him away." Jesus said to her, "Mary." Turning around, she said to him in Aramaic, "Rabboni!"—which means "Teacher." "Don't cling to me," Jesus told her, "since I have not yet ascended to the Father. But go to my brothers and tell them that I am ascending to my Father and your Father, to my God and your God." (John 20:11–17, CSB)

In this very special moment, Mary Magdalene was the first person to see the risen Savior. Rejoining the group of women, Mary had big news HE IS RISEN!

> "So the women hurried away from the tomb, afraid yet filled with joy, and ran to tell his disciples. **Suddenly Jesus met them**. "Greetings," he said. They came to him, clasped his feet and worshiped him. Then Jesus said to them, "Do not be afraid. **Go and tell my brothers to go to Galilee**; there they will see me." (Matt 28:8–10, NIV)

This is now the second time Jesus has mentioned a great Galilean meeting between Him and the apostles, but that meeting would apparently have to wait. The apostles' unbelief was fueling their fear as they barricaded themselves behind closed doors—so Jesus went to them.

> "When it was evening on that first day of the week, the disciples were gathered together with the doors locked because they feared the Jews. Jesus came, stood among them, and said to them, "Peace be with you." Having said this, he showed them his hands and his side. So the disciples rejoiced when they saw the Lord. Jesus said to them again, "Peace be with you. As the Father has sent me, I also send you." After saying this, he breathed on them and said, "Receive the Holy Spirit. If you forgive the sins of any, they are forgiven them; if you retain the sins of any, they are retained." (John 20:19–23, CSB)

But all was not okay. Jesus also rebuked them for not believing the testimony of the women who excitedly shouted, "He is risen!" (Mark 16:14).

The Gospel writers go on to narrate that Christ made many more appearances to hundreds of others, who also marveled at the man who conquered death (Luke 24:34; John 20:24–29; 21:1–14).

And, oh yes… Whatever happened to the scheduled Galilean meeting, you ask? Matthew tells us:

> "Now the eleven disciples went to Galilee, to the mountain to which Jesus had directed them. And when they saw him they worshiped him, but some doubted. And Jesus came and said to them, "**All authority in heaven and on earth has been given to me**. (Matt 28:16–18, ESV)

The implications of what all that means is the anchor of the age-old gospel. All the mysterious and lingering questions surrounding Jesus' claim and resurrection will be illuminated and magnified throughout the rest of the chapter. As you'll discover, it's truly transforming and eternity-altering for all of God's created imagers. It's how Jesus took back the nations and how you'll be saved.

ANSWERING YOUR QUESTIONS

WHY DID JOSEPH BURY JESUS IN A TOMB GARDEN?

Our story began in a mountainous garden. God, our Creator an King, walked in His paradise garden with Adam and Eve, His create imagers. When they sinned, falling victim to the serpent's deception, a transgressors were kicked out of His garden. The template of the King garden was ubiquitously recycled in antiquity. Ancient Near Easter kings were often even thought of as gardeners who provided for the people. When King David died, according to the Septuagint's renderin of Nehemiah 3:16, he was buried in a tomb garden.

> 16 Behind him Nehemiah, son of Azbuk, ruler around the area of Beth-zur, took possession as far as **the garden of the tomb of David** and as far as the artificial reservoir and as far as Bethang-abarim. (EsdB 13:16, LES)

Unsurprisingly, it became traditional to bury the Davidic kings i the city of David; this same lush, mountainous site was known as th tombs of the kings, or the tombs of the sons of David. Deceased Davidi kings were then placed there together. Note the following verses an their verbiage.

SOLOMON	REHOBOAM
43 Then Solomon rested with his fathers, and was buried in the City of David his father. And Rehoboam his son reigned in his place. (1 Kgs 11:43, NKJV)	31 So Rehoboam rested with his fathers, and was buried with his fathers in the City of David. His mother's name was Naamah, an Ammonitess. Then Abijam his son reigned in his place. (1 Kgs 14:31, NKJV)

ABIJAM	ASA
8 So Abijam rested with his fathers, and they buried him in the City of David. Then Asa his son reigned in his place. (1 Kgs 15:8, NKJV)	24 So Asa rested with his fathers, and was buried with his fathers in the City of David his father. Then Jehoshaphat his son reigned in his place. (1 Kgs 15:24, NKJV)
JEHOSHAPHAT	**JORAM (a.k.a., Jehoram)**
50 And Jehoshaphat rested with his fathers, and was buried with his fathers in the City of David his father. Then Jehoram his son reigned in his place. (1 Kgs 22:50, NKJV)	24 So Joram rested with his fathers, and was buried with his fathers in the City of David. Then Ahaziah his son reigned in his place. (2 Kgs 8:24, NKJV)
AHAZIAH	**JOASH**
28 And his servants carried him [Ahaziah] in the chariot to Jerusalem, and buried him in his tomb with his fathers in the City of David. (2 Kgs 9:28, NKJV)	21 For Jozachar the son of Shimeath and Jehozabad the son of Shomer, his servants, struck him. So he died, and they buried him [Joash] with his fathers in the City of David. Then Amaziah his son reigned in his place. (2 Kgs 12:21, NKJV)
AMAZIAH	**AZARIAH (a.k.a., UZZIAH)**
20 Then they brought him [Amaziah] on horses, and he was buried at Jerusalem with his fathers in the City of David. (2 Kgs 14:20, NKJV)	7 So Azariah rested with his fathers, and they buried him with his fathers in the City of David. Then Jotham his son reigned in his place. (2 Kgs 15:7, NKJV)
JOTHAM	**AHAZ**
38 So Jotham rested with his fathers, and was buried with his fathers in the City of David his father. Then Ahaz his son reigned in his place. (2 Kgs 15:38, NKJV)	20 So Ahaz rested with his fathers, and was buried with his fathers in the City of David. Then Hezekiah his son reigned in his place (2 Kgs 16:20, NKJV)

The majority of the rulers in the above subsequent king list were implicitly buried in the tombs of the Davidic kings. The Chronicler makes a couple of exceptions, however. While wicked Judean kings like Joram, Joash, Uzziah, and Ahaz were buried in Jerusalem with their fathers, they weren't granted acceptance into the sepulcher of the kings. Note:

> 20 He [Joram/Jehoram] was thirty-two years old when he began to reign, and he reigned eight years in Jerusalem. And he departed with no one's regret. They buried him in the city of David, **but not in the tombs of the kings**. (2 Chr 21:20, ESV)

> 25 … So he [Joash] died. And they buried him in the City of David, **but they did not bury him in the tombs of the kings**. (2 Chr 24:25, NKJV)

> 23 So Uzziah rested with his fathers, and they buried him with his fathers **in the field of burial which belonged to the kings**, for they said, "He is a leper." Then Jotham his son reigned in his place. (2 Chr 26:23, NKJV)

> 27 And Ahaz slept with his fathers, and they buried him in the city, in Jerusalem, for **they did not bring him into the tombs of the kings** of Israel. And Hezekiah his son reigned in his place. (2 Chr 28:27, ESV)

Additional righteous Davidic kings like Hezekiah are specifically said to have been buried in the tombs of the sons of David.

> 33 And Hezekiah slept with his fathers, and **they buried him in the upper part of the tombs of the sons of David**, and all Judah and the inhabitants of Jerusalem did him honor at his death. And Manasseh his son reigned in his place. (2 Chr 32:33, ESV)

hat's the point? Joseph burying Jesus in a tomb garden inside the city f David telegraphed that the slain Christ was in fact the son of David, e royal heir of the Davidic line. It meant Jesus rightfully carried the atus of King of all kings, the promised Jewish Messiah. Furthermore, e fact that Nicodemus brought seventy-five pounds of myrrh to the mb spoke loudly of Jesus' high kingly status. To grasp the significance f the large quantity of spices, Brown wrote,

> *The biblical background is Jer 34:5 where the Lord promised the soon-to-be exiled King Zedekiah that "as spices were burned for your fathers, the former kings before you, so shall spices be burned for you." The idea that Jesus was accorded a burial fit for a king would correspond well to the solemn proclamation that on the cross he was truly "the King of the Jews" (John 19:19–20) and to the contention that he was buried in a garden*[1]

n what's perhaps the strongest correlation to Jesus' Davidic kingly urial, in Peter's Pentecost sermon, he specifically links David's tomb vith the resurrection of Christ.

> 29 "Fellow Israelites, I can tell you confidently that the patriarch
> **David died and was buried, and his tomb is here to this day**.
> 30 But he was a prophet and knew that God had promised him on
> oath that **he would place one of his descendants on his throne**.
> 31 Seeing what was to come, he spoke of the resurrection of the
> Messiah, that he was not abandoned to the realm of the dead,
> nor did his body see decay. 32 **God has raised this Jesus to life,**
> **and we are all witnesses of it**. 33 Exalted to the right hand of

1 R. E. Brown, vol. 1 of *The Death of the Messiah and 2: From Gethsemane to the Grave, A Commentary on the Passion Narratives in the Four Gospels* (New York; London: Yale University Press, 1994), 1260–1261.

> God, he has received from the Father the promised Holy Spirit
> and has poured out what you now see and hear. 34 For David
> did not ascend to heaven, and yet he said, "'The Lord said to
> my Lord: "Sit at my right hand 35 until I make your enemies a
> footstool for your feet."' 36 "**Therefore let all Israel be assured of
> this: God has made this Jesus, whom you crucified, both Lord
> and Messiah**." (Acts 2:29–36, NIV)

All of the subtleties of the passion narrative are intentional, not coinci dental—Christ praying in a "garden" before His death, His burial i a "tomb garden" like His royal ancestors, and Him being mistake for "the gardener" by Mary. All of this matters. It all ties into the matri of ideas that telegraphs Jesus is King, and as such, He welcomes a created imagers who kneel before Him back into the Edenic kingdon of God.

WHAT IS THE RESURRECTION BODY LIKE?

The nature of the resurrected body of Christ was obviously unique He literally walked around with fresh holes in his hands, feet, an side, totally unharmed. That's not normal. But why leave visibl reminders of the cross on Christ's resurrected body? John Chrysoston (349–407 A.D.) addressed this in *Homilies on John* by writing,

> *But, one might understandably be puzzled as to* ***how an incorruptible body could show marks of the nails and be capable of being touched by a mortal hand****. However, do not be disturbed, for the phenomenon was an evidence of Christ's condescension. To be sure, a body so tenuous and unsubstantial that it entered through doors that were shut was entirely lacking in density.* ***But Christ made His appearance as He did so that the Resurrection would be believed and so that they would know that it was He—the very one who had been crucified—and not someone***

> ***else who had arisen instead of Him****. That is why He arose with the marks of the crucifixion still evident...*[2]

his showed the world that His earthly body had changed into an nharmable, glorified body. What once harmed Him in His crucifixion ody no longer did in His resurrection body. The "stuff" His new body onsisted of was different. Author David Litwa wrote at length about hrist's resurrected body of glory:

> *According to Paul, Christ has a "body of glory" (sōma tēs doxēs) (Phil 3:21)—or, as it can be translated, a "body constituted by glory."* ***This is the body that Christ gained in his resurrection,*** *when he was raised by the "glory" of the Father (Rom 6:4). Accordingly in 1 Corinthians, Christ is called the "Lord of glory" (2:8). When believers "behold the glory of the Lord" (2 Cor 3:18), they behold Christ himself, who is the image of God (2 Cor 4:4; cf. 4:6; Col 1:15).*
>
> *Yet if Christ has a body of glory, why does Paul call him a "life-making spirit" (pneuma zōopoioun) (1 Cor 15:45; cf. 2 Cor 3:17)? The word translated "spirit" here is again the Greek word pneuma. Scholars and exegetes are more and more coming to the conclusion that pneuma did not mean a Platonic, immaterial "spirit." It is more suitably translated by "breath" or "wind." Among ancient philosophers and medical professionals, it was thought of as a corporeal substance, though not a solid, earthly substance like earth and water. It was much more like air. Air, however, was thought to be naturally cold and misty, whereas pneuma was hot, fiery, fine, and extremely subtle. Many Stoics described pneuma as a fine mixture of air and fire, and identified*

---

2 John Chrysostom, vol. 41 of *Commentary on Saint John the Apostle and Evangelist: Homilies 48–88*, 460 (Goggin).

> *it with the substance of aether, or the fiery air thought to exist in the upper reaches of the universe.*
>
> *That Christ's pneuma is also his body is indicated by the fact that those conformed to Christ (v. 49) are said to inherit a "pneumatic body" (sōma pneumatikon) (1 Cor 15:44). Christians become like Christ by conforming to Christ's pneuma (vv. 48–49). Elsewhere Paul speaks of assimilation to Christ's body of glory (Phil 3:21).* ***Pneuma and glory thus appear to be parallel expressions—both describe the "stuff" of a resurrection body.***[3]

In 1 Corinthians 15, Paul takes a deep dive into the subject of deification, where he discusses how the bodies of the human sons of God will all be changed at the resurrection to their eternal glorified states. He writes,

> 39 Not all flesh is the same flesh; there is one flesh for humans,
> another for animals, another for birds, and another for fish.
> 40 There are heavenly bodies and earthly bodies, but the splendor
> of the heavenly bodies is different from that of the earthly ones.
> 41 There is a splendor of the sun, another of the moon, and
> another of the stars; in fact, one star differs from another star in
> splendor. 42 So it is with the resurrection of the dead: Sown in
> corruption, raised in incorruption; 43 sown in dishonor, raised
> in glory; sown in weakness, raised in power; 44 sown a natural
> body, raised a spiritual body. If **there is a natural body, there
> is also a spiritual body.** 45 So it is written, The first man Adam
> became a living being; the last Adam became a life-giving spirit.
> 46 However, the spiritual is not first, but the natural, then the
> spiritual. 47 The first man was from the earth, a man of dust; the

3 M. D. Litwa, *Becoming Divine: An Introduction to Deification in Western Culture* (Eugene, OR: Cascade Books, 2013), 59–60.

> second man is from heaven. 48 Like the man of dust, so are those who are of the dust; **like the man of heaven, so are those who are of heaven.** 49 And just as we have borne the image of the man of dust, we will also bear the image of the man of heaven.
> 50 What I am saying, brothers and sisters, is this: Flesh and blood cannot inherit the kingdom of God, nor can corruption inherit incorruption. 51 Listen, I am telling you a mystery: We will not all fall asleep, but we will all be changed, 52 in a moment, in the twinkling of an eye, at the last trumpet. For the trumpet will sound, and the dead will be raised incorruptible, and we will be changed. 53 For this corruptible body must be clothed with incorruptibility, and this mortal body must be clothed with immortality. (1 Cor 15:39–53, CSB)

Litwa explained,

> *Paul characterizes the pneumatic body by incorruptibility, glory, and power (1 Cor 15:42–43)—all divine qualities. It is also conformed to Christ's body, consisting of "life-making" pneuma (v. 45) associated with "heaven" (v. 47). The nature of the pneumatic body is thus celestial (v. 48);* ***it is not, Paul adds, made up of "flesh and blood"****—the constituents of present bodily life (v. 50).*[4]

Furthermore, Litwa pointed out that Paul makes an implicit,

> *contrast between heavenly and earthly bodies underlying 1 Cor 15:39–49, and Paul associates the future pneumatic body of believers with the heavenly bodies. The mention of the heavenly nature of Christ's body in 1 Cor 15:47 recalls the contrast between earthly and heavenly bodies in 15:40. Paul seems, then,*

---

4 Litwa, *Becoming Divine*, 59–60.

> *to be alluding to the fact that the pneumatic bodies of Christ and believers show the same brilliance (doxa) as the heavenly bodies. In a word, they are "glorified." In a later letter, Paul promises believers a "glorification" (doxazō) of their bodies in conformity to the resurrected body of Christ (Rom 8:29–30). This passage from Romans is structurally similar to 1 Cor 15:49: "Just as we have borne the image of the one of dust (Adam), we will also bear the image of the celestial one (Christ)." In Paul's letter to the Romans, to be conformed to Christ's image means to be glorified; in 1 Corinthians, to bear Christ's image is to become celestial (like the pneumatic Christ).*[5]

Litwa concluded by saying,

> *...In short, a pneumatic body is a glory body. Pneuma, like the aether in ancient cosmology, shines like the stars. Since Christ is pneuma (1 Cor 15:45), he has a body of glory (Phil 3:21).* ***In short, to receive a pneumatic body is to gain a body of glory like the divine Christ.***[6]

The aim of salvation is to grant mortals immortality, just as Jesus prescribed.

> 34 And Jesus said to them, "The sons of this age marry and are given in marriage, 35 but those who are considered worthy to attain to that age and to the resurrection from the dead neither marry nor are given in marriage, 36 for they cannot die anymore, because they are equal to angels and are sons of God, being sons of the resurrection. (Luke 20:34–36, ESV)

---

5 Litwa, *Becoming Divine*, 62.

6 Litwa, *Becoming Divine*, 61.

n that glorious day, we will forever say goodbye to our mortal flesh s we bask in our eternal super bodies as joint heirs with Christ 1 Cor 4:8; Rom 8:17), partakers of the divine nature (2 Pet 1:3–4). n the words of John of Damascus (675–749 A.D.), we will,

> *...shine like the sun together with the angels unto eternal life with our Lord Jesus Christ, ever seeing Him and being seen, enjoying the unending bliss which is from Him, and praising Him together with the Father and the Holy Ghost unto the endless ages of ages. Amen.*[7]

CONNECTING THE GOSPEL

DEFEATING DEATH & RECLAIMING AUTHORITY

While Jesus' death signaled victory over the gods, as we studied in the ast chapter, that was technically only half of the equation. Caesarius of Arles (470–542 A.D.) once said in a sermon,

> *He [Christ] was wounded in order to heal our wounds; He died to free us from everlasting death. He descended into hell to shatter the jaws and ulcerated heart of hell and to* ***bring back*** *to heaven* ***the booty which the Devil had carried away.***[8]

What he says is key. While Christ willingly died to free us from everlasting death, His roundtrip flight to the underworld "brought back" what the devil had carried away—freedom from sin and authority over the nations. You see, if Christ was never raised incorruptible, neither could we be. If His descent was merely a one-way ticket, His

---

7 John Damascene, vol. 37 of *Writings*, 406 (Chase, Jr.).

8 Caesarius of Arles, *Saint Caesarius of Arles: Sermons*, 133 (Mueller).

death must be chalked up to nothing more than a meaningless sacrific by a sick and delirious man, but it's not. His resurrection to glory wa the lifesaving lynchpin to rescuing both Jews and Gentiles alike. Pau makes this abundantly clear in 1 Corinthians 15:13–19.

> 13 If there is no resurrection of the dead, then not even Christ has
> been raised. 14 And if Christ has not been raised, our preaching is
> useless and so is your faith. 15 More than that, we are then found
> to be false witnesses about God, for we have testified about God
> that he raised Christ from the dead. But he did not raise him if
> in fact the dead are not raised. 16 For if the dead are not raised,
> then Christ has not been raised either. 17 And if Christ has not
> been raised, your faith is futile; you are still in your sins. 18 Then
> those also who have fallen asleep in Christ are lost. 19 If only for
> this life we have hope in Christ, we are of all people most to be
> pitied. (1 Cor 15:13–19, NIV)

That's why Jesus is our quintessential Savior—He did what no on else could do when He defeated the very grave in which He was buried

Another familiar passage to believers is 1 Corinthians 15:54–55.

> 54 When the perishable puts on the imperishable, and the
> mortal puts on immortality, then shall come to pass the saying
> that is written: "Death is swallowed up in victory." 55 "O death,
> where is your victory? O death, where is your sting?"
> (1 Cor 15:54–55, ESV)

All of these subjects sound personified, don't they? Paul makes it seem like death, victory, and sting are real entities. That's because they are. Paul isn't just being creative and cute; he's communicating Christ's defeat of three specific Canaanite gods—Mot, Deber, and Qeteb. To grasp this, you simply need to study Paul's source material, Hosea 13:14.

Hosea 13:14 (ESV)	1 Corinthians 15:54–55 (ESV)
[14] I shall ransom them from the power of Sheol [UNDER-WORLD]; I shall redeem them from Death [**MOT**]. O Death [**MOT**], where are your plagues [**DEBER**]? O Sheol, where is your sting [**QETEB**]? Compassion is hidden from my eyes.	[54] … then shall come to pass the saying that is written: "Death is swallowed up in victory." [55] "O death, where is your victory? O death, where is your sting?"

We became acquainted with Deber and Qeteb back in chapter 16. They're two powerful demons; Psalm 91 promises Yahweh will protect His people from them when they dwell in the shelter of the Most High. So, who's Mot?

> *māwet/mōt is the Hebrew word for 'death'. It is also, however, the name of a specific Canaanite deity or →demon, Mot (more precisely Mōtu), known especially from the Ugaritic literature.*[9]

In ancient Ugaritic texts, Mot and Baal are often painted as enemies, not in purpose, but in power for control of the Underworld. The Underworld is Mot's home.

> *This is most explicit in KTU 1.4 viii, in which Baal despatches messengers to Mot in his subterranean realm, a city which is reached through an entrance at the base of the mountains and of which Mot is king (see KTU 1.6 vi:27–29). Descent into the gullet of Mot is the equivalent of descent into the underworld.*[10]

9 J. F. Healey, "Mot," *Dictionary of Deities and Demons in the Bible*, 2nd ed., 598.
10 Healey, "Mot," 599.

Eventually, Mot yields to Baal's/Satan's power, forfeits the scepte of his rule, and is demoted to playing the honorary role of "siniste manager" of the Underworld. Ugaritic text *KTU 1.6:6:25–3* asks Mot,

> *How can you fight with Valiant Baal?*
> *How will Bull El your father not hear you?*
> *He will surely pull down the pillars of your dwelling,*
> *he will surely overturn the throne of your kingship,*
> *he will surely break the sceptre of your rule!'*
> *Divine Mot was afraid;*
> *the Beloved of El, the hero was in dread.*
> *Mot started at her voice.*
> *[He lifted up his voice and cried:]*
> *'Let Baal be installed [on the throne of] his kingship,*
> *on [the back-rest, on the siege of] his dominion!'*[11]

However, Mot remained faithful to the cause of misleading Yahweh's people. Isaiah 28:15–18 records that Israel made a covenant with Mot and the Underworld like they once had with Yahweh and heaven.

> 15 Because you have said, "We have made a covenant with death [MOT], and with Sheol [UNDERWORLD] we have an agreement, when the overwhelming whip passes through it will not come to us, for we have made lies our refuge, and in falsehood we have taken shelter"; 16 therefore thus says the Lord GOD, "Behold, I am the one who has laid as a foundation in Zion, a stone, a tested stone, a precious cornerstone, of a sure foundation: 'Whoever believes will not be in haste.' 17 And

11 Wyatt, *Religious Texts from Ugarit*, 143.

> I will make justice the line, and righteousness the plumb line; and hail will sweep away the refuge of lies, and waters will overwhelm the shelter." [18] Then your covenant with death [MOT] will be annulled, and your agreement with Sheol [UNDERWORLD] will not stand; when the overwhelming scourge passes through, you will be beaten down by it. (Isa 28:15–18, ESV)

They had rejected Yahweh as their solo Shepherd (Ps 23). Like all the nations around them, they had turned to be tended by another shepherd—Mot.

> [14] Like sheep they are appointed for Sheol [UNDERWORLD]; death [MOT] shall be their shepherd, and the upright shall rule over them in the morning. Their form shall be consumed in Sheol, with no place to dwell. [15] But God will ransom my soul from the power of Sheol, for he will receive me. Selah (Ps 49:14–15, ESV)

But Mot is a dark and ruthless shepherd. He's not like the Lord. He doesn't make His sheep lie down in green pastures or lead them beside still waters; he swallows them whole through the mouth of the unsated Underworld, as depicted in *KTU 1.4:8:15–20.*

> *But take care, attendants of the god,*
> *do not draw near divine Mot,*
> *lest he offer you up like a lamb in his mouth,*
> *like a kid in the opening of his maw!*[12]

The Bible depicts Mot's home in the same way.

---

12 Wyatt, *Religious Texts from Ugarit*, 113.

Isaiah 5:14 (ESV)	Proverbs 1:12 (ESV)	Psalm 141:7 (ESV)
14 Therefore Sheol [UNDERWORLD] has enlarged its appetite and opened its mouth beyond measure, and the nobility of Jerusalem and her multitude will go down, her revelers and he who exults in her.	12 like Sheol [UNDERWORLD] let us swallow them alive, and whole, like those who go down to the pit;	7 As when one plows and breaks up the earth, so shall our bones be scattered at the mouth of Sheol [UNDERWORLD].

Old Testament prophets like Isaiah longed for the day when Mot would be the one who was swallowed up. They yearned for an age when the veil of deception would be ripped from the eyes of every nation.

> 6 On this mountain the Lord of hosts will make for all peoples a feast of rich food, a feast of well-aged wine, of rich food full of marrow, of aged wine well refined. 7 **And he will swallow up on this mountain [Mount Zion] the covering that is cast over all peoples, the veil that is spread over all nations.** 8 **He will swallow up death [MOT] forever**; and the Lord God will wipe away tears from all faces, and the reproach of his people he will take away from all the earth, for the Lord has spoken.
> 9 It will be said on that day, "Behold, this is our God; we have waited for him, that he might save us. This is the Lord; we have waited for him; let us be glad and rejoice in his salvation." (Isa 25:6–9, ESV)

Jesus, the good Shepherd, swallowed up Mot and the holding power of the Underworld through His resurrection and departure from it, saving every lost sheep who would name His name (2 Tim 2:19), following

Him (John 10:27). It begs the questions, "O Mot, where is Deber? O Sheol, where is Qeteb?"

In layman's terms, *Hey, big, bad, sinister guys—not so tough now, are you?* As Paul stated, they are defeated through our Lord Jesus Christ!

> [57] But thanks be to God, who gives us the victory through our Lord Jesus Christ. (1 Cor 15:57, ESV)

The "rising up" of Christ as the chosen method through which the Lord would deliver all the nations from their merciless gods was foreshadowed in Psalm 82—that intriguing psalm about the divine council and the judgment of the nations' gods. Once more, the passage reads,

> [1] God has taken his place in the divine council; in the midst of
> the gods he holds judgment: [2] "How long will you judge unjustly
> and show partiality to the wicked? Selah [3] Give justice to the
> weak and the fatherless; maintain the right of the afflicted and
> the destitute. [4] Rescue the weak and the needy; deliver them
> from the hand of the wicked." [5] They have neither knowledge
> nor understanding, they walk about in darkness; all the founda-
> tions of the earth are shaken. [6] I said, "You are gods, sons of
> the Most High, all of you; [7] nevertheless, like men you shall die,
> and fall like any prince." [8] **Arise (ἀνάστα,** anasta)**, O God, judge
> the earth; for you shall inherit all the nations**! (Ps 82, ESV)

The word "arise" in the Greek Septuagint's rendering of Psalm 82:8 is the word *anastasis*. It's the result of coming to life after death. It's the word used in the New Testament for "resurrection." The Lexham Theological Wordbook states,

> *Most instances of the word anastasis in the NT refer either to Jesus' own resurrection or the general resurrection of the dead at*

> *the end of the age (e.g., Luke 14:14; Acts 1:22)... In John, Jesus is "the resurrection (anastasis) and the life" (John 11:25; see also John 5:29; 11:24).*[13]

The Psalmist subtly threw out a clue as to HOW God would "inherit all the nations"; God in the flesh would "rise" from the dead and take them back from their "principalities," "rulers," "authorities," "powers," "dominions," and so forth that had ruled their allotted peoples unjustly. The New Testament writers hammer this point home persistently.

> 18 having the eyes of your hearts enlightened, that you may know what is the hope to which he has called you, what are the riches of his glorious inheritance in the saints,
> 19 and what is the immeasurable greatness of his power toward us who believe, according to the working of his great might
> 20 that he worked in Christ when **he raised him from the dead** and seated him at his right hand in the heavenly places,
> 21 **far above all rule and authority and power and dominion, and above every name that is named**, not only in this age but also in the one to come.
> 22 And **he put all things under his feet** and gave him as head over all things to the church,
> 23 which is his body, the fullness of him who fills all in all. (Eph 1:18–23, ESV)

> 18 For Christ also suffered once for sins, the righteous for the unrighteous, that he might bring us to God, being put to death in the flesh but made alive in the spirit,
> 19 in which he went and proclaimed to the spirits in prison,
> 20 because they formerly did not obey, when God's patience waited in the days of Noah,

13 D. Mangum and J. Spoelstra, "Resurrection," *Lexham Theological Wordbook.*

> while the ark was being prepared, in which a few, that is, eight persons, were brought safely through water. [21] Baptism, which corresponds to this, now saves you, not as a removal of dirt from the body but as an appeal to God for a good conscience, **through the resurrection** (anastasis) **of Jesus Christ,** [22] who has gone into heaven and is at the right hand of God, with **angels, authorities, and powers having been subjected to him.** (1 Pet 3:18–22, ESV)

Indeed, the risen Savior became the light of the world, beckoning all to come to the warmth of His marvelous light.

> [23] that the Christ must suffer and that, by being the first to rise (anastasis) from the dead, he would proclaim light both to our people and to the Gentiles." (Acts 26:23, ESV)

Lastly, recall Jesus' important Galilean meeting.

> [16] Now the eleven disciples went to Galilee, to the mountain to which Jesus had directed them. [17] And when they saw him they worshiped him, but some doubted. [18] And Jesus came and said to them, "**All authority in heaven and on earth has been given to me.**" (Matt 28:16–18, ESV)

Do you know why Jesus chose this verbiage? He articulated His victory with these specific words because of something the devil boasted about to Him in the desert of temptation. Satan said to Christ,

> [6] … "To you I will give all this authority and their glory, for it has been delivered to me, and I give it to whom I will. (Luke 4:6, ESV)

The very words that were once smeared in the face of Jesus in th hour of His temptation were now thrown back in the face of the serper in the hour of his cosmic loss. The language similarity is undeniable.

Satan's Words – Luke 4:6 (ESV)	Jesus' Words – Matthew 28:18 (ESV)
6 "… To you I will give **all this authority** and their glory, for it **has been delivered to me**, and I give it to whom I will.	18 And Jesus came and said to them, "**All authority** in heaven and on earth **has been given to me**.

In a total blindside, Jesus intercepted Satan's authority and took back th nations from the very angels to whom they were allotted. In a matter c three lamenting days, all of his authority was taken from him, thoug not willingly given up by him. In the words of Clement of Alexandri (150–215 A.D.),

> *To Him [Christ] is placed in subjection all the host of angels and gods; He, the paternal Word, exhibiting the holy administration for Him who put [all] in subjection to Him.*[14]

LOOKING AHEAD

Following the preamble to the Great Commission, which establishe Jesus' newly-given status as cosmic ruler, He shared with the apostle their primary objective.

> **Go therefore and make disciples of all nations, baptizing them** in the name of the Father and of the Son and of the Holy Spirit, teaching them to observe all that I have

14 Clement of Alexandria, *The Stromata, or Miscellanies*, 524.

> commanded you. And behold, I am with you always, to the end of the age." (Matt 28:19–20, ESV)

While Jesus took back authority over the nations with His death and resurrection, the people who live in those nations must be individually brought to the light. As a servant specialist to the nations, Paul wrote that his mission was to bring to light the mystery of the gospel to them and that through the help of Christ's church, it would also be made known to their gods (i.e., "rulers" and "authorities").

> 8 To me, though I am the very least of all the saints, this
> grace was given, **to preach to the Gentiles** the unsearchable
> riches of Christ, 9 and to bring to light for everyone what is the
> plan of the mystery hidden for ages in God, who created all
> things, 10 so that **through the church the manifold wisdom
> of God might now be made known to the rulers and author-
> ities in the heavenly places.** 11 This was according to the
> eternal purpose that he has realized in Christ Jesus our Lord,
> (Eph 3:8–11, ESV)

The dark gods were used to battling the antipodal angels of light, as The Epistle of Barnabas (135–138 A.D.) highlights,

> *There are two ways of doctrine and authority, the way of light and the way of darkness. And between these two ways there is a wide difference. For over the one are stationed light-bearing angels of God, but over the other angels of Satan.*[15]

But with Christ's human sons of God joining ranks with His angelic ones, they formed a formidable dyad in the force of light and truth,

---

15 Jackson, *The Apostolic Fathers and the Apologists of the Second Century*, 97.

the likes of which had never been seen before. The powers of darkne
didn't stand a chance against heaven's bright lanterns.

Eusebius (260–339 A.D.) captured the crux of the Gre
Commission and highlighted how Jesus' army of saved human image
fulfilled it.

> *They [the disciples] became too, the Preachers of His Resurrection; because it had prophetically said in the Scriptures of the Prophets, in His Person, "Ask of me, and I will give thee the heathen for thine inheritance, and (for thy) possessions, the uttermost parts of the earth." Just as the testimony of this prophecy has now been fulfilled in fact, He said to His Disciples; "All power is given to me, as in heaven, so in earth." For, He had possessed the sovereignty of the things which are in heaven from eternity; but now, He said was given to Him, by His Father, those upon earth, in conformity with this (viz.) "Ask of me, and I will give thee the nations for thy possession. For, from ancient times,—as Moses attests,—"The most High, when dividing the nations, appointed the boundary of the people, according to the number of the angels." So that the Angels of God were, from ancient times, Rulers over all that was on the earth. But, when mankind had been perverted to the error of many Gods, and the Angels, who were the Rulers, were unable to afford any remedy for this; the common Saviour of all Himself taught, by means of His Divine manifestation, and after His victory over Death, that* ***the empire of the nations upon earth, should no more be given by his Father to the Angels, but to Himself****. And on this account, He commanded his Disciples,—not from ancient times—but now, that* ***they should make the circuit, and make Disciples, of all nations****. And He necessarily added the mystery of cleansing. For it was necessary to those, who should be converted from*

among the heathen, that they should be cleansed by His power from every pollution and uncleanness; because they had been defiled by the error of Demons, and had been holden by the worship of Idols, and by uncleanness of every sort, but had now first been changed from that life of abomination, and of lawless practices.[16]

In Romans 8, Paul envisions the whole "creation" on the edge of its seat, waiting for the reveal of the new sons of God who would undo the counter-covenant of the rebellious angelic sons of God.

> [19] For the creation waits with eager longing for the revealing
> of the sons of God. [20] For the creation was subjected to futility,
> not willingly, but because of him who subjected it, in hope
> [21] that the creation itself will be set free from its bondage
> to corruption and obtain the freedom of the glory of the
> children of God. [22] For we know that the whole creation has
> been groaning together in the pains of childbirth until now.
> (Rom 8:19–22, ESV)

Author Margaret Barker explained,

Paul accepted that the subjugation of the creation was part of the divine plan. He was explaining the role of the (new) sons of God. Those who had received the Spirit were sons of God, and 'creation waits with eager longing for the revealing of the sons of God' (Rom. 8:19). The creation had been subjected to 'futility' and was in bondage to decay, the counter-covenant. Instead of pattern and purpose there was 'futility', a Greek word that shows what was in

---

16 Eusebius of Caesarea, *Eusebius Bishop of Cæsarea on the Theophanīa or Divine Manifestation of Our Lord and Savior Jesus Christ*, 223–225 (Lee).

> *Paul's mind as he wrote. Its equivalent in Hebrew was hebel, used for worthless idols and what they brought: 'idols' (Deut. 32:21); worthless idols (Jer. 10:15); ill-gotten money (Prov. 13:11); worthless help (Isa. 30:7); pointless worry (Ps. 39:6); and, perhaps the most telling: a wasted life of 'nothing and vanity', tohu and hebel, (Isa. 49:4).*[17]

She continued,

> *For Paul, the first result of receiving the Spirit and becoming a son of God was releasing the creation from its bondage to the fallen angels, and, by implication, restoring the right use of knowledge. This was 'the glorious liberty of the children of God'. John expressed the same idea differently: establishing the Kingdom meant destroying the destroyers of the earth (Rev. 11:18). John knew the leader of the fallen angels as Satan, and described him as 'the deceiver of the whole world' (Rev. 12:9).*
>
> *...The result of the fallen angels' teaching was that 'the world was changed... we need to rediscover and emphasize Paul's picture of Christians as the new angels who have to heal the world and set it free.*[18]

Every soul that is brought out of darkness into the light, like Barker said is set free. Irenaeus (130–203 A.D.) wrote in *Against Heresies 3.12.9*,

> ***but that people which believes in God is not now under the power of angels, but under the Lord's [rule].***[19]

---

17 M. Barker, Creation: *A Biblical Vision for the Environment* (London; New York: T&T Clark, 2010), 146.

18 Barker, *Creation*, 147–148.

19 Irenaeus of Lyons, *Irenæus Against Heresies*, 434 (Roberts, Donaldson, and Coxe).

Consequently, every time a lost soul shifts their belief and obedient loyalty from the fallen angels to the Lord's rule, the head of the vile serpent is repeatedly crushed (Rom 16:20). Cyril of Alexandria (375–444 A.D.) really rallied the troops when he screamed the battle cry,

> *let us trample Satan under foot; let us raise the shout of victory over him now he is thrown and fallen: let us exult over the crafty reptile, caught in an inextricable snare: let us too say of him in the words of the prophet Jeremiah, "How is the hammer of all the earth broken and beaten small! Thou art found and hast been taken, because thou stoodest against the Lord."*[20]

But like the first-generation disciples, your mission of going into all the world is your choice. The Lord won't force you; He wants your joint, voluntary participation. Eusebius (260–339 A.D.) wrote,

> *The disciples were not forced to go to the nations. Rather, they freely and zealously accepted the command to make disciples of all nations in his name (Matt 28:19). This is why the text says, Because you shall not go out with confusion, nor shall you go in flight (52:12). They journeyed with complete serenity, carrying with them what Christ had said to them: Behold, I am with you always, even to the end of the age (Matt 28:20).*[21]

In Jesus' commencement speech, He told His graduating students,

> "... you will be my witnesses in Jerusalem, in all Judea and Samaria, and to the ends of the earth." After he had said this, he was taken up as they were watching, and a cloud took

20 Cyril of Alexandria, *A Commentary upon the Gospel According to S. Luke*, 49 (Smith).

21 Wilken, Christman, and Hollerich, *Isaiah*, 407.

> him out of their sight. While he was going, they were gazing into heaven, and suddenly **two men in white clothes** stood by them. They said, "Men of Galilee, why do you stand looking up into heaven? This same Jesus, who has been taken from you into heaven, will come in the same way that you have seen him going into heaven." (Acts 1:8–11, CSB)

And just like that, their master, mentor, and friend faded into the magni icent clouds of glory and was crowned the King of kings, the Lord c lords, and the God of gods (Dan 7:13–14). As for Jesus' disciples, the stopped at nothing to complete their mission. As Paul later reveale the good news did in fact reach all nations, just as Jesus knew it woul (Col 1:23; Rom 16:25–26).

***

Well, I suppose our ancient journey has run its winding course. I wan to thank you for having the courage to care like David, the dare t dream like Joseph, and the willingness to work like Paul. Finishin this book was no small task. I've truly enjoyed hiking the hills o history with you as we've probed, dug, and recovered many of th lost supernatural treasures of the Bible. Just remember—with grea knowledge comes great responsibility. This book has undoubtedl awakened your spirit and sparked your fire to make disciples lik never before. However, the power of the Great Commission doesn't li in your own diligence to fulfill it, though that's vitally important. It power source is in the divine name behind it: Jesus Christ, our Lord Eusebius (260–339 A.D.) hypothesized,

> *It is likely too, His Disciples would thus address their Lord, by way of answer 8:* ***How can we do this?*** *For, How can we preach to the Romans? And, How can we discourse with the Egyptians?*

> *What diction can we use against the Greeks; being brought up in the Syrian language only? How can we persuade the Persians, the Armenians, the Chaldeans, the Scythians, the Hindoos, and other nations called Barbarians,* ***to desert the gods of their forefathers****, and to worship the one Creator of all things? And, upon What superiority of words can we rely, that we shall succeed in this? Or,* ***How can we hope, that we shall prevail in the things attempted? (viz.) that we shall legislate for all nations****, in direct opposition to the laws laid down from ancient times,* ***(and this) against their gods****? And,* ***What power have we upon which to trust****, that we shall succeed in this enterprise? These things therefore, the Disciples of our Saviour would either have thought, or said. But He who was their Lord solved, by one additional word, the aggregate of the things of which they doubted, (and) pledged them by saying, "****Ye shall conquer in my name****." For it was not that He commanded them, simply and indiscriminately, to go and make Disciples of all nations; but with this excellent addition which He delivered, (viz):* ***"In my name."***[22]

And believe me, there's a lot left to conquer in His name. The devil's angels and demons haven't relinquished the fight just yet. Though legally defeated, they're not done deceiving. They're still recruiting God's created imagers and winning souls in every nation, but you know what? So are we.

Every day, Jesus' army of light liberates more imprisoned captives around the world, waving the banner of the Savior's cross in the heart of the enemy's camp. Besides, there's a new, dangerous disciple on the battlefield—YOU! If our paths never cross again in this lifetime, I plan

22 Eusebius of Caesarea, *Eusebius Bishop of Cæsarea on the Theophanīa or Divine Manifestation of Our Lord and Savior Jesus Christ*, 332–334.

on seeing you in Glory in the next one. Until then, go save the worl soldier, for God so loved the world.

In His Light,
Tyler Gilreath

P.S. – If you want to continue the conversation, let's connect. Turn th page to learn how.

CONTACT PAGE

NOW CONDUCTING SUPERNATURAL SEMINARS!

Is your church eager to learn more about the supernatural war of the Bible? Are there difficult questions in God's Word that your members often face which touch on the realm of spiritual warfare? Author and speaker Tyler Gilreath wants to help.

When you book a seminar delving into the supernatural war of the Bible, Tyler will engage with and guide your members through their many questions. He will present in-depth material about God's divine rescue mission that your church members have been longing to hear their entire lives. Tyler would love to partner with you and your congregation and experience the supernatural story of God's Word together.

If you're ready to rejuvenate the body of believers where you worship and increase their love for God's Word, **contact Tyler today!**

Website: gospelovergods.com
Email: gospelovergods@gmail.com

BIBLIOGRAPHY

Abegg, M., Jr., Flint, P., and Ulrich, E., trans. *The Dead Sea Scrolls Bibl The Oldest Known Bible Translated for the First Time into Englis* New York: HarperOne, 1999.

Annus, A. "Are There Greek Rephaim? On the Etymology of Gree Meropes and Titanes." Pages 13–30 in vol. 31 of *Ugarit Forschunge* Kevelaer, Germany: Verlag Butzon & Bercker, 2000.

Arav, R. "Hermon, Mount (Place)." *The Anchor Yale Bible Dictionary* 3

Athanasius the Great of Alexandria. Vol. 44a of *On the Incarnatio Translation*. Edited and translated by J. Behr. Yonkers, NY: St Vladimir's Seminary Press, 2011.

Athenagoras. *Athenagoras: Embassy for the Christians, The Resurrection of the Dead*. Translated by J. H. Crehan. In vol. 23 of *Ancien Christian Writers*. Edited by J. Quasten and J. C. Plumpe. New York Ramsey, NJ: Newman Press, 1956.

Augustine of Hippo. *The City of God, Books VIII–XVI*. Translated by G G. Walsh and G. Monahan. In vol. 14 of The Fathers of the Church Edited by H. Dressler. Washington, DC: The Catholic University o America Press, 1952.

Balogh, A. L., and D. Mangum. "Baal Cycle." *Lexham Bible Dictionary*.

Barker, M. *Creation: A Biblical Vision for the Environment*. London New York: T&T Clark, 2010.

Basil of Caesarea. *Against Eunomius*. Translated by Radde-Gallwitz In vol. 122 of *The Fathers of the Church*. Edited by M. DelCogliano Washington, DC: The Catholic University of America Press, 2011.

asil of Caesarea. *Letters*. Translated by B. Jackson. In vol. 8 of *St. Basil: Letters and Select Works*. Edited by P. Schaff and H. Wace. New York: Christian Literature Company, 1895.

rand, C., C. Draper, A. England, S. Bond, E. R. Clendenen, and T. C. Butler, eds. "Magi." *Holman Illustrated Bible Dictionary*.

rown, R. E. Vol. 1 of *The Death of the Messiah and 2: From Gethsemane to the Grave, A Commentary on the Passion Narratives in the Four Gospels*. New York; London: Yale University Press, 1994.

ullinger, E. W. Vol. 2 of *The Companion Bible: Being the Authorized Version of 1611 with the Structures and Notes, Critical, Explanatory and Suggestive and with 198 Appendixes*. Bellingham, WA: Faithlife, 2018.

aesarius of Arles. *Saint Caesarius of Arles: Sermons*. Translated by M. M. Mueller. Pages 1–238 in vol. 1 of *The Fathers of the Church*. Edited by H. Dressler and B. M. Peebles. Washington, DC: The Catholic University of America Press; Consortium Books, 1956–1973.

harles, R. H., ed. *The Book of Enoch or 1 Enoch: Translation*. Translated by R. H. Charles. Oxford: The Clarendon Press, 1912.

harles, R. H., ed. *The Book of Jubilees*. Translated by R. H. Charles. London: Adam and Charles Black, 1902.

Charlesworth, J. H. Vol. 1 of *The Old Testament Pseudepigrapha*. New York; London: Yale University Press, 1983.

Chrysostom, John. In Vol. 41 of *Commentary on Saint John the Apostle and Evangelist: Homilies 48–88*. Translated by T. A. Goggin. Washington, DC: The Catholic University of America Press, 1959.

Clement of Alexandria. *The Stromata, or Miscellanies*. Translated by A. Roberts. In vol. 2 of *Fathers of the Second Century: Hermas, Tatian, Athenagoras, Theophilus, and Clement of Alexandria*. Edited by J. Donaldson and A. C. Coxe. Buffalo, NY: Christian Literature Company, 1885.

Clendenen, E. R., and C. Chris. "Only Begotten." *Holman Illustrated Bible Dictionary* 1223.

Cobern, C. M. "Calf, Golden." *The International Standard Bible Encyclo-paedia* 1–5.

Cobern, C. M. "Images." *The International Standard Bible Encyclopaedia* 1–5.

Commodian. *The Instructions of Commodianus.* Translated by R. E. Wallis. In vol. 4 of *Fathers of the Third Century: Tertullian, Part Fourth; Minucius Felix; Commodian; Origen, Parts First and Second.* Edited by A. Roberts, J. Donaldson, and A. C. Coxe. Buffalo, NY: Christian Literature Company, 1885.

Currid, J. D. *Against the Gods: The Polemical Theology of the Old Testament.* Wheaton, IL: Crossway, 2013.

Cyprian. *To Demetrian.* Translated by R. J. Deferrari. In vol. 36 of *Treatises.* Edited by R. J. Deferrari. Washington, DC: The Catholic University of America Press, 1958.

Cyril of Alexandria. *A Commentary upon the Gospel According to S. Luke.* Translated by R. P. Smith. Oxford: Oxford University Press, 1859.

Cyril of Alexandria. *Festal Letters, 13–30.* Translated by P. R. Amidon. In vol. 127 of *Fathers of the Church.* Edited by J. J. O'Keefe and D. G. Hunter. Washington, DC: The Catholic University of America Press, 2013.

Cyril of Alexandria. *Isaiah: Interpreted by Early Christian and Medieval Commentators.* Translated by R. L. Wilken, A. R. Christman, and M. J. Hollerich. Edited by R. L. Wilken, A. R. Christman, and M. J. Hollerich. Grand Rapids, MI; Cambridge, UK: William B. Eerdmans Publishing Company, 2007.

Damascene, John. *An Exact Exposition of the Orthodox Faith.* Translated by S. D. F. Salmond. In vol. 9b of *St. Hilary of Poitiers, John of Damascus.* Edited by P. Schaff and H. Wace. New York: Christian Literature Company, 1899.

Damascene, John. Vol. 37 of *Writings.* Translated by F. H. Chase, Jr. Edited by H. Dressler. Washington, DC: The Catholic University of America Press, 1958.

Didymus the Blind. *Commentary on Zechariah*. Translated by R. C. Hill. In vol. 111 of *The Fathers of the Church*. 1st ed. Edited by T. P. Halton. Washington, DC: The Catholic University of America Press, 2006.

DiFransico, L. "Repentance." *Lexham Theological Wordbook*. Bellingham, WA: Lexham Press, 2014.

Elowsky, J. C., ed. *John 11–21*. Downers Grove, IL: InterVarsity Press, 2007.

Elwell, W. A., and B. J. Beitzel. "Babel." *Baker Encyclopedia of the Bible* 1.

Elwell, W. A., and B. J. Beitzel. "Tree of Life." *Baker Encyclopedia of the Bible* 2.

Elwell, W. A., and B. J. Beitzel. "Wise Men." *Baker Encyclopedia of the Bible* 2.

Embry, B., R. Herms, and A. T. Wright, eds. Vol. 1 of *Early Jewish Literature: An Anthology*. Grand Rapids, MI: William B. Eerdmans Publishing Company, 2018.

Embry, B., R. Herms, and A. T. Wright, eds. Vol. 2 of *Early Jewish Literature: An Anthology*. Grand Rapids, MI: William B. Eerdmans Publishing Company, 2018.

Ephrem. *Hymns on Paradise*. Translated by S. Brock. Crestwood, NY: St. Vladimir's Seminary Press, 1990.

Erickson, R. J. *Ephesians*. Vol. 3 of *Evangelical Commentary on the Bible*. Edited by W. Elwell. Grand Rapids, MI: Baker Book House, 1995.

Eusebius of Caesarea. *Commentary on Isaiah*. Translated by J. J. Armstrong. Edited by J. C. Elowsky, T. C. Oden, and G. L. Bray. Downers Grove, IL: IVP Academic: An Imprint of InterVarsity Press, 2013.

Eusebius of Caesarea. *Eusebius Bishop of Cæsarea on the Theophanīa or Divine Manifestation of Our Lord and Savior Jesus Christ*. Translated by S. Lee. Cambridge; London: Cambridge University Press; Duncan and Malcolm, 1843.

Eusebius of Caesarea. *Evangelicae Praeparationis Libri XV*. Edited by H. Gifford. Oxford: Oxford University Press, 1903.

Eusebius of Cæsarea. Vol. 1 of *The Proof of the Gospel: Being the Demonstratio Evangelica of Eusebius of Cæsarea*. Translated by W. J. Ferra Edited by W. J. Sparrow-Simpson and W. K. L. Clarke. London; Ne York: Society for Promoting Christian Knowledge; The Macmilla Company, 1920.

Faithlife Study Bible. Bellingham, WA: Lexham Press, 2012, 2016.

Feldmeth, N. P. *Pocket Dictionary of Church History: Over 3C Terms Clearly and Concisely Defined*. Downers Grove, IL: IV Academic, 2008.

Felix, Minucius. *The Octavius of Marcus Minucius Felix*. Translated b G. W. Clarke. In vol. 39 of *Ancient Christian Writers*. Edited by Quasten, W. J. Burghardt, and T. C. Lawler. New York; Ramsey, N Newman Press, 1974.

Ferguson, E. *Baptism in the Early Church: History, Theology, and Liturg in the First Five Centuries*. Grand Rapids, MI; Cambridge, U.K William B. Eerdmans Publishing Company, 2009.

Fleming, D. "If El Is a Bull, Who Is a Calf? Reflections on Religion i Second Millennium Syria-Palestine." Quoted in Frank Moore Cros Volume. Edited by B. A. Levine, et al. ErIsr 26; Jerusalem: Israe Exploration Society, 1999.

Flint, P. W., J. Duhaime, and K. S. Baek, eds. *Celebrating the Dead Se Scrolls: A Canadian Contribution*. Vol. 30 of *Early Judaism and It Literature*. Atlanta: Society of Biblical Literature, 2011.

France, R. T. *The Gospel of Matthew*. Grand Rapids, MI: William B Eerdmans Publishing Company, 2007.

Gilbert, D. P. *The Great Inception: Satan's Psyops from Eden to Armageddon*. Crane, MO: Defender, 2017. Kindle edition.

Gilbert, D. P. *Last Clash of the Titans: The Second Coming of Hercules Leviathan, and the Prophesied War Between Jesus Christ and the Gods of Antiquity*. Crane, MO: Defender Publishing, 2018. Kindle edition

odawa, B. *Psalm 82: The Divine Council of the Gods, the Judgment of the Watchers and the Inheritance of the Nations*. Los Angeles, CA: Embedded Pictures Publishing, 2018. Kindle edition.

odawa, B. *The Spiritual World of Jezebel and Elijah: Biblical Background to the Novel Jezebel: Harlot Queen of Israel*. Los Angeles, CA: Embedded Pictures Publishing, 2019. Kindle edition.

odawa, B. *When Watchers Ruled the Nations: Pagan Gods at War with Israel's God and the Spiritual World of the Bible*. Los Angeles, CA: Embedded Pictures Publishing, 2020. Kindle edition.

raf, F. "Heroes." *Dictionary of Deities and Demons in the Bible*. 2nd ed.

rether, H. G. "Apollyon." *The Anchor Yale Bible Dictionary* 1.

allo, W. W., and K. L. Younger. *The Context of Scripture*. Leiden; New York: Brill, 1997.

allo, W. W., and K. L. Younger. *The Context of Scripture*. Leiden; Boston: Brill, 2003.

ays, C. B. *Hidden Riches: A Sourcebook for the Comparative Study of the Hebrew Bible and Ancient Near East*. 1st ed. Louisville, KY: Westminster John Knox Press, 2014.

ealey, J. F. "Mot." *Dictionary of Deities and Demons in the Bible*. 2nd ed.

eiser, M. S. "Divine Council." *The Lexham Bible Dictionary*.

eiser, M. S. "The Nephilim." SITCHIN IS WRONG.COM. n.d. http://www.sitchiniswrong.com/nephilim/nephilim.htm.

eiser, M. S. *Reversing Hermon: Enoch, The Watchers & The Forgotten Mission of Jesus Christ*. Bellingham, WA: Lexham Press, 2017.

Heiser, M. S. *The Unseen Realm: Recovering the Supernatural Worldview of the Bible*. 1st ed. Bellingham, WA: Lexham Press, 2015.

Heiser, M. S., H. H. Hardy, and C. Otte. *Hebrew and Canaanite Inscriptions in English Translation*. Bellingham, WA: Lexham Press, 2008.

Hiers, R. H. "'Binding' and 'Loosing': The Matthean Authorizations." *JBL* 104 (1985).

Hundley, M. B. "Divine Presence in Ancient Near Eastern Temples." *Religion Compass* 9.7 (2015): 205–206. doi: 10.1111/rec3.12154.

Irenaeus of Lyons. *The Demonstration of the Apostolic Preachin* Translated by J. A. Robinson. Edited by W. J. S. Simpson and W K. L. Clarke. London; New York: Society for Promoting Christia Knowledge; The Macmillan Co., 1920.

Irenaeus of Lyons. *Irenæus Against Heresies*. In vol. 1 of *The Apostolic Fathe with Justin Martyr and Irenaeus*. Edited by A. Roberts, J. Donaldso and A. C. Coxe. Buffalo, NY: Christian Literature Company, 1885.

Irenaeus of Lyons. Vol. 2 of *The Writings of Irenæus*. Translated by A Roberts and W. H. Rambaut. Edited by A. Roberts and J. Donaldson Edinburgh; London; Dublin: T&T Clark; Hamilton & Co.; Joh Robertson & Co., 1868–1869.

Jackson, G. A. *The Apostolic Fathers and the Apologists of the Secon Century*. Edited by G. P. Fisher. New York: D. Appleton an Company, 1879.

Jerome. *St. Jerome: Commentary on Isaiah: Including St. Jerome's Trans lation of Origen's Homilies 1–9 on Isaiah*. Translated by T. P. Schecl In vol. 68 of *Ancient Christian Writers*. New York; Mahwah, NJ: Th Newman Press, 2015.

Johnson, K., ed. *Ancient Paganism. Biblefacts.org*. Kindle edition.

Johnson, K., ed. *Recognitions of Clement*. In vol. 4 of *Ancient Paganism Biblefacts.org*. Kindle edition.

Josephus, F. *The Works of Josephus: Complete and Unabridged*. Trans lated by W. Whiston. Peabody: Hendrickson, 1987.

Kelley, J. L. "Nehushtan." *The Lexham Bible Dictionary*.

Kelley, J. L. "Resheph." *The Lexham Bible Dictionary*.

Lactantius. *The Divine Institutes*. Translated by W. Fletcher. In vol. 7 o *Fathers of the Third and Fourth Centuries: Lactantius, Venantius Asterius, Victorinus, Dionysius, Apostolic Teaching and Constitu tions, Homily, and Liturgies*. Edited by A. Roberts, J. Donaldson and A. C. Coxe. Buffalo, NY: Christian Literature Company, 1886

Lake, K., ed. Vol. 1 of *The Apostolic Fathers*. Cambridge, MA; London Harvard University Press, 1912–1913.

ake, K., ed. Vol. 2 of *The Apostolic Fathers*. Cambridge, MA; London: Harvard University Press, 1912–1913.

eo the Great. *Sermons*. Translated by C. L. Feltoe. In vol. 12a of *Leo the Great, Gregory the Great*. Edited by P. Schaff and H. Wace. New York: Christian Literature Company, 1895.

.ete, del O. G. "Deber." *Dictionary of Deities and Demons in the Bible*. 2nd ed.

.evine, L. I. "Herod the Great (Person)." *The Anchor Yale Bible Dictionary* 3.

.itwa, M. D. *Becoming Divine: An Introduction to Deification in Western Culture*. Eugene, OR: Cascade Books, 2013.

.outh, A., and M. Conti, eds. *Genesis 1–11*. Downers Grove, IL: InterVarsity Press, 2001.

.ouw, J. P., and E. A. Nida. Vol. 1 of *Greek-English Lexicon of the New Testament: Based on Semantic Domains*. 2nd ed. New York: United Bible Societies, 1996. Electronic edition.

MacArthur, Jr., J. F. *Strange Fire: The Danger of Offending the Holy Spirit with Counterfeit Worship*. Nashville: Thomas Nelson, 2013.

Malina, B. J., and J. J. Pilch. *Social-Science Commentary on the Deutero-Pauline Letters*. Minneapolis, MN: Fortress Press, 2013.

Malul, M. "Terror of the Night." *Dictionary of Deities and Demons in the Bible*. 2nd ed.

Mangum, D., and J. Spoelstra. "Resurrection." *Lexham Theological Wordbook*. Bellingham, WA: Lexham Press, 2014.

Martin, J. A. "Luke." In vol. 2 of *The Bible Knowledge Commentary: An Exposition of the Scriptures*. Edited by J. F. Walvoord and R. B. Zuck. Wheaton, IL: Victor Books, 1985.

Martyr, J. *The First Apology, The Second Apology, Dialogue with Trypho, Exhortation to the Greeks, Discourse to the Greeks, The Monarchy or The Rule of God*. Translated by T. B. Falls. In vol. 6 of *The Fathers of the Church*. Washington, DC: The Catholic University of America Press, 1948.

Martyr, J. *The Second Apology of Justin*. In vol. 1 of *The Apostol[ic] Fathers with Justin Martyr and Irenaeus*. Edited by A. Robert[s], J. Donaldson, and A. C. Coxe. Buffalo, NY: Christian Literatu[re] Company, 1885.

Matthews, V. H., M. W. Chavalas, and J. H. Walton. *The IVP Bib[le] Background Commentary: Old Testament*. Downers Grove, I[L]: InterVarsity Press, 2000. Electronic edition.

Mayor, A. *The First Fossil Hunters: Dinosaurs, Mammoths, and Myth i[n] Greek and Roman Times*. Princeton, NJ: Princeton University Pres[s], 2011. Kindle edition.

McGowan, A. B. *Ancient Christian Worship: Early Church Practices i[n] Social, Historical, and Theological Perspective*. Grand Rapids, M[I]: Baker Academic, 2014.

Moran, W. L., ed. *The Amarna Letters*. Translated by W. L. Moran. Baltimore: Johns Hopkins University Press, 1992.

Morris, L. Vol. 3 of *Luke: An Introduction and Commentary*. Downer[s] Grove, IL: InterVarsity Press, 1988.

Mussies, G. "Giants." *Dictionary of Deities and Demons in the Bibl[e]*. 2nd ed.

Myers, A. C. "Asherah." *Eerdmans Dictionary of the Bible.*

The NET Bible First Edition Notes. Richardson, TX: Biblical Studie[s] Press, 2006.

Neusner, J., ed. *The Jerusalem Talmud: A Translation and Commentary*. Peabody, MA: Hendrickson Publishers, 2008.

Nickelsburg, G. W. E. "1 Enoch: A Commentary on the Book of 1 Enoch," in Hermeneia Commentary Series—a Critical and Historica[l] Commentary on the Bible. Edited by Klaus Baltzer. Minneapolis, MN: Fortress, 2001.

Niehr, H. "Baal-Zaphon." *Dictionary of Deities and Demons in the Bible*. 2nd ed.

Noegel, S. B. "The Egyptian 'Magicians.'" *The Torah.com*. 2017. https://www.thetorah.com/article/the-egyptian-magicians

Oden, T. C., and G. L. Bray, eds. Vol. 1 and 2 *Incomplete Commentary on Matthew (Opus Imperfectum)*. Translated by J. A. Kellerman. Downers Grove, IL: IVP Academic: An Imprint of InterVarsity Press, 2010.

Oden, T. C., and C. A. Hall, eds. *Mark*. Rev. edition. Downers Grove, IL: InterVarsity Press, 1998.

Olmo, G. del. "From Baal to Yahweh." *The Bull in the Mediterranean World* (2004). https://www.academia.edu/4887401/2004_From_Baal_to_Yahweh_The_Bull_in_the_Mediterranean_World

Origen. *Commentary on the Epistle to the Romans, Books 6–10*. Translated by T. P. Scheck. In vol. 4 of *The Fathers of the Church*. Edited by T. P. Halton. Washington, DC: The Catholic University of America Press, 2002.

Origen. *De Principiis*. Translated by F. Crombie. In vol. 4 of *Fathers of the Third Century: Tertullian, Part Fourth; Minucius Felix; Commodian; Origen, Parts First and Second*. Edited by A. Roberts, J. Donaldson, and A. C. Coxe. Buffalo, NY: Christian Literature Company, 1885.

Origen. *Homilies on Genesis and Exodus*. Translated by R. E. Heine. In vol. 71 of *The Fathers of the Church*. Edited by H. Dressler. Washington, DC: The Catholic University of America Press, 1982.

Origen. *Homilies on Leviticus 1–16*. Translated by G. W. Barkley. In vol. 83 of *The Fathers of the Church*. Edited by T. P. Halton. Washington, DC: The Catholic University of America Press, 1990.

Origen. *Origen Against Celsus*. Translated by F. Crombie. In vol. 4 of *Fathers of the Third Century: Tertullian, Part Fourth; Minucius Felix; Commodian; Origen, Parts First and Second*. Edited by A. Roberts, J. Donaldson, and A. C. Coxe. Buffalo, NY: Christian Literature Company, 1885.

Origen. *The Philocalia of Origen*. Translated by G. Lewis. Edinburgh: T&T Clark, 1911.

Philo of Alexandria. *The Works of Philo: Complete and Unabridged*. Translated by C. D. Yonge. Peabody, MA: Hendrickson, 1995.

Piper, J. "The Covenant of Abraham." *Desiring God* (website 18 October 1981. https://www.desiringgod.org/messages/the-covenant-of-abraham.

Pitterson, R. *Judgment of the Nephilim*. Days of Noe Publishing, 201 Kindle edition.

Plato. Vol. 3 of *The Dialogues of Plato*. 3rd ed. Translated by B. Jowet Oxford: The Clarendon Press, 1892.

Plato. Vol. 5 of *The Dialogues of Plato*. 3rd ed. Translated by B. Jowet New York; London: Macmillan and Co., 1892.

Pseudo-Clement of Rome. *The Clementine Homilies*. Translated by T. Smith In vol. 8 of *The Ante-Nicene Fathers: Fathers of the Third and Fourt Centuries: The Twelve Patriarchs, Excerpts and Epistles, the Clementine Apocrypha, Decretals, Memoirs of Edessa and Syriac Document Remains of the First Ages*. Edited by A. Roberts, J. Donaldson, and A C. Coxe. Buffalo, NY: Christian Literature Company, 1886.

Richter, A. E. "The Enochic Watchers' Template and the Gospel c Matthew." PhD diss., Marquette University, 2010. http://epublications.marquette.edu/dissertations_mu/45

Ridley, B. "Hermon, Mount." *The Lexham Bible Dictionary*.

Riley, G. J. "Midday Demon." *Dictionary of Deities and Demons in the Bible*. 2nd ed.

Ritner, R. K. *The Mechanics of Ancient Egyptian Magical Practice* Chicago, IL: The Oriental Institute of Chicago, 1993.

Roberts, R. D. "Magic." *The Lexham Bible Dictionary*.

Rufinus. *The Commentary*. Translated by R. P. Lawson. In vol. 26 o *Origen: The Song of Songs, Commentary and Homilies*. Edited by J Quasten and J. C. Plumpe. New York; Mahwah, NJ: The Newman Press, 1957.

Rufinus. *A Commentary on the Apostles' Creed*. Translated by W. H Fremantle. In vol. 3 of *Theodoret, Jerome, Gennadius, Rufinus Historical Writings, etc*. Edited by P. Schaff and H. Wace. New York Christian Literature Company, 1892.

ufinus. *Rufinus: A Commentary on the Apostles' Creed*. Translated by J. N. D. Kelly. In vol. 20 of *Ancient Christian Writers*. Edited by J. Quasten and J. C. Plumpe. New York; Mahwah, NJ: Newman Press, 1955.

yrie, C. C. *Basic Theology: A Popular Systematic Guide to Understanding Biblical Truth*. Chicago, IL: Moody Press, 1999.

everus, S. *The Sacred History of Sulpitius Severus*. Translated by A. Roberts. In vol. 11 of *Sulpitius Severus, Vincent of Lérins, John Cassian*. Edited by P. Schaff and H. Wace. New York: Christian Literature Company, 1894.

picq, C., and J.D. Ernest. *Theological Lexicon of the New Testament*. Peabody, MA: Hendrickson Publishers, 1994.

tewart, T. A. "Fallen Angels, Bastard Spirits, and the Birth of God's Son: An Enochic Etiology of Evil in Galatians 3:19–4:11." Paper presented at the annual meeting of the Society of Biblical Literature. 2014.

Tertullian. *On the Veiling of Virgins*. Translated by S. Thelwall. In vol. 4 of *Fathers of the Third Century: Tertullian, Part Fourth; Minucius Felix; Commodian; Origen, Parts First and Second*. Edited by A. Roberts, J. Donaldson, and A. C. Coxe. Buffalo, NY: Christian Literature Company, 1885.

Thomas, M. A. "Bull." *Eerdmans Dictionary of the Bible*.

Tidball, D. J. "Church." *New Dictionary of Biblical Theology*.

Van den Broek, R. "Apollo." *Dictionary of Deities and Demons in the Bible*. 2nd ed.

VanderKam, J. C. *The Dead Sea Scrolls Today*. Grand Rapids, MI: Eerdmans, 1994.

Van Dorn, Douglas. *Giants: Sons of the Gods*. Erie, CO: Waters of Creation, 2013. Kindle edition.

Victorinus of Pettau. *Commentary on the Apocalypse of the Blessed John*. Translated by R. E. Wallis. In vol. 7 of *Fathers of the Third and Fourth Centuries: Lactantius, Venantius, Asterius, Victorinus, Dionysius, Apostolic Teaching and Constitutions, Homily, and Liturgies*. Edited by A. Roberts, J. Donaldson, and A. C. Coxe. Buffalo, NY: Christia Literature Company, 1886.

Voicu, S. J., ed. *Apocrypha*. Downers Grove, IL: InterVarsity Press, 201

Walls, D. Vol. 11 of *I & II Peter, I, II & III John, Jude*. Edited by M Anders. Nashville, TN: Broadman & Holman Publishers, 1999.

Wayne, G. *The Genesis 6 Conspiracy: How Secret Societies and th Descendants of Giants Plan to Enslave Humankind*. Trusted Book 2014. Kindle edition.

Weinrich, W. C., ed. *Revelation*. Downers Grove, IL: InterVarsit Press, 2005.

Wierenga, M. "Church Fathers." *The Lexham Bible Dictionary*.

Wilken, R. L., A. R. Christman, and M. J. Hollerich, eds. *Isaiah: Inter preted by Early Christian and Medieval Commentators*. Translate by R. L. Wilken, A. R. Christman, and M. J. Hollerich. Gran Rapids, MI; Cambridge, UK: William B. Eerdmans Publishin Company, 2007.

Wise, M. O., M. G. Abegg, Jr., and E. M. Cook, eds. *The Dead Sea Scrolls A New Translation*. New York: HarperOne, 2005.

Witthoff, D., ed. *The Lexham Cultural Ontology Glossary*. Bellingham WA: Lexham Press, 2014.

Wyatt, N. *Religious Texts from Ugarit*. 2nd ed. London; New York Sheffield Academic Press, 2002.

Xella, P. "Resheph." *Dictionary of Deities and Demons in the Bible* 2nd ed.

INDEX

HE OLD 'ESTAMENT

;ENESIS

EXODUS

LEVITICUS

NUMBERS

DEUTERONOMY

JOSHUA

JUDGES

1 SAMUEL

2 SAMUEL

1 KINGS

2 KINGS

1 CHRONICLES

2 CHRONICLES

EZRA

NEHEMIAH

JOB

PSALMS

PROVERBS

ECCLESIASTES

SONG OF SOLOMON

ISAIAH

JEREMIAH

EZEKIEL

ACTS

ROMANS

1 CORINTHIANS

2 TIMOTHY

TITUS

HEBREWS

JAMES

1 PETER

2 PETER

1 JOHN

JUDE

REVELATION

OTHER CITATIONS

BARUCH

ENOCH

JUBILEES

3 MACCABEES

NAPHTALI

REUBEN

SIRACH

TOBIT

Made in the USA
Columbia, SC
18 March 2021